Society: A User's Guide
Readings and Applications

Susan L. Wortman
University of Nebraska

KENDALL/HUNT PUBLISHING COMPANY
4050 Westmark Drive P.O. Box 1840 Dubuque, Iowa 52004-1840

Cover images © 2006 Jupiter Images Corporation

Copyright © 2006 by Susan L. Wortman

ISBN 13: 978-0-7575-3111-8
ISBN 10: 0-7575-3111-3

Kendall/Hunt Publishing Company has the exclusive rights to reproduce this work, to prepare derivative works from this work, to publicly distribute this work, to publicly perform this work and to publicly display this work.

All rights reserved. No part of this publication may be reproduced, stored in a retrieval system, or transmitted, in any form or by any means, electronic, mechanical, photocopying, recording, or otherwise, without the prior written permission of the copyright owner.

Printed in the United States of America
10 9 8 7 6 5 4 3 2 1

CONTENTS

SECTION I   The Sociological Puzzle: Our Society in Us and the "Us" in Our Society

Chapter 1   Understanding Society through Sociology: An Invitation and Application   1

Sociology as an Individual Pastime, PETER L. BERGER
The Urban Inferno, ERIC KLINENBERG

Chapter 2   Learning Societal Lessons: Socialization and Culture   17

Extreme Social Isolation of a Child, KINGSLEY DAVIS
An Introduction to McDonaldization, GEORGE RITZER

Chapter 3   Creating and Interpreting Society   35

Performances, ERVING GOFFMAN
Making Fantasies Real: Producing Woman and Men on the Maquila Shop Floor, LESLIE SALZINGER

Chapter 4   Breaking Away: Deviance and Social Control   53

The Good Mother: Neutralization Techniques Used by Pageant Mothers, MARTHA HELTSLEY & THOMAS C. CALHOUN
On Being Sane in Insane Places, D.L. ROSENHAN

SECTION II   The Sociological Lens: Seeing Social Inequalities

Chapter 5   Can Money Buy Happiness: Stratification by Social Class   79

Life at the Top in America Isn't Just Better, It's Longer, JANNY SCOTT
Learning the Ropes: The Childhood and College Years of Elite Women, DIANA KENDALL

Chapter 6   Are Men Really from Mars and Women from Venus? Stratification by Sex/Gender   101

Barbie Girls verses Sea Monsters: Children Constructing Gender, MICHAEL A. MESSNER
Because she looks like a Child, KEVIN BALES

Chapter 7   Race Matters: Stratification by Race   127

Racism and Research: The Case of the Tuskegee Syphilis Experiment, ALLAN M. BRANDT
Experiences of Discrimination among African American, Asian American, and Latino Adolescents in an Urban High School, SUSAN RAKOSI ROSENBLOOM & NIOBE WAY

SECTION III   The Sociological Map: Locating Sources of Societal Stability, Conflict, Change

Chapter 8   Fries with that? Economy and Work in the 21st Century   **159**

Nickel-and-Dimed: On (not) getting by in America, Barbara Ehrenreich
Maytag in Mexico, David Moberg

Chapter 9   In Decline or Doing Fine? American Families and Religion   **179**

Marriage: Then and Now, Stephanie Coontz
The Desecularization of the World: A Global Overview, Peter L. Berger

Chapter 10   Education and Health   **193**

Hitting Them Hardest When They're Small, Jonathan Kozol
Let Them Eat: The Heavy Truths about American Obesity, Greg Critser

Chapter 11   Emerging Issues: Media and Environment   **209**

Gangstas, Thugs, and Hustlas: Identity and the Code of the Street in Rap Music, Charis A. Kubrin
Stuff: The Secret Lives of Everyday Things,
John C. Ryan & Alan Thein Durning

The Sociological Puzzle: Our Society in Us and the "Us" in Our Society

Chapter 1

Sociology as an Individual Pastime

By PETER L. BERGER

■ What is sociology? Can it be useful even if you are not a sociology major? In this excerpt, sociologist Peter L. Berger answers these questions as he introduces the sociological way of viewing society. By the end of your journey with Berger you should have an understanding of how sociologists view the world, what they study, and what insights they can offer.

There are very few jokes about sociologists. This is frustrating for the sociologists, especially if they compare themselves with their more favored second cousins, the psychologists, who have pretty much taken over that sector of American humor that used to be occupied by clergymen. A psychologist, introduced as such at a party, at once finds himself the object of considerable attention and uncomfortable mirth. A sociologist in the same circumstance is likely to meet with no more of a reaction than if he had been announced as an insurance salesman. He will have to win his attention the hard way, just like everyone else. This is annoying and unfair, but it may also be instructive. The dearth of jokes about sociologists indicates, of course, that they are not as much part of the popular imagination as psychologists have become. But it probably also indicates that there is a certain ambiguity in the images that people do have of them. It may thus be a good starting point for our considerations to take a closer look at some of these images.

If one asks undergraduate students why they are taking sociology as a major, one often gets the reply, "because I like to work with people." If one then goes on to ask such students about their occupational future, as they envisage it, one often hears that they intend to go into social work. Of this more in a moment. Other answers are more vague and general, but all indicate that the student in question would rather deal with people than with things. Occupations mentioned in this connection include personnel work, human relations in industry, public

---

From *An Invitation to Sociology* by Peter Berger, copyright © 1963 by Peter L. Berger. Used by permission of Doubleday, a division of Random House, Inc.

Berger's "An Invitation to Sociology," was written in a historical period before the movement for inclusive language. The pronoun "he" in this article applies to both women and men.

relations, advertising, community planning or religious work of the unordained variety. The common assumption is that in all these lines of endeavor one might "do something for people," "help people," "do work that is useful for the community." The image of the sociologist involved here could be described as a secularized version of the liberal Protestant ministry, with the YMCA secretary perhaps furnishing the connecting link between sacred and profane benevolence. Sociology is seen as an up-to-date variation on the classic American theme of "uplift." The sociologist is understood as one professionally concerned with edifying activities on behalf of individuals and of the community at large.

One of these days a great American novel will have to be written on the savage disappointment this sort of motivation is bound to suffer in most of the occupations just mentioned. There is moving pathos in the fate of these likers of people who go into personnel work and come up for the first time against the human realities of a strike that they must fight on one side of the savagely drawn battle lines, or who go into public relations and discover just what it is that they are expected to put over in what experts in the field have called "the engineering of consent," or who go into community agencies to begin a brutal education in the politics of real estate speculation. But our concern here is not with the despoiling of innocence. It is rather with a particular image of the sociologist, an image that is inaccurate and misleading.

It is, of course, true that some Boy Scout types have become sociologists. It is also true that a benevolent interest in people could be the biographical starting point for sociological studies. But it is important to point out that a malevolent and misanthropic outlook could serve just as well. Sociological insights are valuable to anyone concerned with action in society. But this action need not be particularly humanitarian. Some American sociologists today are employed by governmental agencies seeking to plan more livable communities for the nation. Other American sociologists are employed by governmental agencies concerned with wiping communities of hostile nations off the map, if and when the necessity should arise. Whatever the moral implications of these respective activities may be, there is no reason why interesting sociological studies could not be carried on in both. Similarly, criminology, as a special field within sociology, has uncovered valuable information about processes of crime in modern society. This information is equally valuable for those seeking to fight crime as it would be for those interested in promoting it. The fact that more criminologists have been employed by the police than by gangsters can be ascribed to the ethical bias of the criminologists themselves, the public relations of the police and perhaps the lack of scientific sophistication of the gangsters. It has nothing to do with the character of the information itself. In sum, "working with people" can mean getting them out of slums or getting them into jail, selling them propaganda or robbing them of their money (be it legally or illegally), making them produce better automobiles or making them better bomber pilots. As an image of the sociologist, then, the phrase leaves something to be desired, even though it may serve to describe at least the initial impulse as a result of which some people turn to the study of sociology.

Another image of the sociologist, related to the two already discussed, is that of social reformer. Again, this image has historical roots, not only in America but also in Europe. Auguste Comte, the early nineteenth-century French philosopher who invented the name of the discipline, thought of sociology as the doctrine of progress, a secularized successor to theology as the mistress of the sciences. The sociologist in this view plays the role of arbiter of all branches of knowledge for the welfare of men. This notion, even when stripped of its more fantastic pretensions, died especially hard in the development of French sociology. But it had its repercussions in America too, as when, in the early days of American sociology, some transatlantic disciples of Comte seriously suggested in a memorandum to the president of Brown University that all the departments of the latter should be reorganized under the department of sociology. Very few sociologists today, and probably none in this country, would think of their role in this way. But something of this conception survives when sociologists are expected to come up with blueprints for reform on any number of social issues.

It is gratifying from certain value positions (including some of this writer's) that sociological insights have served in a number of instances to improve the lot of groups of human beings by uncovering morally shocking conditions or by clearing away collective Illusions or by showing that socially desired results could be obtained in more humane fashion. One might point, for example, to some applications of sociological knowledge in the penological practice of Western countries. Or one might cite the use made of sociological studies in the Supreme Court decision of 1954 on racial segregation in the public schools. Or one could look at the applications of other sociological studies to the humane planning of urban redevelopment. Certainly the sociologist who is morally and politically sensitive will derive gratification from such instances. But, once more, it will be well to keep in mind that what is at issue here is not sociological understanding as such but certain applications of this understanding. It is not difficult to see how the same understanding could be applied with opposite intentions. Thus the sociological understanding of the dynamics of racial prejudice can be applied effectively by those promoting intragroup hatred as well as by those wanting to spread tolerance. And the sociological understanding of the nature of human solidarity can be employed in the service of both totalitarian and democratic regimes. It is sobering to realize that the same processes that generate consensus can be manipulated by a social group worker in a summer camp in the Adirondacks and by a Communist brainwasher in a prisoner camp in China. One may readily grant that the sociologist can sometimes be called upon to give advice when it comes to changing certain social conditions deemed undesirable. But the image of the sociologist as social reformer suffers from the same confusion as the image of him as social worker.

The sociologist, then, is someone concerned with understanding society in a disciplined way. The natures of this discipline is scientific. This means that what the sociologist finds and says about the social phenomena he studies occurs within a certain rather strictly defined frame of reference. One of the main characteristics of this scientific frame of reference is that operations are bound by certain rules of evidence. As a scientist, the sociologist tries to be objective, to control his personal preferences and prejudices, to perceive clearly rather than to judge normatively. This restraint, of course, does not embrace the totality of the sociologist's existence as a human being, but is limited to his operations *qua* sociologist. Nor does the sociologist claim that his frame of reference is the only one within which society can be looked at. For that matter, very few scientists in any field would claim today that one should look at the world only scientifically. The botanist looking at a daffodil has no reason to dispute the right of the poet to look at the same object in a very different manner. There are many ways of playing. The point is not that one denies other people's games but that one is clear about the rules of one's own. The game of the sociologist, then, uses scientific rules. As a result, the sociologist must be clear in his own mind as to the meaning of these rules. That is, he must concern himself with methodological questions. Methodology does not constitute his goal. The latter, let us recall once more, is the attempt to understand society. Methodology helps in reaching this goal. In order to understand society, or that segment of it that he is studying at the moment, the sociologist will use a variety of means. Among these are statistical techniques. Statistics can be very useful in answering certain sociological questions. But statistics does not constitute sociology. As a scientist, the sociologist will have to be concerned with the exact significance of the terms he is using. That is, he will have to be careful about terminology. This does not have to mean that he must invent a new language of his own, but it does mean that he cannot naively use the language of everyday discourse. Finally, the interest of the sociologist is primarily theoretical. That is, he is interested in understanding for its own sake. He may be aware of or even concerned with the practical applicability and consequences of his findings, but at that point he leaves the sociological frame of reference as such and moves into realms of values, beliefs and ideas that he shares with other men who are not sociologists.

We daresay that this conception of the sociologist would meet with very wide consensus within the discipline today. But we would like to go a little bit further here and ask a somewhat more personal (and therefore, no doubt, more controversial) question. We would like to ask not only what it is that the sociologist is doing but also what it is that drives him to it. Or, to use the phrase Max Weber used in a similar connection, we want to inquire a little into the nature of the sociologist's demon. In doing so, we shall evoke an image that is not so much ideal-typical in the above sense but more confessional in the sense of personal commitment. Again, we are not interested in excommunicating anyone. The game of sociology goes on in a spacious playground. We are just describing a little more closely those we would like to tempt to join our game.

We would say then that the sociologist (that is, the one we would really like to invite to our game) is a person intensively, endlessly, shamelessly interested in the doings of men. His natural habitat is all the human gathering places of the world, wherever men come together. The sociologist may be interested in many other things. But his consuming interest remains in the world of men, their institutions, their history, their passions. And since he is interested in men, nothing that men do can be altogether tedious for him. He will naturally be interested in the events that engage men's ultimate beliefs, their moments of tragedy and grandeur and ecstasy. But he will also be fascinated by the common-place, the everyday. He will know reverence, but this reverence will not prevent him from wanting to see and to understand. He may sometimes feel revulsion or contempt. But this also will not deter him from wanting to have his questions answered. The sociologist, in his quest for understanding, moves through the world of men without respect for the usual lines of demarcation. Nobility and degradation, power and obscurity, intelligence and folly—these are equally *interesting* to him, however unequal they may be in his personal values or tastes. Thus his questions may lead him to all possible levels of society, the best and the least known places, the most respected and the most despised. And, if he is a good sociologist, he will find himself in all these places because his own questions have so taken possession of him that he has little choice but to seek for answers.

It would be possible to say the same things in a lower key. We could say that the sociologist, but for the grace of his academic title, is the man who must listen to gossip despite himself, who is tempted to look through keyholes, to read other people's mail, to open closed cabinets. Before some otherwise unoccupied psychologist sets out now to construct an aptitude test for sociologists on the basis of sublimated voyeurism, let us quickly say that we are speaking merely by way of analogy. Perhaps some little boys consumed with curiosity to watch their maiden aunts in the bathroom later become inveterate sociologists. This is quite uninteresting. What interests us is the curiosity that grips any sociologist in front of a closed door behind which there are human, voices. If he is a good sociologist, he will want to open that door, to understand these voices. Behind each closed door he will anticipate some new facet of human life not yet perceived and understood.

The sociologist will occupy himself with matters that others regard as too sacred or as too distasteful for dispassionate investigation. He will find rewarding the company of priests or of prostitutes, depending not on his personal preferences but on the questions he happens to be asking at the moment. He will also concern himself with matters that others may find much too boring. He will be interested in the human interaction that goes with warfare or with great intellectual discoveries, but also in the relations between people employed in a restaurant or between a group of little girls playing with their dolls. His main focus of attention is not the ultimate significance of what men do, but the action in itself, as another example of the infinite richness of human conduct. So much for the image of our playmate.

In these journeys through the world of men the sociologist will inevitably encounter other professional Peeping Toms. Sometimes these will resent his presence, feeling that he is poaching on their preserves. In some places the sociologist will meet up with the economist, in others with the political scientist, in yet others with the psychologist or the ethnologist. Yet chances are that the questions that have brought him to these same places are different from the ones that propelled his fellow-trespassers. The sociologist's questions always remain essentially the same: "What are people doing with each other here?" "What are their relationships to each other?" "How are these relationships organized in institutions?" "What are the collective ideas that move men and institutions?" In trying to answer these questions in specific instances, the sociologist will, of course, have to deal with economic or political matters, but he will do so in a way rather different from that of the economist or the political scientist. The scene that he contemplates is the same human scene that these other scientists concern themselves with. But the sociologist's angle of vision is different. When this is understood, it becomes clear that it makes little sense to try to stake out a special enclave within which the sociologist will carry on business in his own right. Like Wesley the sociologist will have to confess that his parish is the world. But unlike some latter-day Wesleyans he will gladly share this parish with others. There is, however, one traveler whose path the sociologist will cross more often than anyone else's on his journeys. This is the historian. Indeed, as soon as the sociologist turns from the present to the past, his preoccupations are very hard indeed to distinguish from those of the historian. However, we shall leave this relationship to a later part of our considerations. Suffice it to say here that the sociological journey will be much impoverished unless it is punctuated frequently by conversation with that other particular traveler.

Any intellectual activity derives excitement from the moment it becomes a trail of discovery. In some fields of learning this is the discovery of worlds previously unthought and unthinkable. This is the excitement of the astronomer or of the nuclear physicist on the antipodal boundaries of the realities that man is capable of conceiving. But it can also be the excitement of bacteriology or geology. In a different way it can be the excitement of the linguist discovering new realms of human expression or of the anthropologist exploring human customs in faraway countries. In such discovery, when undertaken with passion, a widening of awareness, sometimes a veritable transformation of consciousness, occurs. The universe turns out to be much more wonder-full than one had ever dreamed. The excitement of sociology is usually of a different sort. Sometimes, it is true, the sociologist penetrates into worlds that had previously been quite unknown to him—for instance, the world of crime, or the world of some bizarre religious sect, or the world fashioned by the exclusive concerns of some group such as medical specialists or military leaders or advertising executives. However, much of the time the sociologist moves in sectors of experience that are familiar to him and to most people in his society. He investigates communities, institutions and activities that one can read about every day in the newspapers. Yet there is another excitement of discovery beckoning in his investigations. It is not the excitement of coming upon the totally unfamiliar, but rather the excitement of finding the familiar becoming transformed in its meaning. The fascination of sociology lies in the fact that its perspective makes us see in a new light the very world in which we have lived all our lives. This also constitutes a transformation of consciousness. Moreover, this transformation is more relevant existentially than that of many other intellectual disciplines, because it is more difficult to segregate in some special compartment of the mind. The astronomer does not live in the remote galaxies, and the nuclear physicist can, outside his laboratory, eat and laugh and marry and vote without thinking about the insides of the atom. The geologist looks at rocks only at appropriate times, and the linguist speaks English with his wife. The sociologist lives in society, on the job and off it. His own life; inevitably, is part of his subject matter. Men being what they are, sociologists too manage to segregate their professional insights from their everyday affairs. But it is a rather difficult feat to perform in good faith.

The sociologist moves in the common world of men, close to what most of them would call real. The categories he employs in his analyses are only refinements of the categories by which other men live—power, class, status, race, ethnicity. As a result, there is a deceptive simplicity and obviousness about some sociological investigations. One reads them, nods at the familiar scene, remarks that one has heard all this before and don't people have better things to do than to waste their time on truisms—until one is suddenly brought up against an insight that radically questions everything one had previously assumed about this familiar scene. This is the point at which one begins to sense the excitement of sociology.

Let us take a specific example. Imagine a sociology class in a Southern college where almost all the students are white Southerners. Imagine a lecture on the subject of the racial system of the South. The lecturer is talking here of matters that have been familiar to his students from the time of their infancy. Indeed, it may be that they are much more familiar with the minutiae of this system than he is. They are quite bored as a result. It seems to them that he is only using more pretentious words to describe what they already know. Thus he may use the term "caste," one commonly used now by American sociologists to describe the Southern racial system. But in explaining the term he shifts to traditional Hindu society, to make it clearer. He then goes on to analyze the magical beliefs inherent in caste tabus, the social dynamics of commensalism and connubium, the economic interests concealed within the system, the way in which religious beliefs relate to the tabus, the effects of the caste system upon the industrial development of the society and vice versa—all in India. But suddenly India is not very far away at all. The lecture then goes back to its Southern theme. The familiar now seems not quite so familiar any more. Questions are raised that are new, perhaps raised angrily, but raised all the same. And at least some of the students have begun to understand that there are functions involved in this business of race that they have not read about in the newspapers (at least not those in their home-towns) and that their parents have not told them—partly, at least, because neither the newspapers nor the parents knew about them.

It can be said that the first wisdom of sociology is this—things are not what they seem. This too is a deceptively simple statement. It ceases to be simple after a while. Social reality turns out to have many layers of meaning. The discovery of each new layer changes the perception of the whole.

Anthropologists use the term "culture shock" to describe the impact of a totally new culture upon a newcomer. In an extreme instance such shock will be experienced by the Western explorer who is told, halfway through dinner, that he is eating the nice old lady he had been chatting with the previous day—a shock with predictable physiological if not moral consequences. Most explorers no longer encounter cannibalism in their travels today. However, the first encounters with polygamy or with puberty rites or even with the way some nations drive their automobiles can be quite a shock to an American visitor. With the shock may go not only disapproval or disgust but a sense of excitement that things can *really* be that different from what they are at home. To some extent, at least, this is the excitement of any first travel abroad. The experience of sociological discovery could be described as "culture shock" minus geographical displacement. In other words, the sociologist travels at home—with shocking results. He is unlikely to find that he is eating a nice old lady for dinner. But the discovery, for instance, that his own church has considerable money invested in the missile industry or that a few blocks from his home there are people who engage in cultic orgies may not be drastically different in emotional impact. Yet we would not want to imply that sociological discoveries are always or even usually outrageous to moral sentiment. Not at all. What they have in common with exploration in distant lands, however, is the sudden illumination of new and unsuspected facets of human existence in society. This is the excitement and, as we shall try to show later, the humanistic justification of sociology.

People who like to avoid shocking discoveries, who prefer to believe that society is just what they were taught in Sunday School, who like the safety of the rules and the maxims of what Alfred Schuetz has called the "world-taken–for-granted," should stay away from sociology. People who feel no temptation before closed doors, who have no curiosity about human beings, who are content to admire scenery without wondering about the people who live in those houses on the other side of that river, should probably also stay away from sociology. They will find it unpleasant or, at any rate, unrewarding. People who are interested in human beings only if they can change, convert or reform them should also be warned, for they will find sociology much less useful than they hoped. And people whose interest is mainly in their own conceptual constructions will do just as well to turn to the study of little white mice. Sociology will be satisfying, in the long run, only to those who can think of nothing more entrancing than to watch men and to understand things human.

It may now be clear that we have, albeit deliberately, understated the case in the title of this chapter. To be sure, sociology is an individual pastime in the sense that it interests some men and bores others. Some like to observe human beings, others to experiment with mice. The world is big enough to hold all kinds and there is no logical priority for one interest as against another. But the word "pastime" is weak in describing what we mean. Sociology is more like a passion. The sociological perspective is more like a demon that possesses one, that drives one compellingly, again and again, to the questions that are its own. An introduction to sociology is, therefore, an invitation to a very special kind of passion. No passion is without its dangers. The sociologist who sells his wares should make sure that he clearly pronounces a *caveat emptor* quite early in the transaction.

QUESTIONS

? Berger claims that sociology uses a "scientific frame of reference." What does he mean?

? Where do sociologists find their information? How do they gather it?

? Societal puzzle question: Berger states that sociology can be used for social good, but that it can just as easily be used for "malevolent or misanthropic purposes." What does he mean? Make a list of the ways in which sociology could be used to benefit society and ways in which it could be used to harm society.

The Urban Inferno

By ERIC KLINENBERG

■ Did you know that sociologists can conduct autopsies? In this selection, taken from his book *Heat Wave: A Social Autopsy of Disaster in Chicago,* Eric Klinenberg uses his sociological skills to examine the social patterns that contributed to the over 700 heat wave deaths occurring within just one week in Chicago during the summer of 1995. Although official reports blamed the deaths specifically on the heat wave, Klinenberg reveals that the weather conditions alone were not the only cause of death. He seeks to understand the experiences of those who were most at risk for dying, showing us that when we enlist a sociological perspective, we find that even in death, things are not always as they seem.

On Wednesday morning, 12 July 1995, the *Chicago Sun Times* reported that a heat wave was heading for the city. An article proclaiming "Heat Wave on the Way—And It Can Be a Killer" ran on page 3 of the news section instead of on the weather page. Forecasters were predicting that the temperature would reach the mid-nineties that afternoon and stay near one hundred degrees Fahrenheit for the next two days. The humidity and ozone levels also would be high, making the air feel tropical, as if Chicago were in Fiji or Guam. The heat index, which measures the temperature that a typical person would feel, could top 120 degrees.

On Thursday the temperature hit 106 degrees and the heat index climbed to 126. Brick houses and apartment buildings baked like ovens, and indoor thermometers in high-rises topped 120 degrees even when windows were open. Thousands of cars broke down in the streets. Several roads buckled. City workers watered bridges spanning the Chicago River to prevent them from locking when their plates expanded. Train rails detached from their moorings and commuters endured long delays.

In the newspapers and on television, meteorologists recommended that Chicago residents use air conditioners, drink plenty of water each day and relax; "Stake out your tuck at the nearest beach, pool, or air-conditioned

---

From *Heat Wave: A Social Autopsy of Disaster in Chicago* by Eric Klinenberg. Copyright © 2002 by The University of Chicago. Reprinted by permission of The University of Chicago Press. All rights reserved.

store. Slow down.... Think cool thoughts." Appliance stores throughout the city sold out their air conditioners and home pools. "This is the kind of weather we pray for," remarked one spokesperson for a regional supplier. Nearly one hundred thousand people crowded into a small downtown beach. Others took boat trips onto Lake Michigan, only to return when passengers became dehydrated and ill. Hundreds of children riding in school buses developed heat exhaustion when they got stuck in mid-day traffic. Adults carried many of the children out of the vehicles, firefighters hosed them down, and paramedics provided emergency assistance. Those with the worst illnesses were hospitalized.

The city soon experienced scattered power outages as a result of unprecedented electrical use. As lights, air conditioners, radios, and television sets were rendered useless, news, weather updates, and health advice were hard to get. Elevators stopped, making it necessary for members of the Police and Fire Departments to carry elderly high-rise residents down from the stifling beat of their apartments. Many people with no power or simply no air-conditioning packed bags and stayed with family or friends. On Friday three power transformers failed at the Northwest Substation of Commonwealth Edison, the city's primary electric delivery services company, causing forty-nine thousand customers to lose power—some for as long as two days.

In neighborhoods with few air-conditioned public spaces, young residents opened fire hydrants and showered themselves in the spray to keep cool. At one point more than three thousand hydrants spouted freely, contributing to an expenditure of almost two billion gallons of water, double Chicago's consumption on a typical summer day. Water pressure fell. Neighborhoods where several hydrants were open lost all pressure for hours; malfunctioning pumps left, buildings without water for days. Police announced that anyone found tampering with hydrants would be arrested and fined, and the city dispatched one hundred field crews to seal these emergency water sources. In some places people saw the crews coming and threw bricks and rocks to keep them away. Some shot at the trucks; and four workers received minor injuries.

On Friday, 14 July, the heat index exceeded one hundred degrees for the third consecutive day, and temperatures remained high at night. Because the body's defenses can take only about forty-eight hours of uninterrupted exposure to such heat before they break down, city residents were becoming ill. Many more people than usual grew sick enough to be hospitalized: between 13 and 19 July ambulance services received several thousand transport requests above the norm. In thirty nine-hundred cases, no vehicles were available, so the city sent fire trucks to handle the calls. Although the average response time for Chicago's emergency health services had been less than seven minutes that year, now the paramedics were often delayed. Some residents who phoned for ambulances were told that that they would have to wait because the vehicles were all booked. Fifty-five emergency callers were left unattended for thirty minutes or longer; some endured a two-hour wait. In a few cases of heat stress the victims waited so long for medical attention that they died.

Hospitals and other health-care providers also had trouble meeting the demand for their services. The number of people admitted to emergency rooms and inpatient units began to rise on Wednesday and continued to increase through the weekend. Some emergency rooms ran out of beds and their staffs could not handle more work. More than twenty hospitals, most on the South and Southeast Sides of the city, went on bypass status, closing the doors of their emergency facilities and refusing to accept new admissions. There was no reliable way for citizens or paramedics to learn which emergency rooms were still open, so ambulances and private cars continued to arrive at the hospital ports. Often their passengers required urgent treatment, but facilities on bypass could not tell drivers where such care was available. Some hospitals reported that patients had traveled more than ten miles before finding a facility that could treat them. Medical workers grew anxious. What would happen to the diverted cases? Where could they go?

Many heat victims were not discovered or taken to hospitals until it was too late for doctors to help. On Friday, for example, Margaret Ortiz, the owner of a small day-care service that she operated from her home, took a group of ten small children to an air-conditioned movie theater in her Ford Bronco. After the movie ended, Ortiz took the children back to the center and brought them indoors. Everyone was exhausted and the toddlers napped. An hour and a half passed before Ortiz went to her Bronco on her way to picking up more children. When she reached her vehicle, she discovered that two boys had been left inside. Ortiz carried the children indoors and called 911. The boys were already dead, though, and when the paramedics arrived, they determined that the body temperatures were 107 and 108 degrees. Chicago newspapers and television news programs featured stories of the children's deaths prominently in their heat wave coverage. The Cook County Medical Examiner scheduled autopsies on the children for the next morning, but there was little question about the cause of death.

As the day wore on, more Chicagoans succumbed to the heat. By comparison, on Wednesday, 12 July, and Thursday 13 July, 74 and 82 people, respectively, lost their lives, figures that are only slightly above the July norm of about 72 deaths per day. When the effects of the continuous heat began to accumulate, however, the death toll increased substantially. On Friday, 14 July, 188 Chicago residents perished. On Saturday the reported mortality was 365, five times the typical rate. Two hundred forty-one people died on Sunday, 193 on Monday, and 106 on Tuesday. On Wednesday, 19 July, citywide deaths dropped to 92, then to 91 on Thursday. City agencies, already scrambling to manage the crisis, searched for a place that could hold the dead. According to emergency workers, the task was equivalent to handling one fatal jetliner crash per day for three consecutive days.

In the end, the city reported that between 14 and 20 July, 485 Chicago residents died directly from heat-related causes, bringing the total mortalities for the month to 521. (These numbers were based on medical autopsies and police examinations that officially established causes of death for each case.) More than one thousand people in excess of the July norm were admitted to inpatient units in local hospitals because of heatstroke, dehydration, heat exhaustion, renal failure, and electrolytic imbalances. Those who developed heatstroke suffered permanent damage, such as loss of independent, function and multisystem organ failures. Thousands of other stricken by heat-related illnesses were treated in emergency rooms.

After the heat had subsided, epidemiologists compiled statistics on the mortality patterns during July, taking into account the deaths of people who had not been taken to the Medical Examiners Office. They determined that the death count based solely on the medical autopsies had underestimated the damage. Between 14 and 20 July, 739 more Chicago residents died than in a typical week for that month. In fact, public health scholars have established that the proportional death toll from the heat wave in Chicago has no equal in the record of U.S. heat disasters.

Comparisons with other historic catastrophes help to establish the magnitude of the trauma. More than twice as many people died in the heat wave than in the Great Chicago Fire of 1871, when approximately three hundred people perished. More recent U.S. environmental disasters, such as California's Northridge earthquake of 1994 and Florida's Hurricane Andrew in 1992, caused the deaths of one-tenth and one-twentieth the heat wave total, respectively. The Oklahoma City bombing in April 1995, which killed 168, and the crash of TWA Flight 800 in 1996, which killed 230, were several times less fatal. Reporters, public officials, and scientific authorities have developed compelling and straightforward accounts of the reasons that so many people died in these other environmental or technological disasters. In the Chicago heat tragedy, however, the causes of the mortality are more elusive and complex.

In recent years, a number of meteorological studies and journalistic reports have examined the reasons for the historic mortality figures. According to the National Oceanic and Atmospheric Administration, "The principal cause of the July 1995 heat wave was a slow-moving, hot, and humid air mass produced by the chance occurrence at the same time of an unusually strong upper-level ridge of high pressure and unusually moist ground conditions." The geographer Laurence Kalkstein provided a deeper analysis of the weather. Using a new air mass-based synoptic procedure to pinpoint the meteorological conditions that impose serious health hazards, Kalkstein found that a moist tropical system, with high humidity, low winds, and high minimum temperatures, created an unusually dangerous July climate.

But does the severe weather fully account for Chicago's human catastrophe? According to the meteorologists and epidemiologists who have studied the event, the answer is decidedly no. In an article published by the *American Journal of Public Health*, a group of scholars headed by the former epidemiology director of the Chicago Department of Public Health reported that it had "examined some weather variables but failed to detect relationships between the weather and mortality that would explain what happened in July 1995 in Chicago." Even the most sophisticated meteorological analyses "still leave a fair amount of variance in the mortality measure unexplained." The weather, in other words, accounts for only part of the human devastation that arose from the Chicago heat wave. The disaster also has a social etiology, which no meteorological study, medical autopsy, or epidemiological report can uncover. The human dimensions of the catastrophe remain unexplored.

This book is organized around a social autopsy of the 1995 Chicago heat wave. Just as the medical autopsy opens the body to determine the proximate physiological causes of mortality, this inquiry aims to examine the social organs of the city and identify the conditions that contributed to the deaths of so many Chicago residents that July. If the idea of conducting a social autopsy sounds peculiar, this is largely because modern political and medical institutions have attained monopolistic roles in officially explaining, defining, and classifying life and death, in establishing the terms and categories that structure the way we see and do not see the world. As Gaston Bachelard has written, "It quite often happens that a phenomenon is insignificant only because one fails to take it into account." The missing dimension in our current understanding of the heat wave stems precisely from this kind of diagnostic failure.

What happened in Chicago was more than a natural disaster, and its story is more than a catalogue of urban horrors. The 1995 heat wave was a social drama that played out and made visible a series of conditions that are always present but difficult to perceive. Investigating the people, places, and institutions most affected by the heat wave—the homes of the decedents, the neighborhoods and buildings where death was concentrated or prevented, the city agencies that forged an emergency response system, the Medical Examiners Office and scientific research centers that searched for causes of death, and the newsrooms where reporters and editors symbolically reconstructed the event—helps to reveal the social order of a city in crisis. This study establishes that the heat wave deaths represent what Paul Farmer calls "biological reflections of social fault lines" for which we, and not nature, are responsible. We have collectively created the conditions that made it possible for so many Chicago residents to die in the summer of 1995, as well as the conditions that make these deaths so easy to overlook and forget. We can collectively unmake them, too, but only once we recognize and scrutinize the cracks in our social foundations that we customarily take for granted and put out of sight.

THE SOCIAL PRODUCTION OF ISOLATION

Although the epidemiological reports on the heat wave established the relationship between isolation and mortality in the disaster, they offer little explanation for the deeper question of why so many Chicagoans lived and died alone. The political commissions that studied the heat wave, however, provided two major conclusions. The first was that relative to earlier times, more frail people are aging alone and living with everyday vulnerabilities that render them susceptible to the heat. The second was that most people who live alone take great pride in their independence and tend to refrain from asking for or accepting assistance, because doing so would spoil their identity as self-sufficient individuals. The result, as the Mayor's Commission on Extreme Weather Conditions states, is that "those most at risk may be least likely to want or accept help from government."

There is some degree of truth in both of these explanations, and I will consider them seriously in this chapter. Yet even together they fail to provide a satisfying account of the reasons that so many Chicago residents died in solitude during the heat wave and that so many others continue to live in isolation. According to urban critic Jane Jacobs, "It took a lot of effort to make people this isolated." But the ways in which Americans have engineered such extreme forms of individuation and social segmentation remain mysterious. Looking more closely at the conditions that made Chicagoans vulnerable to the heat helps to make visible a series of social transformations that contribute to the emerging phenomenon of being alone in the city.

This chapter focuses on four trends, all of which contribute to the vulnerability of the growing number of Americans who are old and poor:

- *a demographic shift*, the increasing number of people living alone and, in particular, of seniors who are aging alone, often with disabilities and barriers to mobility and sociability;

- *a cultural condition* related to crime, the coupling of a "culture of fear" stemming from the violence and perceived violence of everyday life with the longstanding American valuation of privacy, individualism, and self-sufficiency, particularly among the elderly and men;
- *a spatial transformation*, the degradation, fortification, or elimination of public spaces and supported housing arrangements such as public housing clusters or SRO dwellings, especially in areas with concentrated poverty, violence, and illness;
- *a gendered condition*, the tendency for older men, particularly single men without children and men with substance abuse problems, to lose crucial parts of their social networks and valuable sources of social support as they age.

Together, these conditions create a new set of risks for a rising segment of the urban population, an everyday state of danger and deprivation whose impact on the life of the city is as severe as it is unspoken.

"THE CLOSEST I'VE COME TO DEATH"

Pauline Jankowitz survived the heat wave, but her story helps to illustrate some of the fundamental features of aging alone and being afraid in the city. I first met Pauline on her eighty-fifth birthday, when I was assigned to be her companion for a day by Little Brothers Friends of the Elderly, a secular, nonprofit, international organization that supports seniors living alone by linking them up with volunteer companions and inviting them to the organization's center for a birthday party and a Thanksgiving and Christmas dinner every year. Although a stranger before the day began, I became her closest companion for the milestone occasion when I picked her up at the Northeast Side apartment where she had lived for thirty years.

Pauline and I had spoken on the phone the previous day, so she was expecting me when I arrived late in the morning. She lives on a quiet residential street dominated by the small three- and four-flat apartment buildings common in Chicago. Her neighborhood, a key site of departure and arrival for urban migrants, has changed dramatically in the time she has lived there. Her block has shifted from a predominantly white ethnic area in which Pauline was a typical resident to a mixed street with a sizable Asian and increasingly Mexican population. The small urban enclave remains home to her, but she is less comfortable in it because the neighbors are no longer familiar to her. "They are good people," she explained, "but I just don't know them." Her situation is similar to that of thousands of Chicago residents and millions of seniors across the country who have *aged in place* while the environment around them changes and their local friends leave.

Other major sources of discomfort for Pauline are her physical infirmities, which worsen as she ages: a bladder problem that left her incontinent, and a weak leg that requires her to walk with a crutch and drastically reduces her mobility. Pauline's fear of crime, which she hears about daily on the radio and television, contributes to her confinement. "Chicago is just a shooting gallery," she told me, "and I am a moving target because I walk so slowly." Acutely aware of her vulnerability, Pauline reorganized her life to limit her exposure to the threats outside, bunkering herself in a third-floor apartment in a building that has no elevator. The stairs give her trouble when she enters and leaves her home, but she prefers the high floor because "it is much safer than the first floor.... If I were on the first floor I'd be even more vulnerable to a break-in." With a home-care support worker, delivered meals, and a publicly subsidized helper visiting weekly to do her grocery shopping and help with errands, Pauline has few reasons to leave home. "I go out of my apartment about six times a year," she told me, "and three of them are for Little Brothers celebrations."

Little Brothers Friends of the Elderly is one of the few organizations in the United States whose mission is to address the problems related to aging alone and to assist isolated seniors in their efforts to make or remake connections to a world that has left them behind. In 1997 the Little Brothers Friends of the Elderly Chicago operation coordinated more than 8,000 personal visits and 11,000 calls to isolated and reclusive seniors; brought more than 2,000 isolated elderly to their various holiday activities; and welcomed about 1,800 to birthday celebrations. "The problem," the organization states clearly in its reports, "is isolation and loneliness.... Our old friends don't have a social network of family and friends. They identify themselves as lonely and they seek companionship and friendship.... Our role is to become the family and friends the elderly have outlived, never had, or from whom they are estranged."

It is, I would learn, a challenge for Little Brothers to help even the seniors with whom they have contact. Pauline and I made it to the birthday celebration after a difficult and painful trip down her stairway, during which we had to turn around and return to the apartment so that she could address "a problem" that she experienced on the stairs—one apparently too embarrassing to discuss with me. Pauline's grimaces and sighs betrayed the depth of the pain that the walk had inflicted, but she was so excited to be going out, and going to her party, that she urged me to get us to the center quickly. I was supposed to have brought two other seniors to the celebration who had confirmed their intention to me the day before, but when I arrived at their apartments they both told me that they had decided to stay home.

Pauline had an extra incentive to get to the party. Edna, one of her two "phone buddies" who lived a few blocks away but saw her only at Little Brothers events, would also be there for the day. The two were thrilled to see each other, and at the end of the excellent meal and sing-along that highlighted the joyous event, Edna arranged to get a ride back with me so that she could extend the visit.

Edna got out more than Pauline, but both explained that the telephone has become their primary link to the world outside. Pauline has two phone buddies with whom she speaks regularly; one is a romantic albeit physically distant attachment. A few other friends and family members also call occasionally. Pauline has two children, who both live out of the state and visit infrequently but call about once a week. Although they phoned to wish their mother a happy birthday, neither could make it to Chicago to celebrate the occasion.

Pauline's other main sources of companionship are the major media, mostly television and radio, and the odd things she receives in the mail, which a neighbor brings up to her apartment and leaves on a pile of boxes outside the door so she doesn't have to bend over to pick it up. Recently, Pauline has started to phone in to talk shows, where she likes to discuss political scandals and local issues. These contacts helped keep her alive during the 1995 heat wave, as she and her friends checked up on one another often to make sure they were taking care of themselves.

Pauline knew that I was studying the disaster and during one visit she announced that she wanted to tell me her story. "It was," she said softly, "the closest I've come to death." Pauline has one air conditioner in her apartment, which gets especially hot during the summer because it is on the third floor. But the machine "is old and it doesn't work too well," which left her place uncomfortably, if not dangerously, warm during the heat wave. A friend had told her that it was important for her to go outside if she was too hot indoors, so she arose very early ("it's safer then") on what would become the hottest day of the heat wave, to visit the local grocer to buy cherries ("my favorite fruit, but I rarely get fresh food so they're a real treat for me") and cool down in the air-conditioned store. "I was so exhausted by the time I got down the stairs that I wanted to go straight back up again," she recounted, "but instead I walked to the corner and took the bus a few blocks to the store. When I got there I could barely move. I had to lean on the shopping cart to keep myself up." But the cool air revived her enough to buy a bag of cherries and return home on the bus.

"Climbing the stairs was almost impossible," she remembered. "I was hot and sweaty and so tired." Pauline called a friend as soon as she made it into her place. As they spoke she began to feel her hands going numb and swelling, a sensation that quickly extended into other parts of her body, alerting her that something was wrong. "I asked my friend to stay on the line but I put the phone down and lied down." Several minutes later, her friend still on the line but the receiver on the floor, Pauline got up, soaked her head in water, directed a fan toward her bed, lay down again, and placed a number of wet towels on her body and face. Remembering that she had left her friend waiting, Pauline got up, picked up the receiver to report that she was feeling better and to thank her buddy for waiting, and then hung up. Finally, she lay down once more to cool off and rest in earnest. Before long she had fully recovered.

"Now," she concluded, "I have a special way to beat the heat. You're going to laugh, but I like to go on a Caribbean cruise"—alone and, as she does nearly everything else, without leaving her home. "I get several washcloths and dip them in cold water. I then place them over my eyes so that I can't see. I lie down and set the fan directly on me. The wet towels and the wind from the fan give a cool breeze, and I imagine myself on a cruise around the islands. I do this whenever it's hot, and you'd be surprised at how nice it is. My friends know about my cruises too. So when they call me on hot days they all say, 'Hi Pauline, how was your trip?' We laugh about it, but it keeps me alive."

Pauline's case is hardly unique. Sharon Keigher, a professor at the University of Wisconsin who conducted a multiyear study of housing risks for the Chicago elderly, reports the following case study of a woman identified through Chicago's Emergency Services program. Her account of Viola Cooper suggests how much more difficult isolation can be when it is compounded by extreme poverty:

> *At similar risk…is Viola Cooper, a thin 70-year-old black woman who continues to live alone in isolation in her basement apartment. She greeted us in the hallway with a toothless, pleasant smile. Her three-room apartment, furnished with odd items of run-down furniture, was cluttered, dirty, and in poor condition.… This apartment, for which she pays $250 of her $490 monthly income, was not much of an improvement over the last apartment where ES [Emergency Services] workers found her.*
>
> *She had just come home from the hospital after 8 days in intensive care for treatment of an infected bite on her face received from a rabid rat. She had been bitten while sleeping in her apartment. After the fire (2 years before), ES determined that repairs on her apartment were 'in process' and 'relocation (was) not needed,' although follow-up (sic) services record the deplorable conditions she was living in.*
>
> *Fortunately, she was referred by the City to a private agency which helped her move and gave her some furniture.… She now lives too far from her church to attend, for the first few months she had no running water or working toilet, her only friend in the building died a few months ago.… Alone, sick, and depressed, her condition is aggravated by the unhealthy conditions under which she lives.*

VIOLENCE AND ISOLATION

Pauline Jankowitz and Viola Cooper are merely two of the 110,000 seniors who lived alone in Chicago during the 1990s; and despite her many barriers to social integration, Pauline's location in the northeast part of the city makes her relatively safer than seniors living in other regions. Nonetheless, urban areas with high levels of violent crime impose real barriers to mobility for their residents, and during this period Chicago was among the most dangerous cities in the country. In 1995, for example, Chicago ranked sixth in robberies and fifth in aggravated assaults among all U.S. cities with populations exceeding 350,000; and in 1998 it was the national leader in homicides at 698—exceeding New York City's figure for that year by about 100, although it is roughly one-third as populous.

Most important for the story of the heat wave, though, is that during the week before the event Chicago experienced a spurt of homicides that put people living near the crossfire on alert. From Friday 7 July to Thursday 13 July 1995, there were twenty-four homicides in the city. Under the headline "City Murders on Rise with the Thermometer," the *Chicago Tribune* reported that the annual summer upsurge in violence had begun, with most killings "concentrated in South Side neighborhoods that carry a disproportionate share of the city's deadly violence." The same areas produced an inordinate number of heat-wave-related deaths the next week. Though they were unlikely targets for the shootings, older residents of violent areas who refused to leave their homes during the heat wave had reason to be concerned about the risks they faced in the city streets.

In recent years a number of studies have shown that older people living in violent and deteriorated urban areas tend to be more isolated and afraid of crime than those in more robust regions. Among the mechanisms producing this concentrated fear and isolation in ecologically depleted and politically underserved places are the lack of local commercial venues and service providers to draw people into the streets; barriers to physical mobility, such as broken stairs, crumbling sidewalks, and poor lighting; the psychological impact of living amidst signs of disorder; indifferent government agencies who neglect the local infrastructure; and the decrease of trusting and reciprocal relationships in areas with high levels of crime. In extreme cases, social gerontologists Estina Thompson and Neal Krause report, "avoidance behavior" encouraged by degraded public areas "is so great among older people that many live in a virtual state of 'self-imposed house arrest.' " But "even if people only partially restrict their outdoor activities in response to their fear of crime, they still have fewer opportunities than those with lower levels of fear to establish the face-to-face contact that appears to be so important to receiving support."

THE CULTURE OF FEAR

The urban elderly are hardly the only Americans to reduce their vulnerability to the dangers of the street by limiting their time in public as well as their social contacts. In recent decades, as sociologists including Elijah Anderson show, social avoidance and reclusion have become essential protective strategies for city residents whose concentration in high-crime neighborhoods places them directly in harm's way. More-over, Americans who live in objectively safer areas have been influenced by a sweeping culture of fear that is borne of both direct experience and sensationalistic representations of crime and danger in the media. In cities like Chicago a pervasive concern with crime is now a fundamental part of the cultural substratum of everyday life, playing a key role in organizing the temporal and spatial boundaries of mundane activities—many people refuse to go out at night or to visit "no-go" areas—as well as in shaping major decisions about where to live, work, and send children to school.

According to several commentators who wrote about the heat wave, one barometer of the extent to which Chicagoans have adapted to the threats of contemporary urban life is that during the heat wave most of the city's public parks and beaches were empty at night. Throughout the city, but especially in the areas with high rates of violent crimes, people chose to suffer through the intense heat rather than cool themselves in the same areas in which their predecessors had congregated in severe heat waves of previous decades. "You'd have to be crazy, suicidal, or homeless these days to spend a sultry night sleeping in a park or on a porch," opined Bob Secter in a *Sun-Times* article placed beneath a photograph of two men resting by a harbor during a balmy night in 1964. "But Chicagoans once did it by the tens of thousands to survive blistering heat waves."

In an especially intense heat wave during 1955, for example, thousands of families packed up their bedding and beverages and camped outdoors in parks, on beaches, or simply on their front porches. Fewer than 10 percent of Chicago homes at the time had air conditioners, but the simple strategy of sleeping outside helped to keep the mortality rate during the 1955 crisis down to roughly half the level of the 1995 disaster. Alan Ehrenhalt argues that in the 1950s the streets and public areas in Chicago's ghettos supported vigorous social activity and provided safe spaces for residents to come together. Ehrenhalt depicts Bronzeville, Chicago's black metropolis, as typical of a 1950s city environment that was "an unrelentingly public world" in which "summer evenings were one long community festival, involving just about everybody on the block" and ending with people "sleeping on fire escapes to avoid the heat."

There is good reason to be cautious about an overly romantic, even nostalgic view in this kind of account. But if the image of sleeping outdoors in summer is a central element of conventional portraits of urban decline, it is such a powerful and pervasive memory among older Chicago residents—including those who lived in the city's ghettos during the 1940s and 1950s—that it is difficult to discount. Eugene Richards, a seventy-year-old African-American man who has lived in North Lawndale since the late 1950s, recalled that in the early days "when it got hot, the whole block would go to Garfield Park and sleep outside. We'd take out blankets and pillows, people would sleep on benches and in the grass. And we just left the dogs in the yard. And that was it." I asked Eugene whether people went to the parks during the 1995 heat wave. He looked at me incredulously and chuckled to himself. "Over here? Now? Are you kidding me? No, no, no. No one would sleep. I won't even walk at night around here. It's too dangerous. You can't trust your luck too much. People out at 2 or 3 in the morning will do anything. You have to be cautious."

Another indication of the extent to which this cautiousness has spread in Chicago is that during the heat wave many Chicago seniors refused to open their doors or respond to volunteers and city workers who had tracked them down and tried to check on them. Although the Mayor's Commission on Extreme Weather Conditions complained that such behavior was a sign of seniors' refusal to compromise their independence and face up to their own vulnerability, there is more to the story than this. According to seniors throughout the city, turning strangers away at the door has become part of a survival strategy for living alone in the city. "If someone comes to the door I won't open it," a woman in her seventies told me during a discussion in a local church. "I'll talk through the door because you never know."

In an environment where preying on the elderly is a standard and recurrent practice of neighborhood deviants as well as legitimate corporations, mail-order businesses, and salespersons, seniors report feeling besieged on an everyday basis. Whether the aggressors are local hoodlums who pay them special attention around the beginning of the month when Social Security checks are delivered, or outsiders who try to visit, or phone and convince them to spend scarce dollars, the cumulative impact for the elderly of exposure to such threats is increased suspicion, especially when it comes to greeting unannounced and unknown visitors at the door.

Criminologists have long puzzled over the question of why the elderly, who are statistically less likely to be victimized by crime than almost all other demographic groups, are generally the most afraid of crime. But seniors in Chicago can explain the basis of their concerns. Many of the elderly people I interviewed acknowledged that they were unlikely to be robbed or burgled, yet argued that they had special concerns about the consequences of being victimized that younger and more adaptable people did not share. Economic insecurity is one source of their fear. Seniors living on fixed and limited incomes worry about making ends meet most of the time, and for them a robbery or burglary could result in a loss of food, medication, rent, or resources to pay for utilities. In Chicago, where roughly 16 percent of the elderly live below the official poverty line and housing is in short supply, these are well-founded concerns. Physical insecurity is another source of disquiet. The seniors I got to know expressed great concerns about their health, and awareness of their own frailty made them especially fearful of an act of aggression. Not only were they worried that they would be unable to defend themselves or flee from an attack, they also feared the possibility that an assault would leave them disabled or even dead.

Sensationalized media representations of crime, particularly local television news stories about violence and danger in the city, fuel these concerns. George Gebner, former dean of the Annenberg School of Communication at the University of Pennsylvania, has shown that "people who watch a lot of TV are more likely than others to believe their neighborhoods are unsafe, to assume that crime rates are rising, and overestimate their own odds of becoming a victim." Chicago television stations contributed to anxiety about crime during the early days of the heat wave. The one local network affiliate, for example, opened its 5:00 P.M. news broadcast on 14 July with a warning that "the heat is also giving opportunities to thieves," accompanied by video footage of a home with open windows and an interview with police officers cautioning residents to look out for trouble.

In fact, another reason that seniors are especially fearful of crime is that older Americans are among the greatest consumers of the media, including broadcast news on radio and television, which are the greatest sources of urban crime stories. Barry Glassner sums up the research on the elderly, media consumption, and fear in language that resonates strikingly with the story of Chicago's heat wave. "Ample real-world evidence can be found among the nation's elderly, many of whom are so upset by all the murder and mayhem they see on their television screens that they are terrified to leave their homes. Some become so isolated, studies found, that they do not get enough exercise and their physical and mental health deteriorates. In the worst cases they actually suffer malnutrition as a consequence.... Afraid to go out and buy groceries, they literally waste away in their homes."

These pressures to withdraw from public life in U.S. cities are especially dangerous because they join forces with another fundamental feature of American culture that fosters isolation: the idealization and valuation of independence and self-sufficiency. The myth of the independent individual who determines his own fate and needs no help from others has evolved from frontier legend to become one of foundations of U.S. popular thought. Americans not only deny the extent to which their fate is shaped by their support networks and their ties with others, but also stigmatize people—historically women and the elderly—who are thought to be especially dependent. The elderly in general, but old men in particular, face the challenge of maintaining their sense of self-worth and dignity in a society that denigrates people having visible needs. For older men, most of whom built their identities around the role of the breadwinner, perhaps the primary struggle of aging is warding off the role of the dependent old-timer who is unable to provide for others or even himself. Many seniors find that retreating into isolation and refusing support is the best means of saving face. Better to be alone, they conclude, than to be disgraced.

Although fear and isolation are more prevalent in areas where violence is most prevalent, the conditions of insecurity and concern about crime penetrate every part of a city. As a consequence, a pervasive bunker mentality has emerged on a smaller scale throughout Chicago, affecting a broad set of buildings, blocks, and housing facilities. It is now common for city residents to protect their neighborhoods, streets, and homes with walls, cul-de-sacs, bright lighting, and alarms, and to patrol their territory with neighborhood watches and crime-control groups. The fortress architecture of gated communities is the most public symbol of this trend, but it is also marked by the make-shift home-security devices common in poor neighborhoods where residents face a greater risk of burglary or violent attack, and by the rise of private alarm systems and security workers in all realms of American life.

Spatial degradation combined with concentrated criminal activity helped produce isolation and reclusion in some of the settings where heat wave deaths were concentrated, such as senior public housing units and SROs.

QUESTIONS

? Who was most at risk for dying in the heat wave? Why?

? The Mayor's Commission on Extreme Weather report makes the statement that "those most at risk may be least likely to want or accept help from the government." Does Klinenberg's research support this statement? Why or why not?

? Societal puzzle question: Identify a recent natural disaster that has claimed many lives. Explain the disaster and how it has been described in the news. How might Klinenberg's social autopsy method be used to gain a more complex understanding of how and why the deaths occurred?

Chapter 2

Extreme Social Isolation of a Child[1]

By KINGSLEY DAVIS

■ Imagine that you could go back to the time when you were only a few weeks old. Now, imagine that your mother or father decide, for whatever reason, to leave you in a room, by yourself. No one talks to you, no one plays with you, and the only time you are visited is to be fed, changed, or bathed. You are experiencing social isolation (the process of being set apart and having limited or no interaction with other people). Would "you" still be who "you" are? Such an example of social isolation—the case of five-year old Anna, caught the attention of sociologist Kingsley Davis. In 1940, he researched Anna's story, publishing his observations in *The American Journal of Sociology*. For Davis, Anna's isolation provided an exemplary case study to highlight the importance of socialization—the process by which we come to learn our culture and become human.

The present paper, dealing with an incarcerated child, is of the nature of a progress report. The girl it describes is still under observation and is likely to remain so for many years. Hence the present results are necessarily inconclusive.

According to the *New York Times* for February 6, 1938, a girl of more than five years had been found "tied to an old chair in a storage room on the second floor" of a farm home seventeen miles from a small Pennsylvania city. The child, said the report, was wedged into the chair, which was tilted backwards to rest on a coal bucket, her spindly arms tied above her head. She was unable to talk or move.... "The child was dressed in a dirty shirt and napkin," the officer said. "Her hands, arms and legs were just bones, with skin drawn over them, so frail she couldn't use them. She never had enough nourishment. She never grew normally, and the chair on which she lay, half reclining and half sitting, was so small the child had to double her legs partly under her."

The reason for this situation was that the child, Anna,[2] was illegitimate. She was the second illegitimate child the mother had borne, and since the mother resided with her father and other relatives in the paternal

---

From *The American Journal of Sociology*, Vol. 45, No. 4, January 1940 by Kingsley Davis. Copyright © 1940 by University of Chicago Press. Reprinted by permission.

homestead, she found her father so angry that he was averse even to seeing this second child. Hence she kept it in an out-of-the-way room.

Upon reading this report the writer and a student assistant, Richard G. Davis, went to see the child. Later, subsequent trips were made, and between visits reports from various persons connected with the child were received by mail. Our records now seem reasonably complete and confirm the salient facts in the *Times* account.[3]

By the time we arrived on the scene, February 7, Anna had been in her new abode, the county home,[4] for only three days. But she was already beginning to change. When first brought to the county home she had been completely apathetic—had lain in a limp, supine position, immobile, expressionless, indifferent to everything. Her flaccid feet had fallen forward, making almost a straight line with the skeleton-like legs, indicating that the child had long lain on her back to the point of exhaustion and atrophy of her foot muscles. She was believed to be deaf and possibly blind. Her urine, according to the nurse, had been extremely concentrated and her stomach exceedingly bloated. It was thought that she had suffered at one time from rickets, though later medical opinion changed the diagnosis to simple malnutrition. Her blood count had been very low in haemoglobin. No sign of disease had been discovered.

Upon our arrival, three days after she was brought to the county home, most of these conditions still prevailed. But her stomach had retracted a little and she had become fairly active, being able to sit up (if placed in a sitting position) and to move her hands, arms, head, eyes, and mouth quite freely. These changes had resulted from a high vitamin diet, massage, and attention. In spite of her physical condition she had an attractive facial appearance, with no discernible stigmata. Her complexion, features, large blue eyes, and even teeth (in good shape though not quite normal in size) gave her a favorable appearance.

Since Anna turned her head slowly toward a loud-ticking clock held near her, we concluded that she could hear. Other attempts to make her notice sounds, such as clapping hands or speaking to her, elicited no response; yet when the door was opened suddenly she tended to look in that direction. Her feet were sensitive to touch. She exhibited the plantar, patellar, and pupillary reflexes. When sitting up she jounced rhythmically up and down on the bed—a recent habit of which she was very fond. Though her eyes surveyed the room, especially the ceiling, it was difficult to tell if she was looking at anything in particular. She neither smiled nor cried in our presence, and the only sound she made—a slight sucking intake of breath with the lips—occurred rarely. She did frown or scowl occasionally in response to no observable stimulus; otherwise she remained expressionless.

Next morning the child seemed more alert. She liked food and lay on her back to take it. She could not chew or drink from a cup but had to be fed from a bottle or spoon—this in spite of the fact that she could grasp and manipulate objects with her hands. Toward numerous toys given her by well-wishers all over the country she showed no reaction. They were simply objects to be handled in a distracted manner; there was no element of play. She liked having her hair combed. When physically restrained she exhibited considerable temper. She did not smile except when coaxed and did not cry.

She had thus made some progress during her three days in the county home. Subsequently her progress in the home was slower. But before dealing with her later history, let us first review more completely the background facts in the case.

Anna was born March 6, 1932, in a private nurse's home. Shortly thereafter she was taken to a children's home. For a time she was boarded with a practical nurse. To those who saw and cared for her, she seemed an entirely normal baby—indeed, a beautiful child, as more than one witness has asserted. At the age of six to ten months she was taken back to her mother's home because no outside agency wished the financial responsibility of caring for her. In her mother's home she was perpetually confined in one room, and here she soon began to suffer from malnutrition, living solely on a diet of milk and getting no sunshine. She developed impetigo. The doctor, according to the mother, prescribed some external medicine which made the child "look like a nigger," and which the mother ceased to use for that reason. The mother,[5] a large woman of twenty-seven, alleges that she tried to get the child welfare agency to take Anna, but that she was refused for financial reasons. The mother, resenting the trouble which Anna's presence caused her and wanting to get rid of the girl, paid little attention to her. She apparently did nothing but feed the child, not taking the trouble to bathe, train, supervise, or caress her. Though she denies tying the child at any time, it is perhaps true that the child was restrained in some way (by tying, confining in a crib, or otherwise) and gradually, as her physical condition became worse, due to confinement and poor diet, became so apathetic that she could be safely left unrestrained without danger of moving from her chair. Anna's brother, the first illegitimate child, seems to have ignored her except to mistreat her occasionally.

The bedroom in which Anna was confined was reported to have been extraordinarily dirty and contained a double bed on which the mother and son slept while Anna reclined in a broken chair. The mother carried up and fed to Anna huge quantities of milk. Toward Anna's fifth birthday the mother, apparently on advice, began feeding her thin oatmeal with a spoon, but Anna never learned to eat solid food.

Anna's social contacts with others were then at a minimum. What few she did have were of a perfunctory or openly antagonistic kind, allowing no opportunity for *Gemeinschaft* to develop. She affords therefore an excellent subject for studying the effects of extreme social isolation.

Ten days after our first visit Anna showed some improvement. She was more alert, had more ability to fix her attention, had more expression, handled herself better, looked healthier. Moreover, she had found her tongue—in a physical sense. Whereas it had formerly lain inactive back in her mouth, she now stuck it out frequently and with enjoyment. She showed taste discrimination, for she now resisted taking cod-liver oil, which she had previously not distinguished from milk. She was beginning, in fact, to dislike any new type of food. Visual discrimination was attested by the fact that she apparently preferred a green pencil to a yellow one. She smiled more often, regularly followed with her eye the movements of the two other small children temporarily quartered in her room, and handled her toys in a more definite fashion. She could sit up better and, while lying down, could raise her head from the pillow. She liked now to sit on the edge of the bed and dangle her feet. The doctor claimed that she had a new trick every day.

She had not, however, learned any way to seek attention, to manifest wants, to chew, or to control her elimination. Only one sociable stunt had she begun to learn—rubbing foreheads with the nurse, a sport of which she later became very fond. On the other hand, her ritualistic hand play, a noticeable trait at this time, was entirely asocial.[6]

On this second visit we took along a clinical psychologist, Edward Carr. He began by checking the reflexes, finding none that were defective. He then gave Anna a three-figure form board test used in the Form L Revision of the Stanford-Binet. Anna was unable to place the blocks in the appropriately shaped holes, though apparently by chance she did once place the round piece satisfactorily. She more readily removed the blocks from the board and played with them idly for a time. When Mr. Carr first attempted by pantomime to get her to place the blocks, she seemed to concentrate, but only momentarily; and this concentration, so limited in results, apparently tired her too greatly for further efforts.[7]

The next visit, on March 22, revealed little change, except for slight physical improvement. She could lift her hips from the bed; the nurse had induced her to laugh outright by tickling her and laughing uproariously herself; and the nurse believed that Anna recognized her. The doctor had changed his early optimistic opinion; he now believed the child was congenitally deficient.

After another month Anna was five pounds heavier, more energetic, given to laughing a good deal, and credited with having made a sound like "da." But that was all.

On June 9, another month later, she had scarcely improved in any respect. When tested by the writer according to the items of the Gesell schedule, she seemed to rank with a one-year-old or better in motor activities involving hands and eyes. But with regard to linguistic and purposive behavior, she lagged behind. If any estimate were made, it could be said that she definitely ranked below the one-year-old child.

By August 12 she was still improving physically. Her legs had calves in them, and she liked to exhibit her strength in rough-housing. She would laugh heartily, often make a "tsha-tsha-tsha" sound with her lips, once or twice making a verbal type of sound, though meaningless. When held by someone, she could "walk" by putting one foot in front of the other in ostentatious steps. Her interest in other persons had become more obvious, her responses more definite and discriminating.[8]

Until removed from the county home on November 11, there were few additional changes. By this time she could barely stand while holding to something. When put on a carpet she could scoot but not crawl. She visibly liked people, as manifested by smiling, rough-housing, and hair-pulling. But she was still an unsocialized individual, for she had learned practically nothing.

If we ask why she had learned so little—not even to chew or drink from a glass—in nine months, the answer probably lies in the long previous isolation and in the conditions at the county home. At the latter institution she was early deprived of her two little roommates and was left alone. In the entire establishment there was only one nurse, who had three hundred and twenty-four other inmates to look after. Most of Anna's care was turned over to adult inmates, many of whom were mentally deficient and scarcely able to speak themselves. Part of the time Anna's door was shut. In addition to this continued isolation, Anna was given no stimulus to learning. She was fed, clothed, and cleaned without having to turn a hand in her own behalf. She was never disciplined or rewarded, because nobody had the time for the tedious task. All benefits were for her in the nature of things and therefore not rewards. Thus she remained in much the same animal-like stage, except that she did not have the animal's inherently organized structure, and hence remained in a more passive, inadequate state.

On our visit of December 6 a surprise awaited us, for Anna had undergone what was for her a remarkable transformation—she had begun to learn. Not that she could speak, but she could do several things formerly considered impossible. She could descend the stairs (by sitting successively on each one), could hold a doughnut in her hand and eat it (munching like a normal child), could grasp a glass of tomato juice and drink it by herself, could take a step or two while holding to something, and could feed herself with a spoon. These accomplishments, small indeed for a child of seven, represented a transformation explainable, no doubt, by her transference from the county home to a private family where she was the sole object of one woman's assiduous care.

Anna had been in the foster-home less than a month, but the results were plain to see. Her new guardian was using the same common-sense methods by which mothers from time immemorial have socialized their infants—unremitting attention, repetitive correction, and countless small rewards and punishments, mixed always with sympathetic interest and hovering physical presence. These Anna was getting for the first time in her life.

One thing seemed noticeable. Anna was more like a one-year-old baby than she had been before. She was responsive in the untutored, random, energetic way of a baby. When one beckoned and called her, she would make an effort to come, smiling and going through excited extra motions.

A month later more improvement along the same lines was noted. Though grave limitations remained, Anna was definitely becoming more of a human being.

Still later, on March 19, 1939, her accomplishments were the following: she was able to walk alone for a few steps without falling; she was responsive to the verbal commands of her foster-mother, seeming to understand in a vague sort of way what the latter wanted her to do; she definitely recognized the social worker who took her weekly to the doctor and who therefore symbolized to her the pleasure of an automobile ride; she expressed by anxious bodily movements her desire to go out for a ride; she seemed unmistakably to seek and to like attention, though she did not sulk when left alone; she was able to push a doll carriage in front of her and to show some skill in manipulating it. She was, furthermore, much improved physically, being almost fat, with chubby arms and legs and having more energy and alertness. On the visit prior to this one she had shown that she could quickly find and eat candy which she saw placed behind a pillow, could perform a knee-bending exercise, could use ordinary utensils in eating (e.g., could convey liquid to her mouth in a spoon), could manifest a sense of neatness (by putting bread back on a plate after taking a bite from it). Limitations still remaining, however, were as follows: she said nothing—could not even be taught to say "bye-bye"; she had to be watched to tell when elimination was imminent; she hardly played when alone; she had little curiosity, little initiative; it seemed still impossible to establish any communicative contact with her.

On August 30, 1939, Anna was taken from the foster-home and moved to a small school for defective children. Observations made at this time showed her to have become a fat girl twenty pounds overweight for her age. Yet she could walk better and could almost run. Her toilet habits showed that she understood the whole procedure. She manifested an obvious comprehension of many verbal instructions, though she could not speak.

Comparison of Anna with other cases of isolated children reveals several interesting parallels, both in their histories and in the interpretation of them. First of all, we note the almost universal failure to learn to talk with any facility, and hence the failure to master much of the cultural heritage. Second, we note the nearly universal presence of sensory abnormalities. Finally, we note, and also question, the usual interpretation of these recurrent facts—namely, that they are due to congenital feeble-mindedness.

Though Anna at present cannot speak, she is not an unusual member of her peculiar class. The feral child, Kamala, found at the age of eight, was able to utter only forty words after six years of tutoring,[9] and somewhat similar slowness is encountered in other cases.[10] Inability to walk or run and pronounced peculiarities of gait are also exceedingly characteristic; and some sort of abnormality of the senses, either as acuteness or dulness, appears in nearly every instance.[11]

In view of these similarities it is not surprising that a standard interpretation has been applied to practically every case—namely, that the child was innately feeble-minded. Pinel declared the Wild Boy of Aveyron to be a fake as to wildness and an incurable idiot as to mentality, and Itard, after five years of exasperating effort, ultimately admitted that the boy may have been mentally deficient from the start, though he still attributed great importance to his long isolation.[12] Popular interest in feeble-mindedness and in biological determinism led to general agreement with Pinel's verdict. But recently scientific opinion has been changing. F. S. Freeman, an authority on individual differences, believes that the Aveyron boy's stupidity was due to his long period of social isolation.

Even if it is granted that the boy was quite dull to begin with, it should have been possible to achieve much more with him than was the case, unless one allows for the peculiar conditions under which he lived, and for the "fixing" process resulting from these conditions.... Itard's reports present the case of an individual whose early life so shaped his behavior and fixed his abilities that even five years of painstaking, devoted, and intelligent instruction were inadequate to produce the mental manifestations of even a low-grade moron.[13]

Similarly, W. N. Kellog argues for the innate normality of this and other feral children. He assumes that they probably possessed an entirely normal equipment—otherwise survival in a harsh environment would have been impossible. They developed responses suitable to their surroundings. Hence their subsequent inability to learn is attributable to the difficulty of uprooting fundamental, basically intrenched habits formed by earlier experience.[14]

There is one actual case in which the hypothesis was disproved. This was the case of Edith Riley, who, after incarceration in a closet for some years, was said at twelve to be feeble-minded. She recovered complete normality within two year.[15]

CONCLUSIONS

1. Comparing Anna with other isolated children, bearing in mind that she seemed normal in infancy, and noting her progress to date, one can maintain that though she is still at the idiot level in mentality this fact is largely the result of social isolation.

2. But if the striking parallel with other known cases diminishes the probability of congenital deficiency, it also diminishes the chance of a favorable outcome, for it seems almost impossible for any child to learn to speak, think, and act like a normal person after a long period of early isolation. Yet Anna is in one respect a marginal case: she was discovered before she had reached six years of age. This is young enough to allow for some plasticity. In fact, she has made a good many adjustments.

3. The comparative facts seem to indicate that the stages of socialization are to some extent necessarily related to the stages of organic development. If the delicate, complex, and logically prior stages of socialization are not acquired when the organism is plastic, they will never be acquired and the later stages never achieved (except crudely).

4. Anna's history, like others, seems to demonstrate the Cooley-Mead-Dewey-Faris theory of personality—namely, that human nature is determined by the child's communicative social contacts as much as by his organic equipment and that the system of communicative symbols is a highly complex business acquired early in life as the result of long and intimate training. It is not enough that other persons be merely present; these others must have an intimate, primary-group relationship with the child.

5. Other than this, however, the theories of socialization are generally neither wrong nor right with respect to Anna, but simply inapplicable. The psychoanalytic theory, in so far as it assumes certain wishes as given inherently in the organism and responsible for a series of subsequent developmental states, seems wrong; but in so far as it talks in terms of dynamic mechanisms, such as conflict and anxiety, it simply does not apply—because such mechanisms assume that socialization has already begun; that the initial stages have been traversed. The latter characteristic seems indeed true of most theories of socialization. The central problem of how the organism first acquires a self, first begins the communicative process, is skipped and taken for granted, the theory going on from this point.

---

[1] Condensed from a paper read at the annual meeting of the American Sociological Society in Detroit, 1938.

[2] Out of regard for the parties concerned, correct names of persons and places are not given.

[3] It is doubtful that the child's hands at the time of discovery were tied. It is more likely that she was confined to her crib in the first period of life and at all times kept locked in her room to keep her from falling down the steep stairs leading immediately from the door and to keep the grandfather from seeing her. It is doubtful if the child was ever kept in the attic, as the report also stated.

[4] She remained in the home more than nine months, being removed on November 11 to a foster-home. The institution is primarily for the aged and infirm in the county where Anna lived, but contains cases of nearly all types.

[5] The mother was reported to have the mentality of a child of ten. We did not interview the persons who gave the intelligence test but did interview the mother herself. She seems probably subnormal, and this is the opinion of most people who know her. But it is doubtful if her status is any lower than that of a high-grade moron, and she may be merely a dull normal.

Anna's father, according to one story, is a wealthy farmer living in the same rural section as the mother, distantly kin to her. Another story has it, however, that a syphilitic married man in the near-by town is the father.

[6] She would hold one hand in front of her with the little finger pressed against the palm, the other three fingers close together and straight out, and would then manipulate the hand shaped in this way close to her eyes. Often when doing this she would hold a finger of her other hand in her ear. These actions gave her an idiotic appearance. She showed more skill in bending the fingers than any of us could exhibit.

[7] Mr. Carr, who represented the Psycho-educational Clinic at Pennsylvania State College, found that Anna showed accommodation for both light and distance, that she winked when a pencil was suddenly shoved toward her eyes and when a tumbler was struck with a spoon just behind her ear, and that the patellar and plantar reflexes were present. It being impossible to administer any standardized tests involving language, he examined her with reference to the motor-behavior items in Gesell's developmental scale. The items passed included the following: resisting head pressure (appears normally at four months), lifting head while in prone position (six months), sitting up (nine months), clasping cubes (six months), picking up cube (six months), scribbling (eighteen months—but this "scribbling" appeared to us to be an accident).

[8] Anna had for weeks been without any playmates in her room. As a test a little boy (age five) was brought in. We all left the room and peered back. Anna took a definite interest in him. She tried her trick of looking hard into his eyes and moving her head near his to rub foreheads. She clapped her hands, manifesting more interest in him than he in her.

The nurse said that Anna had played with kittens a few days previously by swinging them by their tails. We secured two kittens and put them on her bed. This time she became paralyzed with fright. She made little noise, except a stifled yell once or twice, and she made no effort to get away or push the kittens off.

This paralyzed type of reaction was characteristic. Initiative seemed virtually impossible for her. A temper tantrum previously exhibited had this character. She waved her head from side to side and flipped her hands up and down—a nervous, futile sort of tantrum behavior. It was as if she had no channels of expression or action, no mode of dealing with the environment.

As soon as the kittens were out of sight she forgot about them, but the fright returned whenever they were placed in her presence. During her fright she broke into the first crying spell the writer had witnessed. It was a real child's cry.

[9] P. C. Squires, " 'Wolf Children' of India," *American Journal of Psychology*, XXXVIII (1927), 313–15.

[10] Sanichar, found at about the age of seven, could not speak even as a grown man. He merely uttered incomprehensible sounds (G. C. Ferris, *Sanichar, the Wolf-Boy of India* [New York: Published by the Author, 1902], pp. 31–33). The girl of Songi, discovered at about ten years of age, learned after several years to speak, but apparently not very well (Madam Hecquet, *The History of a Savage Girl* [London: Dursley, Davison, Mauson, Bland, & Jones], pp. 23, 34–35, and 61–63). Caspar Hauser, who might seem an exception to the rule, actually remained, to the last, awkward in language (Anselm von Feuerbach, *Caspar Hauser*, trans. from German [2d ed.; Boston: Allen & Ticknor, 1833], 1, 54). His case is not clear, however, for it appears he could

pronounce some words when first discovered (*ibid.*, pp. 4–5). Other instances of speech difficulties seem as numerous as the cases of isolated children, though the evidence is scanty and dubious.

[11] Kamala possessed extremely acute hearing when discovered and an animal-like sense of smell. She could smell meat at a great distance. After six years in civilization she could still see better at night than in the daytime (Squires, *op. cit.*). Sanichar's sense of hearing seemed practically destroyed (Ferris, *op. cit.*, p. 28). The senses of the boy of Aveyron "were extraordinarily apathetic. His nostrils were filled with snuff without making him sneeze. He picked up potatoes from boiling water. A pistol fired near him provoked hardly any response though the sound of cracking a walnut caused him to turn round" (J. M. G. Itard, *The Wild Boy of Aveyron*, trans. with Introd. by George Humphrey [New York and London, 1932]). The resemblance to Anna is obvious. Months after Anna had been in the county home we blew up a paper bag, exploded it suddenly behind her head, and found that she winced a bit, but did not really mind a loud sound near to her ear. This in spite of the fact that nothing seemed wrong with her hearing apparatus. Like many isolated children, she was fond of music. The conclusion seems inescapable that her deafness was functional, not organic, just as that of the boy of Aveyron. Caspar Hauser's senses "appeared at first to be in a state of torpor, and only gradually to open to the perception of external objects." Yet he had an extraordinary ability to see in the dark (Feuerbach, *op. cit.*, pp. 26 and 166–67).

[12] Itard, *op. cit.*, pp. vii and 99–101.

[13] *Individual Differences* (New York: Henry Holt & Co., 1934), p. 117.

[14] This agrees with the general opinion concerning the importance of the early years in development. "A large percentage of children previously diagnosed as feeble-minded have been proven to be sound in all respects except in…acquired reactions. If discovered at an early age the 'inherited' deficiencies of these individuals have been satisfactorily corrected through specialized education, although this has not been possible if they have persisted too long in their original habits" ("Humanizing the Ape," *Psychological Review*, XXXVIII [1931], 160–76). Similar arguments are contained in Humphrey's Introduction to Itard's work (*op. cit.*), pp. x–xi.

[15] *New York Times*, November 17, 1931, sec. 4, p. 6, and December 24, 1931, sec. 12, p. 1; *New York Daily Mirror*, magazine section, March 27, 1938, p. 6. This is an interesting case, differing from most of the others in that the child was incarcerated at the late age of eight. She lost the capacity for speech and vision. But since she had once acquired these abilities, she recovered them again fairly rapidly.

QUESTIONS

? How did Anna's lack of socialization show? Give examples from the article.

? Does Davis believe that Anna can overcome her early lack of socialization? Why or why not?

? Societal puzzle question: How does the Cooley-Mead-Faris theory of personality help us understand our friends and acquaintances? What are its limitations? Apply this theory to one of your friends or acquaintances to explain how they became the person they are today.

An Introduction to McDonaldization

By GEORGE RITZER

■ When you think of the term "culture" what images come to your mind? Sociologists define culture as those elements of our society that we learn through the process of socialization—including symbols such as language, appropriate behaviors, and social values. One "symbol" of contemporary American culture is the fast-food restaurant McDonalds. In this article, sociologist George Ritzer illustrates how McDonalds has not only become a cultural symbol that we widely recognize and share, but how it also has become part of a "wide ranging process" that he calls McDonaldization. Ritzer further claims that McDonaldization is one of the most influential global developments in recent years. As you read, you will not only discover how McDonaldization works, but also some of the benefits and problems it brings.

McDonald's is the basis of one of the most influential developments in contemporary society. Its reverberations extend far beyond its point of origin in the United States and in the fast-food business. It has influenced a wide range of undertakings, indeed the way of life, of a significant portion of the world. And that impact is likely to expand at an accelerating rate.

However, this is not...about McDonald's, or even about the fast-food business.... Rather, McDonald's serves here as the major example, the paradigm, of a wide-ranging process I call McDonaldization—that is,

> *the process by which the principles of the fast-food restaurant are coming to dominate more and more sectors of American society as well as of the rest of the world.*

As you will see, McDonaldization affects not only the restaurant business but also...virtually every other aspect of society. McDonaldization has shown every sign of being an inexorable process, sweeping through seemingly impervious institutions and regions of the world.

George Ritzer, excerpts from *The McDonaldization of Society*, pages 1–19, copyright © 2000 by George Ritzer, Reprinted by permission of Pine Forge Press, Inc.

McDONALD'S AS A GLOBAL ICON

McDonald's has come to occupy a central place in American popular culture, not just the business world. A new McDonald's opening in a small town can be an important social event. Said one Maryland high school student at such an opening, "Nothing this exciting ever happens in Dale City." Even big-city newspapers avidly cover developments in the fast-food business.

Fast-food restaurants also play symbolic roles on television programs and in the movies. A skit on the television show *Saturday Night Live* satirized specialty chains by detailing the hardships of a franchise that sells nothing but Scotch tape.... In *Falling Down*, Michael Douglas vents his rage against the modern world in a fast-food restaurant dominated, by mindless rules designed to frustrate customers.... In *Sleeper*, Woody Allen awakens in the future only to encounter a McDonald's.

Further proof that McDonald's has become a symbol of American culture is to be found in what happened when plans were made to raze Ray Kroc's first McDonald's restaurant. Hundreds of letters poured into McDonald's headquarters, including the following:

> *Please don't tear it down!... Your company's name is a household word, not only in the United States of America, but all over the world. To destroy this major artifact of contemporary culture would, indeed, destroy part of the faith the people of the world have in your company.*

In the end, the restaurant was not only saved but turned into a museum. A McDonald's executive explained the move: "McDonald's...is really a part of Americana."

Americans aren't the only ones who feel this way. At the opening of the McDonald's in Moscow, one journalist described the franchise as the "ultimate icon of Americana."... Reflecting on the growth of fast-food restaurants in Brazil, an executive associated with Pizza Hut of Brazil said that his nation "is experiencing a passion for things American."

One could go further and argue that in at least some ways McDonald's has become *more important* than the United States itself. Take the following story about a former U.S. ambassador to Israel who was officiating at the opening of the first McDonald's, in Jerusalem wearing a baseball hat with the McDonald's golden arches logo:

> *An Israeli teenager walked up to him, carrying his own McDonald's hat, which he handed to Ambassador Indyk with a pen and asked, "Are you the Ambassador? Can I have your autograph?" Somewhat sheepishly, Ambassador Indyk replied, "Sure. I've never been asked for my autograph before."*
>
> *As the Ambassador prepared to sign his name, the Israeli teenager said to him, "Wow, what's it like to be the ambassador from McDonald's, going around the world opening McDonald's restaurants everywhere?"*
>
> *Ambassador Indyk looked at the Israeli youth and said, "No, no. I'm the American ambassador—not the ambassador from McDonald's!" Ambassador Indyk described what happened next: "I said to him, 'Does this mean you don't want my autograph?' And the kid said, 'No, I don't want your autograph,' and he took his hat back and walked away."*

Two other indices of the significance of McDonald's (and, implicitly, McDonaldization) are worth mentioning. The first is the annual "Big Mac Index" (part of "burgernomics") published by a prestigious magazine, *The Economist*. It indicates the purchasing power of various currencies around the world based on the local price (in dollars) of the Big Mac. The Big Mac is used because it is a uniform commodity sold in many (115) different nations. In the 1998 survey, a Big Mac in the United States cost $2.56; in Indonesia and Malaysia it cost $1.16; in Switzerland it cost $3.87. This measure indicates, at least roughly, where the cost of living is high or low, as well as which currencies are undervalued (Indonesia and Malaysia) and which are overvalued (Switzerland). Although *The Economist* is calculating the Big Mac Index tongue-in-cheek, at least in part, the index represents the ubiquity and importance of McDonald's around the world.

The second indicator of McDonald's global significance is the idea developed by Thomas J. Friedman that "no two countries that both have a McDonald's have ever fought a war since they each got McDonald's." Friedman calls this the "Golden Arches Theory of Conflict Prevention." Another half-serious idea, it implies that the path to world peace lies through the continued international expansion of McDonald's. Unfortunately, it was proved wrong by the NATO bombing of Yugoslavia in 1999, which had 11 McDonald's restaurants as of 1997.

To many people throughout the world, McDonald's has become a sacred institution. At that opening of the McDonald's in Moscow, a worker spoke of it "as if it were the Cathedral in Chartres,...a place to experience 'celestial joy.' "... Similarly, a visit to another central element of McDonaldized society, Walt Disney World, has been described as "the middle-class hajj, the compulsory visit to the sunbaked holy city."

McDonald's has achieved its exalted position because virtually all Americans, and many others, have passed through its golden arches on innumerable occasions. Furthermore, most of us have been bombarded by commercials extolling McDonald's virtues, commercials tailored to a variety of audiences and that change as the chain introduces new foods, new contests, and new product tie-ins. These ever-present commercials, combined with the fact that people cannot drive very far without having a McDonald's pop into view, have embedded McDonald's deeply in popular consciousness. A poll of school-age children showed that 96% of them could identify Ronald McDonald, second only to Santa Claus in name recognition.

Over the years, McDonald's has appealed to people in many ways. The restaurants themselves are depicted as spick-and-span, the food is said to be fresh and nutritious, the employees are shown to be young and eager, the managers appear gentle and caring, and the dining experience itself seems fun-filled. People are even led to believe that they contribute through their purchases, at least indirectly, to charities such as the Ronald McDonald Houses for sick children.

THE LONG ARM OF MCDONALDIZATION

McDonald's strives to continually extend its reach within American society and beyond. As the company's chairman said, "Our goal: to totally dominate the quick service restaurant industry worldwide.... I want McDonald's to be more than a leader. I want McDonald's to dominate."

McDonald's began as a phenomenon of suburbs and medium-sized towns, but in recent years, it has moved into smaller towns that supposedly could not support such a restaurant and into many big cities that are supposedly too sophisticated. You can now find fast-food outlets in New York's Times Square as well as on the Champs Elysees in Paris. Soon after it opened in 1992, the McDonald's in Moscow sold almost 30,000 hamburgers a day and employed a staff of 1,200 young people working 2 to a cash register. In early 1992, Beijing witnessed the opening of the world's largest McDonald's restaurant with 700 seats, 29 cash registers, and nearly 1,000 employees. On its first day of business, it set a new one-day record for McDonald's by serving about 40,000 customers.

Small satellite, express, or remote outlets, opened in areas that cannot support full-scale fast-food restaurants, are also expanding rapidly. They have begun to appear in small store fronts in large cities and in nontraditional settings such as department stores, service stations, and even schools. These satellites typically offer only limited menus and may rely on larger outlets for food storage and preparation. McDonald's is considering opening express outlets in museums, office buildings, and corporate cafeterias. A flap occurred recently over the placement of a McDonald's in the new federal courthouse in Boston.

No longer content to dominate the strips that surround many college campuses, fast-food restaurants have moved onto many of those campuses. The first campus fast-food restaurant opened at the University of Cincinnati in 1973. Today, college cafeterias often look like shopping-mall food courts. In conjunction with a variety of "branded partners" (for example, Pizza Hut and Subway), Marriott now supplies food to many colleges and universities. The apparent approval of college administrations puts fast-food restaurants in a position to further influence the younger generation.

More recently, another expansion has occurred: People no longer need to leave the highway to obtain fast food quickly and easily. Fast food is now available at convenient rest stops along the highway. After "refueling," we can proceed with our trip, which is likely to end in another community that has about the same density and mix of fast-food restaurants as the locale we left behind.

Fast food is also increasingly available in hotels, railway stations, airports, and even on the trays for in-flight meals. The following advertisement appeared in *The Washington Post* and *The New York Times* a few years ago: "Where else at 35,000 feet can you get a McDonald's meal like this for your kids? Only on United's Orlando flights." Now, McDonald's so-called Friendly Skies Meals are generally available to children on Delta flights. Similarly, in December 1994, Delta began to offer Blimpie sandwiches on its North American flights and Continental now offers Subway sandwiches. How much longer before McDonaldized meals will be available on all flights everywhere by every carrier? In fact, on an increasing number of flights, prepackaged "snacks" have already replaced hot main courses.[1]

In other sectors of society, the influence of fast-food restaurants has been subtler but no less profound. Food produced by McDonald's and other fast-food restaurants has begun to appear in high schools and trade schools; 13% of school cafeterias are serving branded fast food. Said the director of nutrition for the American School Food Service Association, "'Kids today live in a world where fast food has become a way of life. For us to get kids to eat, period, we have to provide some familiar items.'" Few lower-grade schools as yet have in-house fast-food restaurants. However, many have had to alter school cafeteria menus and procedures to make fast food readily available. Apples, yogurt, and milk may go straight into the trash can, but hamburgers, fries, and shakes are devoured. Furthermore, fast-food chains are now trying to market their products in school cafeterias. The attempt to hook school-age children on fast food reached something of a peak in Illinois, where McDonald's operated a program called "A for Cheeseburger." Students who received A's on their report cards received a free cheeseburger, thereby linking success in school with rewards from McDonald's.

The military has also been pressed to offer fast food on both bases and ships. Despite the criticisms by physicians and nutritionists, fast-food outlets increasingly turn up inside hospitals. Though no homes yet have a McDonald's of their own, meals at home often resemble those available in fast-food restaurants. Frozen, microwavable, and prepared foods, which bear a striking resemblance to meals available at fast-food restaurants, often find their way to the dinner table. Then there is also home delivery of fast foods, especially pizza, as revolutionized by Domino's.

McDonald's is such a powerful model that many businesses have acquired nicknames beginning with Mc. Examples include "McDentists" and "McDoctors," meaning drive-in clinics designed to deal quickly and efficiently with minor dental and medical problems; "McChild" care centers, meaning child care centers such as KinderCare; "McStables," designating the nationwide racehorse-training operation of Wayne Lucas; and "McPaper," designating the newspaper *USA TODAY*....

So powerful is McDonaldization that the derivatives of McDonald's in turn exert their own influence. For example, the success of *USA TODAY* has led many newspapers across the nation to adopt, for example, shorter stories and colorful weather maps. As one *USA TODAY* editor said, "The same newspaper editors who call us McPaper have been stealing our McNuggets." Even serious journalistic enterprises such as *The New York Times* and *The Washington Post* have undergone changes (for example, the use of color) as a result of the success of *USA TODAY*. The influence of *USA TODAY* is blatantly manifested in *The Boca Raton News*, which has been described as "a sort of smorgasbord of snippets, a newspaper that slices and dices the news into even smaller portions than does *USA TODAY,* spicing it with color graphics and fun facts and cute features like 'Today's Hero' and 'Critter Watch.'" As in *USA TODAY,* stories in *The Boca Raton News* usually start and finish on the same page. Many important details, much of a story's context, and much of what the principals have to say, are severely cut back or omitted entirely. With its emphasis on light news and color graphics, the main function of the newspaper seems to be entertainment.

Like virtually every other sector of society, sex has undergone McDonaldization. In the movie *Sleeper*, Woody Allen not only created a futuristic world in which McDonald's restaurants were an important and highly visible element, but he also envisioned a society in which people could enter a machine called an "orgasmatron" to experience an orgasm without going through the muss and fuss of sexual intercourse.

Similarly, real-life "dial-a-porn" allows people to have intimate, sexually explicit, even obscene conversations with people they have never met and probably never will meet. There is great specialization here: Dialing numbers such as 555-FOXX will lead to a very different phone message than dialing 555-SEXY. Those who answer the phones mindlessly and repetitively follow "scripts" that have them say such things as "Sorry, tiger, but your Dream Girl has to go.... Call right back and ask for me." Less scripted are phone sex systems that permit erotic conversations between total strangers. As Woody Allen anticipated with his "orgasmatron," participants can experience an orgasm without ever meeting or touching one another. "In a world where convenience is king, disembodied sex has its allure. You don't have to stir from your comfortable home. You pick up the phone or log onto the computer and, if you're plugged in, a world of unheard of sexual splendor rolls out before your eyes." In New York City, an official called a three-story pornographic center "the McDonald's of sex" because of its "cookie-cutter cleanliness and compliance with the law." These examples suggest that no aspect of people's lives is immune to McDonaldization.

THE DIMENSIONS OF McDONALDIZATION

Why has the McDonald's model proven so irresistible? Eating fast food at McDonald's has certainly become a "sign" that, among other things, one is in tune with the contemporary lifestyle. There is also a kind of magic or enchantment associated with such food and their settings. However, what will be focused on here are the four alluring dimensions that lie at the heart of the success of this model and, more generally, of McDonaldization. In short, McDonald's has succeeded because it offers consumers, workers, and managers efficiency, calculability, predictability, and control.

Efficiency

One important element of McDonald's success is *efficiency*, or the optmum method for getting from one point to another. For consumers, McDonald's offers the best available way to get from being hungry to being full. In a society where both parents are likely to work or where a single parent is struggling to keep up, efficiently satisfying hunger is very attractive. In a society where people rush from one spot to another, usually by car, the efficiency of a fast-food meal, perhaps even a drive-through meal, often proves impossible to resist.

The fast-food model offers, or at least appears to offer, an efficient method for satisfying many other needs as well. Woody Allen's orgasmatron offered an efficient method for getting people from quiescence to sexual gratification. Other institutions fashioned on the McDonald's model offer similar efficiency in losing weight, lubricating cars, getting new glasses or contacts, or completing income tax forms.

Like their customers, workers in McDonaldized systems function efficiently following the steps in a predesigned process. They are trained to work this way by managers, who watch over them closely to make sure that they do. Organizational rules and regulations also help ensure highly efficient work.

Calculability

Calculability is an emphasis on the quantitative aspects of products sold (portion size, cost) and services offered (the time it takes to get the product). In McDonaldized systems, quantity has become equivalent to quality; a lot of something, or the quick delivery of it, means it must be good.... "As a culture, we tend to believe deeply that in general 'bigger is better.'" Thus, people order the Quarter Pounder, the Big Mac, the large fries. More recent lures are the "double this" (for instance, Burger King's "Double Whopper with Cheese") and the "triple that." People can quantify these things and feel that they are getting a lot of food for what appears to be a nominal sum of money. This calculation does not take into account an important point, however: The high profits of fast-food chains indicate that the owners, not the consumers, get the best deal.

People also tend to calculate how much time it will take to drive to McDonald's, be served the food, eat it, and return home; then, they compare that interval to the time required to prepare food at home. They often conclude, rightly or wrongly, that a trip to the fast-food restaurant will take less time than eating at home. This sort of calculation particularly supports home delivery franchises such as Domino's, as well as other chains that emphasize time saving. A notable example of time saving in another sort of chain is Lens Grafters, which promises people "Glasses fast, glasses in one hour."

Some McDonaldized institutions combine the emphases on time and money. Domino's promises pizza delivery in half an hour, or the pizza is free. Pizza Hut will serve a personal pan pizza in five minutes, or it, too, will be free.

Workers in McDonaldized systems also tend to emphasize the quantitative rather than the qualitative aspects of their work. Since the quality of the work is allowed to vary little, workers focus on things such as how quickly tasks can be accomplished. In a situation analogous to that of the customer, workers are expected to do a lot of work, very quickly, for low pay.

Predictability

McDonald's also offers *predictability*, the assurance that products and services will be the same over time and in all locales. The Egg McMuffin in New York will be, for all intents and purposes, identical to those in Chicago and Los Angeles. Also, those eaten next week or next year will be identical to those eaten today. Customers take great comfort in knowing that McDonald's offers no surprises. People know that the next Egg McMuffin they eat will not be awful, although it will not be exceptionally delicious, either. The success of the McDonald's model suggests that many people have come to prefer a world in which there are few surprises. "This is strange," notes a British observer, "considering [McDonald's is] the product of a culture which honours individualism above all."

The workers in McDonaldized systems also behave in predictable ways. They follow corporate rules as well as the dictates of their managers. In many cases, what they do, and even what they say, is highly predictable. McDonaldized organizations often have scripts that employees are supposed to memorize and follow whenever the occasion arises. This scripted behavior helps create highly predictable interactions between workers and customers. While customers do not follow scripts, they tend to develop simple recipes for dealing with the employees of McDonaldized systems....

> *McDonald's pioneered the routinization of interactive service work and remains an exemplar of extreme standardization. Innovation is not discouraged...at least among managers and franchisees. Ironically, though, "the object is to look for new, innovative ways to create an experience that is exactly the same no matter what McDonald's you walk into, no matter where it is in the world."*

Control Through Nonhuman Technology

The fourth element in McDonald's success, *control*, is exerted over the people who enter the world of McDonald's. Lines, limited menus, few options, and uncomfortable seats all lead diners to do what management wishes them to do—eat quickly and leave. Furthermore, the drive-through (in some cases, walk-through) window leads diners to leave before they eat. In the Domino's model, customers never enter in the first place.

The people who work in McDonaldized organizations are also controlled to a high degree, usually more blatantly and directly than customers. They are trained to do a limited number of things in precisely the way they are told to do them. The technologies used and the way the organization is set up reinforce this control. Managers and inspectors make sure that workers toe the line.

McDonald's also controls employees by threatening to use, and ultimately using, technology to replace human workers. No matter how well they are programmed and controlled, workers can foul up the system's operation. A slow worker can make the preparation and delivery of a Big Mac inefficient. A worker who refuses to follow the rules might leave the pickles or special sauce off a hamburger, thereby making for unpredictability. And a distracted worker can put too few fries in the box, making an order of large fries seem skimpy. For these and other reasons, McDonald's and other fast-food restaurants have felt compelled to steadily replace human beings with machines, such as the soft drink dispenser that shuts itself off when the glass is full, the French fry machine that rings and lifts the basket out of the oil when the fries arc crisp, the preprogrammed cash register that eliminates the need for the cashier to calculate prices and amounts, and perhaps at some future time, the robot capable of making hamburgers. Technology that increases control over workers helps McDonaldized systems assure customers that their products and service will be consistent.

THE ADVANTAGES OF McDONALDIZATION

This discussion of four fundamental characteristics of McDonaldization makes it clear that McDonald's has succeeded so phenomenally for good, solid reasons. Many knowledgeable people such as the economic columnist, Robert Samuelson, strongly support McDonald's business model. Samuelson confesses to "openly worship[ing] McDonald's," and he thinks of it as "the greatest restaurant chain in history." In addition, McDonald's offers many praiseworthy programs that benefit society, such as its Ronald McDonald Houses, which permit parents to stay with children undergoing treatment for serious medical problems; job-training programs for teenagers; programs to help keep its employees in school; efforts to hire and train the handicapped; the McMasters program, aimed at hiring senior citizens; and an enviable record of hiring and promoting minorities.

The process of McDonaldization also moved ahead dramatically, undoubtedly because it has led to positive changes. Here are a few specific examples:

- A wider range of goods and services is available to a much larger portion of the population than ever before.
- Availability of goods and services depends far less than before on time or geographic location; people can do things, such as obtain money at the grocery store or a bank balance in the middle of the night, that were impossible before.
- People are able to get what they want or need almost instantaneously and get it far more conveniently.
- Goods and services are of a far more uniform quality; at least some people get better goods and services than before McDonaldization.
- Far more economical alternatives to high-priced, customized goods and services are widely available; therefore, people can afford things they could not previously afford.
- Fast, efficient goods and services are available to a population that is working longer hours and has fewer hours to spare.
- In a rapidly changing, unfamiliar, and seemingly hostile world, the comparatively stable, familiar, and safe environment of a McDonaldized system offers comfort.
- Because of quantification, consumers can more easily compare competing products.
- Certain products (for example, diet programs) are safer in a carefully regulated and controlled system.
- People are more likely to be treated similarly, no matter what their race, gender, or social class.
- Organizational and technological innovations are more quickly and easily diffused through networks of identical operators.
- The most popular products of one culture are more easily diffused to others.

A CRITIQUE OF McDONALDIZATION: THE IRRATIONALITY OF RATIONALITY

Although McDonaldization offers powerful advantages, it has a downside. Efficiency, predictability, calculability, and control through nonhuman technology can be thought of as the basic components of a rational system. However, rational systems inevitably spawn irrationalities. The downside of McDonaldization will be dealt with most systematically under the heading of the irrationality of rationality; in fact, paradoxically, the irrationality of rationality can be thought of as the fifth dimension of McDonaldization. The basic idea here is that rational systems inevitably spawn irrational consequences. Another way of saying this is that rational systems serve to deny human reason; rational systems are often unreasonable.

For example, McDonaldization has produced a wide array of adverse effects on the environment. One is a side effect of the need to grow uniform potatoes from which to create predictable French fries. The huge farms of the Pacific Northwest that now produce such potatoes rely on the extensive use of chemicals. In addition, the need to produce a perfect fry means that much of the potato is wasted, with the remnants either fed to cattle or used for fertilizer. The underground water supply in the area is now showing high levels of nitrates, which may be traceable to the fertilizer and animal wastes. Many other ecological problems are associated with the McDonaldization of the fast-food industry: the forests felled to produce paper wrappings, the damage caused by polystyrene and other packaging materials, the enormous amount of food needed to produce feed cattle, and so on.

Another unreasonable effect is that fast-food restaurants are often dehumanizing settings in which to eat or work. Customers lining up for a burger or waiting in the drive-through line and workers preparing the food often feel as though they are part of an assembly line. Hardly amenable to eating, assembly lines have been shown to be inhuman settings in which to work.

Such criticisms can be extended to all facets of the McDonaldizing world. For example, at the opening of Euro Disney, a French politician said that it will "bombard France with uprooted creations that are to culture what fast food is to gastronomy."

As you have seen, McDonaldization offers many advantages. However, this book will focus on the great costs and enormous risks of McDonaldization. McDonald's and other purveyors of the fast-food model spend billions of dollars each year outlining the benefits of their system. However, critics of the system have few outlets for their ideas. For example, no one is offering commercials between Saturday-morning cartoons warning children of the dangers associated with fast-food restaurants.

Nonetheless, a legitimate question may be raised about this critique of McDonaldization: Is it animated by a romanticization of the past and an impossible desire to return to a world that no longer exists? Some critics do base their critiques on nostalgia for a time when life was slower and offered more surprises, when people were freer, and when one was more likely to deal with a human being than a robot or a computer. Although they have a point, these critics have undoubtedly exaggerated the positive aspects of a world without McDonald's, and they have certainly tended to forget the liabilities associated with earlier eras. As an example of the latter, take the following anecdote about a visit to a pizzeria in Havana, Cuba, which in some respects is decades behind the United States:

> *The pizza's not much to rave about—they scrimp on tomato sauce, and the dough is mushy.*
>
> *It was about 7:30 P.M., and as usual the place was standing-room-only, with people two deep jostling for a stool to come open and a waiting line spilling out onto the sidewalk.*
>
> *The menu is similarly Spartan.... To drink, there is tap water. That's it—no toppings, no soda, no beer, no coffee, no salt, no pepper. And no special orders.*
>
> *A very few people are eating. Most are waiting.... Fingers are drumming, flies are buzzing, the clock is ticking. The waiter wears a watch around his belt loop, but he hardly needs it; time is evidently not his chief concern. After a while, tempers begin to fray.*

But right now, it's 8:45 P.M. at the pizzeria, I've been waiting an hour and a quarter for two small pies.

Few would prefer such a restaurant to the fast, friendly, diverse offerings of, say, Pizza Hut. More important, however, critics who revere the past do not seem to realize that we are not returning to such a world. In fact, fast-food restaurants have begun to appear in Havana. The increase in the number of people crowding the planet, the acceleration of technological change, the increasing pace of life—all this and more make it impossible to go back to the world, if it ever existed, of home-cooked meals, traditional restaurant dinners, high-quality foods, meals loaded with surprises, and restaurants run by chefs free to express their creativity.

It is more valid to critique McDonaldization from the perspective of the future. Unfettered by the constraints of McDonaldized systems, but using the technological advances made possible by them, people would have the potential to be far more thoughtful, skillful, creative, and well-rounded than they are now. In short, if the world were less McDonaldized, people would be better able to live up to their human potential.

We must therefore look at McDonaldization as both "enabling" and "constraining." McDonaldized systems enable us to do many things that we were not able to do in the past. However, these systems also keep us from doing things we otherwise would do. McDonaldization is a "double-edged" phenomenon. We must not lose sight of that fact, even though this book will focus on the constraints associated with McDonaldization—its "dark side."

WHAT ISN'T McDONALDIZED?

This chapter should be giving you a sense not only of the advantages and disadvantages of McDonaldization but also of the range of phenomena that will be discussed throughout this book. In fact, such a wide range of phenomena can be linked to McDonaldization that you may be led to wonder what isn't McDonaldized. Is McDonaldization the equivalent of modernity? Is everything contemporary McDonaldized?

Although much of the world has been McDonaldized, at least three aspects of contemporary society have largely escaped the process:

- Those aspects traceable to an earlier, "premodern" age. A good example is the mom-and-pop grocery store.
- New businesses that have sprung up, at least in part, as a reaction against McDonaldization. For instance, people fed up with McDonaldized motel rooms in Holiday Inns or Motel 6s can instead stay in a bed-and-breakfast, which offers a room in a private home with personalized attention and a homemade breakfast from the proprietor.
- Those aspects suggesting a move toward a new, "postmodern" age. For example, in a postmodern society, "modern" high-rise housing projects make way for smaller, more livable communities.

Thus, although McDonaldization is ubiquitous, there is more to the contemporary world than McDonaldization. It is a very important social process, but it is far from the only process transforming contemporary society.

Furthermore, McDonaldization is not an all-or-nothing process. There are degrees of McDonaldization. Fast-food restaurants, for example, have been heavily McDonaldized, universities moderately McDonaldized, and mom-and-pop groceries only slightly McDonaldized. It is difficult to think of social phenomena that have escaped McDonaldization totally, but some local enterprise in Fiji may yet be untouched by this process.

NOTE

1. Of course, as a result of the plane crashes on September 11, 2001, all meals on most flights within the United States have been eliminated.

QUESTIONS

- Explain the four dimensions of McDonaldization. Give examples of each dimension.
- Why does Ritzer think McDonaldization has become so widespread? Do you agree?
- Societal puzzle question: If Ritzer is correct, you should easily be able to apply McDonaldization to your social world. Pick one of the following areas: music, sports, Internet, recreation. Apply each of the dimensions of McDonaldization to the topic that you have chosen.

Chapter 3

Performances

By ERVING GOFFMAN

■ Throughout the day you commonly encounter and talk to a variety of people. During the course of your conversations, you don't just exchange pleasantries. You and those you talk to are actually engaging in a sophisticated process of gathering and giving information. Sociologists call this mutual process "interaction." In the following classical statement about human interaction, taken from his 1959 book "The Presentation of Self in Everyday Life," sociologist Erving Goffman uses "dramaturgical analysis" to explain how we create and project images about ourselves to others. That is, he compares people to performers, interaction to an act, and the place where interactions occur as a stage. In doing, so he builds a framework for you to consider a diverse range of social interactions—for instance, from a father disciplining his child to a doctor conducting a surgical procedure. When you see the social world through Goffman's eyes, you will probably view your own interactions in a very different way.

BELIEF IN THE PART ONE IS PLAYING

When an individual plays a part he implicitly requests his observers to take seriously the impression that is fostered before them. They are asked to believe that the character they see actually possesses the attributes he appears to possess, that the task he performs will have the consequences that are implicitly claimed for it, and that, in general, matters are what they appear to be. In line with this, there is the popular view that the individual offers his performance and puts on his show "for the benefit of other people." It will be convenient to begin a consideration of performances by turning the question around and looking at the individual's own belief in the impression of reality that he attempts to engender in those among whom he finds himself.

From *The Presentation of Self in Everyday Life* by Erving Goffman, copyright © 1959 by Erving Goffman. Used by permission of Doubleday, a division of Random House, Inc.

At one extreme, one finds that the performer can be fully taken in by his own act; he can be sincerely convinced that the impression of reality which he stages is the real reality. When his audience is also convinced in this way about the show he puts on—and this seems to be the typical case—then for the moment at least, only the sociologist or the socially disgruntled will have any doubts about the "realness" of what is presented.

At the other extreme, we find that the performer may not be taken in at all by his own routine. This possibility is understandable, since no one is in quite as good an observational position to see through the act as the person who puts it on. Coupled with this, the performer may be moved to guide the conviction of his audience only as a means to other ends, having no ultimate concern in the conception that they have of him or of the situation. When the individual has no belief in his own act and no ultimate concern with the beliefs of his audience, we may call him cynical, reserving the term "sincere" for individuals who believe in the impression fostered by their own performance. It should be understood that the cynic, with all his professional disinvolvement, may obtain unprofessional pleasures from his masquerade, experiencing a land of gleeful spiritual aggression from the fact that he can toy at will with something his audience must take seriously.[1]

It is not assumed, of course, that all cynical performers are interested in deluding their audiences for purposes of what is called "self-interest" or private gain. A cynical individual may delude his audience for what he considers to be their own good, or for the good of the community, etc. For illustrations of this we need not appeal to sadly enlightened showmen such as Marcus Aurelius or Hsun Tzǔ. We know that in service occupations practitioners who may otherwise be sincere are sometimes forced to delude their customers because their customers show such a heartfelt demand for it. Doctors who are led into giving placebos, filling station attendants who resignedly check and recheck tire pressures for anxious women motorists, shoe clerks who sell a shoe that fits but tell the customer it is the size she wants to hear—these are cynical performers whose audiences will not allow them to be sincere. Similarly, it seems that sympathetic patients in mental wards will sometimes feign bizarre symptoms so that student nurses will not be subjected to a disappointingly sane performance.[2] So also, when inferiors extend their most lavish reception for visiting superiors, the selfish desire to win favor may not be the chief motive; the inferior may be tactfully attempting to put the superior at ease by simulating the kind of world the superior is thought to take for granted.

I have suggested two extremes: an individual may be taken in by his own act or be cynical about it.

FRONT

I have been using the term "performance" to refer to all the activity of an individual which occurs during a period marked by his continuous presence before a particular set of observers and which has some influence on the observers. It will be convenient to label as "front" that part of the individual's performance which regularly functions in a general and fixed fashion to define the situation for those who observe the performance. Front, then, is the expressive equipment of a standard kind intentionally or unwittingly employed by the individual during his performance. For preliminary purposes, it will be convenient to distinguish and label what seem to be the standard parts of front.

First, there is the "setting," involving furniture, décor, physical layout, and other background items which supply the scenery and stage props for the spate of human action played out before, within, or upon it. A setting tends to stay put, geographically speaking, so that those who would use a particular setting as part of their performance cannot begin their act until they have brought themselves to the appropriate place and must terminate their performance when they leave it. It is only in exceptional circumstances that the setting follows along with the performers; we see this in the funeral cortège, the civic parade, and the dreamlike processions that kings and queens are made of. In the main, these exceptions seem to offer some kind of extra protection for performers who are, or who have momentarily become, highly sacred. These worthies are to be distinguished, of course, from quite profane performers of the peddler class who move their place of work between performances, often being forced to do so. In the matter of having one fixed place for one's setting, a ruler may be too sacred, a peddler too profane.

In thinking about the scenic aspects of front, we tend to think of the living room in a particular house and the small number of performers who can thoroughly identify themselves with it. We have given insufficient attention to assemblages of sign-equipment which large numbers of performers can call their own for short periods of time. It is characteristic of Western European countries, and no doubt a source of stability for them, that a large number of luxurious settings are available for hire to anyone of the right kind who can afford them. One illustration of this may be cited from a study of the higher civil servant in Britain:

> *The question how far the men who rise to the top in the Civil Service take on the "tone" or "color" of a class other than that to which they belong by birth is delicate and difficult. The only definite information bearing on the question is the figures relating to the membership of the great London clubs. More than three-quarters of our high administrative officials belong to one or more clubs of high status and considerable luxury, where the entrance fee might be twenty guineas or more, and the annual subscription from twelve to twenty guineas. These institutions are of the upper class (not even of the upper-middle) in their premises, their equipment, the style of living practiced there, their whole atmosphere. Though many of the members would not be described as wealthy, only a wealthy man would unaided provide for himself and his family space, food and drink, service, and other amenities of life to the same standard as he will find at the Union, the Travellers', or the Reform.*[3]

Another example can be found in the recent development of the medical profession where we find that it is increasingly important for a doctor to have access to the elaborate scientific stage provided by large hospitals, so that fewer and fewer doctors are able to feel that their setting is a place that they can lock up at night.[4]

If we take the term "setting" to refer to the scenic parts of expressive equipment, one may take the term "personal front" to refer to the other items of expressive equipment, the items that we most intimately identify with the performer himself and that we naturally expect will follow the performer wherever he goes. As part of personal front we may include: insignia of office or rank; clothing; sex, age, and racial characteristics; size and looks; posture; speech patterns; facial expressions; bodily gestures; and the like. Some of these vehicles for conveying signs, such as racial characteristics, are relatively fixed and over a span of time do not vary for the individual from one situation to another. On the other hand, some of these sign vehicles are relatively mobile or transitory, such as facial expression, and can vary during a performance from one moment to the next.

It is sometimes convenient to divide the stimuli which make up personal front into "appearance" and "manner," according to the function performed by the information that these stimuli convey. "Appearance" may be taken to refer to those stimuli which function at the time to tell us of the performer's social statuses. These stimuli also tell us of the individual's temporary ritual state, that is, whether he is engaging in formal social activity, work, or informal recreation, whether or not he is celebrating a new phase in the season cycle or in his life-cycle. "Manner" may be taken to refer to those stimuli which function at the time to warn us of the interaction role the performer will expect to play in the oncoming situation. Thus a haughty, aggressive manner may give the impression that the performer expects to be the one who will initiate the verbal interaction and direct its course. A meek, apologetic manner may give the impression that the performer expects to follow the lead of others, or at least that he can be led to do so.

We often expect, of course, a confirming consistency between appearance and manner; we expect that the differences in social statuses among the interactants will be expressed in some way by congruent differences in the indications that are made of an expected interaction role. This type of coherence of front may be illustrated by the following description of the procession of a mandarin through a Chinese city:

> *Coming closely behind…the luxurious chair of the mandarin, carried by eight bearers, fills the vacant space in the street. He is mayor of the town, and for all practical purposes the supreme power in it. He is an ideal-looking official, for he is large and massive in appearance, whilst he has that stern and uncompromising look that is supposed to be necessary in any magistrate who would hope to keep his subjects in order. He has a stern and forbidding aspect, as though he were on his way to the execution ground to have some criminal*

decapitated. This is the kind of air that the mandarins put on when they appear in public. In the course of many years' experience, I have never once seen any of them, from the highest to the lowest, with a smile on his face or a look of sympathy for the people whilst he was being carried officially through the streets.[5]

But, of course, appearance and manner may tend to contradict each other, as when a performer who appears to be of higher estate than his audience acts in a manner that is unexpectedly equalitarian, or intimate, or apologetic, or when a performer dressed in the garments of a high position presents himself to an individual of even higher status.

In addition to the expected consistency between appearance and manner, we expect, of course, some coherence among setting, appearance, and manner.[6] Such coherence represents an ideal type that provides us with a means of stimulating our attention to and interest in exceptions. In this the student is assisted by the journalist, for exceptions to expected consistency among setting, appearance, and manner provide the piquancy and glamor of many careers and the salable appeal of many magazine articles. For example, a *New Yorker* profile on Roger Stevens (the real estate agent who engineered the sale of the Empire State Building) comments on the startling fact that Stevens has a small house, a meager office, and no letterhead stationery.[7]

In order to explore more fully the relations among the several parts of social front, it will be convenient to consider here a significant characteristic of the information conveyed by front namely, its abstractness and generality.

However specialized and unique a routine is, its social front, with certain exceptions will tend to claim facts that can be equally claimed and asserted of other, somewhat different routines. For example many service occupations offer their clients a performance that is illuminated with dramatic expressions of cleanliness, modernity, competence, and integrity. While in fact these abstract standards have a different significance in different occupational performances the observer is encouraged to stress the abstract similarities. For the observer this is a wonderful, though sometime, disastrous, convenience. Instead of having to maintain a different pattern of expectation and responsive treatment for each slightly different performer and performance he can place the situation in a broad category around which it is easy for him to mobilize his past experience and stereo-typical thinking. Observers then need only be familiar with a small and hence manageable vocabulary of fronts, and know how to respond to them, in order to orient themselves in a wide variety of situations. Thus in London the current tendency for chimney sweeps[8] and perfume clerks to wear white lab coats tends to provide the client with an understanding that the delicate tasks performed by these persons will be performed in what has become a standardized, clinical confidential manner.

There are grounds for believing that the tendency for a large number of different acts to be presented from behind a small number of fronts is a natural development in social organization. Radcliffe-Brown has suggested this in his claim that a "descriptive" kinship system which gives each person a unique place may work for very small communities, but, as the number of persons becomes large, clan segmentation becomes necessary as a means of providing a less complicated system of identifications and treatments.[9] We see this tendency illustrated in factories, barracks, and other large social establishments. Those who organize these establishments find it impossible to provide a special cafeteria, special modes of payment, special vacation rights, and special sanitary facilities for every line and staff status category in the organization, and at the same time they feel that persons of dissimilar status ought not to be indiscriminately thrown together or classified together. As a compromise, the full range of diversity is cut at a few crucial points, and all those within a given bracket are allowed or obliged to maintain the same social front in certain situations.

In addition to the fact that different routines may employ the same front, it is to be noted that a given social front tends to become institutionalized in terms of the abstract stereotyped expectations to which it gives rise, and tends to take on a meaning and stability apart from the specific tasks which happen at the time to be performed in its name. The front becomes a "collective representation" and a fact in its own right.

When an actor takes on an established social role, usually he finds that a particular front has already been established for it. Whether his acquisition of the role was primarily motivated by a desire to perform the given task or by a desire to maintain the corresponding front, the actor will find that he must do both.

Further, if the individual takes on a task that is not only new to him but also unestablished in the society, or if he attempts to change the light in which his task is viewed, he is likely to find that there are already several well-established fronts among which he must choose. Thus, when a task is given a new front we seldom find that the front it is given is itself new.

Since fronts tend to be selected, not created, we may expect trouble to arise when those who perform a given task are forced to select a suitable front for themselves from among several quite dissimilar ones. Thus, in military organizations, tasks are always developing which (it is felt) require too much authority and skill to be carried out behind the front maintained by one grade of personnel and too little authority and skill to be carried out behind the front maintained by the next grade in the hierarchy. Since there are relatively large jumps between grades, the task will come to "carry too much rank" or to carry too little.

An interesting illustration of the dilemma of selecting an appropriate front from several not quite fitting ones may be found today in American medical organizations with respect to the task of administering anesthesia.[10] In some hospitals anesthesia is still administered by nurses behind the front that nurses are allowed to have in hospitals regardless of the tasks they perform—a front involving ceremonial subordination to doctors and a relatively low rate of pay. In order to establish anesthesiology as a speciality for graduate medical doctors, interested practitioners have had to advocate strongly the idea that administering anesthesia is a sufficiently complex and vital task to justify giving to those who perform it the ceremonial and financial reward given to doctors. The difference between the front maintained by a nurse and the front maintained by a doctor is great; many things that are acceptable for nurses are *infra dignitatem* for doctors. Some medical people have felt that a nurse "under-ranked" for the task of administering anesthesia and that doctors "over-ranked"; were there an established status midway between nurse and doctor, an easier solution to the problem could perhaps be found.[11] Similarly, had the Canadian Army had a rank halfway between lieutenant and captain, two and a half pips instead of two or three, then Dental Corps captains, many of them of a low ethnic origin, could have been given a rank that would perhaps have been more suitable in the eyes of the Army than the captaincies they were actually given.

I do not mean here to stress the point of view of a formal organization or a society; the individual, as someone who possesses a limited range of sign-equipment, must also make unhappy choices. Thus, in the crofting community studied by the writer, hosts often marked the visit of a friend by offering him a shot of hard liquor, a glass of wine, some home-made brew, or a cup of tea. The higher the rank or temporary ceremonial status of the visitor, the more likely he was to receive an offering near the liquor end of the continuum. Now one problem associated with this range of sign-equipment was that some crofters could not afford to keep a bottle of hard liquor, so that wine tended to be the most indulgent gesture they could employ. But perhaps a more common difficulty was the fact that certain visitors, given their permanent and temporary status at the time, outranked one potable and under-ranked the next one in line. There was often a danger that the visitor would feel just a little affronted or, on the other hand, that the host's costly and limited sign-equipment would be misused. In our middle classes a similar situation arises when a hostess has to decide whether or not to use the good silver, or which would be the more appropriate to wear, her best afternoon dress or her plainest evening gown.

I have suggested that social front can be divided into traditional parts, such as setting, appearance, and manner, and that (since different routines may be presented from behind the same front) we may not find a perfect fit between the specific character of a performance and the general socialized guise in which it appears to us. These two facts, taken together, lead one to appreciate that items in the social front of a particular routine are not only found in the social fronts of a whole range of routines but also that the whole range of routines in which one item of sign-equipment is found will differ from the range of routines in which another item in the same social front will be found. Thus, a lawyer may talk to a client in a social setting that he employs only for this purpose (or for a study), but the suitable clothes he wears on such occasions he will also employ, with equal suitability, at dinner with colleagues and at the theater with his wife. Similarly, the prints that hang on his wall and the carpet on his floor may be found in domestic social establishments. Of course, in highly ceremonial occasions, setting, manner, and appearance may all be unique and specific, used only for performances of a single type of routine, but such exclusive use of sign-equipment is the exception rather than the rule.

DRAMATIC REALIZATION

While in the presence of others, the individual typically infuses his activity with signs which dramatically highlight and portray confirmatory facts that might otherwise remain unapparent or obscure. For if the individual's activity is to become significant to others, he must mobilize his activity so that it will express *during the interaction* what he wishes to convey. In fact, the performer may be required not only to express his claimed capacities during the interaction but also to do so during a split second in the interaction. Thus, if a baseball umpire is to give the impression that he is sure of his judgment, he must forgo the moment of thought which might make him sure of his judgment; he must give an instantaneous decision so that the audience will be sure that he is sure of his judgment.[12]

It may be noted that in the case of some statuses dramatization presents no problem, since some of the acts which are instrumentally essential for the completion of the core task of the status are at the same time wonderfully adapted, from the point of view of communication, as means of vividly conveying the qualities and attributes claimed by the performer. The roles of prizefighters, surgeons, violinists, and policemen are cases in point These activities allow for so much dramatic self-expression that exemplary practitioners—whether real or fictional—become famous and are given a special place in the commercially organized fantasies of the nation.

In many cases, however, dramatization of one's work does constitute a problem. An illustration of this may be cited from a hospital study where the medical nursing staff is shown to have a problem that the surgical nursing staff does not have:

> *The things which a nurse does for post-operative patients on the surgical floor are frequently of recognizable importance, even to patients who are strangers to hospital activities. For example, the patient sees his nurse changing bandages, swinging orthopedic frames into place, and can realize that these are purposeful activities. Even if she cannot be at his side, he can respect her purposeful activities.*

Medical nursing is also highly skilled work.... The physician's diagnosis must rest upon careful observation of symptoms over time where the surgeon's are in larger part dependent on visible things. The lack of visibility creates problems on the medical. A patient will see his nurse stop at the next bed and chat for a moment or two with the patient there. He doesn't know that she is observing the shallowness of the breathing and color and tone of the skin. He thinks she is just visiting. So, alas, does his family who may thereupon decide that these nurses aren't very impressive. If the nurse spends more time at the next bed than at his own, the patient may feel slighted.... The nurses are "wasting time" unless they are darting about doing some visible thing such as administering hypodermics.[13]

Similarly, the proprietor of a service establishment may find it difficult to dramatize what is actually being done for clients because the clients cannot "see" the overhead costs of the service rendered them. Undertakers must therefore charge a great deal for their highly visible product—a coffin that has been transformed into a casket—because many of the other costs of conducting a funeral are ones that cannot be readily dramatized.[14] Merchants, too, find that they must charge high prices for things that look intrinsically expensive in order to compensate the establishment for expensive things like insurance, slack periods, etc., that never appear before the customers' eyes.

The problem of dramatizing one's work involves more than merely making invisible costs visible. The work that must be done by those who fill certain statuses is often so poorly designed as an expression of a desired meaning, that if the incumbent would dramatize the character of his role, he must divert an appreciable amount of his energy to do so. And this activity diverted to communication will often require different attributes from the ones which are being dramatized. Thus to furnish a house so that it will express simple quiet dignity, the householder may have to race to auction sales, haggle with antique dealers, and doggedly canvass all the local shops for proper wallpaper and curtain materials. To give a radio talk that will sound genuinely informal, spontaneous, and relaxed, the speaker may have to design his script with painstaking care, testing one phrase after another, in order to follow the content, language, rhythm, and pace of everyday talk.[15] Similarly, a *Vogue* model, by her clothing, stance, and facial expression, is able expressively to portray a cultivated understanding of the book she poses in her hand; but those who trouble to express themselves so appropriately will have very little time left over for reading. As Sartre suggested: "The attentive pupil who wishes to *be* attentive, his eyes riveted on the teacher, his ears open wide, so exhausts himself in playing the attentive role that he ends up by no longer hearing anything."[16] And so individuals often find themselves with the dilemma of expression *versus* action. Those who have the time and talent to perform a task well may not, because of this, have the time or talent to make it apparent that they are performing well. It may be said that some organizations resolve this dilemma by officially delegating the dramatic function to a specialist who will spend his time expressing the meaning of the task and spend no time actually doing it.

If we alter our frame of reference for a moment and turn from a particular performance to the individuals who present it, we can consider an interesting fact about the round of different routines which any group or class of individuals helps to perform. When a group or class is examined, one finds that the members of it tend to invest their egos primarily in certain routines, giving less stress to the other ones which they perform. Thus a professional man may be willing to take a very modest role in the street, in a shop, or in his home, but, in the social sphere which encompasses his display of professional competency, he will be much concerned to make an effective showing. In mobilizing his behavior to make a showing, he will be concerned not so much with the full round of the different routines he performs but only with the one from which his occupational reputation derives. It is upon this issue that some writers have chosen to distinguish groups with aristocratic habits (whatever their social status) from those of middle-class character. The aristocratic habit, it has been said, is one that mobilizes all the minor activities of life which fall outside the serious specialities of other classes and injects into these activities an expression of character, power, and high rank.

> *By what important accomplishments is the young nobleman instructed to support the dignity of his rank, and to render himself worthy of that superiority over his fellow-citizens, to which the virtue of his ancestors had raised them: Is it by knowledge, by industry, by patience, by self-denial, or by virtue of any kind? As all his words, as all his motions are attended to, he learns a habitual regard to every circumstance of ordinary behavior, and studies to perform all those small duties with the most exact propriety. As he is conscious of how much he is observed, and how much mankind are disposed to favor all his inclinations, he acts, upon the most indifferent occasions, with that freedom and elevation which the thought of this naturally inspires. His air, his manner, his deportment, all mark that elegant, and graceful sense of his own superiority, which those who are born to inferior stations can hardly ever arrive at. These are the arts by which he proposes to make mankind more easily submit to his authority, and to govern their inclinations according to his own pleasure: and in this he is seldom disappointed. These arts, supported by rank and preeminence, are, upon ordinary occasions, sufficient to govern the world.[17]*

If such virtuosi actually exist, they would provide a suitable group in which to study the techniques by which activity is transformed into a show.

REALITY AND CONTRIVANCE

In our own Anglo-American culture there seems to be two common-sense models according to which we formulate our conceptions of behavior: the real, sincere, or honest performance; and the false one that thorough fabricators assemble for us, whether meant to be taken unseriously, as in the work of stage actors, or seriously, as in the work of confidence men. We tend to see real performances as something not purposely put together at all, being an unintentional product of the individual's unselfconscious response to the facts in his situation. And contrived performances we tend to see as something painstakingly pasted together, one false item on another, since there is no reality to which the items of behavior could be a direct response. It will be necessary to see now that these dichotomous conceptions are by way of being the ideology of honest performers, providing strength to the show they put on, but a poor analysis of it.

First, let it be said that there are many individuals who sincerely believe that the definition of the situation they habitually project is the real reality. In this report I do not mean to question their proportion in the population but rather the structural relation of their sincerity to the performances they offer. If a performance is to come off, the witnesses by and large must be able to believe that the performers are sincere. This is the structural place of sincerity in the drama of events. Performers may be sincere—or be insincere but sincerely convinced of their own sincerity-but this land of affection for one's part is not necessary for its convincing performance. There are not many French cooks who are really Russian spies, and perhaps there are not many women who play the part of wife to one man and mistress to another but these duplicities do occur, often being sustained successfully for long periods of time. This suggests that while persons usually are what they appear to be, such appearances could still have been managed. There is, then, a statistical relation between appearances and reality, not an intrinsic: or necessary one. In fact, given the unanticipated threats that play upon a performance, and given the need (later to be discussed) to maintain solidarity with one's fellow performers and some distance from the witnesses, we find that a rigid incapacity to depart from one's inward view of reality may at times endanger one's performance. Some performances are carried off successfully with complete dishonesty, others with complete honesty; but for performances in general neither of these extremes is essential and neither, perhaps, is dramaturgically advisable.

The implication here is that an honest, sincere, serious performance is less firmly connected with the solid world than one might first assume. And this implication will be strengthened if we look again at the distance usually placed between quite honest performances and quite contrived ones. In this connection take, for example, the remarkable phenomenon of stage acting. It does take deep skill, long training, and psychological capacity to become a good stage actor. But this fact should not blind us to another one: that almost anyone can quickly learn a script well enough to give a charitable audience some sense of realness in what is being contrived before them. And it seems this is so because ordinary social intercourse is itself put together as a scene is put together, by the exchange of dramatically inflated actions, counteractions, and terminating replies. Scripts even in the hands of unpracticed players can come to life because life itself is a dramatically enacted thing. All the world is not, of course, a stage, but the crucial ways in which it isn't are not easy to specify.

The recent use of "psychodrama" as a therapeutic technique illustrates a further point in this regard. In these psychiatrically staged scenes patients not only act out parts with some effectiveness, but employ no script in doing so. Their own past is available to them in a form which allows them to stage a recapitulation of it. Apparently a part once played honestly and in earnest leaves the performer in a position to contrive a showing of it later. Further, the parts that significant others played to him in the past also seem to be available, allowing him to switch from being the person that he was to being the persons that others were for him. This capacity to switch enacted roles when obliged to do so could have been predicted; everyone apparently can do it. For in learning to perform our parts in real life we guide our own productions by not too consciously maintaining an incipient familiarity with the routine of those to whom we will address ourselves. And when we come to be able properly to manage a real routine we are able to do this in part because of "anticipatory socialization,"[18] having already been schooled in the reality that is just coming to be real for us.

When the individual does move into a new position in society and obtains a new part to perform, he is not likely to be told in full detail how to conduct himself, nor will the facts of his new situation press sufficiently on him from the start to determine his conduct without his further giving thought to it. Ordinarily he will be given only a few cues, hints, and stage directions, and it will be assumed that he already has in his repertoire a large number of bits and pieces of performances that will be required in the new setting. The individual will already have a fair idea of what modesty, deference, or righteous indignation looks like, and can make a pass at playing these bits when necessary. He may even be able to play out the part of a hypnotic subject[19] or commit a "compulsive" crime[20] on the basis of models for these activities that he is already familiar with.

A theatrical performance or a staged confidence game requires a thorough scripting of the spoken content of the routine; but the vast part Involving "expression given off" is often determined by meager stage directions.

It is expected that the performer of illusions will already know a good deal about how to manage his voice, his face, and his body, although he—as well as any person who directs him—may find it difficult indeed to provide a detailed verbal statement of this land of knowledge. And to this, of course, we approach the situation of the straightforward man in the street. Socialization may not so much involve a learning of the many specific details of a single concrete part—often there could not be enough time or energy for this. What does seem to be required of the individual is that he learn enough pieces of expression to be able to "fill in" and manage, more or less, any part that he is likely to be given. The legitimate performances of everyday life are not "acted" or "put on" in the sense that the performer knows in advance just what he is going to do, and does this solely because of the effect it is likely to have. The expressions it is felt he is giving off will be especially "inaccessible" to him.[21] But as in the case of less legitimate performers, the incapacity of the ordinary individual to formulate in advance the movements of his eyes and body does not mean that he will not express himself through these devices in a way that is dramatized and pre-formed in his repertoire of actions. In short, we all act better than we know how.

When we watch a television wrestler gouge, foul, and snarl at his opponent we are quite ready to see that, in spite of the dust, he is, and knows he is, merely playing at being the "heavy," and that in another match he may be given the other role, that of clean-cut wrestler, and perform this with equal verve and proficiency. We seem less ready to see, however, that while such details as the number and character of the falls may be fixed beforehand, the details of the expressions and movements used do not come from a script but from command of an idiom, a command that is exercised from moment to moment with little calculation or forethought.

In reading of persons in the West Indies who become the "horse" or the one possessed of a voodoo spirit,[22] it is enlightening to learn that the person possessed will be able to provide a correct portrayal of the god that has entered him because of "the knowledge and memories accumulated in a life spent visiting congregations of the cult";[23] that the person possessed will be in just the right social relation to those who are watching; that possession occurs at just the right moment in the ceremonial undertakings, the possessed one carrying out his ritual obligations to the point of participating in a kind of skit with persons possessed at the time with other spirits. But in learning this, it is important to see that this contextual structuring of the horse's role still allows participants in the cult to believe that possession is a real thing and that persons are possessed at random by gods whom they cannot select.

And when we observe a young American middle-class girl playing dumb for the benefit of her boy friend, we are ready to point to items of guile and contrivance in her behavior. But like herself and her boy friend, we accept as an unperformed fact that this performer is a young American middle-class girl. But surely here we neglect the greater part of the performance. It is commonplace to say that different social groupings express in different ways such attributes as age, sex, territory, and class status, and that in each case these bare attributes are elaborated by means of a distinctive complex cultural configuration of proper ways of conducting oneself. To *be* a given land of person, then, is not merely to possess the required attributes, but also, to sustain the standards of conduct and appearance that one's social grouping attaches thereto. The unthinking ease with which performers consistently carry off such standard-maintaining routines does not deny that a performance has occurred, merely that the participants have been aware of it.

A status, a position, a social place is not a material thing, to be possessed and then displayed; it is a pattern of appropriate conduct, coherent, embellished, and well articulated. Performed with ease or clumsiness, awareness or not, guile or good faith, it is none the less something that must be enacted and portrayed, something that must be realized. Sartre, here, provides a good illustration:

Let us consider this waiter in the café. His movement is quick and forward, a little too precise, a little too rapid. He comes toward the patrons with a step a little too quick. He bends forward a little too eagerly; his voice, his eyes express an interest a little too solicitous for the order of the customer. Finally there he returns, trying to imitate in his walk the inflexible stiffness of some kind of automaton while carrying his tray with the recklessness of a tightrope-walker by putting it in a perpetually unstable, perpetually broken equilibrium which he perpetually re-establishes by a light movement of the arm and hand. All his behavior seems to us a game. He applies himself to chaining his movements as if they were mechanisms, the one regulating the other; his gestures and even his voice seem to be mechanisms; he gives himself the quickness and pitiless rapidity of things. He is playing, he is amusing himself. But what is he playing? We need not watch long before we can explain it: he is playing at being a waiter in a café. There is nothing there to surprise us. The game is a kind of marking out and investigation. The child plays with his body in order to explore it, to take inventory of it; the waiter in the café plays with his condition in order to realize it. This obligation is not different from that which is imposed on all tradesmen. Their condition is wholly one of ceremony. The public demands of them that they realize it as a ceremony; there is the dance of the grocer, of the tailor, of the auctioneer, by which they endeavor to persuade their clientele that they are nothing but a grocer, an auctioneer, a tailor. A grocer who dreams is offensive to the buyer, because such a grocer is not wholly a grocer. Society demands that he limit himself to his function as a grocer, just as the soldier at attention makes himself into a soldier-thing with a direct regard which does not see at all, which is not longer meant to see, since it is the rule and not the interest of the moment which determines the point he must fix his eyes on (the sight "fixed at ten paces"). There are indeed many precautions to imprison a man in what he is, as if we lived in perpetual fear that he might escape from it, that he might break away and suddenly elude his condition.[24]

NOTES

1. Perhaps the real crime of the confidence man is not that he takes money from his victims but that he robs all of us of the belief that middle-class-manners, and appearance can be sustained only by middle-class people. A disabused professional can be cynically hostile to the service relation his clients expect him to extend to them the confidence man is in a position to hold the whole "legit" world in this contempt.

2. See Taxel, *op. cit.*, p. 4. Harry Stack Sullivan has suggested that the tact of institutionalized performers can operate in the other direction, resulting in a kind of *noblesse-oblige* sanity.

3. H. E. Dale, *The Higher Civil Service of Great Britain* (Oxford: Oxford University Press, 1941), p. 50.

4. David Solomon, "Career Contingencies of Chicago Physicians" (unpublished Ph.D. dissertation, Department of Sociology, University of Chicago, 1952), p. 74.

5. J. Macgowan, *Sidelights on Chinese Life* (Philadelphia: Lippincott, 1908), p. 187.

6. Cf. Kenneth Burke's comments on the "scene-act-agent ratio," *A Grammar of Motives* (New York: Prentice-Hall, 1945), pp. 6–9.

7. E. J. Kahn, Jr., "Closings and Openings," *The New Yorker*, February 13 and 20, 1954.

8. See Mervyn Jones, "White as a Sweep," *The New Statesman and Nation*, December 6, 1952.

9. A. R. Radcliffe-Brown, "The Social Organization of Australian Tribes," *Oceania*, 1, 440.

10. See the thorough treatment of this problem in Dan C. Lortie, "Doctors without Patients: The Anesthesiologist, a New Medical Specialty" (unpublished Master's thesis, Department of Sociology. University of Chicago, 1950). See also Mark Murphy's three-part Profile of Dr. Rovenstine, "Anesthesiologist," *The New Yorker*, October 25, November 1, and November 8, 1947.

11. In some hospitals the intern and the medical student perform tasks that are beneath a doctor and above a nurse. Presumably such tasks do not require a large amount of experience and practical training, for while this Intermediate status of doctor-in-training is a permanent part of hospitals, all those who hold it do so temporarily.

12. See Babe Pinelli, as told to Joe King, Mr. Ump (Philadelphia: Westminster Press, 1953), p. 75.

13. Edith Lentz, "A Comparison of Medical and Surgical Floors" (Mimeo: New York State School of Industrial and Labor Relations. Cornell University, 1954), pp. 2–3.

14. Material on the burial business used throughout this report is taken from Robert W. Habenstein, "The American Funeral Director" (unpublished Ph.D. dissertation, Department of Sociology, University of Chicago, 1954). I owe much to Mr. Habenstein's analysis of a funeral as a performance.

15. John Hilton, "Calculated Spontaneity," *Oxford Book of English Talk* (Oxford: Clarendon Press, 1953), pp, 399–404.

16. Sartre, *op. cit.*, p. 60.

17. Adam Smith, *The Theory of Moral Sentiments* (London: Henry Bohn, 1853), p. 75.

18. See R. K. Merton, *Social Theory and Social Structure* (Glencoe: The Free Press, revised and enlarged edition, 1957), P-265 ff.

19. This view of hypnosis is neatly presented by T. R. Sarbin, "Contributions to Role Taking Theory. 1: Hypnotic Behavior," *Psychological Review*, 57, pp. 255–70.

20. See D. R. Cressey, "The Differential Association Theory and Compulsive Crimes," *Journal of Criminal Law, Criminology and Police Science*, 45, pp. 29–40.
21. This concept derives from T. R. Sarbin, "Role Theory," in Gardner Lindzey, *Handbook of Social Psychology* (Cambridge: Addison-Wesley, 1954), Vol. 1, pp. 235–36.
22. See, for example, Alfred Métraux, "Dramatic Elements in Ritual Possession," Diogenes, 11, pp. 18–36.
23. Ibid., p. 24.
24. Sartre, *op. cit.*, p. 59.

QUESTIONS

? For Goffman, a performance consists of many different aspects including the front, setting, sign equipment, manners, appearances and gestures. Give examples of each of these.

? Goffman says that certain roles (expectations and behaviors associated with your job or status) have dramatic qualities and attributes attached to them. Identify and describe a role played by you or someone you know. List the dramatic qualities and attributes attached to that role.

? Societal puzzle question: Describe a recent interaction that you had with a friend or acquaintance. Now, using what you have learned from the article, conduct a dramaturgical analysis of this interaction. Then, identify one benefit and one problem with using such an analysis to understand this interaction.

Making Fantasies Real
Producing Women and Men on the Maquila Shop Floor

By LESLIE SALZINGER

■ At some point in your life you probably worked for pay. To earn this pay, you performed certain tasks constituting what sociologists would call your "role" (expectations and behaviors associated with your job or status). For instance, if you worked as a server, you role might have called for you to perform the following tasks: waiting on customers including seating them, taking their orders, bringing food and drink to their tables, and presenting them with a bill. But merely performing work-related duties was probably not enough, your employer also probably expected you to display a certain type of image. For example, she may have singled out the way you dress. In this article, sociologist Leslie Salzinger explores the projection of required images at a Juarez *maquiladora* (an American-owned assembly plant located in Mexico and Central America where low-wage production workers transform imported components into exportable products). She shows how Mexican men and women workers are asked not only to perform the tasks at their factory jobs, but also to perform a particular gender role (a social expectation of behavior and attitude based on sex).

In the early 1990s, I went to Mexico's northern border to study the role of gender in global production.[1] In Mexico, the bulk of such production takes place in maquiladoras (or maquilas)—export-processing tactories owned by foreign (usually U S) capital First established in 1965 on Mexico's northern border, maquilas employ low-paid Mexican workers to assemble U.S -produced parts into goods to be sold on the U.S. market.

"Panoptimex" was the first plant I saw, and its shop floor fulfilled my most stereotypical expectations.[2] The "docile women" of managerial dreams and feminist ethnography, theory and nightmare were there in the flesh.[3] Rows of them, smiling lips drawn red, darkened lashes lowered to computer boards, male supervisors looking

---

From *NACLA Report on the Americas*, Vol. 34, Issue 5, Mar/Apr 2001 by Leslie Salzinger. Copyright © 2001 by the North American Congress on Latin America, 38 Greene St. New York, NY 10013, www.nacla.org. Reprinted by permission.

over their shoulders—monitoring finger speed and manicure in a single look. It was visible at a glance: femininity incarnate in the service of capitalism.

But the story would not prove to be so straightforward. Although the femininity enacted at Panoptimex appears to be imported from the women workers' homes and family lives, what is most noticeable over time spent in the plant is the amount of work dedicated to creating appropriately gendered workers. It has become a truism to note that globalization is fueled by the search for docile, dextrous and cheap labor, and Third World women are understood as "cheap labor" par excellence. Nonetheless, a closer look at an actual, live global factory suggests that this formulation puts the cart before the horse. Women workers are not always and already father-cowed, mother-trained and husband-supported. Rather, productive femininity is a paradigm through which managers view, and therefore structure, assembly work and through which they imagine, describe and define job applicants and workers. The people we think of as classic "women workers" are formed within these ways of thinking and being. Thus, it is a mistake to think that their presence in the factory makes global production possible. To the contrary, they are global production's finished product. Gender indeed is a significant aspect of globalization, but it is the rhetoric of "femininity," rather than the presence of flesh-and-blood women, that enables low-cost production.

All this is nowhere more apparent than in Mexico's maquila industry, where the image of the "woman worker" persists in shaping shop-floor relations, even in the face of a massive influx of young men into these feminized jobs. A closer look at the history of this paradox, and more importantly, an exploration of how the image of "femininity" operates on a particular maquila shop floor, make it possible to see the construction of "Third World women workers" in action and thereby to better grasp the role of gender in globalization.

The gendering of the maquila industry has a long and contradictory history. When the industry was first established in 1965, it was already framed in highly publicized, gendered rhetorics. Supposedly, its main purpose was to absorb the large number of Mexican men (*braceros*) who at the time were being expelled from their migrant farmworker jobs in the western United States. However, like managers of other export-processing factories in free-trade zones around the world, maquila hiring departments already had an image of "assembly workers," and male farmworkers were not part of it.[4] Advertising for "*señoritas*" and "*damitas*" throughout the border areas made clear—only young women need apply.[5] These policies were repeatedly, if indirectly, legitimated in public discussions by managers, union bosses, and political commentators, who all persistently invoked the superiority of women workers and the deficiencies of their male counterparts. In a typical article, a manager commented matter-of-factly "Eighty-five percent of the labor force is made up of women, since they're more disciplined, pay more attention to what they do, and get bored less than men do."[6]

In the early 1980s, the image of the docile young woman began to crack. Interunion conflicts led to several strikes, bringing anomalous pictures of defiant women workers, sticks in hand, to the front pages of local newspapers. Shortly thereafter, peso devaluations dramatically cut wage costs in dollar terms, and the demand for maquila workers soared. This led to a shortage of young women willing to work at maquila wages and to an increasingly assertive attitude on the part of those already employed. Confronted by young women workers who did not behave like "women" at all, some managers faced by shortages turned to young men. By the end of the decade, men made up close to half the maquila work force.[7]

As a result of this history, a tour of the industry in the early 1990s revealed an increasingly paradoxical situation. Despite the large numbers of male workers, descriptions of the prototypically malleable female worker emerged again and again. In an interview held more than a decade after men began entering maquila jobs in large numbers, the head of labor relations for the Association of Maquiladoras still advocated hiring women, commenting: "Men are not inclined to sit. Women are calmer about sitting." Despite the increasing scarcity of the women purportedly described, the rhetoric of femininity persisted, shaping the decisions and expectations of managers and workers alike.

It was in this context that I began to ask how this persistent image operated in production, and how it was related to the emblematic, but—as I gradually came to realize—unusual women of Panoptimex. Over 18 months I studied four maquila shop floors. Three of these, including Panoptimex, were in Crudad Juárez, the border city containing the largest number of maquila workers in Mexico.[8] One was farther south, having moved in search of the docile women workers who had become increasingly elusive at the border. Managers in three of these maquilas remained committed to the idea that assembly work is necessarily "women's work," and the fourth had let the image go, but only under pressure.[9] Thus, the image had effects across the board. Nonetheless, its impact varied dramatically across the plants, creating different types of shop-floor subjects with differing levels of productivity.

In the Juárez auto parts assembly plant, a group of U.S. managers were deeply wedded to the notion that the work was appropriately "women's work". Yet they could not attract enough female workers and succeeded only in antagonizing most of their male employees and provoking them to interfere with their female coworkers production. In another auto parts plant located outside Juárez, Mexican managers were intent on showing that they were cosmopolitan. They dismissed the notion that their rural women workers were merely "traditional Mexican women" and organized them into teamwork and leadership training. This training used the rhetoric to assertiveness and self-discipline—all, of course, in the service of work output, and it evoked a distinctive, and highly productive, shop-floor "femininity." And in a Juárez-based hospital-garment assembly factory, responding to a distinctly "unfeminine" strike, Mexican managers deliberately turned to male workers scrapping completely the image of the "feminine" assembly worker and consciously working outside that framework.

Thus, the rhetoric of productive femininity was always meaningful on these shops floors; yet it had distinctive effects in each of them, depending on the managers' senses of who they themselves were. Such managerial self-concepts set both the rhetoric of feminity and the labor control strategies within which it was communicated, in motion. It was only at Panoptimex, though, that I saw women workers who actually resembled the ones described in transnational accounts. At Panoptimex, therefore, we can excavate the construction to the paradigmatic feminine subject—by tracing the multiple forces that come together to bring her into being.

Panoptimex makes televisions, and it is managers' consequent obsession with the visual, in the context of the transnational rhetoric of feminine productivity, that decides what is the appropriate way to be a woman (or a man) in a particular place. At Panoptimex, labor control practices based on the heightened visibility of workers create self-conscious and self-monitoring women on the one hand, and emasculated men on the other. In this process, managerial framing generates, rather than simply takes advantage of a particular set of gendered subjectivities and in so doing establishes order on the shop floor.

The plant manager is an ash-blond South American who has his sights set on being promoted to the company's metropolitan headquarters. He is obsessed with the aesthetics of "his" factory—repainting the shop floor his trademark colors and insisting on ties for supervisors and uniforms for workers. The plant is the company's showpiece in Mexico a state-of-the-art facility whose design has been so successful that its blueprint was recently bought by a competitor building a second factory in Juárez.

The factory floor is organized for visibility—a panopticon in which everything is marked.[10] Yellow tape lines the walkways, red arrows point to test sites; green, yellow and red lights glow above the machines. On the walls hang large, shiny white graphs documenting quality levels in red, yellow, green and black. Just above each worker's head is a chart full of dots: green for one defect, red for three defects, gold stars for perfect days. Workers' bodies, too, are marked: yellow, sleeveless smocks for new workers; light blue smocks for more seasoned women workers; dark blue jackets for male workers and mechanics; orange smocks for (female) "special" workers; red smocks for (female) group chiefs; lipstick, mascara, eyeliner, rouge, high heels, miniskirts, identity badges… Everything is signaled.

Ringing the top of the production floor are windows. One flight up sit the managers, behind glass, looking—or perhaps not. From on high, they "keep track of the flow of production," calling down to a supervisor to ask about a slowdown, which is easily visible from above in the accumulation of televisions in one part of the line, gaps further along or in a mound of sets in the center of a line that also has technicians clustered nearby. Late afternoons, the plant manager and his assistant descend. Hands clasped behind their backs, they stroll the plant floor, stopping to chat and joke—just as everyone says—with "the young and pretty ones." The personnel department (its staff are titled "social workers") is entirely focused on questions of appropriate appearance and behavior, rather than on the work itself. 'That's not manly. A man with trousers wouldn't behave like that' one of the social workers tells a young male worker who showed his ex-girlfriend's letter to others on the line.

"Remember this. It's nice to be important, but more important to be nice," she counsels a young woman who keeps getting into arguments with her coworkers. Behavior, attitude, demeanor—typically in highly gendered form—is evaluated here Skill, speed and quality rarely come up.

Managerial focus on the look of things is reflected in the demographics of the workplace as well. Close to 80% of the plant's direct line workers are women. They sit in long lines, always observed, repeating the same meticulous gestures a thousand times over the nine-hour day. During the 1980s, when it became difficult to hire women workers and most Juárez maquilas began hiring men, the company went so far as to recruit a busload of young women from a rural village 45 minutes away. The company, calmed by the sight of the familiarly populated lines, for years provided the workers with free transportation to and from the factory. This economic decision, one not made by most companies in the area, suggests the way in which Panoptimex managers' visually oriented attentional practices heightened their commitment to the transnational image of the woman worker.

Lines are "operator controlled." The chassis comes to a halt in front of the worker; she inserts her components and pushes a button to send it on. There is no piece rate, no moving assembly line to hurry her along. But in this fishbowl, no one wants to be seen with the clogged line behind her, an empty space ahead of her and managers peering from their offices above. If she does slow momentarily, the supervisor materializes. "Ah, here's the problem. What's wrong, my dear?" For the supervisor is, of course, watching as well as watched. He circles behind seated workers, monitoring efficiency and legs simultaneously—his gaze focused sometimes on "nimble fingers" at work and sometimes on the quality of a hairstyle. Often he will stop by a favorite operator—chatting, checking quality, flirting. His approval marks "good worker" and "desirable woman" in a single gesture.

"Did you see him talking to her?" For the eyes of workers are also at work, quick side-glances registering a new style, making note of wrinkles that betray ironing undone. "Uuf, look how she's dressed!" With barely a second thought, women workers can produce five terms for "give her the once over." A young woman comments that when she started work she used no makeup and only wore dresses below the knee. But then her coworkers started telling her she looked bad, that she should "fix herself up." As she speaks, her best friend affectionately surveys her painted face and nails, and her miniskirted physique. "They say one's appearance reveals a lot," she remarks. Two lines down, another young woman mentions she missed work the day before because she slept too late. Too late, that is, to do her hair and makeup and still make the bus. To come to work is to be seen, to watch and so to watch and see yourself.[11]

The ultimate arbiter of desirability, of course, is neither one's self nor one's coworkers, but supervisors and managers. Workers gossip constantly about who is or is not chosen. For those (few) who are so anointed, the experience is one of personal power. "If you've got it. flaunt it!" a worker comments gleefully, looking from her lace bodysuit to the supervisor hovering nearby. This power is often used more instrumentally as well. On my first day in the plant, a young woman—known as one of the "young and pretty ones" favored by managerial notice—is stopped by guards for lateness. She slips upstairs and convinces the plant manager to intercede for her. She is allowed to work after all. The lines sizzle with gossip.

The few men on the line are not part of these games Physically segregated from the women workers, they stand rather than sit, attaching screen and chassis to the television cabinet at one end of the line, packing the finished product at the other. They move relatively freely, joking and laughing and calling out—noisy but ignored. The supervisor is glaringly absent from their section of the line, and they comment disdainfully that he's afraid to bother them Nonetheless, when they get too obviously boastful, he brings their behavior to a halt. Abruptly he moves the loudest of them, placing them in soldering, where they sit in conspicuous discomfort among the "girls," while the men who have not been moved make uneasy jokes about how boring it is "over there."

One young man says he came here intentionally for all the women. "I thought I'd find a girlfriend. I thought it would be fun" "And was it?" I ask. There's a pause "No one paid any attention to me," he responds finally, a bit embarrassed, laughing and downcast. His experience reminds me of a story told by one of the women workers who returned to the factory after having quit. "It's a good environment here," she says. "In the street they [men] mess with us, but here, we mess with them a little. We make fun of them and they get embarrassed."

In the factory, to be male is to have the right to look, to be a "super-visor." As for the male line worker, standing facing the line, eyes trained on his work, he does not count as a man. In the plant's central game, he is neither subject nor object. As a result, he has no location from which to act—either in his relation to the women in the plant or in relation to factory managers.

What is striking once inside the plant is how much work is involved in the ongoing labor of constructing appropriate "young women"—and "young men"—out of new hires, gendered meanings are forged within the context of panoptic labor control strategies in which women are constituted as desirable objects and male managers as desiring subjects. Male workers become not-men, with no standing in the game. These identities are defined by management in the structure of the plant, but they are reinforced by workers Young women workers take pleasure in the experience of being desirable and in their use of this delicious if limited power in attempting to evade the most egregious aspects of managerial control. As male workers attempt to assert masculinity, they become vulnerable to managerial ability lo undercut these assertions.

The gendered meanings and subjectivities developed here are familiar. It appears that Panoptimex managers have indeed found their ideal feminine workers, and simply supplemented them with the predictably rebellious young men of international repute. Certainly that is the managers' own understanding Nonetheless, managers' beliefs are also a product of external rhetorics—in this case, discourses from their own national cultures and from the transnational industry they work for Closer inspection reveals instead the localized operations of the expectation of femininity, as managers who are committed to the look of things go to unusual lengths to create the subjects they expect to see.[12] Thus, Panoptimex's docile women and emasculated men are local products, created through the self-fulfilling prophecy of management's hiring and labor-control tactics Here we see the transnational rhetoric of femininity put into local practice.

Panoptimex is a compelling case not because it is typical, but because it is unusual. It stands out for the remarkable accuracy with which its workers incarnate—literally bring lo life—the image of homegrown feminine docility, an image that in fact is generated not it their homes, but in transnational managerial rhetoric and imagination. Panoptimex workers are classic simulacra, embodiments of a fantasized reality.[13]

In focusing on the symbolic practices and formative descriptions of shop-floor life, rather than on gender demographics or managerial portrayals of workers, a distinctive set of social processes come into focus. We can see how subjects are evoked on the shop floor, rather than imported from outside the factory. And we can begin to describe the local conditions necessary for transnational images of docile feminity to be construed and acted upon. The workers of Panoptimex do not enter the factory with a gender identity that is already set, but neither do they automatically reflect managerial fantasy Rather, managers are located within many discourses—the feminine worker is only one Panoptimex managers also participate in a work world in which the visual is disproportionately highlighted. It is at the intersection of those two frameworks that the painted, permed and plant Panoptimex woman emerges—born not of a Mexican father and mother, but of transnational perspectives Panoptimex workers are as much global products as are the televisions they assemble.

NOTES

1. The research on which this article is based as part of a larger study of four maquilas done over 18 months in the early 1990s. I spent three of those months in Panoptimex. During that time, I spent every weekday wandering the shop floor, sitting in the personnel office or interviewing managers. Later, I interviewed ten workers I knew well in my home.

2. All the proper names used here are fictitious.

3. Donald Baerresen. *The Border Industrialization Program of Mexico* (Lexington, MA; Health Lexington Books, 1971); also see Rachel Kamel, *The Global Factory: Analysis and Action for a New Economic Era* (Philadelphia: American Friends Service Committee, 1990); Norma Iglesras Pneto, *La flor mas bella de la maquiladora* (Mexico City Secretaria de Education Publica, 1987); Lourdes Beneria and Martha Roldan, *The Crossroads of Class and Gender* (Chicago: University of Chicago Press, 1987); Diane Elson and Ruth Pearson, "Third World Manufacturing," in *Feminist Review* (London: Virago, 1986), pp. 67–92. Maria Patncia Fernandez-Kelly, *For We Are Sold, I and My people: Women and Industry in Mexico's Frontier* (Albany: State University of New York Press, 1983); Annette Fuentes and Barbara Ehrenreich, *Women in the Global Factory* (Boston, South End Press, 1983).

4. Ruth Pearson, "Male Bias and Women's Work in Mexico Border Industries," in Diane Elson (ed.,) *Male Bias in the Development Process* (Manchester: Manchester University Press. 1991), pp. 133–163; Altha Cravey, *Women and Work in Mexico's Maquiladoras* (Lanbam: Rowmen and Littlefield, 1998).

5. For excellent histories of this labor market process, see large Carnilla and Alberto Hernandez, *Mujeres tranterizas end industria maquiladora* (Mexico City SEPCEFNOMEX, 1985) and Fernandez Kelly, *For We Are Sold*. For an overview of the varied ways in which gender has figured in contemporary transnational production, see Aihwa Ong, "The Gender and Labor Politics of Postmodernity," *Annual Review of Anthropology*, No. 20(1991), pp. 279–309.

6. *El Fronterizo*, (Cludad Juárez), March 16, 1981.

7. In the late 1980s, the percentage of men on maquila production lines stabilized at close to 45% . See *Avance de Information Economica*, (Mexico City Institute National de Estadistica, Geografia e Informática [INEGI], 1991). Since then, the percentage has remained roughly the same. See *Estadistica de la Industria Maquiladora de Exportacion*, 1990–1995 (Mexico City: INEGI, 1996).

8. INEGI, 1996.

9. For a more complete discussion of these issues, see Leslie Salzinger, "From High Heels to Swathed Bodies: Gendered Meanings Under Production in Mexico's Export-Processing Industry," *Feminist Studies* Vol. 23 No. 3 (1997), pp. 549–574; and Leslie Salzinger, *Gender Under Production: Making Subjects in Medico's Global Factories* (Berkeley: University of California Press, forthcoming).

10. See Michel Foucault. *Discipline and Punish* (New York Vintage Books, 1997).

11. For further discussion of the role of sexuality in this process, see Salzinger, "Manufacturing Sexual Objects: 'Harassment, Desire and Discipline on a Maquiladora Shop Floor," *Ethnography*, Vol. 1, No. 1 (2000), pp. 67–92.

12. See Salzinger, "From High Heels to Swathed Bodies," for an analysis of other modes of copying with the disjuncture between expectation and reality, as the managerial meteoric of femininity produces recalcitrant subjects in the hands of less consistent managers.

13. "Simulacra and Simulations," in Mark Poster, (ed.), *Jean Baudrillard. Selected Writings* (Stanford: Stanford University Press, 1988), pp. 166–184.

QUESTIONS

? What does it mean that the work in the maquiladora industry is "feminized?" Give examples.

? Salzinger argues that it is ultimately the *image* of femininity that makes low cost workers possible, even though women workers do not necessarily fit the description and even though men are also working in these jobs. How can an image make low cost workers possible?

? Societal puzzle question: Identify a job that you think is "feminized." Explain the general tasks associated with this job. Explain the tasks that are "feminized." How do the men who do this job carry out such feminized tasks? The women? What impact does working in a feminized job have on men?

Chapter 4

The Good Mother:
Neutralization Techniques Used by Pageant Mothers

By MARTHA HELTSLEY & THOMAS C. CALHOUN

■ Usually we follow the written and unwritten rules of our society, but there are times when we deliberately or unwittingly deviate (break away) from these societal expectations. If our actions cause others to label us deviant, how do we explain and manage this label? Sociologists Martha Heltsley and Tom Calhoun address such a question in the following selection. During their study of mothers of young beauty pageant participants, a highly publicized crime occurred. A five year-old beauty pageant winner, Jon Benet Ramsey, was murdered. No one was found guilty of the crime, but images of a highly sexualized Jon Benet and other young pageant contestants flooded national media following the murder. Consequently, mothers who entered their daughters in such events found that they were labeled deviant. Read this article carefully to understand the ways in which Heltsley and Calhoun's beauty pageant mothers enlisted "techniques of neutralization" to manage the deviant label.

INTRODUCTION

The December 26, 1996 murder of JonBenet Ramsey, was the perfect case for capturing the attention of the press: a millionaire father, a Miss America finalist for a mother, and the alleged sexual abuse and murder of a tiny beauty queen. Media coverage focused initially on an alleged connection between the murder and pageants. A former Florida state representative asserted that children's pageants provide "an attractive package for somebody looking to violate a young person" (Briggs 1997:A4, A1). Child contestants were portrayed with a combination of sexuality and innocence—"exactly what a pedophile would do with a little girl" (Henetz 1997:A1). The question often asked was: "Could the pageants' sly sexuality have aroused her killer?" (Reed 1997:16:6).

Copyright 2003 from *Deviant Behavior* by Martha Heltsley and Thomas C. Calhoun. Reproduced by permission of Taylor & Francis Group, LLC., http://www.taylorandfrancis.com

Camille Pagalia believed the pageants represent "a deep sexual disturbance in the society" (Davidson 1997:61) and *New York Times* columnist Frank Rich declared, "the merchandising of children as sexual commodities is ubiquitous" (Rich 1997:23). The movie, television, fashion, and advertising industries were thought to share some of the blame (Davidson 1997; Giroux 1998). It is difficult to hold an entire society culpable and consequently mothers receive the brunt of criticism. Holding mothers responsible for the social and moral welfare of children is not unusual, as sex role tasks for specific traits, beliefs, and attitudes that include responsibility for protecting and socializing children characterize motherhood. For many, the measure of a good mother is reflected in her children.

The pageant controversy garnered media attention for a relatively short time. By the end of January, the connection between the murder of JonBenet and her involvement in pageants was discounted in the murder investigation and the media followed suit. The following statement summarizes the month long coverage of the Ramsey case.

> *JonBenet was horribly murdered, apparently with sexual motives…The killing has baffled the police and no arrest has been made. Nonetheless, the American media have decided that the beauty pageants were to blame. News organizations have waded in, deploring the use of make-up on little girls' cheeks and analyzing the parents who allow their daughters to enter beauty pageants. We have been urged to censure "mothers who live through their children," and to condemn the organizers of such events. The word "sick" has been widely used and polemicists have decried the "merchandising of children as sexual commodities." Feminists have sighed that this is what happens when you force pre-pubescent girls to act like supermodels. (Letts 1997:18)*

By late January 1997 the media shifted its focus from pageants being responsible for Ramsey's death to the plight of little pageant girls who were "robbed of their girlhood" (Berman 1997:E:1).

> *I know that children are not malleable lumps of clay, that they are smarter and tougher than we give them credit for. But I prefer to err on the side on caution any day of the week because at the bottom line, they are still children. Not vessels for adult fulfillment, not a second chance for faded parental dreams, not miniature women and men, but children. That has to mean something. It has to be inviolate. Sadly, that was not the case with JonBenet Ramsey. So far as I'm concerned, she was the victim of two crimes. On the day after Christmas, she was murdered. But long before that, she was robbed. (Pitts 1997:2)*

JonBenet allegedly suffered from a syndrome called "premature adulthood" (Berger 1997:E12). Lost childhood brought with it a multitude of problems including eating disorders ("Girls…" 1997:A6) and an array of other dysfunctions. "At best, such pageants put little girls at risk for delays in most major areas of development. At worst, the experience will lead to serious academic, behavioral, and emotional problems" (Elder, Digirolamo, and Thompson 1997:B7:2).

Popular culture articles focusing primarily on the evils of child pageantry began to slowly fade in the following months as attention was focused more on the botched murder investigation. Several documentaries produced since the first few months of 1997 closely investigate the social world of children's pageants, but for the most part these contests remain unexplored in scholarly research. Cohen, Wilk, and Stoeltje (1996) suggest that pageants have long been ignored by academia because they have been viewed as merely examples of popular culture. This article is concerned with how pageant mothers responded to the deviant label placed on them during the first few months of negative media attention. Specifically, this article addresses the neutralization techniques utilized by mothers whose daughters participate in pageants.

TECHNIQUES OF NEUTRALIZATION

According to Sykes and Matza (1957) neutralization techniques protect the actor from self-blame and deflect moral culpability. Five neutralization techniques identified by Sykes and Matza include denial of responsibility, denial of injury, denial of the victim, condemnation of the condemners, and an appeal to higher loyalties. The denial of responsibility is a technique where the actor denies responsibility for the behavior because of circumstances beyond his or her control. When applied successfully, the technique functions to deflect blame and lessen guilt to buttress the self-image of the actor. The denial of injury neutralization technique enables individuals to view their action as not really causing any harm. If another person is not seen as being injured, then the culprit cannot be seen as a victimizer. Denial of the victim, the third technique, involves transforming the victim into a person who somehow deserves injury. The victim becomes the wrongdoer. In cases where this type of neutralization technique is used, the deviant views his or her behavior as justified—as though he or she has taken an almost heroic stance against the wrongs committed by others. The deviant accepts responsibility for the act but deflects social disapproval because the act was viewed as justified.

The condemnation of condemners is a neutralization technique where one shifts attention from his or her deviant act by pointing out behaviors and motives of those who may judge the behavior. The infidel caught cheating on his spouse, for example, might point out that judges, lawyers, prosecutors, and even policemen cheat on their wives. He concludes that he is no worse than the people judging him. Appealing to higher loyalties is the final technique used by deviants to shield blame. The demands of the larger society are sacrificed for the demands of the smaller group to which the deviant belongs. Subcultural norms sometimes conflict with those of the greater society, and the offender imagines himself or herself to be seen in a better light by affirming loyalties to the group that support the particular act.

Sykes and Matza's (1957) neutralization techniques are used as a guide to examine the accounts offered by mothers who place their children in beauty contests. These accounts were collected during the first five months (January through May of 1997) after JonBenet Ramsey's murder when mothers were aware of how the media portrayed them.

METHODOLOGY

This study involves analyzing the latter part of a pageant survey conducted by the first author that began four months before the Ramsey murder. A 48-item questionnaire was distributed at six national children's pageants between September 14, 1996 to May 25, 1997. These national competitions were held in Kentucky (Owensboro), Indiana (Clarksville), Alabama (Cullman and Decatur), and Tennessee (Jackson and Pigeon Forge). Because of their geographic proximity to the researcher, mothers of competing daughters 16 years of age or younger were asked to complete the questionnaire. A total of 371 forms were distributed with 122 returned after the competitions were completed. In the last section of the four-page survey space was provided for additional commentary about the respondents' involvement in pageants. The questions asked: "What do you like best about pageants?" and "What do you like least about pageants?" Forty-three mothers answered the questions and did so *only after the death of Ramsey*. The data used in this study were derived from their responses.

In the analysis of this section of the questionnaire the space seemed to take on a different character after JonBenet Ramsey's murder than its intended purpose. Instead of answering the questions specifically, the area allowed respondents to vent their dismay at the treatment of pageants by the media and public. Almost one-half of the responses found in that section of the questionnaire referred directly to childhood sexuality or exploitation, sexual predators, the Ramsey murder case, or the media—topics not generally connected to children's beauty pageants until after the murder of Ramsey. Perhaps because of its location the mothers had more space to express their sentiments. Many participants may have also assumed that the study was being conducted as a reaction to the pageant controversy that began with Ramsey's death. Additionally, the media's presence at two contests may have also accounted for the opinions expressed. The media was kept out of the ballroom where these contests were held, but their presence in the hallway was a constant reminder that the participants' behavior was being scrutinized.

Population Studied

The population studied were mothers who place their daughters, aged from infancy to 16 years of age, in Southern-style national beauty pageants. "Southern" is a style rather than a location. These contests are more complex than "Little Miss" contests at a county fair that require a minimum of stage performance, emphasizing facial beauty and personality. Southern pageants also judge facial attractiveness and personality, but have a strong emphasis on stage performance and glitzy attire. The emphasis on expensive attire, cosmetics use, and vibrant modeling techniques for children further separate Southern from Northern competitions and scholarship pageants that prefer a more natural appearing contestant.

Unlike other types of pageants where individuality is promoted, Southern style contestants are trained to fit "The Look," the dominating image for the last decade (Vernetti 2001). "Think of it as candied red hots, Tabasco, Pepsodent smiles and Alka-Seltzer all rolled up into a glittering tornado of motion on the stage" (Vernetti 2001: 40). Vernetti (2001) suggests to find competitors who are not professionally trained and polished is rare, and it is rarer to find a contestant that has an original stage persona and appearance. A national competition in this research was defined as one in which children from any state were eligible to compete, where entry fees were $250 or more, where competitions included a beauty, modeling, and photogenic event, and where the grand prize equaled $1,000 or more.

Responding to the questionnaire were women from 19 states, with the greatest response coming from Tennessee (21.9 percent), Kentucky (19.0 percent), and Alabama (17.5 percent). The typical pageant mother was White (88.6 percent), married (80.3 percent), and between 29 and 39 years of age (79.1 percent). Approximately 28 percent of the mothers had high school diplomas, 37 percent had some college experience, and 27 percent were college graduates. The majority of the mothers (74.8 percent) were employed and reported a family income in the range of $20,000 to $49,000 (56 percent).

RESULTS

Before examining the accounts provided by the respondents, a table was constructed to illustrate the overall patterns that emerged from analyzing the data contained in the responses to "What do you like best about pageants?" and "What do you like least about pageants?" Table 2 lists the type of neutralization, the frequency of use, and the percentage of responses that fit the category. The results indicated that condemnation of the condemner was the most frequently used technique (46.5 percent), the denial of injury followed at 25.6 percent with denial of responsibility and appeal to higher loyalties each with 13.9 percent. The neutralization technique of denying the victim was absent, therefore no discussion of this technique is provided.

TABLE 2: NEUTRALIZATION TECHNIQUE, FREQUENCY, AND PERCENTAGE

Techniques	Frequency	Percent
Denial of responsibility	06	13.9
Denial of injury	11	25.6
Denial of victim	00	00.0
Condemnation of condemners	20	46.5
Appeal to higher loyalty	06	13.9
(N)	43	99.9

Condemnation of the Condemners

As previously stated, the condemnation of condemners is a strategy that diverts negative attention from the deviant and focuses on parties standing in judgment. This neutralization technique was employed most frequently by 46.5 percent of the mothers. Many mothers proffered that those pointing an accusing finger were probably pedophiles or suffering from some mental disorder. Attention is diverted from the mothers' actions to the perversions of the sex offender. One mother said: "People are sick if they can see anything sexy about a little girl." This theme was echoed by others. According to a few subjects, the spotlight on pageants *will create* deviance in the social world as the following example illustrates:

> *Only a sick person would see these children as sexual. There is nothing sexy about these little girls. All girls like to play dress up. I wonder about the mentality of those people who have never been to a pageant but pretend to know what is going on. Pageants have never had to worry about pedophiles but now all those perverts will be trying to get in. It's sick.*

The neutralization technique of deflecting the actions of the accused onto the accuser by questioning their motives and behaviors may reflect the opinion that many of these women believe it was JonBenet Ramsey's death that aroused public concern. While the overall theme of the media was to point out that these contests were sexualizing youth, some mothers seemed to fixate on the media's linkage of pageants to the murder. One example:

> *JonBenet's death had nothing to do with pageants. I am sick of hearing people say that pageant girls are looked at sexually. Nobody better ever tell me that my daughter looks sexy— they'll be sorry they ever messed with me.*

Another version of the same theme:

> *It is sad that JonBenet was killed. It probably was a pervert. I watch my daughter like crazy now—now that perverts know about these contests.*

Several mothers directed their anger at the media, a forum where appearance plays a great role in who is portrayed on screen. One mother viewed a television news reporter who interviewed her daughter as a hypocrite.

> *They [television media] came to interview us about pageants from our local station. They asked about the fake hair, suntanned skin and all. My daughter is bi-racial, we don't go to tanning beds. The girl asked if we were obsessed with beauty or something like that. Did she think I did not know who she was? She was in pageants herself! How do you think she got her job—she got it on her looks. We all know that. And how about her bleached hair, tanned skin, and the boob job, talk about the pot calling the kettle black!*

Denial of Injury

The denial of injury technique was used by 25.6 percent of the mothers. As previously stated, denial of injury results in eliminating the guilt or blame when no victimization occurs. If the daughter is not a victim, the mother cannot be causing her harm. Responses included statements that referred to the exaggeration of the media's claims about pageants. These respondents insisted their daughters were helped—not harmed. Many mothers attributed their daughters' accomplishments to their involvement in pageants. A middle-class mother admitted that her daughter's hair is lightened, that she also wears make-up on stage, and uses hair extensions. Beyond her school activities the five-year-old takes modeling classes and practices at home at least twice a week. She commented:

My daughter loves pageants. Her teacher tells us she is far ahead of other children her age. She has better concentration than most her age. I think pageants brought that about. We put all her winnings back for college, and she has won two cars and several thousand in cash. That will go a long way to finance her education.

The mother seems successful in her attempt to point out the monetary gains of her daughter's involvement in pageants and the financial security for her daughter's education. Although some may still question the vast amount of money she has invested in these contests that would likely exceed the child's winnings—others may believe that the money invested for college indicates these events are not harmful.

Another "denial of injury" theme focuses on alleged child abuse. This working class mother is aware of what others think about pageant participation for children, but how she situates her argument mutes the consequences of harm.

I am sick of people saying that my daughter is abused. She really looks abused. She has the finest clothes that money can buy, parents that adore her, and she is doing well in school. How many people can say that they have won a car, and lots of money? I wish someone would abuse me like that.

The injury to the child is difficult to see by this response alone. The mother points out the material gains from pageants and the financial and emotional support from family. The image she describes is not what most people would recognize as abusive.

Denial of Responsibility

Ideally, the denial of responsibility takes place when the actor recognizes the behavior as wrong, but outside circumstances intervened to influence the deviant's actions. However, this definition did not adequately explain what was found in the case of the pageant mothers. Instead of an outright affirmation that pageants were wrong, 13.9 percent of these mothers indicated that they *personally* did not care for pageants. Responses falling in the denial of responsibility category were ones in which the mother acknowledges that pageant participation is viewed as wrong, but the mother contends she would not put her child in these contests if it was up to her alone. Outside forces are the "real" cause of the child's involvement in these contests.

A college professor and mother of a 16-year-old who competes in 7 to 12 pageants a year, implied forces beyond her control have placed her in this situation. She said:

My daughter used to come home in tears when she was in the eighth grade. Her classmates used to make fun of her and call her ugly. Appearance makes a big difference to girls her age. Pageants have brought self-esteem and self-confidence to my daughter. Today her peers think she is pretty and she is a much happier girl. I never cared for pageants but I was willing to do anything I could to help her feel better about herself.

This mother recognizes that being stigmatized by peers can be particularly hurtful to young children, and most adults can relate to incidents in their own lives where others (or they) were mistreated because of appearance norms. This neutralization technique allows the mother to deny responsibility because she is merely trying to help her daughter avoid peer criticism. Some may envision this woman as a caring mother who wants only for her daughter to be treated well.

Four other mothers of older children made similar statements, but placed blame solely on the media and unobtainable beauty standards. One comments:

I'm okay about how I look. I guess fat looks good on an older woman. But my daughter is not okay about her looks and she is slim and beautiful. But according to Cosmo she is not good enough.

Although mothers with children over 12 years of age used this technique most often, a 7 year-old's mother also chose it. She said:

My daughter saw a pageant on television and begged to be in them! She wants to be Miss America too. I never wanted to be a queen. What else could I do? Blame t.v.

Appeal to Higher Loyalties

The appeal to higher loyalties was identified by 13.9 percent of the mothers, suggesting that the norms and values of the greater society are understood and appreciated, yet when they conflict with the normative actions of the subculture loyalty is given to the subculture. In the social world of pageants, the mother is faced with a dilemma: Her actions may not be considered appropriate by society in general, but if she wishes her child to do well in these contests, she must conform to the norms operating in the pageant subculture. For example:

I do not care for the pressure of making my 4-year-old daughter look and act like a 25-year-old woman. The requirements to compete are a little much. I'll quit when she finally gets tired of doing them.

Apparently to this mother, when the child becomes an independent thinker, and is not influenced as much by the group she will no longer compete. She seems to be indicating her daughter's current fascination with pageants—but the child is hardly old enough to be making her own decisions. Similarly, a five-year old's mother is much clearer as why she continues in these contests—she wants her daughter to excel at them.

I really do not like making small children look grown. But that's what it takes to win.

A mother of an eight-year-old who has participated in pageants for over three years admits her daughter wears make-up, hair extensions, and a "flipper" (dental partial) when appearing on stage. This mother is clearly deeply involved in competitions, but hopes the subculture will change.

It is getting hard to keep up in pageants. There is too much emphasis on money and clothes. Spending $1,000 on a dress and another $1,000 on a picture is ridiculous! Modeling is another thing that has gotten out of control. We keep doing them hoping that the time will come when a simple dress, real hair, and missing front teeth can win a pageant.

The use of "we" in the above statement implies that both the child and the mother are tired of the escalating costs and beauty enhancements necessary for competition. It is unlikely that the daughter is concerned with financial matters, but in making a united plea to the organizers of these events it appears as if the mother is in touch with her child's feelings concerning pageants. The team remains loyal to the subculture, but are ready for a change in the structure of these events. Like parents with children in sports, pageant mothers have been accused of living vicariously through their children. In the above statement the interconnection between mother and daughter is evident by the use of the pronoun "we." Surprisingly, few accounts were stated in this fashion and most mothers separated their role from their daughter's role as contestant.

DISCUSSION

Beauty pageants for children illustrate the ambiguous and ever-changing nature of deviance. Pageants for children may or may not be considered deviant today. The controversy over these contests has faded and little scholarly research can be found on the phenomenon. The purpose of this research was to make a sociological contribution in understanding this subculture by examining the neutralization techniques utilized by mothers of participants. This study indicated that during the peak of negative press in 1997 the mothers were aware that the media viewed them as deviants. The presence of the media at two of these contests studied further reflected, we argue, the perception of being labeled deviant. The mothers in this study generally saw little wrong with pageants but were adamant the media played a major role in creating the perception that pageants were arenas exploiting young girls.

The data presented in this article demonstrate that mothers of children who participate in pageants use "condemnation of condemners" as the main neutralizing technique responsible for the negative perception associated with beauty pageants. The majority of these mothers discussed the positive and more functional dimension of pageants. Pageants were seen as mechanisms to help their daughters achieve culturally valued skills such as self-esteem, confidence, or future educational funding. Consequently, they were convinced that participation did not result in injury to their daughters; therefore, "denial of injury" was the second most identified neutralizing technique used.

Since respondents' denied that 'Southern' pageants were deviant activities for children, some of the categories designed by Sykes and Matza (1957) took a different form or were excluded from the analysis. The "denial of responsibility" neutralization technique was somewhat altered. For example, the mothers stated that they would not enter these contests themselves, but did not admit the contests were deviant for their daughters to enter. The "denial of victim" technique was not used by any mothers and thus was excluded in the analysis since no mother intentionally set out to cause her daughter any harm. The accounts suggested these were good mothers who only wanted the best for their daughters. Their sentiments are perhaps not that different from other women in our society who grew up knowing the importance of appearance norms. Many of these women likely watched television, read magazines, and experienced in their own lives just how valuable beauty is in our society. The emphasis on beauty has permeated much of our society, but while many of us publicly condemn the overemphasis of beauty in our society, we privately strive for physical attractiveness through weight loss and exercise programs, and fashionable attire. While many "right minded" people in our society condemn it, beauty still has its advantages.

> *Some say it's sick to put a child in a contest of physical beauty, because it teaches her the wrong values. Yet beauty contests teach something true: Beauty gets you places.... Certified beauties get movie deals, endorsements, their own television shows, modeling gigs and a shot at some very desirable mates. They do Broadway and get invited to state dinners. They are people like Vanessa Williams, Phyllis George, Kathy Lee Gifford, Diane Sawyer and hundreds of other women who parlayed their sashes and tiaras into enviable careers, (Leach 1997:A7)*

Finally, these mothers felt that there were norms associated with the pageant subculture and although some did not like these norms they still complied. In this instance "appeal to higher loyalties" was identified as a justification for their daughter's participation.

The structuring of this particular form of deviance by the media and general public deserves greater attention. According to media programming, pageants themselves are not deviant—Miss America, Miss USA, and Miss Universe are televised annually to millions of appreciative viewers. Similarly, some pageants for children are not deviant—attend any county or state fair and watch the crowds appear at these events. The media insinuated that only Southern pageants for children deserved the label of deviant. It was the mothers who the media held as primarily responsible for creating a glamorized and sexualized image of children.

The data suggest that the media played an important role in the creation of deviance. The amount of time allotted this construction was also a variable in the stability of the deviant label. While the attention may have initially been negative, we speculate that media exposure may have increased the popularity of these contests and encourage future researchers to examine this phenomenon more closely.

Future researchers should examine more closely the contributions of others connected to these contests that the media neglected such as the dentists who supply the "flippers," or to the clothing designers who supply the children's costumes. No one has yet questioned the operators of the tanning beds that allow six-years-olds to use their facilities. There has been no outrage directed at the photographers (or the makeup artists who work with them) who sculpt the child into adulthood while charging fees of $400 or more. These peripheral contributors deserve greater attention, but pale in comparison to the contributions made by the media in sexualizing and glamorizing young females.

As in the game of "Clue" where specifics are necessary in defining the villain: it was the mothers, at the Southern children's pageants in 1997, with the curling iron and mascara wand—or so the story went, as children's pageants faded from the limelight into obscurity. The temporal state of deviance is in part due to the reactions of the media and public toward beauty pageants in general. Perhaps it was because they were so reluctant to denounce pageants as deviance that the definition of what was inappropriate became very narrow. Such a narrow boundary represents only a marginal group of people who qualify as being deviant. With so few people involved in this specific form of deviance, according to some, they are hardly worth studying, and certainly not worthy of media attention or censorship by legislators. Sociologists must share some of the blame in this assessment. Instead of trivializing these events as simply popular culture, it should be recognized that the pageant world *reflects* what is found in the greater society. Valuable information can be obtained from this group concerning the changing nature of childhood, appearance norms, sexuality, gender, and deviance.

REFERENCES

Berger, Alexandria. 1997. "Pageants Emotionally Cripple Girls." *Norfolk Virginia Pilot*, 19 January, E12.

Berman, Laura. 1997. "Pageant Problems: Former Michigan Beauty Queen Says Her Years on the Circuit Robbed Her of Her Childhood." *Detroit News*, 17 January, E1.

Brennan, William C. 1974. "Abortion and the Techniques of Neutralization." *Journal of Health and Social Behavior* 15:358–65.

Briggs, Bill. 1997. "Talk Swirls about Merits of Child Beauty Pageants." *Denver Post*, 12 January, A,4.

Cohen, Collen B., Richard Wilk, and Beverly Stoeltje. 1996. "Introduction." pp. 1–11 in *Beauty Queens on the Global Stage: Gender, Contests, and Power*. New York: Routledge.

Davidson, Mark. 1997. "Is the Media to Blame for Child Sex Victims?" *USA Today*, 126(2628):60–3.

DeYoung, Mary. 1989. "The World According to NAMBLA: Accounting for Deviance." *Journal of Sociological and Social Welfare* 16:111–26.

Durkin, Keith F. and Clifton D. Bryant. 2001. "On-Line Accounts of Unrepentant Pedophiles." pp. 305–13 in *Readings in Deviant Behavior*, edited by Alex Thio and Thomas C. Calhoun. Boston: Allyn and Bacon.

Elder, Rebecca A., Ann Digirolamo, and Suzanne Thompson. 1997. "Is Winning a Pageant Worth a Lost Childhood?" *St. Louis Dispatch*, 24 February, p. B7.

Eliason, Stephan L. and Richard A. Dodder. 2001. "The Techniques of Neutralization Among Deer Poachers. pp. 339–46 in *Readings in Deviant Behavior*, edited by Alex Thio and Thomas C. Calhoun. Boston: Allyn and Bacon.

Forsyth, Craig J. and Rhonda D. Evans. 1998. "Dogmen: The Rationalization of Deviance." *Society and Animals* 6(3):203–18.

Forsyth, Craig J., Robert Gramling, and George Wooddell. 1997. "The Game of Poaching: Folk Crimes in Southwest Louisiana." *Society and Natural Resources* 11(1): 25–38.

Forsyth, Craig J. and Thomas A. Marckese. 1993. "Folk Outlaws: Vocabularies of Motive." *International Review of Modern Sociology* 23(1): 17–31.

"Girls Are the Losers in Children's Pageants." 1997. *Tacoma News Tribune*, 22 January, p. A6.

Giroux, Henry A. 1998. "Nymphet Fantasies: Child Beauty Pageants and the Politics of Innocence." *Social Text* 16(4):31–53.

Henetz, Patty. 1997. "Naughty or Nice? At Child Pageants, Utah Girls Aims for Cute, Not Carnal." *Salt Lake Tribune* 17 January, p. A1.

Hewitt, John P. and Randall Stokes. 1975. "Disclaimers." *American Sociological Review* 40(1):1–11.

LaBeff, Emily E., Robert E. Clark, Valerie J. Haines, and George M. Diekhoff. 2001. "Situational Ethics and College Student Cheating." pp. 225–28 in *Readings in Deviant Behavior*, edited by Alex Thio and Thomas C. Calhoun. Boston: Allyn and Bacon.

Leach, Ruth Ann. 1997 "Some Kids Fit, Some Don't in Child Beauty Pageants." *The Nashville Banner*, 30 January, p. A7.

Letts, Quentin. 1997. "Daughters on the Catwalk?" *The London Times*, 28 January, p. 18.

Mills C. Wright. 1940. "Situated Actions and Vocabulary of Motive." *American Sociological Review* 5(6):904–13.

Pitts, Leonard, Jr. 1997. "The Girl Who was Already a Crime Victim." *Fort Worth Star-Telegram*, 19 January, p. 2.

Reed, Christopher. 1997. "'Little Miss' Murder Casts Pall Over Child Glamour." *The Manchester Guardian*, 17 January, p. 16:6.

Rich, Frank. 1997. "Let Me Entertain You." *New York Times*, 18 January, p. 1.

Scott, Marvin B. and Stanford M. Lyman. 1968. "Accounts." *American Sociological Review* 33(1):46–62.

Scully, Diana and Joseph Marolla. 1984. "Rapist's Vocabulary of Motive." *Social Problems* 31(5):530–44.

Sykes, Gresham and David Matza. 1957. "Techniques of Neutralization: A Theory of Delinquency." *American Sociological Review* 22:664–70.

Vernetti, Larry. 2001. "Northern Sparkle or Southern Charm? And the Winning Pageant Queen is…" *Babettes: Pageant and Talent Gazette* 12(2): 40–1.

QUESTIONS

- How did the researchers in this article gather their information?
- List and explain each of the five techniques of neutralization. How do pageant mothers use each technique to neutralize their deviance?
- Societal puzzle question: It has been almost a decade since the Jon Benet Ramsey case. Think of a recent example of a mother or father who has been labeled deviant by the media. What did they do? Why were they considered deviant? What does their deviant label tell us about social norms surrounding "good mothers" or "good fathers"?

On Being Sane in Insane Places

By D. L. ROSENHAN

■ Is it possible to make a distinction between the sane and the insane? Most of us believe that we can, and this thought is somehow comforting to us. However, in this article, psychologist D. L. Rosenhan indicates that differentiating between the sane and insane may not be so easy. To test this idea, eight "pseudopatients" each deliberately report the same vague symptoms in order to gain admission to mental hospitals. What they find there should make you consider the ways in which we take for granted labels that experts apply to people, the "stickiness" of these labels, and the way in which labeled people become "socially controlled" by such labels.

If sanity and insanity exist, how shall we know them?

The question is neither capricious nor itself insane. However much we may be personally convinced that we can tell the normal from the abnormal, the evidence is simply not compelling. It is commonplace, for example, to read about murder trials wherein eminent psychiatrists for the defense are contradicted by equally eminent psychiatrists for the prosecution on the matter of the defendant's sanity. More generally, there are a great deal of conflicting data on the reliability, utility, and meaning of such terms as "sanity," "insanity," "mental illness," and "schizophrenia."[1] Finally, as early as 1934, Benedict suggested that normality and abnormality are not universal.[2] What is viewed as normal in one culture may be seen as quite aberrant in another. Thus, notions of normality and abnormality may not be quite as accurate as people believe they are.

To raise questions regarding normality and abnormality is in no way to question the fact that some behaviors are deviant or odd. Murder is deviant. So, too, are hallucinations. Nor does raising such questions deny the existence of the personal anguish that is often associated with "mental illness." Anxiety and depression exist. Psychological suffering exists. But normality and abnormality, sanity and insanity, and the diagnoses that flow from them may be less substantive than many believe them to be.

At its heart, the question of whether the sane can be distinguished from the insane (and whether degrees of insanity can be distinguished from each other) is a simple matter: do the salient characteristics that lead to diagnoses reside in the patients themselves or in the environments and contexts in which observers find them? From Bleuler, through Kretchmer, through the formulators of the recently revised *Diagnostic and Statistical Manual* of the American Psychiatric Association, the belief has been strong that patients present symptoms, that those symptoms can be categorized, and, implicitly, that the sane are distinguishable from the insane. More recently, however, this belief has been questioned. Based in part on theoretical and anthropological considerations, but also on philosophical, legal, and therapeutic ones, the view has grown that psychological categorization of mental illness is useless at best and downright harmful, misleading, and pejorative at worst. Psychiatric diagnoses, in this view, are in the minds of the observers and are not valid summaries of characteristics displayed by the observed.[3-5]

Gains can be made in deciding which of these is more nearly accurate by getting normal people (that is, people who do not have, and have never suffered, symptoms of serious psychiatric disorders) admitted to psychiatric hospitals and then determining whether they were discovered to be sane and, if so, how. If the sanity of such pseudo-patients were always detected, there would be prima facie evidence that a sane individual can be distinguished from the insane context in which he is found. Normality (and presumably abnormality) is distinct enough that it can be recognized wherever it occurs, for it is carried within the person. If, on the other hand, the sanity of the pseudopatients were never discovered, serious difficulties would arise for those who support traditional modes of psychiatric diagnosis. Given that the hospital staff was not incompetent, that the pseudopatient had been behaving as sanely as he had been outside of the hospital, and that it had never been previously suggested that he belonged in a psychiatric hospital, such an unlikely outcome would support the view that psychiatric diagnosis betrays little about the patient but much about the environment in which an observer finds him.

This article describes such an experiment. Eight sane people gained secret admission to 12 different hospitals.[6] Their diagnostic experiences constitute the data of the first part of this article; the remainder is devoted to a description of their experiences in psychiatric institutions. Too few psychiatrists and psychologists, even those who have worked in such hospitals, know what the experience is like. They rarely talk about it with former patients, perhaps because they distrust information coming from the previously insane. Those who have worked in psychiatric hospitals are likely to have adapted so thoroughly to the settings that they are insensitive to the impact of that experience. And while there have been occasional reports of researchers who submitted themselves to psychiatric hospitalization[7] these researchers have commonly remained in the hospitals for short periods of time, often with the knowledge of the hospital staff. It is difficult to know the extent to which they were treated like patients or like research colleagues. Nevertheless, their reports about the inside of the psychiatric hospital have been valuable. This article extends those efforts.

PSEUDOPATIENTS AND THEIR SETTINGS

The eight pseudopatients were a varied group. One was a psychology graduate student in his 20's. The remaining seven were older and "established." Among them were three psychologists, a pediatrician, a psychiatrist, a painter, and a housewife. Three pseudopatients were women, five were men. All of them employed pseudonyms, lest their alleged diagnoses embarrass them later. Those who were in mental health professions alleged another occupation in order to avoid the special attentions that might be accorded by staff, as a matter of courtesy or caution, to ailing colleagues.[8] With the exception of myself (I was the first pseudopatient and my presence was known to the hospital administrator and chief psychologist and, so far as I can tell, to them alone), the presence of pseudopatients and the nature of the research program was not known to the hospital staffs.[9]

The settings were similarly varied. In order to generalize the findings, admission into a variety of hospitals was sought. The 12 hospitals in the sample were located in five different states on the East and West coasts. Some were old and shabby, some were quite new. Some were research-oriented, others not. Some had good staff-patient ratios, others were quite understaffed. Only one was a strictly private hospital. All of the others were supported by state or federal funds or, in one instance, by university funds.

After calling the hospital for an appointment, the pseudopatient arrived at the admissions office complaining that he had been hearing voices. Asked what the voices said, he replied that they were often unclear, but as far as he could tell they said "empty," "hollow," and "thud." The voices were unfamiliar and were of the same sex as the pseudopatient. The choice of these symptoms was occasioned by their apparent similarity to existential symptoms. Such symptoms are alleged to arise from painful concerns about the perceived meaninglessness of one's life. It is as if the hallucinating person were saying, "My life is empty and hollow." The choice of these symptoms was also determined by the *absence* of a single report of existential psychoses in the literature.

Beyond alleging the symptoms and falsifying name, vocation, and employment, no further alterations of person, history, or circumstances were made. The significant events of the pseudopatient's life history were presented as they had actually occurred. Relationships with parents and siblings, with spouse and children, with people at work and in school, consistent with the aforementioned exceptions, were described as they were or had been. Frustrations and upsets were described along with joys and satisfactions. These facts are important to remember. If anything, they strongly biased the subsequent results in favor of detecting sanity, since none of their histories or current behaviors were seriously pathological in any way.

Immediately upon admission to the psychiatric ward, the pseudopatient ceased simulating *any* symptoms of abnormality. In some cases, there was a brief period of mild nervousness and anxiety, since none of the pseudopatients really believed that they would be admitted so easily. Indeed, their shared fear was that they would be immediately exposed as frauds and greatly embarrassed. Moreover, many of them had never visited a psychiatric ward; even those who had, nevertheless had some genuine fears about what might happen to them. Their nervousness, then, was quite appropriate to the novelty of the hospital setting, and it abated rapidly.

Apart from that short-lived nervousness, the pseudopatient behaved on the ward as he "normally" behaved. The pseudopatient spoke to patients and staff as he might ordinarily. Because there is uncommonly little to do on a psychiatric ward, he attempted to engage others in conversation. When asked by staff how he was feeling, he indicated that he was fine, that he no longer experienced symptoms. He responded to instructions from attendants, to calls for medication (which was not swallowed), and to dining-hall instructions. Beyond such activities as were available to him on the admissions ward, he spent his time writing down his observations about the ward, its patients, and the staff. Initially these notes were written "secretly," but as it soon became clear that no one much cared, they were subsequently written on standard tablets of paper in such public places as the dayroom. No secret was made of these activities.

The pseudopatient, very much as a true psychiatric patient, entered a hospital with no foreknowledge of when he would be discharged. Each was told that he would have to get out by his own devices, essentially by convincing the staff that he was sane. The psychological stresses associated with hospitalization were considerable, and all but one of the pseudopatients desired to be discharged almost immediately after being admitted. They were, therefore, motivated not only to behave sanely, but to be paragons of cooperation. That their behavior was in no way disruptive is confirmed by nursing reports, which have been obtained on most of the patients. These reports uniformly indicate that the patients were "friendly," "cooperative," and "exhibited no abnormal indications."

THE NORMAL ARE NOT DETECTABLY SANE

Despite their public "show" of sanity, the pseudopatients were never detected. Admitted, except in one case, with a diagnosis of schizophrenia[10], each was discharged with a diagnosis of schizophrenia "in remission." The label "in remission" should in no way be dismissed as a formality, for at no time during any hospitalization had any question been raised about any pseudopatient's simulation. Nor are there any indications in the hospital records that the pseudopatient's status was suspect. Rather, the evidence is strong that, once labeled schizophrenic, the pseudopatient was stuck with that label. If the pseudopatient was to be discharged, he must naturally be "in remission"; but he was not sane, nor, in the institution's view, had he ever been sane.

The uniform failure to recognize sanity cannot be attributed to the quality of the hospitals, for, although there were considerable variations among them, several are considered excellent. Nor can it be alleged that there was simply not enough time to observe the pseudopatients. Length of hospitalization ranged from 7 to 52 days, with an average of 19 days. The pseudopatients were not, in fact, carefully observed, but this failure clearly speaks more to traditions within psychiatric hospitals than to lack of opportunity.

Finally, it cannot be said that the failure to recognize the pseudopatients' sanity was due to the fact that they were not behaving sanely. While there was clearly some tension present in all of them, their daily visitors could detect no serious behavioral consequences—nor, indeed, could other patients. It was quite common for the patients to "detect" the pseudopatients' sanity. During the first three hospitalizations, when accurate counts were kept, 35 of a total of 118 patients on the admissions ward voiced their suspicions, some vigorously. "You're not crazy. You're a journalist, or a professor [referring to the continual note-taking]. You're checking up on the hospital." While most of the patients were reassured by the pseudopatient's insistence that he had been sick before he came in but was fine now, some continued to believe that the pseudopatient was sane throughout his hospitalization[11]. The fact that the patients often recognized normality when staff did not raises important questions.

Failure to detect sanity during the course of hospitalization may be due to the fact that physicians operate with a strong bias toward what statisticians call the type 2 error[5]. This is to say that physicians are more inclined to call a healthy person sick (a false positive, type 2) than a sick person healthy (a false negative, type 1). The reasons for this are not hard to find: it is clearly more dangerous to misdiagnose illness than health. Better to err on the side of caution, to suspect illness even among the healthy.

But what holds for medicine does not hold equally well for psychiatry. Medical illnesses, while unfortunate, are not commonly pejorative. Psychiatric diagnoses, on the contrary, carry with them personal, legal, and social stigmas[12]. It was therefore important to see whether the tendency toward diagnosing the sane insane could be reversed. The following experiment was arranged at a research and teaching hospital whose staff had heard these findings but doubted that such an error could occur in their hospital. The staff was informed that at some time during the following 3 months, one or more pseudopatients would attempt to be admitted into the psychiatric hospital. Each staff member was asked to rate each patient who presented himself at admissions or on the ward according to the likelihood that the patient was a pseudopatient. A 10-point scale was used, with a 1 and 2 reflecting high confidence that the patient was a pseudopatient.

Judgments were obtained on 193 patients who were admitted for psychiatric treatment. All staff who had had sustained contact with or primary responsibility for the patient—attendants, nurses, psychiatrists, physicians, and psychologists—were asked to make judgments. Forty-one patients were alleged, with high confidence, to be pseudopatients by at least one member of the staff. Twenty-three were considered suspect by at least one psychiatrist. Nineteen were suspected by one psychiatrist *and* one other staff member. Actually, no genuine pseudopatient (at least from my group) presented himself during this period.

The experiment is instructive. It indicates that the tendency to designate sane people as insane can be reversed when the stakes (in this case, prestige and diagnostic acumen) are high. But what can be said of the 19 people who were suspected of being "sane" by one psychiatrist and another staff member? Were these people truly "sane," or was it rather the case that in the course of avoiding the type 2 error the staff tended to make more errors of the first sort—calling the crazy "sane"? There is no way of knowing. But one thing is certain: any diagnostic process that lends itself so readily to massive errors of this sort cannot be a very reliable one.

THE STICKINESS OF PSYCHODIAGNOSTIC LABELS

Beyond the tendency to call the healthy sick—a tendency that accounts better for diagnostic behavior on admission than it does for such behavior after a lengthy period of exposure—the data speak to the massive role of labeling in psychiatric assessment. Having once been labeled schizophrenic, there is nothing the pseudopatient can do to overcome the tag. The tag profoundly colors others' perceptions of him and his behavior.

From one viewpoint, these data are hardly surprising, for it has long been known that elements are given meaning by the context in which they occur. Gestalt psychology, made this point vigorously, and Asch[13] demonstrated that there are "central" personality traits (such as "warm" versus "cold") which are so powerful that they markedly color the meaning of other information in forming an impression of a given personality.[14] "Insane," "schizophrenic," "manic-depressive," and "crazy" are probably among the most powerful of such central traits. Once a person is designated abnormal, all of his other behaviors and characteristics are colored by that label. Indeed, that label is so powerful that many of the pseudopatients' normal behaviors were overlooked entirely or profoundly misinterpreted. Some examples may clarify this issue.

Earlier I indicated that there were no changes in the pseudopatient's personal history and current status beyond those of name, employment, and, where necessary, vocation. Otherwise, a veridical description of personal history and circumstances was offered. Those circumstances were not psychotic. How were they made consonant with the diagnosis of psychosis? Or were those diagnoses modified in such a way as to bring them into accord with the circumstances of the pseudopatient's life, as described by him?

As far as I can determine, diagnoses were in no way affected by the relative health of the circumstances of a pseudopatient's life. Rather, the reverse occurred: the perception of his circumstances was shaped entirely by the diagnosis. A clear example of such translation is found in the case of a pseudopatient who had had a close relationship with his mother but was rather remote from his father during his early childhool. During adolescence and beyond, however, his father became a close friend, while his relationship with his mother cooled. His present relationship with his wife was characteristically close and warm. Apart from occasional angry exchanges, friction was minimal. The children had rarely been spanked. Surely there is nothing especially pathological about such a history. Indeed, many readers may see a similar pattern in their own experiences, with no markedly deleterious consequences. Observe, however, bow such a history was translated in the psychopathological context, this from the case summary prepared after the patient was discharged.

This white 39-year-old male...manifests a long history of considerable ambivalence in close relationships, which begins in early childhood. A warm relationship with his mother cools during his adolescence. A distant relationship to his father is described as becoming very intense. Affective stability is absent. His attempts to control emotionality with his wife and children are punctuated by angry outbursts and, in the case of the children, spankings. And while he says that he has several good friends, one senses considerable ambivalence embedded in those relationships also....

The facts of the case were unintentionally distorted by the staff to achieve consistency with a popular theory of the dynamics of a schizophrenic reaction.[15] Nothing of an ambivalent nature had been described in relations with parents, spouse, or friends. To the extent that ambivalence could be inferred, it was probably not greater than is found in all human relationships. It is true the pseudopatient's relationships with his parents changed over time, but in the ordinary context that would hardly be remarkable—indeed, it might very well be expected. Clearly, the meaning ascribed to his verbalizations (that is, ambivalence, affective instability) was determined by the diagnosis: schizophrenia. An entirely different meaning would have been ascribed if it were known that the man was "normal."

All pseudopatients took extensive notes publicly. Under ordinary circumstances, such behavior would have raised questions in the minds of observers, as, in fact, it did among patients. Indeed, it seemed so certain that the notes would elicit suspicion that elaborate precautions were taken to remove them from the ward each day. But the precautions proved needless. The closest any staff member came to questioning these notes occurred when one pseudopatient asked his physician what kind of medication he was receiving and began to write down the response. "You needn't write it," he was told gently. "If you have trouble remembering, just ask me again."

If no questions were asked of the pseudopatients, how was their writing interpreted? Nursing records for three patients indicate that the writing was seen as an aspect of their pathological behavior. "Patient engages in writing behavior" was the daily nursing comment on one of the pseudopatients who was never questioned about his writing. Given that the patient is in the hospital, he must be psychologically disturbed. And given that he is disturbed, continuous writing must be a behavioral manifestation of that disturbance, perhaps a subset of the compulsive behaviors that are sometimes correlated with schizophrenia.

One tacit characteristic of psychiatric diagnosis is that it locates the sources of aberration within the individual and only rarely within the complex of stimuli that surrounds him. Consequently, behaviors that are stimulated by the environment are commonly misattributed to the patient's disorder. For example, one kindly nurse found a pseudopatient pacing the long hospital corridors. "Nervous, Mr. X?" she asked. "No, bored," he said.

The notes kept by pseudopatients are full of patient behaviors that were misinterpreted by well-intentioned staff. Often enough, a patient would go "berserk" because he had, wittingly or unwittingly, been mistreated by, say, an attendant. A nurse coming upon the scene would rarely inquire even cursorily into the environmental stimuli of the patient's behavior. Rather, she assumed that his upset derived from his pathology, not from his present interactions with other staff members. Occasionally, the staff might assume that the patient's family (especially when they had recently visited) or other patients had stimulated the outburst. But never were the staff found to assume that one of themselves or the structure of the hospital had anything to do with a patient's behavior. One psychiatrist pointed to a group of patients who were sitting outside the cafeteria entrance half an hour before lunchtime. To a group of young residents he indicated that such behavior was characteristic of the oral-acquisitive nature of the syndrome. It seemed not to occur to him that there were very few things to anticipate in a psychiatric hospital besides eating.

A psychiatric label has a life and an influence of its own. Once the impression has been formed that the patient is schizophrenic, the expectation is that he will continue to be schizophrenic. When a sufficient amount of time has passed, during which the patient has done nothing bizarre, he is considered to be in remission and available for discharge. But the label endures beyond discharge, with the unconfirmed expectation that he will behave as a schizophrenic again. Such labels, conferred by mental health professionals, are as influential on the patient as they are on his relatives and friends, and it should not surprise anyone that the diagnosis acts on all of them as a self-fulfilling prophecy. Eventually, the patient himself accepts the diagnosis, with all of its surplus meanings and expectations, and behaves accordingly.[15]

The inferences to be made from these matters are quite simple. Much as Zigler and Phillips have demonstrated that there is enormous overlap in the symptoms presented by patients who have been variously diagnosed[16], so there is enormous overlap in the behaviors of the sane and the insane. The sane are not "sane" all of the time. We lose our tempers "for no good reason." We are occasionally depressed or anxious, again for no good reason. And we may find it difficult to get along with one or another person—again for no reason that we can specify. Similarly, the insane are not always insane. Indeed, it was the impression of the pseudopatients while living with them that they were sane for long periods of time—that the bizarre behaviors upon which their diagnoses were allegedly predicated constituted only a small fraction of their total behavior. If it makes no sense to label ourselves permanently depressed on the basis of an occasional depression, then it takes better evidence than is presently available to label all patients insane or schizophrenic on the basis of bizarre behaviors or cognitions. It seems more useful, as Mischel[17] has pointed out, to limit our discussions to *behaviors*, the stimuli that provoke them, and their correlates.

It is not known why powerful impressions of personality traits, such as "crazy" or "insane," arise. Conceivably, when the origins of and stimuli that give rise to a behavior are remote or unknown, or when the behavior strikes us as immutable, trait labels regarding the *behaver* arise. When, on the other hand, the origins and stimuli are known and available, discourse is limited to the behavior itself. Thus, I may hallucinate because I am sleeping, or I may hallucinate because I have ingested a peculiar drug. These are termed sleep-induced hallucinations, or dreams, and drug-induced hallucinations, respectively. But when the stimuli to my hallucinations are unknown, that is called craziness, or schizophrenia—as if that inference were somehow as illuminating as the others.

THE EXPERIENCE OF PSYCHIATRIC HOSPITALIZATION

The term "mental illness" is of recent origin. It was coined by people who were humane in their inclinations and who wanted very much to raise the station of (and the public's sympathies toward) the psychologically disturbed from that of witches and "crazies" to one that was akin to the physically ill. And they were at least partially successful, for the treatment of the mentally ill *has* improved considerably over the years. But while treatment has improved, it is doubtful that people really regard the mentally ill in the same way that they view the physically ill. A broken leg is something one recovers from, but mental illness allegedly endures forever[18]. A broken leg does not threaten the observer, but a crazy schizophrenic? There is by now a host of evidence that attitudes toward the mentally ill are characterized by fear, hostility, aloofness, suspicion, and dread.[19] The mentally ill are society's lepers.

That such attitudes infect the general population is perhaps not surprising, only upsetting. But that they affect the professionals—attendants, nurses, physicians, psychologists, and social workers—who treat and deal with the mentally ill is more disconcerting, both because such attitudes are self-evidently pernicious and because they are unwitting. Most mental health professionals would insist that they are sympathetic toward the mentally ill, that they are neither avoidant nor hostile. But it is more likely that an exquisite ambivalence characterizes their relations with psychiatric patients, such that their avowed impulses are only part of their entire attitude. Negative attitudes are there too and can easily be detected. Such attitudes should not surprise us. They are the natural offspring of the labels patients wear and the places in which they are found.

Consider the structure of the typical psychiatric hospital. Staff and patients are strictly segregated. Staff have their own living space, including their dining facilities, bathrooms, and assembly places. The glassed quarters that contain the professional staff, which the pseudopatients came to call "the cage," sit out on every dayroom. The staff emerge primarily for caretaking purposes—to give medication, to conduct a therapy or group meeting, to instruct or reprimand a patient. Otherwise, staff keep to themselves, almost as if the disorder that afflicts their charges is somehow catching.

So much is patient-staff segregation the rule that, for four public hospitals in which an attempt was made to measure the degree to which staff and patients mingle, it was necessary to use "time out of the staff cage" as the operational measure. While it was not the case that all time spent out of the cage was spent mingling with patients (attendants, for example, would occasionally emerge to watch television in the dayroom), it was the only way in which one could gather reliable data on time for measuring.

The average amount of time spent by attendants outside of the cage was 11.3 percent (range, 3 to 52 percent). This figure does not represent only time spent mingling with patients, but also includes time spent on such chores as folding laundry, supervising patients while they shave, directing ward cleanup, and sending patients to off-ward activities. It was the relatively rare attendant who spent time talking with patients or playing games with them. It proved impossible to obtain a "percent mingling time" for nurses, since the amount of time they spent out of the cage was too brief. Rather, we counted instances of emergence from the cage. On the average, daytime nurses emerged from the cage 11.5 times per shift, including instances when they left the ward entirely (range, 4 to 39 times). Late afternoon and night nurses were even less available, emerging on the average 9.4 times per shift (range, 4 to 41 times). Data on early morning nurses, who arrived usually after midnight and departed at 8 A.M., are not available because patients were asleep during most of this period.

Physicians, especially psychiatrists, were even less available. They were rarely seen on the wards. Quite commonly, they would be seen only when they arrived and departed, with the remaining time being spent in their offices or in the cage. On the average, physicians emerged on the ward 6.7 times per day (range, 1 to 17 times). It proved difficult to make an accurate estimate in this regard, since physicians often maintained hours that allowed them to come and go at different times.

The hierarchical organization of the psychiatric hospital has been commented on before[20], but the latent meaning of that kind of organization is worth noting again. Those with the most power have least to do with patients, and those with the least power are most involved with them. Recall, however, that the acquisition of role-appropriate behaviors occurs mainly through the observation of others, with the most powerful having the most influence. Consequently, it is understandable that attendants not only spend more time with patients than do any other members of the staff—that is required by their station in the hierarchy—but also, insofar as they learn from their superiors' behavior, spend as little time with patients as they can. Attendants are seen mainly in the cage, which is where the models, the action, and the power are.

I turn now to a different set of studies, these dealing with staff response to patient-initiated contact. It has long been known that the amount of time a person spends with you can be an index of your significance to him. If he initiates and maintains eye contact, there is reason to believe that he is considering your requests and needs. If he pauses to chat or actually stops and talks, there is added reason to infer that he is individuating you. In four hospitals, the pseudopatient approached the staff member with a request which took the following form: "Pardon me, Mr. [or Dr. or Mrs.] X, could you tell me when I will be eligible for grounds privileges?" (or "...when I will be presented at the staff meeting?" or "...when I am likely to be discharged?"). While the content of the question varied according to the appropriateness of the target and the pseudopatient's (apparent) current needs the form was always a courteous and relevant request for information. Care was taken never to approach a particular member of the staff more than once a day, lest the staff member become suspicious or irritated. In examining these data, remember that the behavior of the pseudopatients was neither bizarre nor disruptive. One could indeed engage in good conversation with them.

TABLE 1: SELF-INITIATED CONTACT BY PSEUDOPATIENTS WITH PSYCHIATRISTS AND NURSES AND ATTENDANTS, COMPARED TO CONTACT WITH OTHER GROUPS

Contact	Psychiatric hospitals		University campus (nonmedical)	University medical center		
				Physicians		
	(1) Psychiatrists	(2) Nurses and attendants	(3) Faculty	(4) "Looking for a psychiatrist"	(5) "Looking for an internist"	(6) No additional comment
Responses						
Moves on, head averted (%)	71	88	0	0	0	0
Makes eye contact (%)	23	10	0	11	0	0
Pauses and chats (%)	2	2	0	11	0	10
Stops and talks (%)	4	0.5	100	78	100	90
Mean number of questions answered (out of 6)	*	*	6	3.8	4.8	4.5
Respondents (No.)	13	47	14	18	15	10
Attempts (No.)	185	1283	14	18	15	10

* Not applicable.

The data for these experiments are shown in Table 1, separately for physicians (column 1) and for nurses and attendants (column 2). Minor differences between these four institutions were overwhelmed by the degree to which staff avoided continuing contacts that patients had initiated. By far, their most common response consisted of either a brief response to the question, offered while they were "on the move" and with head averted, or no response at all.

The encounter frequently took the following bizarre form: (pseudopatient) "Pardon me, Dr. X. Could you tell me when I am eligible for grounds privileges?" (physician) "Good morning, Dave. How are you today?" (Moves off without waiting for a response.)

It is instructive to compare these data with data recently obtained at Stanford University. It has been alleged that large and eminent universities are characterized by faculty who are so busy that they have no time for students. For this comparison, a young lady approached individual faculty members who seemed to be walking purposefully to some meeting or teaching engagement and asked them the following six questions.

1. "Pardon me, could you direct me Encina Hall?" (at the medical school: "...to the Clinical Research Center?").
2. "Do you know where Fish Annex is?" (there is no Fish Annex at Stanford).
3. "Do you teach here?"
4. "How does one apply for admission to the college?" (at the medical school: "...to the medical school?").
5. "Is it difficult to get in?"
6. "Is there financial aid?"

Without exception, as can be seen in Table 1 (column 3), all of the questions were answered. No matter how rushed they were, all respondents not only maintained eye contact, but stopped to talk. Indeed, many of the respondents went out of their way to direct or take the questioner to the office she was seeking, to try to locate "Fish Annex," or to discuss with her the possibilities of being admitted to the university.

Similar data, also shown in Table 1 (columns 4, 5, and 6), were obtained in the hospital. Here too, the young lady came prepared with six questions. After the first question, however, she remarked to 18 of her respondents (column 4), "I'm looking for a psychiatrist," and to 15 others (column 5), "I'm looking for an internist." Ten other respondents received no inserted comment (column 6). The general degree of cooperative responses is, considerably higher for these university groups than it was for pseudopatients in psychiatric hospitals. Even so, differences are apparent within the medical school setting. Once having indicated that she was looking for a psychiatrist, the degree of cooperation elicited was less than when she sought an internist.

POWERLESSNESS AND DEPERSONALIZATION

Eye contact and verbal contact reflect concern and individuation; their absence, avoidance and depersonalization. The data I have presented do not do justice to the rich daily encounters that grew up around matters of depersonalization and avoidance. I have records of patients who were beaten by staff for the sin of having initiated verbal contact. During my own experience, for example, one patient was beaten in the presence of other patients for having approached an attendant and told him, "I like you." Occasionally, punishment meted out to patients for misdemeanors seemed so excessive that it could not be justified by the most radical interpretations of psychiatric canon. Nevertheless, they appeared to go unquestioned. Tempers were often short. A patient who had not heard a call for medication would be roundly excoriated, and the morning attendants would often wake patients with, "Come on, you m-----f----s, out of bed!"

Neither anecdotal nor "hard" data can convey the overwhelming sense of powerlessness which invades the individual as he is continually exposed to the depersonalization of the psychiatric hospital. It hardly matters *which* psychiatric hospital—the excellent public ones and the very plush private hospital were better than the rural and shabby ones in this regard, but, again, the features that psychiatric hospitals had in common overwhelmed by far their apparent differences.

Powerlessness was evident everywhere. The patient is deprived of many of his legal rights by dint of his psychiatric commitment[21]. He is shorn of credibility by virtue of his psychiatric label. His freedom of movement is restricted. He cannot initiate contact with the staff, but may only respond to such overtures as they make.

Personal privacy is minimal. Patient quarters and possessions can be entered and examined by any staff member, for whatever reason. His personal history and anguish is available to any staff member (often including the "grey lady" and "candy striper" volunteer) who chooses to read his folder, regardless of their therapeutic relationship to him. His personal hygiene and waste evacuation are often monitored. The water closets may have no doors.

At times, depersonalization reached such proportions that pseudopatients had the sense that they were invisible, or at least unworthy of account. Upon being admitted, I and other pseudopatients took the initial physical examinations in a semipublic room, where staff members went about their own business as if we were not there.

On the ward, attendants delivered verbal and occasionally serious physical abuse to patients in the presence of other observing patients, some of whom (the pseudopatients) were writing it all down. Abusive behavior, on the other hand, terminated quite abruptly when other staff members were known to be coming. Staff are credible witnesses. Patients are not.

A nurse unbuttoned her uniform to adjust her brassiere in the presence of an entire ward of viewing men. One did not have the sense that she was being seductive. Rather, she didn't notice us. A group of staff persons might point to a patient in the dayroom and discuss him animatedly, as if he were not there.

One illuminating instance of depersonalization and invisibility occurred with regard to medications. All told, the pseudopatients were administered nearly 2100 pills, including Elavil, Stelazine, Compazine, and Thorazine, to name but a few. (That such a variety of medications should have been administered to patients presenting identical symptoms is itself worthy of note.) Only two were swallowed. The rest were either pocketed or deposited in the toilet. The pseudopatients were not alone in this. Although I have no precise records on how many patients rejected their medications, the pseudopatients frequently found the medications of other patients in the toilet before they deposited their own. As long as they were cooperative, their behavior and the pseudopatients' own in this matter, as in other important matters, went unnoticed throughout.

Reactions to such depersonalization among pseudopatients were intense. Although they had come to the hospital as participant observers and were fully aware that they did not "belong," they nevertheless found themselves caught up in and fighting the process of depersonalization. Some examples: a graduate student in psychology asked his wife to bring his textbooks to the hospital so he could "catch up on his homework"—this despite the elaborate precautions taken to conceal his professional association. The same student, who had trained for quite some time to get into the hospital, and who had looked forward to the experience, "remembered" some drag races that he had wanted to see on the weekend and insisted that he be discharged by that time. Another pseudopatient attempted a romance with a nurse. Subsequently, he informed the staff that he was applying for admission to graduate school in psychology and was very likely to be admitted, since a graduate professor was one of his regular hospital visitors. The same person began to engage in psychotherapy with other patients—all of this as a way of becoming a person in an impersonal environment.

THE SOURCES OF DEPERSONALIZATION

What are the origins of depersonalization? I have already mentioned two. First are attitudes held by all of us toward the mentally ill—including those who treat them—attitudes, characterized by fear, distrust, and horrible expectations on the one hand, and benevolent intentions on the other. Our ambivalence leads, in this instance as in others, to avoidance.

Second, and not entirely separate, the hierarchical structure of the psychiatric hospital facilitates depersonalization. Those who are at the top have least to do with patients, and their behavior inspires the rest of the staff. Average daily contact with psychiatrists, psychologists, residents, and physicians combined ranged from 3.9 to 25.1 minutes, with an overall mean of 6.8 (six pseudopatients over a total of 129 days of hospitalization). Included in this average are time spent in the admissions interview, ward meetings in the presence of a senior staff member, group and individual psychotherapy contacts, case presentation conferences, and discharge meetings. Clearly, patients do not spend much time in interpersonal contact with doctoral staff. And doctoral staff serve as models for nurses and attendants.

There are probably other sources. Psychiatric installations are presently in serious financial straits. Staff shortages are pervasive, staff time at a premium. Something has to give, and that something is patient contact. Yet, while financial stresses are realities, too much can be made of them. I have the impression that the psychological forces that result in depersonalization are much stronger than the fiscal ones and that the addition of more staff would not correspondingly improve patient care in this regard. The incidence of staff meetings and the enormous amount of record-keeping on patients, for example, have not been as substantially reduced as has patient contact. Priorities exist, even during hard times. Patient contact is not a significant priority in the traditional psychiatric hospital, and fiscal pressures do not account for this. Avoidance and depersonalization may.

Heavy reliance upon psychotropic medication tacitly contributes to depersonalization by convincing staff that treatment is indeed being conducted and that further patient contact may not be necessary. Even here, however, caution needs to be exercised in understanding the role of psychotropic drugs. If patients were powerful rather than powerless, if they were viewed as interesting individuals rather than diagnostic entities, if they were socially significant rather than social lepers, if their anguish truly and wholly compelled our sympathies and concerns, would we not *seek* contact with them, despite the availability of medications? Perhaps for the pleasure of it all?

THE CONSEQUENCES OF LABELING AND DEPERSONALIZATIO

Whenever the ratio of what is known to what needs to be known approaches zero, we tend to invent "knowledge" and assume that we understand more than we actually do. We seem unable to acknowledge that we simply don't know. The needs for diagnosis and remediation of behavioral and emotional problems are enormous. But rather than acknowledge that we are just embarking on understanding, we continue to label patients "schizophrenic," "manic-depressive," and "insane," as if in those words we had captured the essence of understanding. The facts of the matter are that we have known for a long time that diagnoses are often not useful or reliable, but we have nevertheless continued to use them. We now know that we cannot distinguish insanity from sanity. It is depressing to consider how that information will be used.

Not merely depressing, but frightening. How many people, one wonders, are sane but not recognized as such in our psychiatric institutions? How many have been needlessly stripped of their privileges of citizenship, from the right to vote and drive to that of handling their own accounts? How many have feigned insanity in order to avoid the criminal consequences of their behavior, and, conversely, how many would rather stand trial than live interminably in a psychiatric hospital—but are wrongly thought to be mentally ill? How many have been stigmatized by well-intentioned, but nevertheless erroneous, diagnoses? On the last point, recall again that a "type 2 error" in psychiatric diagnosis does not have the same consequences it does in medical diagnosis. A diagnosis of cancer that has been found to be in error is cause for celebration. But psychiatric diagnoses are rarely found to be in error. The label sticks, a mark of inadequacy forever.

Finally, how many patients might be "sane" outside the psychiatric hospital but seem insane in it—not because craziness resides in them, as it were, but because they are responding to a bizarre setting, one that may be unique to institutions which harbor nether people? Goffman *(4)* calls the process of socialization to such institutions "mortification"—an apt metaphor that includes the processes of depersonalization that have been described here. And while it is impossible to know whether the pseudopatients' responses to these processes are characteristic of all inmates—they were, after all, not real patients—it is difficult to believe that these processes of socialization to a psychiatric hospital provide useful attitudes or habits of response for living in the "real world."

SUMMARY AND CONCLUSIONS

It is clear that we cannot distinguish the sane from the insane in psychiatric hospitals. The hospital itself imposes a special environment in which the meanings of behavior can easily be misunderstood. The consequences to patients hospitalized in such an environment—the powerlessness, depersonalization, segregation, mortification, and self-labeling—seem undoubtedly counter-therapeutic.

I do not, even now, understand this problem well enough to perceive solutions. But two matters seem to have some promise. The first concerns the proliferation of community mental health facilities, of crisis intervention centers, of the human potential movement, and of behavior therapies that, for all of their own problems, tend to avoid psychiatric labels, to focus on specific problems and behaviors, and to retain the individual in a relatively non-pejorative environment. Clearly, to the extent that we refrain from sending the distressed to insane places, our impressions of them are less likely to be distorted. (The risk of distorted perceptions, it seems to me, is always present, since we are much more sensitive to an individual's behaviors and verbalizations than we are to the subtle contextual stimuli that often promote them. At issue here is a matter of magnitude. And, as I have shown, the magnitude of distortion is exceedingly high in the extreme context that is a psychiatric hospital.)

The second matter that might prove promising speaks to the need to increase the sensitivity of mental health workers and researchers to the *Catch 22* position of psychiatric patients. Simply reading materials in this area will be of help to some such workers and researchers. For others, directly experiencing the impact of psychiatric hospitalization will be of enormous use. Clearly, further research into the social psychology of such total institutions will both facilitate treatment and deepen understanding.

I and the other pseudopatients in the psychiatric setting had distinctly negative reactions. We do not pretend to describe the subjective experiences of true patients. Theirs may be different from ours, particularly with the passage of time and the necessary process of adaptation to one's environment. But we can and do speak to the relatively more objective indices of treatment within the hospital. It could be a mistake, and a very unfortunate one, to consider that what happened to us derived from malice or stupidity on the part of the staff. Quite the contrary, our overwhelming impression of them was of people who really cared, who were committed and who were uncommonly intelligent. Where they failed, as they sometimes did painfully, it would be more accurate to attribute those failures to the environment in which they, too, found themselves than to personal callousness. Their perceptions and behavior were controlled by the situation, rather than being motivated by a malicious disposition. In a more benign environment, one that was less attached to global diagnosis, their behaviors and judgments might have been more benign and effective.

REFERENCES AND NOTES

1. P. Ash, *J. Abnorm. Soc. Psychol.* 44, 272 (1949); A. T. Beck, *Amer. J. Psychia.* 119, 210 (1962); A. T. Boisen, *Psychiatry* 2, 233 (1938); N. Kreitman, *J. Ment. Sci.* 107, 876 (1961); N. Kreitman, P. Sainsbury, J. Morrisey, J. Towers, J. Scrivener, *Ibid.*, p. 887; H. O. Schmitt and C. P. Fonda, *J. Abnorm. Soc. Psychol.* 52, 262 (1956); W. Seeman, *J. Nerv. Ment. Dis.* 111, 541 (1953). For an analysis of these artifacts and summaries of the disputes, see J. Zubin, *Anna. Rev. Psychol.* 18, 373 (1967); L. Phillips and J. G. Draguns. *Ibid.* 22, 447 (1971).

2. R. Benedict. *J. Gen. Psychol* 10, 59 (1934).

3. See in this regard H. Becker, *Outsiders: Studies in the Sociology of Deviance* (Free Press, New York, 1963); B. M. Braginsky, D. D. Braginsky. K. Ring, *Methods of Madness: The Mental Hospital as a Last Resort* (Holt, Rinehart & Winston, New York, 1969); G. M. Crocetti and P. V. Lemkau, *Amer. Social. Rev.* 30, 577 (1965); E. Goffman, *Behavior in Public Places* (Free Press, New York, 1964); R. D. Laing, *The Divided Self: A Study of Sanity and Madness* (Quadrangle, Chicago, 1960); D. L. Phillips, *Amer. Social. Rev.* 28, 963 (1963); T. R. Sarbin, *Psychol. Today* 6, 18 (1972); E. Schur, *Amer. J. Social.* 75, 309 (1969); T. Szasz, *Law, Liberty and Psychiatry* (Macmillan, New York, 1963); *The Myth of Mental Illness: Foundations of a Theory of Mental Illness* (Hoeber-Harper. New York, 1963). For a critique of some of these views, see W. R. Gove, *Amer. Social. Rev.* 35, 873 (1970).

4. E. Goffman, *Asylums* (Doubleday, Garden City, N.Y., 1961).

5. T. J. Scheff, *Being Mentally Ill: A Sociological Theory* (Aldine, Chicago, 1966).

6. Data from a ninth pseudopatient are not incorporated in this report because, although his sanity went undetected, he falsified aspects of his personal history, including his marital status and parental relationships. His experimental behaviors therefore were not identical to those of the other pseudopatients.

7. A. Barry, *Bellevue Is a State of Mind* (Harcourt Brace Jovanovich, New York, 1971); I. Belknap, *Human Problems of a State Mental Hospital* (McGraw-Hill, New York, 1956); W. Coudill, F. C. Redlich, H. R. Gilmore, E. B. Brody, *Amer. J. Orthopsychiat.* 22, 314 (1952); A. R. Goldman, R. H. Bohr, T. A. Steinberg, *Prof. Psychol.* 1, 427 (1970); un-authored, *Roche Report* 1 (No. 13), 8 (1971).

8. Beyond the personal difficulties that the pseudopatient is likely to experience in the hospital, there are legal and social ones that, combined, require considerable attention before entry. For example, once admitted to a psychiatric institution, it is difficult, if not impossible, to be discharged on short notice, state law to the contrary notwithstanding. I was not sensitive to these difficulties at the outset of the project, nor to the personal and situational emergencies that can arise, but later a writ of habeas corpus was prepared for each of the entering pseudopatients and an attorney was kept "on call" during every hospitalizau'on. I am grateful to John Kaplan and Robert Bartels for legal advice and assistance in these matters.

9. However distasteful such concealment is, it was a necessary first step to examining these questions. Without concealment, there would have been no way to know how valid these experiences were; nor was there any way of knowing whether whatever detections occurred were a tribute to the diagnostic acumen of the staff or to the hospital's rumor network. Obviously, since my concerns are general ones that cut across individual hospitals and staffs, I have respected their anonymity and have eliminated clues that might lead to their identification.

10. Interestingly, of the 12 admissions, 11 were diagnosed as schizophrenic and one, with the identical symptomatology, as manic-depressive psychosis. This diagnosis has a more favorable prognosis, and it was given by the only private hospital in our sample. On the relations between social class and psychiatric diagnosis, see A. deB. Hollingshead and F. C. Redlich, *Social Class and Mental Illness: A Community Study* (Wiley, New York, 1958).

11. It is possible, of course, that patients have quite broad latitudes in diagnosis and therefore are inclined to call many people sane, even those whose behavior, is patently aberrant. However, although we have no hard data on this matter, it was our distinct impression that this was not the case. In many instances, patients not only singled us out for attention, but came to imitate our behaviors and styles.

12. J. Cumming and E. Cummins, *Community Ment. Health* 1, 135 (1965); A. Farina and Ring, *J. Abnorm. Psychol.* 70, 47 (1965); H. E. Freeman and O. G. Simmons, *The Mental Patient Comes Home* (Wiley, New York, 1963): W J. Johannsen. *Ment. Hygiene* 53, 218 (1969); A. S. Linsky, *Soc. Psychiat.* 5, 166 (1970).

13. S. E. Asch, *J. Abnorm. Soc. Psychol.* 41, 258 (1946); *Social Psychology* (Prentice-Hall, New York. 1952).

14. See also I. N. Mensh and J. Wishner, *J. Personality* 16, 188 (1947); J. Wishner, *Psychol. Rev.* 67, 96 (1960); J. S. Bruner and R. Tagiuri, in *Handbook of Social Psychology*, G. Lindzey. Ed. (Addison-Wesley, Cambridge, Mass., 1954), vol. 2, pp. 634–654; J. S. Bruner, D. Shapiro, R. Tagiuri, in *Person Perception and Interpersonal Behavior*, R. Tagiuri and L. Petruilo, Eds. (Stanford Univ. Press, Stanford, Calif., 1958), pp. 277–288.

15. For an example of a similar self-fulfilling prophecy, in this instance dealing with the "central" trait of intelligence, see R. Rosenthai and L. Jacobson, *Pygmalion in the Classroom* (Holt, Rinehart & Winston, New York, 1968).

16. E. Zigler and L. Phillips, *J. Abnorm. Soc. Psychol.* 63, 69 (1961). See also R. K. Freudenberg and J. P. Robertson, *A.M.A. Arch. Neurol. Psychiar.* 76, 14 (1956).

17. W. Mischel, *Personality and Assessment* (Wiley, New York, 1968).

18. The most recent and unfortunate instance of this tenet is that of Senator Thomas Eagleton.

19. T. R. Sarbin and J. C. Mancuso, *J. Clin. Consult. Psychol.* 35, 159 (1970); T. R. Sarbin, *Ibid.* 31, 447 (1967); J. C. Nunnally, Jr., *Popular Conceptions of Mental Health* (Holt, Rinehart & Winston, New York, 1961).

20. A. H. Stanton and M. S. Schwartz, *The Mental Hospital: A Study of Institutional Participation In Psychiatric Illness and Treatment* (Basic, New York, 1954).

21. D. B. Wexler and S. E. Scoville, *Ariz. Law Rev.* 13, 1 (1971).

QUESTIONS

? What patterns do you see in the experiences of the eight pseudopatients?

? What is depersonalization? Who is depersonalized in this article and how are they depersonalized?

? Societal puzzle question: The author says that psychiatric diagnoses are rarely found to be in error. Why is this the case? What other "diagnoses" stick in our contemporary world? To answer this question you might want to think beyond the psychiatric hospital to schools, churches, sports arenas, etc.

Section II

*The Sociological Lens:
Seeing Social Inequalities*

Chapter 5

Life at the Top in America Isn't Just Better, It's Longer

By JANNY SCOTT

■ You've heard people say money can't buy happiness." Perhaps, but in this article, New York Times journalist Janny Scott illustrates that in the United States, money can, to some extent, buy health and longer life. How is this so? This article illustrates that if we adopt a social class lens, we can see that differences in health outcomes are related to where we find ourselves on the social class ladder. After you read the accounts of heart attack survivors Jean G. Miele, an architect, Will L. Wilson, a utility worker, and Ewa Rynczak Gora, a housekeeper, consider the questions at the end of this article.

Jean G. Miele's heart attack happened on a sidewalk in Mid-town Manhattan in May 2004. He was walking back to work along Third Avenue with two colleagues after a several-hundred-dollar sushi lunch. There was the distant rumble of heartburn, the ominous tingle of perspiration. Then Miele, an architect, collapsed onto a concrete planter in a cold sweat.

Will L. Wilson's heart attack came four days earlier in the bedroom of his brownstone in Bedford-Stuyvesant in Brooklyn. He had been regaling his fiancée with the details of an all-you-can-eat dinner he was beginning to regret. Wilson, a Consolidated Edison office worker, was feeling a little bloated. He flopped onto the bed. Then came a searing sensation, like a hot iron deep inside his chest.

Ewa Rynczak Gora's first signs of trouble came in her rented room in the noisy shadow of the Brooklyn-Queens Expressway. It was the Fourth of July. Gora, a Polish-born housekeeper, was playing bridge. Suddenly she was sweating, stifling an urge to vomit. She told her husband not to call an ambulance; it would cost too much. Instead, she tried a home remedy: salt water, a double dose of hypertension pills, and a glass of vodka.

Architect, utility worker, maid: heart attack is the great leveler, and in those first fearful moments, three New Yorkers with little in common faced a single common threat. But in the months that followed, their experiences

---

Copyright © 2005 by The New York Times Co. Reprinted with permission.

diverged. Social class—that elusive combination of income, education, occupation, and wealth—played a powerful role in Miele's, Wilson's, and Gora's struggles to recover.

Class informed everything from the circumstances of their heart attacks to the emergency care each received, the households they returned to, and the jobs they hoped to resume. It shaped their understanding of, their illness, the support they got from their families, their relationships with their doctors. It helped define their ability to change their lives and shaped their odds of getting better.

Class is a potent force in health and longevity in the United States. The more education and income people have, the less likely they are to have and die of heart disease, strokes, diabetes, and many types of cancer. Upper-middle-class Americans live longer and in better health than middle-class Americans, who live longer and better than those at the bottom. And the gaps are widening, say people who have researched social factors in health.

As advances in medicine and disease prevention have increased life expectancy in the United States, the benefits have disproportionately gone to people with education, money, good jobs, and connections. They are almost invariably in the best position to learn new information early, modify their behavior, take advantage of the latest treatments, and have the cost covered by insurance.

Many risk factors for chronic diseases are now more common among the less educated than the better educated. Smoking has dropped sharply among the better educated, but not among the less. Physical inactivity is more than twice as common among high school dropouts as among college graduates. Lower-income women are more likely than other women to be overweight, though the pattern among men may be the opposite.

There may also be subtler differences. Some researchers now believe that the stress involved in so-called high-demand, low-control jobs further down the occupational scale is more harmful than the stress of professional jobs that come with greater autonomy and control. Others are studying the health impact of job insecurity, lack of support on the job, and employment that makes it difficult to balance work and family obligations.

Then there is the issue of social networks and support, the differences in the knowledge, time, and attention that a person's family and friends are in a position to offer. What is the effect of social isolation? Neighborhood differences have also been studied: How stressful is a neighborhood? Are there safe places to exercise? What are the health effects of discrimination?

Heart attack is a window on the effects of class on health. The risk factors—smoking, poor diet, inactivity, obesity, hypertension, high cholesterol, and stress—are all more common among the less educated and less affluent, the same group that research has shown is less likely to receive cardiopulmonary resuscitation, to get emergency room care, or to adhere to lifestyle changes after heart attacks.

"In the last twenty years, there have been enormous advances in rescuing patients with heart attack and in knowledge about how to prevent heart attack," said Ichiro Kawachi, a professor of social epidemiology at the Harvard School of Public Health. "It's like diffusion of innovation: whenever innovation comes along, the well-to-do are much quicker at adopting it. On the lower end, various disadvantages have piled onto the poor. Diet has gotten worse. There's a lot more work stress. People have less time, if they're poor, to devote to health maintenance behaviors when they are juggling two jobs. Mortality rates even among the poor are coming down, but the rate is not anywhere near as fast as for the well-to-do. So the gap has increased."

Bruce G. Link, a professor of epidemiology and socio-medical sciences at Columbia University, said of the double-edged consequences of progress: "We're creating disparities. It's almost as if it's transforming health, which used to be like fate, into a commodity. Like the distribution of BMWs or goat cheese."

THE BEST OF CARE

Jean Miele's advantage began with the people he was with on May 6, when the lining of his right coronary artery ruptured, cutting off the flow of blood to his sixty-six-year-old heart. His two colleagues were knowledgeable enough to dismiss his request for a taxi and call an ambulance instead.

And because he was in Midtown Manhattan, there were major medical centers nearby, all licensed to do the latest in emergency cardiac care. The emergency medical technician in the ambulance offered Miele a choice. He picked Tisch Hospital, part of New York University Medical Center, an academic center with relatively affluent patients, and passed up Bellevue, a city-run hospital with one of the busiest emergency rooms in New York.

Within minutes, Miele was on a table in the cardiac catheterization laboratory, awaiting angioplasty to unclog his artery—a procedure that many cardiologists say has become the gold standard in heart attack treatment. When he developed ventricular fibrillation, a heart rhythm abnormality that can be fatal within minutes, the problem was quickly fixed.

Then Dr. James N. Slater, a fifty-four-year-old cardiologist with some twenty-five thousand cardiac catheterizations under his belt, threaded a catheter through a small incision in the top of Miele's right thigh and steered it toward his heart. Miele lay on the table, thinking about dying. By 3:52 P.M., less than two hours after Miele's first symptoms, his artery was reopened and Slater implanted a stent to keep it that way.

Time is muscle, as cardiologists say. The damage to Miele's heart was minimal.

Miele spent just two days in the hospital. His brother-in-law, a surgeon, suggested a few specialists. His brother, Joel, chairman of the board of another hospital, asked his hospital's president to call New York University. "Professional courtesy," Joel Miele explained later. "The bottom line is that someone from management would have called patient care and said, 'Look, would you make sure everything's okay?'"

Things went less flawlessly for Will Wilson, a fifty-three-year-old transportation coordinator for Con Ed. He imagined fleetingly that he was having a bad case of indigestion, though he had had a heart attack before. His fiancée insisted on calling an ambulance. Again, the emergency medical technician offered a choice of two nearby hospitals—neither of which had state permission to do angioplasty, the procedure Jean Miele received.

Wilson chose the Brooklyn Hospital Center over Wood-hull Medical and Mental Health Center, the city-run hospital that serves three of Brooklyn's poorest neighborhoods. At Brooklyn Hospital, he was given a drug to break up the clot blocking an artery to his heart. It worked at first, said Narinder P. Bhalla, the hospital's chief of cardiology, but the clot re-formed.

So Bhalla had Wilson taken to the Weill Cornell Center of New York-Presbyterian Hospital in Manhattan the next morning. There, Bhalla performed angioplasty and implanted a stent. Asked later whether Wilson would have been better off if he had had his heart attack elsewhere, Bhalla said the most important issue in heart attack treatment was getting the patient to a hospital quickly.

But he added, "In his case, yes, he would have been better off had he been to a hospital that was doing angioplasty."

Wilson spent five days in the hospital before heading home on many of the same high-priced drugs that Miele would be taking and under similar instructions to change his diet and exercise regularly. After his first heart attack, in 2000, he quit smoking; but once he was feeling better, he stopped taking several medications, drifted back to red meat and fried foods, and let his exercise program slip.

This time would be different, he vowed: "I don't think I'll survive another one."

Ewa Gora's experience was the rockiest. First, she hesitated before allowing her husband to call an ambulance; she hoped her symptoms would go away. He finally insisted; but when the ambulance arrived, she resisted leaving. The emergency medical technician had to talk her into going. She was given no choice of hospitals; she was simply taken to Wood-hull, the city hospital Will Wilson had rejected.

Woodhull was busy when Gora arrived around 10:30 P.M. A triage nurse found her condition stable and classified her as "high priority." Two hours later, a physician assistant and an attending doctor examined her again and found her complaining of chest pain, shortness of breath, and heart palpitations. Over the next few hours, tests confirmed she was having a heart attack.

She was given drugs to stop her blood from clotting and to control her blood pressure, treatment that Woodhull officials say is standard for the type of heart attack she was having. The heart attack passed. The next day, Gora was transferred to Bellevue, the hospital Jean Miele had turned down, for an angiogram to assess her risk of a second heart attack.

Chapter 5: Can Money Buy Happiness: Stratification by Social Class   81

But Gora, who was fifty-nine at the time, came down with a fever at Bellevue, so the angiogram had to be canceled. She remained at Bellevue for two weeks, being treated for an infection. Finally, she was sent home. No angiogram was ever done.

COMFORTS AND RISKS

Jean Miele is a member of New York City's upper middle class. The son of an architect and an artist, he worked his way through college, driving an ice-cream truck and upholstering theater seats. He spent two years in the military and then joined his father's firm, where he built a practice as not only an architect but also an arbitrator and an expert witness, developing real estate on the side.

Miele is the kind of person who makes things happen. He bought a $21,000 house in the Park Slope section of Brooklyn, sold it about fifteen years later for $285,000, and used the money to build his current house next door, worth over $2 million. In Brookhaven, on Long Island, he took a derelict house on a single acre, annexed several adjoining lots, and created what is now a four-acre, three-house compound with an undulating lawn and a fifteen-thousand-square-foot greenhouse he uses as a workshop for his collection of vintage Jaguars.

Miele's architecture partners occasionally joked that he was not in the business for the money, which to some extent was true. He had figured out how to live like a millionaire, he liked to say, even before he became one. He had worked four-day weeks for twenty years, spending long weekends with his family, sailing or iceboating on Bellport Bay and rebuilding cars.

Miele had never thought of himself as a candidate for a heart attack—even though both his parents had died of heart disease; even though his brother had had arteries unclogged; and even though he himself was on hypertension medication, his cholesterol levels bordered on high, and his doctor had been suggesting he lose weight.

He was a passionate chef who put great store in the healthfulness of fresh ingredients from the Mieles' vegetable garden or the greengrocers in Park Slope. His breakfasts may have been a cardiologist's nightmare—eggs, sausage, bacon, pastina with a poached egg—but he considered his marinara sauce to be healthy perfection: just garlic, oil, tomatoes, salt, and pepper.

He figured he had something else working in his favor: he was happy. He adored his second wife, Lori, twenty-three years younger, and their six-year-old daughter, Emma. He lived within blocks of his two sisters and two of his three grown children from his first marriage. The house regularly overflowed with guests, including Miele's former wife and her husband. He seemed to know half the people of Park Slope.

"I walk down the street and I feel good about it every day," Miele, a gregarious figure with twinkling blue eyes and a taste for worn T-shirts and jeans, said of his neighborhood. "And yes, that gives me a feeling of well-being."

His approach to his health was utilitarian. When body parts broke, he got them fixed so he could keep doing what he liked to do. So he had had disk surgery, rotator cuff surgery, surgery for a carpal tunnel problem. But he was also not above an occasional bit of neglect. In March 2004, his doctor suggested a stress test after Miele complained of shortness of breath. On May 6, the prescription was still hanging on the kitchen cabinet door.

An important link in the safety net that caught Miele was his wife, a former executive at a sweater manufacturing company who had stopped work to raise Emma but managed the Mieles' real estate as well. While Miele was still in the hospital, she was on the Internet, Googling stents.

She scheduled his medical appointments. She got his prescriptions filled. Leaving him at home one afternoon, she taped his cardiologist's business card to the couch where he was sitting, "Call Dr. Hayes and let him know you're coughing," she said, her fingertips on his shoulder. Thirty minutes later, she called home to check.

She prodded Miele, gently, to cut his weekly egg consumption to two, from seven. She found fresh whole wheat pasta and cooked it with turkey sausage and broccoli rabe. She knew her way around nutrition labels.

Lori Miele took on the burden of dealing with the hospital and insurance companies. She accompanied her husband to his doctor's appointments and retained pharmaceutical dosages in her head.

"I can just leave and she can give you all the answers to all the questions," Miele said to his cardiologist, Dr. Richard M. Hayes, one day.

"Okay, why don't you just leave?" Hayes said back. "Can she also examine you?"

With his wife's support, Miele set out to lose thirty pounds. His pasta consumption plunged to a plate a week from two a day. It was not hard to eat healthfully from the Mieles' kitchens. Even the "junk drawer" in Park Slope was stocked with things like banana chips and sugared almonds. Lunches in Brookhaven went straight from garden to table: tomatoes with basil, eggplant, corn, zucchini flower tempura.

At his doctor's suggestion, Miele enrolled in a three-month monitored exercise program for heart disease patients, called cardiac rehab, which has been shown to reduce the mortality rate among heart patients by 20 percent. Miele's insurance covered the cost. He even managed to minimize the inconvenience, finding a class ten minutes from his country house.

He had the luxury of not having to rush back to work. By early June, he had decided he would take the summer off, and maybe cut back his workweek when he returned to the firm.

"You know, the more I think about it, the less I like the idea of going back to work," he said. "I don't see any real advantage. I mean, there's money. But you've got to take the money out of the equation."

So he put a new top on his 1964 Corvair. He played host to a large family reunion, replaced the heat exchanger in his boat, and transformed the ramshackle greenhouse into an elaborate workshop. His weight dropped to 189 pounds, from 211. He had doubled the intensity of his workouts. His blood pressure was lower than ever.

Miele saw Hayes only twice in six months, for routine follow-ups. He had been known to walk out of doctors' offices if he was not seen within twenty minutes, but Hayes did not keep him waiting. The Mieles were swept into the examining room at the appointed hour. Buoyed by the evidence of Miele's recovery, they would head out to lunch in downtown Manhattan. Those afternoons had the feel of impromptu dates.

"My wife tells me that I'm doing fourteen-hour days," Miele mused one afternoon, slicing cold chicken and piling it with fresh tomatoes on toast. "She said, 'You're doing better now than you did ten years ago.' And I said, 'I haven't had sex in a week.' And she said, 'Well?'"

Just one unpleasant thing happened. Miele's partners informed him in late July that they wanted him to retire. It caught him off guard, and it hurt, He countered by taking the position that he was officially disabled and therefore entitled to be paid for a full year after he began his medical leave. "I mean, the guy has a heart attack," he said later. "So you get him while he's down?"

LUKEWARM EFFORTS TO REFORM

Will Wilson fits squarely in the city's middle class. His parents had been sharecroppers who moved north and became a machinist and a nurse. He grew up in Bedford-Stuyvesant and had spent thirty-four years at Con Ed. He had an income of $73,000, five weeks' vacation, health benefits, a house worth $450,000, and plans to retire to North Carolina when he is fifty-five.

Wilson, too, had imagined becoming an architect. But there had been no money for college, so he found a job as a utility worker. By age twenty-two, he had two children. He considered going back to school, with the company's support, to study engineering. But doing shift work, and with small children, he never found the time.

For years he was a high-voltage cable splicer, a job he loved because it meant working outdoors with plenty of freedom and overtime pay. But on a snowy night in the early 1980s, a car skidded into a stanchion, which hit him in the back. A doctor suggested that Wilson learn to live with the pain instead of having disk surgery, as Jean Miele had done.

So Wilson became a laboratory technician, then a transportation coordinator, working in a cubicle in a low-slung building in Astoria, Queens, overseeing fuel deliveries for the company's fleet. Some people might think of the work as tedious, Wilson said, "but it keeps you busy."

"Sometimes you look back over your past life experiences and you realize that if you would have done something different, you would have been someplace else," he said. "I don't dwell on it too much because I'm not in a negative position. But you do say, 'Well, dag, man, I should have done this or that.'"

Wilson's health was not bad, but far from perfect. He had quit drinking and smoking, but had high cholesterol, hypertension, and diabetes. He was slim, five foot nine, and just under 170 pounds. He traced his first heart attack to his smoking, his diet, and the stress from a grueling divorce.

His earlier efforts to reform his eating habits were halfhearted. Once he felt better, he stopped taking his cholesterol and hypertension drugs. When his cardiologist moved and referred Wilson to another doctor, he was annoyed by what he considered the rudeness of the office staff. Instead of demanding courtesy or finding another specialist, Wilson stopped going.

By the time Dr. Bhalla encountered Wilson at Brooklyn Hospital, there was damage to all three main areas of his heart. Bhalla prescribed a half-dozen drugs to lower Wilson's cholesterol, prevent clotting, and control his blood pressure.

"He has to behave himself," Bhalla said. "He needs to be more compliant with his medications. He has to really go on a diet, which is grains, no red meat, no fat. No fat at all."

Wilson had grown up eating his mother's fried chicken, pork chops, and macaroni and cheese. He confronted those same foods at holiday parties and big events. There were doughnut shops and fried chicken places in his neighborhood; but Wilson's fiancée, Melvina Murrell Green, found it hard to find fresh produce and good fish.

"People in my circle, they don't look at food as, you know, too much fat in it," Wilson said. "I don't think it's going to change. It's custom."

At Red Lobster after his second heart attack, Green would order chicken and Wilson would have salmon—plus a side order of fried shrimp. "He's still having a problem with the fried seafood," Green reported sympathetically.

Whole grains remained mysterious. "That we've got to work on," she said. "Well, we recently bought a bag of grain something. I'm not used to that. We try to put it on the cereal. It's okay."

In August 2004, Green's blood pressure shot up. The culprit turned out to be a turkey chili recipe that she and Wilson had discovered: every ingredient except the turkey came from a can. She was shocked when her doctor pointed out the salt content. The Con Ed cafeteria, too, was problematic. So Wilson began driving to the Best Yet Market in Astoria at lunch to troll the salad bar.

Dr. Bhalla had suggested that Wilson walk for exercise. There was little open space in the neighborhood, so Wilson and Green often drove just to go for a stroll. In the fall of 2004 he entered a cardiac rehab program like Miele's, only less convenient. He would drive into Manhattan after work, during the afternoon rush, three days a week. He would hunt for on-street parking or pay too much for a space in a lot. Then a stranger threatened to damage Wilson's car in a confrontation over a free spot, so Wilson switched to the subway.

For a time, he considered applying for permanent disability. But Con Ed allowed him to return to work "on restrictions," so he decided to go back, with plans to retire in a year and a half. The week before he went back, he and Green took a seven-day cruise to Nassau. It was a revelation.

"Sort of like helped me to see there's a lot more things to do in life," he said. "I think a lot of people deny themselves certain things in life, in terms of putting things off, 'I'll do it later.' Later may never come."

IGNORING THE RISKS

Ewa Gora is a member of the working class. A bus driver's daughter, she arrived in New York City from Kraków in the early 1990s, leaving behind a grown son. She worked as a housekeeper in a residence for the elderly in Manhattan, making beds and cleaning toilets. She said her income was $21,000 to $23,000 a year, with health insurance through her union.

For $365 a month, she rented a room in a friend's Brooklyn apartment on a street lined with aluminum-sided row houses and American flags. She used the friend's bathroom and kitchen. She was in her seventh year on a waiting list for a subsidized one-bedroom apartment in the adjacent Williamsburg neighborhood. In the meantime, she had acquired a roommate: Edward Gora, an asbestos-removal worker newly arrived from Poland and ten years her junior, whom she met and married in 2003.

Like Jean Miele, Ewa Gora had never imagined she was at risk of a heart attack, though she was overweight, hypertensive, and a thirty-year smoker, and heart attacks had killed her father and sister. She had numerous health problems, which she addressed selectively, getting treated for back pain, ulcers, and so on, until the treatment became too expensive or inconvenient, or her insurance declined to pay.

"My doctor said, 'Ewa, be careful with cholesterol,'" recalled Gora, whose vestigial Old World sense of propriety had her dressed in heels and makeup for every visit to Bellevue. "When she said that, I think nothing; I don't care. Because I don't believe this touch me. Or I think she have to say like that because she doctor. Like cigarettes: she doctor, she always told me to stop. And when I got out of the office, lights up."

Gora had a weakness for the peak of the food pyramid. She grew up on her mother's fried pork chops, spare ribs, and meatballs—all cooked with lard—and had become a pizza, hamburger, and french fry enthusiast in the United States. Fast food was not only tasty but also affordable. "I eat terrible," she reported cheerily from her bed at Bellevue. "I like grease food and fast food. And cigarettes."

She loved the feeling of a cigarette between her fingers, the rhythmic rise and fall of it to her lips. Using her home computer, she had figured out how to buy Marlboros online for just $2.49 a pack. Her husband smoked, her friends all smoked. Everyone she knew seemed to love tobacco and steak.

Her life was physically demanding. She would rise at 6:00 A.M. to catch a bus to the subway, change trains three times, and arrive at work by 8:00 A.M. She would make twenty-five to thirty beds, vacuum, cart out trash. Yet she says she loved her life. "I think America is El Dorado," she said. "Because in Poland now is terrible; very little bit money. Here, I don't have a lot of, but I live normal. I have enough, not for rich life but for normal life."

The precise nature of Gora's illness was far from clear to her even after two weeks in Bellevue. In her first weeks home, she remained unconvinced that she had had a heart attack. She arrived at the Bellevue cardiology clinic for her first follow-up appointment imagining that whatever procedure had earlier been canceled would then be done, that it would unblock whatever was blocked, and that she would be allowed to return to work.

Jad Swingle, a doctor completing his specialty training in cardiology, led Gora through the crowded waiting room and into an examining room. She clutched a slip of paper with words she had translated from Polish, using her pocket dictionary: "dizzy," "groin," "perspiration." Swingle asked her questions, speaking slowly. Do you ever get chest discomfort? Do you get short of breath when you walk?

She finally interrupted: "Doctor, I don't know what I have, why I was in hospital. What is this heart attack? I don't know why I have this. What I have to do to not repeat this?"

No one had explained these things, Gora believed. Or, she wondered, had she not understood? She perched on the examining table, ankles crossed, reduced by the setting to an oversize, obedient child. Swingle examined her, then said he would answer her questions "in a way you'll understand." He set about explaining heart attacks: the narrowed artery, the blockage, the partial muscle death.

Gora looked startled.

"My muscle is dead?" she asked.

Swingle nodded.

What about the procedure that was never done?

"I'm not sure an angiogram would help you," he said. She needed to stop smoking, take her medications, walk for exercise, come back in a month.

"My muscle is still dead?" she asked again, incredulous.

"Once it's dead, it's dead," Swingle said. "There's no bringing it back to life."

Outside, Gora tottered toward the subway, fourteen blocks away, on pink high-heeled sandals in 89-degree heat. "My thinking is black," she said, uncharacteristically glum. "Now I worry. You know, you have hand? Now I have no finger."

If Jean Miele's encounters with the health care profession in the first months after his heart attack were occasional and efficient, Ewa Gora's were the opposite. Whereas he saw his cardiologist just twice, Gora, burdened by complications, saw hers a half-dozen times. Meanwhile, her heart attack seemed to have shaken loose a host of other problems.

A growth on her adrenal gland had turned up on a Bellevue CAT scan, prompting a visit to an endocrinologist. An old knee problem flared up; an orthopedist recommended surgery. An alarming purple rash on her leg led to a trip to a dermatologist. Because of the heart attack, she had been taken off hormone replacement therapy and was constantly sweating. She tore open a toe stepping into a pothole and needed stitches.

Without money or connections, moderate tasks consumed entire days. One cardiology appointment coincided with a downpour that paralyzed the city. Gora was supposed to be at the hospital laboratory at 8:00 A.M. to have blood drawn and back at the clinic at 1:00 P.M. In between, she wanted to meet with her boss about her disability payments. She had a 4:00 P.M. appointment in Brooklyn for her knee.

So at 7:00 A.M., she hobbled through the rain to the bus to the subway to another bus to Bellevue. She was waiting outside the laboratory when it opened. Then she took a bus uptown in jammed traffic, changed buses, descended into the subway at Grand Central Terminal, rode to Times Square, found service suspended because of flooding, climbed the stairs to Forty-second Street, maneuvered through angry crowds hunting for buses, and found another subway line.

She reached her workplace an hour and a half after leaving Bellevue; if she had had the money she could have made the trip in twenty minutes by cab. Her boss was not there. So she returned to Bellevue and waited until 2:35 P.M. for her one o'clock appointment. As always, she asked Dr. Swingle to let her return to work. When he insisted she have a stress test first, a receptionist gave her the first available appointment—seven weeks away.

Meanwhile, Gora was trying to stop smoking. She had quit in the hospital, then returned home to a husband and a neighbor who both smoked. To be helpful, her husband smoked in the shared kitchen next door. He was gone most of the day, working double shifts. Alone and bored, Gora started smoking again, then called Bellevue's free smoking cessation program and enrolled.

For the next few months, she trekked regularly to "the smoking department" at Bellevue. A counselor supplied her with nicotine patches and advice, not always easy for her to follow: stay out of the house; stay busy; avoid stress; satisfy oral cravings with, say, candy. The counselor suggested a support group, but Gora was too ashamed of her English to join. Even so, over time her tobacco craving waned.

There was just one hitch: Gora was gaining weight. To avoid smoking, she was eating. Her work had been her exercise and now she could not work. Dr. Swingle suggested cardiac rehab, leaving it up to Gora to find a program and arrange it. Gora let it slide. As for her diet, she had vowed to stick to chicken, turkey, lettuce, tomatoes, and low-fat cottage cheese. But she got tired of that. She began sneaking cookies when no one was looking—and no one was.

She cooked separate meals for her husband, who was not inclined to change his eating habits. She made him meatballs with sauce, liver, soup from spare ribs. Then one day she helped herself to one of his fried pork chops, and was soon eating the same meals he was. As an alternative to eating cake while watching television, she turned to pistachios, and then ate a pound in a single sitting.

Cruising the 99 Cent Wonder store in Williamsburg, where the freezers were filled with products like Budget Gourmet Rigatoni with Cream Sauce, she pulled down a small package of pistachios: two and a half servings, thirteen grams of fat per serving. "I can eat five of these," she confessed, ignoring the nutrition label. Not servings. Bags.

Heading home after a trying afternoon in the office of the apartment complex in Williamsburg, where the long-awaited apartment seemed perpetually just out of reach, Gora slipped into a bakery and emerged with a doughnut, her first since her heart attack. She found a park bench where she had once been accustomed to reading and smoking. Working her way through the doughnut, confectioners' sugar snowing onto her chest, she said ruefully, "I miss my cigarette."

She wanted to return to work. She felt uncomfortable depending on her husband for money. She worried that she was becoming indolent and losing her English. Her disability payments, for which she needed a doctor's letter every month, came to just half of her $331 weekly salary. Once, she spent hours searching for the right person at Bellevue to give her a letter, only to be told to come back in two days.

The copayments on her prescriptions came to about eighty dollars each month. Unnerving computer printouts from the pharmacist began arriving: "Maximum benefit reached." She switched to her husband's health insurance plan. Twice, Bellevue sent bills for impossibly large amounts of money for services her insurance was supposed to cover. Both times she spent hours traveling into Manhattan to the hospital's business office to ask why she had been billed. Both times a clerk listened, made a phone call, said the bill was a mistake, and told her to ignore it.

When the stress test was finally done, Dr. Swingle said the results showed she was not well enough to return to full-time work. He gave her permission for part-time work, but her boss said it was out of the question. By November, four months after her heart attack, her weight had climbed to 197 pounds from 185 in July. Her cholesterol levels were stubbornly high and her blood pressure was up, despite drugs for both.

In desperation, Gora embarked upon a curious, heart-unhealthy diet clipped from a Polish-language newspaper. Day 1: two hardboiled eggs, one steak, one tomato, spinach, lettuce with lemon and olive oil. Another day: coffee, grated carrots, cottage cheese, and three containers of yogurt. Yet another: just steak. She decided not to tell her doctor. "I worry if he don't let me, I not lose the weight," she said.

UNEVEN RECOVERIES

Nearly a year after his heart attack, Jean Miele was, remarkably, better off. He had lost thirty-four pounds and was exercising five times a week and taking subway stairs two at a time. He had retired from his firm on the terms he wanted. He was working from home, billing $225 an hour. More money in less time, he said. His blood pressure and cholesterol were low. "You're doing great," Dr. Hayes had said. "You're doing better than ninety-nine percent of my patients."

Will Wilson's heart attack had been a setback. His heart function remained impaired, though improved somewhat. At one checkup in the spring of 2005, his blood pressure and his weight had been a little high. He still enjoyed fried shrimp on occasion, but he took his medications diligently. He graduated from cardiac rehab with plans to join a health club with a pool. And he was looking forward to retirement.

Ewa Gora's life and health were increasingly complex. With Dr. Swingle's reluctant approval, she returned to work in November 2004. She had moved into the subsidized apartment in Williamsburg, which gave her her own kitchen and bathroom for the first time in seven years. But she began receiving menacing phone calls from a collection agency about an old bill her health insurance had not covered. Her husband, with double pneumonia, was out of work for weeks.

She had her long-awaited knee surgery in January 2005. But it left her temporarily unable to walk. Her weight hit two hundred pounds. When the diet failed, she considered another consisting largely of fruit and vegetables sprinkled with an herbal powder. Her blood pressure and cholesterol remained ominously high. She had been warned that she was now a borderline diabetic.

"You're becoming a full-time patient, aren't you?" Swingle remarked.

QUESTIONS

? How do money, occupation, and education affect the lives of these heart attack survivors? Give examples from each account.

? What does it mean to say that in America, health is "transformed into a commodity?" Is this transformation good, bad, or neutral? Why?

? Societal lens question: Select one of the following illnesses: diabetes, asthma, AIDS. Explain why and how a person's social class standing would affect their experience with such an illness. If you were a health care provider trying to offer the best advice to all of your patients how would you deal with a poor uninsured patient who has the illness you selected?

Learning the Ropes:
The Childhood and College Years of Elite Women

By DIANA KENDALL

■ What types of foods do you eat? Who were your childhood friends? Do you enjoy the symphony? How you answer these questions may reveal more than your personal preference—it also may indicate the social standing of both you and your parents or guardians who were responsible for teaching you "the ropes." In the following excerpt from her book "The Power of Good Deeds," sociologist Diana Kendall uses content analysis, participant observation, and interviews to illustrate how socially elite children are carefully taught "the ropes" that will help them achieve and reproduce their parent's upper class social class position.

Gay, a white woman—who at the time of these remarks was in her mid-20s—from an Old Name family, offered an interesting and informative personal narrative while we were discussing elite children's education:

> After the obstetrician told me I was pregnant, the first phone call I made was to my husband to tell him. The second call I made was to [an elite private school] to put my [unborn] child on the school's waiting list for four years down the road. I've been extremely happy with my choice and have enrolled my other children in the same school because they learn values that are in keeping with what we try to teach the children at home, and they develop playgroups and friendship with other children like themselves, playgroups that help them to know, from an early age, that they will be recognized for their hard work and their personal achievements. I also like it that [name of school] teaches cooperation and sharing, virtues that will be important when they start to be involved in the life of the community.

Some people might find it odd that Gay would have contacted a school about enrolling her future child even before she discussed her pregnancy with friends and other relatives, yet her remarks clearly illustrate an important point: Most elite parents strongly believe that, early on in their children's lives, the parents should start putting

---

From *The Power of Good Deeds: Privileged Women and the Reproduction of the Upper Class* by Diana Kendall. Copyright © 2002 by Rowman and Littlefield. Reprinted by permission.

together all the right "building blocks" that their children will need in order to take their own places in the elite circles in which the parents live, and that the parents need to continue this process of social reproduction as the children grow into adulthood. Although biological reproduction creates new generations of children who are members of upper-class families, this does not guarantee that the attitudes, beliefs, and behaviors of the current generation of elites will be accepted by their offspring and employed in a manner that maintains the privilege of members of this class. For this reason, social reproduction—in this instance, meaning the replication of the social structures and class relationships that characterize a society and, especially, the right to maintain the privileged position of one's family within society—becomes one of the tasks of elite parents, particularly of elite women. Understanding the process of social reproduction of the upper classes helps to explain how the adult women in this study came to be the way they are, why they hold the attitudes and beliefs they hold, and how they bring up their children in a way that reproduces these characteristics in the next generation.[1]

This chapter looks at the childhood and school experiences of some elite women, and of their children, to show how these early experiences may contribute to the norm of exclusivity in elite women's organizations. Typically, elite community volunteers do not question their lifestyle, including the fact that privilege goes with their lives or that certain opportunities just "open up" for them that are not available to people in other classes. Consequently, elite women do not view themselves as having done anything that intentionally discriminates against anyone, such as whom they may—or may not—invite to participate in their clubs and organizations. Rather, they describe themselves as pursuing their everyday lives in a way that they have learned since childhood. Exclusivity and noblesse oblige are among the attitudes and beliefs that many elite women learn from an early age.

The ability to exclude others is a form of social power that privileged young women possess from an early age. Typically, the women in my study grew up in exclusive neighborhoods, attended exclusive schools, dined at exclusive private clubs, and belonged to exclusive organizations as a result of their parents' wealth and social position. Many women who possess this sort of privilege—by being an "insider" with regard to class and/or race—exercise the prerogative of exclusion without necessarily recognizing that they are doing so. Privilege is simply something that they have always had and that they envision they have the right to pass on to their children. One form of privilege is the ability to associate with those—and only those—people with whom one chooses to associate.

Elite women typically do not describe themselves as privileged or see their early childhood socialization as having been vastly different from that of girls in other social classes. In the words of Paula Rothenberg, these women have "invisible privilege" based on their class position, their race, their ethnicity, or some combination of these factors.[2] This invisible privilege, as Rothenberg has noted, provides those in the top tiers of society with advantages that other people do not have and gives their children a head start in life. It is so carefully woven into the fabric of their everyday lives that it becomes, at least to them, invisible.

Such privilege is particularly invisible to elite children, who are surrounded by others (except for servants) similar to themselves and who therefore are unlikely to notice that it even exists. Is this mere happenstance? No, the children are brought up in a social "bubble"—a term used by some of the women in this study to describe their neighborhood (or the neighborhood where they grew up) and the environment in which they desire to raise their children. This "bubble" exists based on a number of perquisites of privilege, including the elite geographic location of the family's residence (or residences), the early friendship groups and peer cliques that the children are allowed to have, the clubs and organizations of which they are members, and the schools—from nursery school through college—that foster their educational and social skills. It is a social bubble that the parents work hard to create and maintain. An example is Highland Park and University Park, wealthy adjacent enclaves surrounded by the city of Dallas. Many people who reside in these affluent cities refer to their neighborhood as "the bubble," a term that journalists have adopted for describing life in this small, exclusive area.

Whether the women in this study were employed full time in a professional career or were full-time moms, most of them were quick to acknowledge that they take—and feel that they should take—an active role in organizing their children's lives. Among the reasons for this belief is the widely held assumption among these women that, for their children merely to grow up in an affluent family is not enough. They typically believe that their children also need—and are entitled to have—accomplishments of their own. Among these accomplishments should be development of the right academic, professional, and social skills to fit into the next generation of the upper-class lifestyle and the accompanying concept of noblesse oblige, of helping the less fortunate. In other words, that the children should follow in the parents' footsteps, at least with regard to doing well for themselves and doing good for others. The unspoken belief or assumption is that the children will not—or will not be allowed to—fail.

Just as privilege and exclusivity are linked, so too are the concepts of control and achievement: Elite women typically believe that their children are most likely to "learn the ropes" for being successful as adults if the parents early on use their money and social power to control the circumstances under which their children grow up. This includes maintaining the social bubble described above—a safe and protective environment from which the children only emerge in supervised and special circumstances. This protective environment surrounds all aspects of the children's lives. In order to learn the concept of noblesse oblige, for example, children in some elite prep schools are encouraged to participate in closely supervised volunteer activities that help the less fortunate in the community in which the school is located. Yet these same children would never be permitted (by their parents or by the school administration) to go alone to an inner-city school, an AIDS hospice, or a homeless shelter to engage in one-on-one volunteering. Doing good for others is always performed within the safe confines of the social bubble or under the immediate supervision of responsible adults who are charged with their care, a concept that is not forgotten by these children in their subsequent adult-life philanthropic endeavors.

Having the social power to control the interactions and early experiences of their children provides elite parents with the unique opportunity not only to ensure the exclusivity of their children's lives but also to make sure that the children have only limited and highly structured involvement with people of other social classes or racial-ethnic groupings. To both the parents and the children, this exclusivity—this form of social exclusion of those who are not considered beneficial to the children—is a matter of entitlement. It is an entitlement based on "good blood," good connections, and/or hard work (in the form of the accumulation of money and status by the parents). Controlling the social environment of the children and teaching them the concept of exclusivity is part of the parents' role in providing them with all the right "building blocks" for the upper-class lifestyle and part of the social reproduction of the upper classes.

Jenny, an active community volunteer from a white Old Name family and the mother of three daughters, introduced me to the building block concept in elite child rearing and of its importance to many elite parents:

The symphony has a program called Building Blocks of the Orchestra, where children are introduced to instruments, music, conductors, and other things that it takes to make up a symphony orchestra. I got to thinking about this during a program one day and realized that children's lives are like building blocks. That, as a mother, I have a responsibility to take one block after another and help my children become the human beings that they have the potential to become. I know that my children have started with more of these blocks than some children have, and through the [Junior] League and other organizations, we try to help children who have fewer blocks than our children do so that they, too, can get a good education and have a happy life. But my primary responsibility is my own kids. It's important that I help them know who they are and why they must be proud of the family of which they are a part. I want to be sure that my children know how to use the building blocks that they have been given.

Previous research[3] has suggested that Jenny is correct: Elite families use the building blocks that they have been given in creating an exclusive environment—a social bubble—for their children and themselves. In the discussion that follows, we will examine some of those building blocks for elite young women and the effect that those blocks have on people both within and outside the social bubble. They include the neighborhood of the family's residence, the young women's friends and in-groups, the behaviors and beliefs that they are taught are appropriate, the educational institutions that they attend, and the Greek-letter sororities that they may join prior to graduation from college. We will also examine the effect that those building blocks have on the attitudes that elite women have regarding the good deeds described elsewhere in this book.

THE PRESTIGIOUS NEIGHBORHOODS THAT ELITE GIRLS CALL "HOME"

The early socialization of elite women usually begins in a residential area that is among the most exclusive or prestigious in the city in which their families reside. Based on location, type, and quality, an elite family's residence may be both a showplace of conspicuous consumption and a part of the social "bubble": a safe haven that provides the family with comfort, safety, and isolation from those of other social classes. As E. Digby Baltzell has noted, elite families place great importance on their place of residence:

> *The higher the social class, the more social distance is reinforced by geographical isolation. The social life of the upper classes, both children and adults, tends to be exclusive.... The exclusive neighborhood, then, with its distinctive architecture, fashionable churches, private schools, and sentimental traditions, is an indispensable factor in the development of an upper class style of life, system of personal values, and distinct character structure.*[4]

Over the half century since Baltzell wrote about the desire of elites for geographic isolation, the concern for social distance has grown more intense among some elites in the Southwest as the cities in which they live have become more racially and ethnically diverse and as fear of crime has risen due to urban population growth and waves of immigration from elsewhere in the United States and from other countries. Geographic isolation and exclusivity may therefore be seen by elite parents as related to safety issues, and often are described to the children as such. A number of women in my study recalled being repeatedly told during their childhoods not to stray outside their own residential areas without the protection and supervision of their own or a friend's parents or household employees.

Elite residences tend to be in exclusive enclaves where housing costs prohibit all but the wealthiest families from acquiring a home. As a result, no middle- or lower-income families and few families of color will be the neighbors of elite white families, with the exceptions being top CEOs, celebrities, or sports stars of color, who are typically viewed as "the exception rather than the rule for minorities," in the words of one white woman. These exclusive residential enclaves usually fit into one of several categories, one of which is a fairly large older area of town with a high enough proportion of very expensive housing to promote the feeling of exclusivity and privilege. Some of these older areas are incorporated cities within the larger city of which they are a part, such as Alamo Heights (surrounded by San Antonio) and Highland Park and University Park (surrounded, as previously noted, by Dallas). These areas have their own school system and police department to enforce the rules, not only as they are set forth "on the books" but also sometimes as the residents see fit. I heard a number of examples of police being encouraged to stop and question people who drove older cars or did not look like "they belonged in our neighborhood," particularly after dark.

Other elite enclaves—such as the River Oaks area of Houston and the "Old Enfield" area of Austin—are located in exclusive older areas of a city rather than constituting an incorporated city in and of themselves. Often, the residents of such areas have been able to get the city to close certain streets, creating a cul de sac, or to create other barriers of one sort or another that discourage or prevent outsiders from driving through the neighborhood. If less expensive housing abuts such an enclave, elite parents may seek to dissuade their children from associating with children who live in the less expensive areas, as Nancy (a white woman in her mid-30s from an Old Name family) recalled from her childhood:

> *We lived in a large brick house on a tree-lined street, but several blocks away there were smaller, wood-frame houses with families living in them. I wanted to play with a child who lived in one of those houses, but my mother repeatedly said, "We don't play with the children who live on [name of street]." When I asked, "Why?" I always got the same answer, "Well, they are different from you and me, and there are plenty of children that you can be friends with on our own street." When I pressed her further, one day Mother blurted out, "Nancy, I wish you'd quit asking me about that. I've told you time after time that "They are not our kind*

of people,' so will you kindly hush up about that?" I have really tried to raise my children to see that we should treat everybody the same regardless of wealth, race, creed, color, national origin, or anything else about them that may be different from us, but I'd have to say that how I'm teaching [my children] is different from what I learned in my own family.

To prevent their children's exposure to those they deem unacceptable, some elite parents choose to live in more closely guarded enclaves than the neighborhood where Nancy grew up. Gated communities located within the city proper and affluent suburbs in outlying areas are examples of such exclusive residential areas. Regardless of the specific geographic location of their residences, the goal of elites—particularly those with children—is sufficient social distance and geographical isolation (to use Baltzell's terminology) to separate themselves from people of other classes, races, or ethnicities and to be in the proximity of others from their own group. Whether parents and significant others explicitly use such terms or not, elite children across racial and ethnic lines quickly learn that some people are "our kind of people" while all of the others are not.[5]

Social geographers such as Stephen Richard Higley[6] have shown how the upper classes shape and control residential land use for their own benefit. Restrictive covenants regarding land use are an example: Affluent suburbs are established beyond central cities and their problems—including high crime rates, deteriorating housing and public schools, and high rates of unemployment—and residential neighborhoods in these separately incorporated suburbs have land use restrictions that specify what size house must be built, the size of the lot on which it can be located, and in some instances even what the minimum cost of building the house must be. Practices such as these protect property values and ensure a certain lifestyle for residents; at the same time, however, they have the effect of excluding families that cannot afford to live in an area with such requirements. Along with upper-middle-class professionals, many of the Old Name and New Rich families in Texas prefer to reside in these wealthy suburban enclaves rather than in the areas historically associated with elites in their geographical area. Wealthy suburbs located near the cities in this study (suburbs in which a number of the women discussed in this book live) include West Lake Hills (near Austin), The Woodlands (near Houston), and Plano and Frisco (near Dallas).

As discussed later in this chapter, the location of a family's residence may have some effect on whether elite parents in the Southwest choose to enroll their children in private schools or in well-regarded local public schools, but another of the building blocks involved in the social reproduction of the upper classes needs to be discussed before reaching that topic.

PARENTAL SELECTION OF ELITE CHILDREN'S FRIENDS AND IN-GROUPS

Consciousness of kind is a central factor when elite mothers help their children establish their first playgroups and friendship networks. Although some friendships may emerge from neighborhood settings, many of the women described how their children's playgroups are more closely tied to the mother's own friendship groups and social networks. As one mother stated, "I like for my kids to play with my friends' children. That way I know I can trust that they will be safe and that they will be around kids with whom they attend school or are involved in other social activities." A number of the mothers were rather outspoken about the fact that they do not encourage their children to find their own friends, sometimes even when the children are teenagers. Nancy, whose recollections regarding her own youth are stated above and who is the mother of several young children, is an example of an elite woman who sees it as her responsibility to help her children choose their friends:

My children don't really select their own friends. They decide who they like most or have the most fun with in playgroups that we set up for them. Young children don't really know how to go out and find friends of their own, but they enjoy doing activities together that the mothers have set up or that are like playday in the summer at the country club. On those days, the kids get to use the club and the facilities, and they don't have to worry about whether they are in the way of adults. My oldest daughter met her friends at some of those activities along with the children of mothers who do volunteer activities with me.

Nancy, like other mothers in this study, provides her children with opportunities to play at the country club and at a private club in their neighborhood, where the only children with whom they will associate are the children of other club members. Neither the women nor their children see this as any form of exclusivity or "snobbishness," but instead view it as going about their everyday lives "just doing what we always do."

Elite mothers typically do not acknowledge that allowing their children to associate only with children of their own class or racial/ethnic group separates them from children of other backgrounds or that this may make it more difficult for the children to interact with those outside their own social circle as they grow up. Rather, the mothers are quick to describe how much diversity exists in the lives of their children, frequently noting the one African American or Asian American family that lives nearby or belongs to some organization of which the parents are members, and how their children have exposure to children from those families.

It must be noted, however, that elite white parents are not alone in promoting class-based (and sometimes race-based) separation of their children: Elite African American parents, for example, also tend to make decisions about their children's schools and playmates that separate their children from young people of other classes, regardless of race. In his best-selling book about the U.S. black upper class, Lawrence Otis Graham describes how children of the black upper class are members (along with their parents) of the exclusive by-invitation-only organization known as Jack and Jill of America, which provides "a great opportunity for [African American] professional parents to introduce their kids to children of similar families." According to Graham, Jack and Jill has served for generations as a "network for parents who want playgroups for their children, as well as a network for young adults who want companionship, dating relationships, and ultimately marriage partners."[7]

The consciousness of kind among African American children that Graham describes provides children of color with a race- and class-based identity as well as giving them a group of people with whom they can associate throughout life. In my own research, Tamara—an affluent African American college student—described the significance of Jack and Jill to her parents and in her own life:

For my parents, missing a Jack and Jill awards banquet or party was as bad as if I played hooky from Sunday school. They thought that I might miss meeting somebody that I would really enjoy knowing or of seeing other black parents be good role models for their kids. I have to admit that when I came to [a predominantly white] University, it was nice that some of the people I had known at Jack and Jill were already in the sorority I wanted to join. Of course, it also helped that I was legacy because my mother had been in the same sorority at [a historically black university] in her day.

Organizations such as Jack and Jill provide African American families with a venue in which to recognize the academic and social achievements of their children. Like predominantly white organizations, elite African American organizations such as this may have the covert (and perhaps unintentional) effect of maintaining and perpetuating a class- and sometimes race-based consciousness that fosters an ingroup-outgroup mind-set even among young children.

Whether the process of inclusion and exclusion influences all children or not, many of the organizations that elite parents encourage their children to join (another of the building blocks of elite status) serve as a means of anticipatory socialization for the kinds of responsibilities that the children will assume and the honors and awards that they will receive for successful accomplishment of their responsibilities later in life. Sociological research has demonstrated the importance of anticipatory socialization—the process by which knowledge and skills are learned for future roles—for people of all classes and racial-ethnic categories, but this process is particularly important for those who assume that they or their children have significant leadership roles, economic responsibilities, and social obligations to fulfill on behalf of themselves, their families, and the larger society.

TEACHING ELITE CHILDREN "APPROPRIATE" BEHAVIORS AND BELIEFS

Anticipatory socialization includes learning what behaviors and beliefs are appropriate for people in particular social locations. Among the elite women in this study, the most frequently mentioned behaviors and beliefs that they sought to teach their children at an early age were good manners, good communication skills, and loyalty. The mothers emphasized time and again the importance of preparing their children to be part of "polite society" and suggested that communication skills should be cultivated so that their children could interact with friends, family members, and other people who may be important to them in later life.

As early as age 5 or 6, some of the children in this study were enrolled in classes to learn good manners, just as their parents had been. The classes were typically taught by "socially acceptable" women who had many years of experience in arbitrating the social manners and customs of elites in their community. These women set up classes and "play" activities where children can learn to interact with other children, learn new social skills, and begin to establish networks beyond the immediate family.

By the time they reach 8 or 9 years of age, a number of the children are involved in junior cotillions, which are started by parents—particularly by mothers—who want their children to continue to learn about "the social graces." Typically held in settings such as the local country club, cotillion classes serve as an extension of earlier lessons in manners and etiquette, and they afford children the opportunity to interact with elite children of the opposite sex. The children in such classes frequently look like little adults, trying to do very adult-like things but lacking the physical stature to do so. At one of the "arranged parties" that a cotillion organizer planned, I saw that many of the children were short enough that their feet did not touch the floor when they sat in the adult-sized chairs in the room. However, the teachers and parental organizers did not see this as a problem: Rather, they issued directives to the children to "act like young adults," to "sit up straight in your chair," and, above all else, to "act like young ladies and gentlemen."

For girls, acting like a young lady includes, according to one organizer, "sitting cross-ankled but never with legs crossed." For young gentlemen, appropriate posture requires, among other things, sitting with their feet flat on the floor or, if they can't touch the floor, not wiggling their feet. My analysis regarding such classes being one of the building blocks of elite privilege is supported by previous accounts. For example, one prominent woman has noted that etiquette and cotillion classes are "a very long-term investment in a child's life. What they learn at cotillion is something they will have with them forever. It enforces the polite training they receive at home."[8]

Despite social critics who believe that the old upper class is dying out or that its social rituals are no longer important, the women in my study do not see it this way. Rather, they are busy encouraging their children (and grandchildren) to participate in playgroups and social learning experiences such as manners and cotillion classes that they believe will help the younger generation learn to live successfully an affluent lifestyle. Moreover, the women believe that what they and their children are doing is fun both for the children doing it and for the parents who watch them as they participate in these rites of anticipatory socialization. Charlotte, a white woman from a New Money family, described how she felt when she watched her son at junior cotillion classes:

It is so much fun to see our young people all dressed up and having a good time. Children learn how to be polite and to interact with other children even though we have a few "casualties" along the way like the little boy who hid under the grand piano when he was supposed to ask one of the young ladies to dance with him. It all works, however. By now he and all of the other children are having a great time at the "little dances" we hold several times a year. You asked me what I think is most important about these classes, and I guess I would have to say that, early on, the children learn the answers to important questions such as "how does one eat hors d'oeuvres without messing up formal attire?" or "how much money should you leave for the maid who provides a towel after you wash your hands in the club's ladies room?" or "how can you make a full court bow in a debutante presentation without getting makeup on your dress?"

Children in socially active elite families learn the answers to such questions many years before they actually perform the activities involved. In addition, they come to see their parents as active players in elite social events even when the children do not attend adult functions. However, some of the women I spoke with about etiquette and cotillion classes don't have a fond recollection of that experience, Sherry—a white woman who at the time of this interview was in her 30s—being one example:

> *I learned dance steps and I learned how to eat like a lady. That is true. But what I really learned is how to compete without appearing to be competitive. The underlying message that I got was that you have to compete for social recognition, you have to compete for boyfriends and for adult adoration, but you have to appear to be cooperative rather than aggressive. I also learned that you have to appear to be loyal to your family and your friends.*

Although Sherry participates in volunteer work in her community and is active on the "social scene," she has distanced her children from some of the activities in which she was involved as a child, believing some of them to be superficial; however, one of the building blocks that she believes her early socialization provided for her, and which she believes is important for her own children, is learning the value of family loyalty.

Although not necessarily different from the behavior of people in other classes, the linkage between class and family loyalty is deeply entrenched in most upper-class families, where the children may become joint owners of the family's assets at some point in the future, or where children may believe that alienating their parents by behavior that appears to be disbelieving or disloyal might cut them off from the social and economic advantages that accrue from being closely identified with that family.

The importance of family as a social building block was evident in the frequent use of the word *legacy* by the women in this study. Legacy is a hereditary form of social power. Children may be informed at an early age that they are "legacy" when it comes to attending schools that their parents or other relatives attended or becoming members of clubs or other organizations where family ties may help a person receive an invitation to join. The term legacy particularly becomes meaningful to college-aged women, who often proudly note that being a member of a particular sorority is a part of their families' legacy. Across racial and ethnic lines, sorority women spoke of the concept of legacy as a "proud heritage." Some women who joined a sorority other than the one their mother had belonged to described themselves as feeling somewhat disloyal for their decision. However, many of the women joined the sorority of which they were legacy.

Family loyalty is also linked to the concept of noblesse oblige. Parents who have made substantial gifts to a particular charity, for example, may extract assurances from their children that the children will use their own money, or money they inherit, on behalf of that particular charity or at least for the betterment of the community. It is a family tradition, a family obligation. It has its rewards as well as its obligations. It also is one of the building blocks that the parents hope their children will utilize in their own lives—building blocks that are further cemented through the educational experiences of young elites.

THE EARLY EDUCATIONAL EXPERIENCES OF ELITE YOUNG WOMEN

Previous studies have often indicated that children of the upper classes exclusively attend private preparatory schools, particularly boarding schools in the northeastern United States. However, this is not always true in the Southwest, where there are a number of highly regarded public schools located in wealthy residential enclaves and attended by many elite children. These schools are not "typical" public schools by any measure: Whether located in separate school districts maintained by wealthy "cities within a city" such as Highland Park, University Park, or Alamo Heights, or by wealthy suburban school districts such as the Eanes school district in Westlake Hills near Austin, these schools are considered to be top-tier schools for elite children who live within those districts' boundaries. Frequently, a "drawing card" for such a school district is a highly regarded sports program and a reputation for many of its graduates attending prestigious public or private universities.

The women in my study who enrolled their children in such public schools typically describe this as being important for the "democratization" of their children, but they also note that their children are receiving the high quality education that only a "special" public school or school district can provide and that the children are not missing out on any opportunities that might be available to children in college preparatory schools. With the exception of what is set forth above, however, I am going to focus primarily on elite girls who attend private schools, since most of the women in my study—at least at some point during their educational experience—attended an elite private day or boarding school.

The education of elite young women is a central factor in self-identity and class affiliation. As noted earlier in this chapter, some parents attempt to arrange—even before the child is born—for their daughters to attend certain prestigious schools. Which school or schools they will attend sometimes has an intergenerational genesis, with mothers (or even grandmothers) passing on tips regarding the selection of "the right school" to attend. Jenny described the system her mother had used in analyzing where she should attend school and stated that she had used a similar method when her own daughter was born:

> *Mother kept a card file on schools in the area, beginning with nursery schools and continuing through private elementary and high schools and colleges. On the cards she wrote down, of course, the names and addresses of the schools, the name of the head of the school, and details such as what the school currently cost, who the alumni of the school were that she knew, and the names of people whose kids currently attended the school. I decided that these cards were a really neat idea because Mother always had references she could list on my applications for those schools, and she could jog her memory if she wanted to contact someone who might be helpful in getting me enrolled. The system worked well for my mother, and so far it's worked well for my children.*

As Jenny's statement indicates, elite women are socialized as young children to understand not only the importance of attaining a good education but also that the particular schools a person attends are important building blocks for the lifestyle to which they have been born. Accordingly, elite women are very anxious to make sure that their daughters (and sons) will attend the right schools, beginning with the nursery school or pre-school experience. In some cases, parents in Old Money and Old Name families may feel that their children are entitled to attend a particular exclusive private school due to the family's longtime connection with that institution or with the church that sponsors it, but this is becoming more difficult—even as to availability of slots in schools they have considered to be "their schools" for generations of family members—due to increasing demands from New Money parents for similar educational opportunities for their children. As a result, new private schools come into existence, hoping to build their reputations over a relatively short period of time. Some parents, accordingly, place their children's names on waiting lists both for old and new schools, hoping for the former but being willing to settle for the latter.

Shared beliefs, values, and social networks are factors that bind many members of the upper classes together. Beliefs and values initially taught at home are strengthened in elite schools, where students are encouraged to develop a sense of collective identity that involves school, peers, and one's place within the larger society. As privileged young people create a web of affiliations in dormitories, sporting events, classrooms, and other settings within their schools, they establish ties that, because they are interwoven in such a way as to become indistinguishable from the students' individual identity, will grow and become even more important after graduation. Consequently, to develop solidarity with one's classmates is to develop a form of class solidarity because of the commonalities in beliefs and lived experiences that have been shared over a period of time, frequently without the students being exposed to countervailing belief systems or social networks. Over time, identity with others in the same class is a stronger link than merely some vague perception that they share similar values. As Baltzell stated, "The character of American upper-class institutions has usually been more a product of interpersonal networks than of ideological affinities."[9]

Cassy, a white woman from a well-connected Old Name family and who—at the time of these comments—was a college student, described how much an interpersonal network forged in prep school helped her and a number of her friends make a comfortable transition to an honors program at a prestigious state university:

The friends I made at [prep school] gave me an instant on-campus network at [university]. I'd say our bond was strongest when we were freshmen because we were in the middle of a sea of strangers. In fact, several people who were not my best friends at [prep school] and I hung out together and went to dinners and parties. When I pledged [sorority], upperclassmen from [prep school] were there to cheer me on. They were very helpful and showed me what I should do and what I should expect.

My content analysis of the catalogs, school literature, and Web sites of eighteen elite prep schools (listed in Appendix 1) showed certain recurring themes at these schools that tend to create and reinforce not only academic rigor but also the development of communications skills and long-term upper-class networks such as Cassy described:

- Emphasis on tradition and the part that children and their families play in the tradition of the school;
- Focus on developing active, responsible citizenship and leadership skills among students;
- Emphasis on cultivating the individual interests and talents of the students while at the same time teaching them to respect the rights and opinions of others; and
- Stressing the importance of alumni and parent activities and associations as they relate to the networks that can be created by students, showing how the child becomes a significant link in the chain between the past, present, and future of that specific institution.

Elite private schools emphasize that they strive to educate the "whole child;" whereas public schools typically view this as the parents' responsibility.[10] The Web site of one elite private school in this study states the "whole child" or "whole person" mission as follows:

Our mission to educate the whole person requires that attention be paid to virtues, ethics, character, and integrity.... [We are] committed to the idea that the proper goal of education is the shaping of free, responsible men and women. To this end, [the school] encourages intellectual curiosity and honesty, while cultivating a respect for the discipline required to pursue truth.[11]

In the process of educating the "whole child," even the simple fact of being accepted into an elite private school shows that the young person has been welcomed into a status group whose members feel a consciousness of kind or a sense of shared social similarities.

My content analysis of the catalogs and Web sites of elite schools also revealed that the schools emphasize how rigorous their curriculum is and how they pride themselves on using varied teaching methods and technologies to produce high academic achievement in a wider variety of courses than are typically available at other types of schools in the same geographic region. According to Peter W. Cookson Jr., and Caroline Hodges Persell, "Being comfortable in the world of ideas and being able to express thoughts in a concise and logical manner are not only the mark of a well-educated person, but are essential skills in the struggle for power today."[12]

Each of the schools included in my research emphasizes the building of the cultural capital that constitutes a source of social power for students who have been exposed to an education rich in the fine arts. As one school states, "In a unique way, experience in the arts promotes positive self-awareness in both the context of our community experience and the celebration of our diverse cultural heritage."[13] Like other elite prep schools, this institution not only wants to prepare those who might choose to become art professionals or to participate in art, music, theater, and dance for their own enjoyment, but it also wants to educate the next generation of active members of the arts audience who might also engage in volunteerism and philanthropy on behalf of their preferred arts organizations.

Previous research has noted how the education that elite children receive reflects the distinct lifestyle of the upper class, and that these schools transmit the traditions of the upper social classes to the next generation of elites.[14] In their study of elite prep schools, for example, Cookson and Persell described how boarding schools reproduce upper-class values and behavior in privileged children:

Boarding school students...are taught that they should be moral and treat life as an exciting challenge, but what they often learn is that life is hard, and that winning is essential for survival. The "muscular Christianity" that so well describes the essence of prep pride is exactly right: speak like a man or woman of God, but act like a man or woman who knows the score and can settle a score without flinching. Preps are taught that right should prevail, but they learn that it often does not.[15]

As Cookson and Persell state, prep students learn that they must be competitive and that they must learn to live with seemingly contradictory concerns in their lives. Above all else, as Cookson and Persell note, prep school students come to believe that privilege is justified. This attitude is essential for maintaining an upper-class outlook, but it often limits the prep school experience so that the students' outlook may not stretch beyond the school's boundaries.[16]

In my discussions with one former prep school student, she referred to her years there as being an example of the "brick wall syndrome." I did not have a chance to follow up with her on this statement, but later came across the writing of another prep school student, Katie Hagedorn, who described the same phenomena in her boarding school experience. Hagedorn stated that the brick wall syndrome isolates boarding school students from the community that surrounds them, supposedly for the purpose of encouraging intensive studying, but that this isolation has another significant consequence for students: It limits their view of the world beyond the brick wall.[17] Thus, for some students at both day and boarding schools, the very educational institution that their parents are paying to enhance the children's cultural capital and broaden their social horizons may also create a brick wall—a wall whose building blocks foster the belief that exclusion of those outside the wall is normal rather than it being something arbitrary or discriminatory. The norm of exclusivity—whether learned in a prestigious private prep school or other elite educational institution—helps explain the exclusive nature of the women's organizations discussed in this book, and why the women who participate in them may not be aware of that exclusivity and the privilege associated with it.

Private schools—and the concept of exclusivity—have been important for children in both elite white and elite black families. Even among early black elite families, private schools were often considered to be essential for one of two reasons: For families living in southern cities, the segregated school districts provided little, if any, educational opportunities for black children; elsewhere, African American parents wanted to offer their children the opportunity to meet children from other high-income black families and to reinforce the idea of their own children's prominent lineage.[18] Although many black elite children today are educated in day schools or boarding schools that previously had primarily white student bodies, the transition for some African American students has not been without its tough times due to racial and ethnic differences in white and black students, including such factors as interests, politics, hobbies, or music, which may leave African American students out of the social groups established by their "overwhelmingly conservative white classmates."[19]

Elite education does not end with graduation from prep school. Upper-class children (whether they attended public or private schools), along with a carefully selected constituency of children from lower income backgrounds, attend prestigious private or state universities, where they not only further their formal education but also establish in-group ties with other members of their own class through by-invitation-only social organizations such as Greek-letter fraternities and sororities, further reinforcing the norm of exclusivity.

NOTES

1. Although some young elites may grow up to follow in their parents' footsteps, others may rebel to the extent that they lose some or all of the economic and social assets that would otherwise accrue to them as a result of their families. As William A. Corsaro's (1997) study of children's sense-making process shows, children develop their own interpretations of situations. They engage in negotiations with others, and they frequently modify or transform the information that they receive from adults. Like children from other classes, elite children do not passively internalize the norms and values of their adult significant others. However, wealthy and privileged parents—who have more economic resources and advantages that they can offer their children from birth through college (or even beyond college) than do parents in other classes—can bring more of those resources to bear on socializing their children in a particular manner. Children who do not "learn the ropes" that would make them

full-fledged members of the social elite run the risk of being estranged from families that typically place a high (but often unacknowledged) value on reproduction into future generations not only of the family itself but also of the lifestyle of the privileged classes in which the parents live.

2. Rothenberg 2000:1.
3. Baltzell 1958, 1964; Cookson and Persell 1985; Daniels 1988; Domhoff 1998; Mills 2000 [1956]; Ostrander 1984.
4. Baltzell 1958:174.
5. Graham 2000.
6. Higley 1995.
7. Graham 2000:23.
8. Quoted in McCready 1988: Southwest Section.
9. Baltzell 1979:278.
10. Cookson and Persell 1985.
11. St. Stephens 2001.
12. Cookson and Persell 1985:30.
13. St. Stephens 2001.
14. Domhoff 1998; Mills 2000 [1956].
15. Cookson and Persell 1985:19.
16. Cookson and Persell 1985.
17. Hagedorn 1996.
18. Graham 2000.
19. Graham 2000:59.

QUESTIONS

? What types of attitudes, beliefs, and behaviors do Kendall's elite parents want to instill in their children? How do they do so?

? Kendall uses a number of terms to discuss elite children's socialization. What does she mean by the following: norm of exclusivity, social bubble, invisible privilege, consciousness of kind, and anticipatory socialization?

? Societal lens question: How did social class play a role in your upbringing? Think about your early attitudes, beliefs, and behaviors. Identify and describe three building blocks that adults in charge of your "ropes" taught to you.

Chapter 6

Barbie Girls versus Sea Monsters
Children Constructing Gender

By MICHAEL A. MESSNER

■ What can a children's soccer game teach us about gender (the social significance given to biological categories of male and female)? In the following selection, sociologist Michael A. Messner uses his gender lens to analyze an event that occurred before his five-year old son's soccer game. Messner describes an incident between a girl's soccer team (Barbie Girls) and a boy's soccer team (Sea Monsters). Calling this episode a "magnified moment" – a small window into the inner workings of our social world that allows him to illustrate the importance of gender in society – he shows you how gender is created and maintained through interactions, cultural symbols, and social structures. When you are done reading you should not only be able to explain how each of these factors (interaction, culture, structure) worked for the children. You should also be able to identify and link them to gender in your daily world.

In the past decade, studies of children and gender have moved toward greater levels of depth and sophistication (e.g., Jordan and Cowan 1995; McGuffy and Rich 1999; Thorne 1993). In her groundbreaking work on children and gender, Thorne (1993) argued that previous theoretical frameworks, although helpful, were limited: The top-down (adult-to-child) approach of socialization theories tended to ignore the extent to which children are active agents in the creation of their worlds—often in direct or partial opposition to values or "roles" to which adult teachers or parents are attempting to socialize them. Developmental theories also had their limits due to their tendency to ignore group and contextual factors while overemphasizing "the constitution and unfolding of *individuals* as boys or girls" (Thorne 1993, 4). In her study of grade school children, Thorne demonstrated a dynamic approach that examined the ways in which children actively construct gender in specific social contexts of the classroom and the playground. Working from emergent theories of performativity, Thorne developed the concept of "gender play" to analyze the social processes through which children construct gender. Her level of analysis was not the individual but "*group life*—with social relations, the organization and meanings of social situations, the collective practices through which children and adults create and recreate gender in their daily interactions" (Thorne 1993, 4).

A key insight from Thorne's research is the extent to which gender varies in salience from situation to situation. Sometimes, children engage in "relaxed, cross sex play"; other times—for instance, on the playground during boys' ritual invasions of girls' spaces and games—gender boundaries between boys and girls are activated in ways that variously threaten or (more often) reinforce and clarify these boundaries. However, these varying moments of gender salience are not free-floating; they occur in social contexts such as schools and in which gender is formally and informally built into the division of labor, power structure, rules, and values (Connell 1987).

The purpose of this article is to use an observation of a highly salient gendered moment of group life among four- and five-year-old children as a point of departure for exploring the conditions under which gender boundaries become activated and enforced. I was privy to this moment as I observed my five-year-old son's first season (including weekly games and practices) in organized soccer. Unlike the long-term, systematic ethnographic studies of children conducted by Thorne (1993) or Adler and Adler (1998), this article takes one moment as its point of departure. I do not present this moment as somehow "representative" of what happened throughout the season; instead, I examine this as an example of what Hochschild (1994, 4) calls "magnified moments," which are "episodes of heightened importance, either epiphanies, moments of intense glee or unusual insight, or moments in which things go intensely but meaningfully wrong. In either case, the moment stands out; it is metaphorically rich, unusually elaborate and often echoes [later]." A magnified moment in daily life offers a window into the social construction of reality. It presents researchers with an opportunity to excavate gendered meanings and processes through an analysis of institutional and cultural contexts. The single empirical observation that serves as the point of departure for this article was made during a morning. Immediately after the event, I recorded my observations with detailed notes. I later slightly revised the notes after developing the photographs that I took at the event.

I will first describe the observation—an incident that occurred as a boys' four- and five-year-old soccer team waited next to a girls' four- and five-year-old soccer team for the beginning of the community's American Youth Soccer League (AYSO) season's opening ceremony. I will then examine this moment using three levels of analysis.

- *The interactional level:* How do children "do gender," and what are the contributions and limits of theories of performativity in understanding these interactions?
- *The level of structural context:* How does the gender regime, particularly the larger organizational level of formal sex segregation of AYSO, and the concrete, momentary situation of the opening ceremony provide a context that variously constrains and enables the children's interactions?
- *The level of cultural symbol:* How does the children's shared immersion in popular culture (and their differently gendered locations in this immersion) provide symbolic resources for the creation, in this situation, of apparently categorical differences between the boys and the girls?

Although I will discuss these three levels of analysis separately, I hope to demonstrate that interaction, structural context, and culture are simultaneous and mutually intertwined processes, none of which supersedes the others.

BARBIE GIRLS VERSUS SEA MONSTERS

It is a warm, sunny Saturday morning. Summer is coming to a close, and schools will soon reopen. As in many communities, this time of year in this small, middle- and professional-class suburb of Los Angeles is marked by the beginning of another soccer season. This morning, 156 teams, with approximately 1,850 players ranging from 4 to 17 years old, along with another 2,000 to 3,000 parents, siblings, friends, and community dignitaries have gathered at the local high school football and track facility for the annual AYSO opening ceremonies. Parents and children wander around the perimeter of the track to find the assigned station for their respective teams. The coaches muster their teams and chat with parents. Eventually, each team will march around the track, behind their new team banner, as they are announced over the loudspeaker system and are applauded by the crowd. For now though, and for the next 45 minutes to an hour, the kids, coaches, and parents must stand, mill around, talk, and kill time as they await the beginning of the ceremony.

The Sea Monsters is a team of four- and five-year-old boys. Later this day, they will play their first-ever soccer game. A few of the boys already know each other from preschool, but most are still getting acquainted. They are wearing their new uniforms for the first time. Like other teams, they were assigned team colors—in this case, green and blue—and asked to choose their team name at their first team meeting, which occurred a week ago. Although they preferred "Blue Sharks," they found that the name was already taken by another team and settled on "Sea Monsters." A grandmother of one of the boys created the spiffy team banner, which was awarded a prize this morning. As they wait for the ceremony to begin, the boys inspect and then proudly pose for pictures in front of their new award-winning team banner. The parents stand a few feet away—some taking pictures, some just watching. The parents are also getting to know each other, and the common currency of topics is just how darned cute our kids look, and will they start these ceremonies soon before another boy has to be escorted to the bathroom?

Queued up one group away from the Sea Monsters is a team of four- and five-year-old girls in green and white uniforms. They too will play their first game later today, but for now, they are awaiting the beginning of the opening ceremony. They have chosen the name "Barbie Girls," and they also have a spiffy new team banner. But the girls are pretty much ignoring their banner, for they have created another, more powerful symbol around which to rally. In fact, they are the only team among the 156 marching today with a team float—a red Radio Flyer wagon base, on which sits a Sony boom box playing music, and a 3-foot-plus-tall Barbie doll on a rotating pedestal. Barbie is dressed in the team colors—indeed, she sports a custom-made green-and-white cheerleader-style outfit, with the Barbie Girls' names written on the skirt. Her normally all-blonde hair has been streaked with Barbie Girl green and features a green bow, with white polka dots. Several of the girls on the team also have supplemented their uniforms with green bows in their hair.

The volume on the boom box nudges up and four or five girls begin to sing a Barbie song. Barbie is now slowly rotating on her pedestal, and as the girls sing more gleefully and more loudly, some of them begin to hold hands and walk around the float, in sync with Barbie's rotation. Other same-aged girls from other teams are drawn to the celebration and, eventually, perhaps a dozen girls are singing the Barbie song. The girls are intensely focused on Barbie, on the music, and on their mutual pleasure.

As the Sea Monsters mill around their banner, some of them begin to notice, and then begin to watch and listen as the Barbie Girls rally around their float. At first, the boys are watching as individuals, seemingly unaware of each other's shared interest. Some of them stand with arms at their sides, slack-jawed, as though passively watching a television show. I notice slight smiles on a couple of their faces, as though they are drawn to the Barbie Girls' celebratory fun. Then, with side-glances, some of the boys begin to notice each other's attention on the Barbie Girls. Their faces begin to show signs of distaste. One of them yells out, "NO BARBIE!" Suddenly, they all begin to move—jumping up and down, nudging and bumping one other—and join into a group chant: "NO BARBIE! NO BARBIE! NO BARBIE!" They now appear to be every bit as gleeful as the girls, as they laugh, yell, and chant against the Barbie Girls.

The parents watch the whole scene with rapt attention. Smiles light up the faces of the adults, as our glances sweep back and forth, from the sweetly celebrating Barbie Girls to the aggressively protesting Sea Monsters. "They are SO different!" exclaims one smiling mother approvingly. A male coach offers a more in-depth analysis: "When I was in college," he says, "I took these classes from professors who showed us research that showed that boys and girls are the same. I believed it, until I had my own kids and saw how different they are." "Yeah," another dad responds, "Just look at them! They are so different!"

The girls, meanwhile, show no evidence that they hear, see, or are even aware of the presence of the boys who are now so loudly proclaiming their opposition to the Barbie Girls' songs and totem. They continue to sing, dance, laugh, and rally around the Barbie for a few more minutes, before they are called to reassemble in their groups for the beginning of the parade.

After the parade, the teams reassemble on the infield of the track but now in a less organized manner. The Sea Monsters once again find themselves in the general vicinity of the Barbie Girls and take up the "NO BARBIE!" chant again. Perhaps put out by the lack of response to their chant, they begin to dash, in twos and threes, invading the girls' space, and yelling menacingly. With this, the Barbie Girls have little choice but to recognize the presence of the boys—some look puzzled and shrink back, some engage the boys and chase them off. The chasing seems only to incite more excitement among the boys. Finally, parents intervene and defuse the situation, leading their children off to their cars, homes, and eventually to their soccer games.

THE PERFORMANCE OF GENDER

In the past decade, especially since the publication of Judith Butler's highly influential *Gender Trouble* (1990), it has become increasingly fashionable among academic feminists to think of gender not as some "thing" that one "has" (or not) but rather as situationally constructed through the performances of active agents. The idea of gender as performance analytically foregrounds the agency of individuals in the construction of gender, thus highlighting the situational fluidity of gender: here, conservative and reproductive, there, transgressive and disruptive. Surely, the Barbie Girls versus Sea Monsters scene described above can be fruitfully analyzed as a moment of crosscutting and mutually constitutive gender performances: The girls—at least at first glance—appear to be performing (for each other?) a conventional four- to five-year-old version of emphasized femininity. At least on the surface, there appears to be nothing terribly transgressive here. They are just "being girls," together. The boys initially are unwittingly constituted as an audience for the girls' performance but quickly begin to perform (for each other?—for the girls, too?) a masculinity that constructs itself in opposition to Barbie, and to the girls, as not feminine. They aggressively confront—first through loud verbal chanting, eventually through bodily invasions—the girls' ritual space of emphasized femininity, apparently with the intention of disrupting its upsetting influence. The adults are simultaneously constituted as an adoring audience for their children's performances and as parents who perform for each other by sharing and mutually affirming their experience-based narratives concerning the natural differences between boys and girls.

In this scene, we see children performing gender in ways that constitute themselves as two separate, opposed groups (boys vs. girls) and parents performing gender in ways that give the stamp of adult approval to the children's performances of difference, while constructing their own ideological narrative that naturalizes this categorical difference. In other words, the parents do not seem to read the children's performances of gender as social constructions of gender. Instead, they interpret them as the inevitable unfolding of natural, internal differences between the sexes. That this moment occurred when it did and where it did is explicable, but not entirely with a theory of performativity. As Walters (1999, 250) argues,

> *The performance of gender is never a simple voluntary act.... Theories of gender as play and performance need to be intimately and systematically connected with the power of gender (really, the power of male power) to constrain, control, violate, and configure. Too often, mere lip service is given to the specific historical, social, and political configurations that make certain conditions possible and others constrained.*

Indeed, feminist sociologists operating from the traditions of symbolic interactionism and/or Goffmanian dramaturgical analysis have anticipated the recent interest in looking at gender as a dynamic performance. As early as 1978, Kessler and McKenna developed a sophisticated analysis of gender as an everyday, practical accomplishment of people's interactions. Nearly a decade later, West and Zimmerman (1987) argued that in people's everyday interactions, they were "doing gender" and, in so doing, they were constructing masculine dominance and feminine deference. As these ideas have been taken up in sociology, their tendencies toward a celebration of the "freedom" of agents to transgress and reshape the fluid boundaries of gender have been put into play with theories of social structure (e.g., Lorber 1994; Risman 1998). In these accounts, gender is viewed as enacted or created through everyday interactions, but crucially, as Walters suggested above, within "specific historical, social, and political configurations" that constrain or enable certain interactions.

The parents' response to the Barbie Girls versus Sea Monsters performance suggests one of the main limits and dangers of theories of performativity. Lacking an analysis of structural and cultural context, performances of gender can all too easily be interpreted as free agents' acting out the inevitable surface manifestations of a natural inner essence of sex difference. An examination of structural and cultural contexts, though, reveals that there was nothing inevitable about the girls' choice of Barbie as their totem, nor in the boys' response to it.

THE STRUCTURE OF GENDER

In the entire subsequent season of weekly games and practices, I never once saw adults point to a moment in which boy and girl soccer players were doing the *same* thing and exclaim to each other, "Look at them! They are *so similar!*" The actual similarity of the boys and the girls, evidenced by nearly all of the kids' routine actions throughout a soccer season—playing the game, crying over a skinned knee, scrambling enthusiastically for their snacks after the games, spacing out on a bird or a flower instead of listening to the coach at practice—is a key to understanding the salience of the Barbie Girls versus Sea Monsters moment for gender relations. In the face of a multitude of moments that speak to similarity, it was this anomalous Barbie Girls versus Sea Monsters moment—where the boundaries of gender were so clearly enacted—that the adults seized to affirm their commitment to difference. It is the kind of moment—to use Lorber's (1994, 37) phrase—where "believing is seeing," where we selectively "see" aspects of social reality that tell us a truth that we prefer to believe, such as the belief in categorical sex difference. No matter that our eyes do not see evidence of this truth most of the rest of the time.

In fact, it was not so easy for adults to actually "see" the empirical reality of sex similarity in everyday observations of soccer throughout the season. That is due to one overdetermining factor: an institutional context that is characterized by informally structured sex segregation among the parent coaches and team managers, and by formally structured sex segregation among the children. The structural analysis developed here is indebted to Acker's (1990) observation that organizations, even while appearing "gender neutral," tend to reflect, re-create, and naturalize a hierarchical ordering of gender. Following Connell's (1987, 98–99) method of structural analysis, I will examine the "gender regime"—that is, the current "state of play of sexual politics"—within the local AYSO organization by conducting a "structural inventory" of the formal and informal sexual divisions of labor and power.[1]

Adult Divisions of Labor and Power

There was a clear—although not absolute—sexual division of labor and power among the adult volunteers in the AYSO organization. The Board of Directors consisted of 21 men and 9 women, with the top two positions—commissioner and assistant commissioner—held by men. Among the league's head coaches, 133 were men and 23 women. The division among the league's assistant coaches was similarly skewed. Each team also had a team manager who was responsible for organizing snacks, making reminder calls about games and practices, organizing team parties and the end-of-the-year present for the coach. The vast majority of team managers were women. A common slippage in the language of coaches and parents revealed the ideological assumptions underlying this position: I often noticed people describe a team manager as the "team mom." In short, as Table 1 shows, the vast majority of the time, the formal authority of the head coach and assistant coach was in the hands of a man, while the backup, support role of team manager was in the hands of a woman.

These data illustrate Connell's (1987, 97) assertion that sexual divisions of labor are interwoven with, and mutually supportive of, divisions of power and authority among women and men. They also suggest how people's choices to volunteer for certain positions are shaped and constrained by previous institutional practices. There is no formal AYSO rule that men must be the leaders, women the supportive followers. And there are, after all, *some* women coaches and *some* men team managers.² So, it may appear that the division of labor among adult volunteers simply manifests an accumulation of individual choices and preferences. When analyzed structurally, though, individual men's apparently free choices to volunteer disproportionately for coaching jobs, alongside individual women's apparently free choices to volunteer disproportionately for team manager jobs, can be seen as a logical collective result of the ways that the institutional structure of sport has differentially constrained and enabled women's and men's previous options and experiences (Messner 1992). Since boys and men have had far more opportunities to play organized sports and thus to gain skills and knowledge, it subsequently appears rational for adult men to serve in positions of knowledgeable authority, with women serving in a support capacity (Boyle and McKay 1995). Structure—in this case, the historically constituted division of labor and power in sport—constrains current practice. In turn, structure becomes an object of practice, as the choices and actions of today's parents re-create divisions of labor and power similar to those that they experienced in their youth.

TABLE 1: ADULT VOLUNTEERS AS COACHES AND TEAM MANAGERS, BY GENDER (in percentages) (*N* = 156 teams)

	Head Coaches	Assistant Coaches	Team Managers
Women	15	21	86
Men	85	79	14

The Children: Formal Sex Segregation

As adult authority patterns are informally structured along gendered lines, the children's leagues are formally segregated by AYSO along lines of age and sex. In each age-group, there are separate boys' and girls' leagues. The AYSO in this community included 87 boys' teams and 69 girls' teams. Although the four- to five-year-old boys often played their games on a field that was contiguous with games being played by four- to five-year-old girls, there was never a formal opportunity for cross-sex play. Thus, both the girls' and the boys' teams could conceivably proceed through an entire season of games and practices in entirely homosocial contexts.³ In the all-male contexts that I observed throughout the season, gender never appeared to be overtly salient among the children, coaches, or parents. It is against this backdrop that I might suggest a working hypothesis about structure and the variable salience of gender: The formal sex segregation of children does not, in and of itself, make gender overtly salient. In fact, when children are absolutely segregated, with no opportunity for cross-sex interactions, gender may appear to disappear as an overtly salient organizing principle. However, when formally sex-segregated children are placed into immediately contiguous locations, such as during the opening ceremony, highly charged gendered interactions between the groups (including invasions and other kinds of border work) become more possible.

Although it might appear to some that formal sex segregation in children's sports is a natural fact, it has not always been so for the youngest age-groups in AYSO. As recently as 1995, when my older son signed up to play as a five-year-old, I had been told that he would play in a coed league. But when he arrived to his first practice and I saw that he was on an all-boys team, I was told by the coach that AYSO had decided this year to begin sex segregating all age-groups, because "during half-times and practices, the boys and girls tend to separate into separate groups. So the league thought it would be better for team unity if we split the boys and girls into separate leagues." I suggested to some coaches that a similar dynamic among racial ethnic groups (say, Latino kids and white kids clustering as separate groups during halftimes) would not similarly result in a decision to create racially segregated leagues. That this comment appeared to fall on deaf ears illustrates the extent to which many adults' belief in the need for sex segregation—at least in the context of sport—is grounded in a mutually agreed-upon notion of boys' and girls' "separate worlds," perhaps based in ideologies of natural sex difference.

The gender regime of AYSO, then, is structured by formal and informal sexual divisions of labor and power. This social structure sets ranges, limits, and possibilities for the children's and parents' interactions and performances of gender, but it does not determine them. Put another way, the formal and informal gender regime of AYSO made the Barbie Girls versus Sea Monsters moment possible, but it did not make it inevitable. It was the agency of the children and the parents within that structure that made the moment happen. But why did this moment take on the symbolic forms that it did? How and why do the girls, boys, and parents construct and derive meanings from this moment, and how can we interpret these meanings? These questions are best grappled within in the realm of cultural analysis.

THE CULTURE OF GENDER

The difference between what is "structural" and what is "cultural" is not clear-cut. For instance, the AYSO assignment of team colors and choice of team names (cultural symbols) seem to follow logically from, and in turn reinforce, the sex segregation of the leagues (social structure). These cultural symbols such as team colors, uniforms, songs, team names, and banners often carried encoded gendered meanings that were then available to be taken up by the children in ways that constructed (or potentially contested) gender divisions and boundaries.

Team Names

Each team was issued two team colors. It is notable that across the various age-groups, several girls' teams were issued pink uniforms—a color commonly recognized as encoding feminine meanings—while no boys' teams were issued pink uniforms. Children, in consultation with their coaches, were asked to choose their own team names and were encouraged to use their assigned team colors as cues to theme of the team name (e.g., among the boys, the "Red Flashes," the "Green Pythons," and the blue-and-green "Sea Monsters"). When I analyzed the team names of the 156 teams by age-group and by sex, three categories emerged:

TABLE 2: TEAM NAMES, BY AGE-GROUPS AND GENDER

	4–5		6–7		8–13		14–17		Total	
	n	%	n	%	n	%	n	%	n	%
Girls										
Sweet names	5	42	3	17	2	7	0	0	10	15
Neutral/paradoxical	5	42	6	33	7	25	5	45	23	32
Power names	2	17	9	50	19	68	6	55	36	52
Boys										
Sweet names	0	0	0	0	1	4	0	0	1	1
Neutral/paradoxical	1	7	4	15	4	12	4	31	13	15
Power names	13	93	22	85	29	85	9	69	73	82

1. Sweet names: These are cutesy team names that communicate small stature, cuteness, and/or vulnerability. These kinds of names would most likely be widely read as encoded with feminine meanings (e.g., "Blue Butterflies," "Beanie Babes," "Sunflowers," "Pink Flamingos," and "Barbie Girls").

2. Neutral or paradoxical names: Neutral names are team names that carry no obvious gendered meaning (e.g., "Blue and Green Lizards," "Team Flubber," "Galaxy," "Blue Ice"). Paradoxical names are girls' team names that carry mixed (simultaneously vulnerable *and* powerful) messages (e.g., "Pink Panthers," "Flower Power," "Little Tigers").

3. Power names: These are team names that invoke images of unambiguous strength, aggression, and raw power (e.g., "Shooting Stars," "Killer Whales," "Shark Attack," "Raptor Attack," and "Sea Monsters").

As Table 2 illustrates, across all age-groups of boys, there was only one team name coded as a sweet name—"The Smurfs," in the 10- to 11-year-old league. Across all age categories, the boys were far more likely to choose a power name than anything else, and this was nowhere more true than in the youngest age-groups, where 35 of 40 (87 percent) of boys' teams in the four-to-five and six-to-seven age-groups took on power names. A different pattern appears in the girls' team name choices, especially among the youngest girls. Only 2 of the 12 four- to five-year-old girls' teams chose power names, while 5 chose sweet names and 5 chose neutral/paradoxical names. At age six to seven, the numbers begin to tip toward the boys' numbers but still remain different, with half of the girls' teams now choosing power names. In the middle and older girls' groups, the sweet names all but disappear, with power names dominating, but still a higher proportion of neutral/paradoxical names than among boys in those age-groups.

Barbie Narrative versus Warrior Narrative

How do we make sense of the obviously powerful spark that Barbie provided in the opening ceremony scene described above? Barbie is likely one of the most immediately identifiable symbols of femininity in the world. More conservatively oriented parents tend to happily buy Barbie dolls for their daughters, while perhaps deflecting their sons' interest in Barbie toward more sex-appropriate "action toys." Feminist parents, on the other hand, have often expressed open contempt—or at least uncomfortable ambivalence—toward Barbie. This is because both conservative and feminist parents see dominant cultural meanings of emphasized femininity as condensed in Barbie and assume that these meanings will be imitated by their daughters. Recent developments in cultural studies, though, should warn us against simplistic readings of Barbie as simply conveying hegemonic messages about gender to unwitting children (Attfield 1996; Seiter 1995). In addition to critically analyzing the cultural values (or "preferred meanings") that may be encoded in Barbie or other children's toys, feminist scholars of cultural studies point to the necessity of examining "reception, pleasure, and agency," and especially "the fullness of reception contexts" (Walters 1999, 246). The Barbie Girls versus Sea Monsters moment can be analyzed as a "reception context," in which differently situated boys, girls, and parents variously used Barbie to construct pleasurable intergroup bonds, as well as boundaries between groups.

Barbie is plastic both in form and in terms of cultural meanings children and adults create around her (Rogers 1999). It is not that there are not hegemonic meanings encoded in Barbie: Since its introduction in 1959, Mattel has been successful in selling millions[4] of this doll that "was recognized as a model of ideal teenhood" (Rand 1998, 383) and "an icon—perhaps *the* icon—of true white womanhood and femininity" (DuCille 1994, 50). However, Rand (1998) argues that "we condescend to children when we analyze Barbie's content and then presume that it passes untransformed into their minds, where, dwelling beneath the control of consciousness or counterargument, it generates self-image, feelings, and other ideological constructs." In fact, people who are situated differently (by age, gender, sexual orientation, social class, race/ethnicity, and national origin) tend to consume and construct meanings around Barbie variously. For instance, some adult women (including many feminists) tell retrospective stories of having rejected (or even mutilated) their Barbies in favor of boys' toys, and some adult lesbians tell stories of transforming Barbie "into an object of dyke desire" (Rand 1998, 386).

Mattel, in fact, clearly strategizes its marketing of Barbie not around the imposition of a singular notion of what a girl or woman should be but around "hegemonic discourse strategies" that attempt to incorporate consumers' range of possible interpretations and criticisms of the limits of Barbie. For instance, the recent marketing of "multicultural Barbie" features dolls with different skin colors and culturally coded wardrobes (DuCille 1994). This strategy broadens the Barbie market, deflects potential criticism of racism, but still "does not boot blond, white Barbie from center stage" (Rand 1998, 391). Similarly, Mattel's marketing of Barbie (since the 1970s) as a career woman raises issues concerning the feminist critique of Barbie's supposedly negative effect on girls.

When the AAUW recently criticized Barbie, adult collectors defended Barbie, asserting that "Barbie, in fact, is a wonderful role model for women. She has been a veterinarian, an astronaut, and a soldier—and even before real women had a chance to enter such occupations" (Spigel forthcoming). And when the magazine *Barbie Bazaar* ran a cover photo of its new "Gulf War Barbie," it served "as a reminder of Mattel's marketing slogan: 'We Girls Can Do Anything'" (Spigel forthcoming). The following year, Mattel unveiled its "Presidential Candidate Barbie" with the statement "It is time for a woman president, and Barbie had the credentials for the job." Spigel observes that these liberal feminist messages of empowerment for girls run—apparently unambiguously—alongside a continued unspoken understanding that Barbie must be beautiful, with an ultraskinny waist and long, thin legs that taper to feet that appear deformed so that they may fit (only?) into high heels.[5] "Mattel does not mind equating beauty with intellect. In fact, so long as the $11^{1/2}$ inch Barbie body remains intact, Mattel is willing to accessorize her with a number of fashionable perspectives—including feminism itself" (Spigel forthcoming).

It is this apparently paradoxical encoding of the all-too-familiar oppressive bodily requirements of feminine beauty alongside the career woman role modeling and empowering message that "we girls can do anything" that may inform how and why the Barbie Girls appropriated Barbie as their team symbol. Emphasized femininity—Connell's (1987) term for the current form of femininity that articulates with hegemonic masculinity—as many Second Wave feminists have experienced and criticized it, has been characterized by girls' and women's embodiments of oppressive conceptions of feminine beauty that symbolize and reify a thoroughly disempowered stance vis-à-vis men. To many Second Wave feminists, Barbie seemed to symbolize all that was oppressive about this femininity—the bodily self-surveillance, accompanying eating disorders, slavery to the dictates of the fashion industry, and compulsory heterosexuality. But Rogers (1999, 14) suggests that rather than representing an unambiguous image of emphasized femininity, perhaps Barbie represents a more paradoxical image of "emphatic femininity" that

> *takes feminine appearances and demeanor to unsustainable extremes. Nothing about Barbie ever looks masculine, even when she is on the police force.... Consistently, Barbie manages impressions so as to come across as a proper feminine creature even when she crosses boundaries usually dividing women from men. Barbie the firefighter is in no danger, then, of being seen as "one of the boys." Kids know that; parents and teachers know that; Mattel designers know that too.*

Recent Third Wave feminist theory sheds light on the different sensibilities of younger generations of girls and women concerning their willingness to display and play with this apparently paradoxical relationship between bodily experience (including "feminine" displays) and public empowerment. In Third Wave feminist texts, displays of feminine physical attractiveness and empowerment are not viewed as mutually exclusive or necessarily opposed realities, but as lived (if often paradoxical) aspects of the same reality (Heywood and Drake 1997). This embracing of the paradoxes of post-Second Wave femininity is manifested in many punk, or Riot Grrrl, subcultures (Klein 1997) and in popular culture in the resounding late 1990s' success of the Spice Girls' mantra of "Girl Power." This generational expression of "girl power" may today be part of "the pleasures of girl culture that Barbie stands for" (Spigel forthcoming). Indeed, as the Barbie Girls rallied around Barbie, their obvious pleasure did not appear to be based on a celebration of quiet passivity (as feminist parents might fear). Rather, it was a statement that they—the Barbie Girls—were here in this public space. They were not silenced by the boys' oppositional chanting. To the contrary, they ignored the boys, who seemed irrelevant to their celebration. And, when the boys later physically invaded their space, some of the girls responded by chasing the boys off. In short, when I pay attention to what the girls *did* (rather than imposing on the situation what I *think* Barbie "should" mean to the girls), I see a public moment of celebratory "girl power."

And this may give us better basis from which to analyze the boys' oppositional response. First, the boys may have been responding to the threat of displacement they may have felt while viewing the girls' moment of celebratory girl power. Second, the boys may simultaneously have been responding to the fears of feminine pollution that Barbie had come to symbolize to them. But why might Barbie symbolize feminine pollution to little boys? A brief example from my older son is instructive. When he was about three, following a fun day of play with the five-year-old girl next door, he enthusiastically asked me to buy him a Barbie like hers. He was gleeful when I took him to the store and bought him one. When we arrived home, his feet had barely hit the pavement getting out of the car before an eight-year-old neighbor boy laughed at and ridiculed him: "A *Barbie*? Don't you know that Barbie is a *girl's toy*?" No amount of parental intervention could counter this devastating peer-induced injunction against boys' playing with Barbie. My son's pleasurable desire for Barbie appeared almost overnight to transform itself into shame and rejection. The doll ended up at the bottom of a heap of toys in the closet, and my son soon became infatuated, along with other boys in his preschool, with Ninja Turtles and Power Rangers.

Research indicates that there is widespread agreement as to which toys are appropriate for one sex and polluting, dangerous, or inappropriate for the other sex. When Campenni (1999) asked adults to rate the gender appropriateness of children's toys, the toys considered most appropriate to girls were those pertaining to domestic tasks, beauty enhancement, or child rearing. Of the 206 toys rated, Barbie was rated second only to Makeup Kit as a female-only toy. Toys considered most appropriate to boys were those pertaining to sports gear (football gear was the most masculine-rated toy, while boxing gloves were third), vehicles, action figures (G. I. Joe was rated second only to football gear), and other war-related toys. This research on parents' gender stereotyping of toys reflects similar findings in research on children's toy preferences (Bradbard 1985; Robinson and Morris 1986). Children tend to avoid cross-sex toys, with boys' avoidance of feminine-coded toys appearing to be stronger than girls' avoidance of masculine-coded toys (Etaugh and Liss 1992). Moreover, preschool-age boys who perceive their fathers to be opposed to cross-gender-typed play are more likely than girls or other boys to think that it is "bad" for boys to play with toys that are labeled as "for girls" (Raag and Rackliff 1998).

By kindergarten, most boys appear to have learned—either through experiences similar to my son's, where other male persons police the boundaries of gender-appropriate play and fantasy and/or by watching the clearly gendered messages of television advertising—that Barbie dolls are not appropriate toys for boys (Rogers 1999, 30). To avoid ridicule, they learn to hide their desire for Barbie, either through denial and oppositional/pollution discourse and/or through sublimation of their desire for Barbie into play with male-appropriate "action figures" (Pope et al. 1999). In their study of a kindergarten classroom, Jordan and Cowan (1995, 728) identified "warrior narratives...that assume that violence is legitimate and justified when it occurs within a struggle between good and evil" to be the most commonly agreed-upon currency for boys' fantasy play. They observe that the boys seem commonly to adapt story lines that they have seen on television. Popular culture—film, video, computer games, television, and comic books—provides boys with a seemingly endless stream of Good Guys versus Bad Guys characters and stories—from cowboy movies, Superman and Spiderman to Ninja Turtles, Star Wars, and Pokémon—that are available for the boys to appropriate as the raw materials for the construction of their own warrior play.

In the kindergarten that Jordan and Cowan studied, the boys initially attempted to import their warrior narratives into the domestic setting of the "Doll Corner." Teachers eventually drove the boys' warrior play outdoors, while the Doll Corner was used by the girls for the "appropriate" domestic play for which it was originally intended. Jordan and Cowan argue that kindergarten teachers' outlawing of boys' warrior narratives inside the classroom contributed to boys' defining schools as a feminine environment, to which they responded with a resistant, underground continuation of masculine warrior play. Eventually though, boys who acquiesce and successfully sublimate warrior play into fantasy or sport are more successful in constructing what Connell (1989, 291) calls "a masculinity organized around themes of rationality and responsibility [that is] closely connected with the 'certification' function of the upper levels of the education system and to a key form of masculinity among professionals."

In contrast to the "rational/professional" masculinity constructed in schools, the institution of sport historically constructs hegemonic masculinity as *bodily superiority* over femininity and nonathletic masculinities (Messner 1992). Here, warrior narratives are allowed to publicly thrive—indeed, are openly celebrated (witness, for instance, the commentary of a televised NFL [National Football League] football game or especially the spectacle of televised professional wrestling). Preschool boys and kindergartners seem already to know this, easily adopting aggressively competitive team names and an us-versus-them attitude. By contrast, many of the youngest girls appear to take two or three years in organized soccer before they adopt, or partially accommodate themselves to, aggressively competitive discourse, indicated by the 10-year-old girls' shifting away from the use of sweet names toward more power names. In short, where the gender regime of preschool and grade school may be experienced as an environment in which mostly women leaders enforce rules that are hostile to masculine fantasy play and physicality, the gender regime of sport is experienced as a place where masculine styles and values of physicality, aggression, and competition are enforced and celebrated by mostly male coaches.

A cultural analysis suggests that the boys' and the girls' previous immersion in differently gendered cultural experiences shaped the likelihood that they would derive and construct different meanings from Barbie—the girls through pleasurable and symbolically empowering identification with "girl power" narratives; the boys through oppositional fears of feminine pollution (and fears of displacement by girl power?) and with aggressively verbal, and eventually physical, invasions of the girls' ritual space. The boys' collective response thus constituted them differently, *as boys*, in opposition to the girls' constitution of themselves *as girls*. An individual girl or boy, in this moment, who may have felt an inclination to dissent from the dominant feelings of the group (say, the Latina Barbie Girl who, her mother later told me, did not want the group to be identified with Barbie, or a boy whose immediate inner response to the Barbie Girls' joyful celebration might be to join in) is most likely silenced into complicity in this powerful moment of border work.

What meanings did this highly gendered moment carry for the boys' and girls' teams in the ensuing soccer season? Although I did not observe the Barbie Girls after the opening ceremony, I did continue to observe the Sea Monsters' weekly practices and games. During the boys' ensuing season, gender never reached this "magnified" level of salience again—indeed, gender was rarely raised verbally or performed overtly by the boys. On two occasions, though, I observed the coach jokingly chiding the boys during practice that "if you don't watch out, I'm going to get the Barbie Girls here to play against you!" This warning was followed by gleeful screams of agony and fear, and nervous hopping around and hugging by some of the boys. Normally, though, in this sex-segregated, all-male context, if boundaries were invoked, they were not boundaries between boys and girls but boundaries between the Sea Monsters and other boys' teams, or sometimes age boundaries between the Sea Monsters and a small group of dads and older brothers who would engage them in a mock scrimmage during practice. But it was also evident that when the coach was having trouble getting the boys to act together, as a group, his strategic and humorous invocation of the dreaded Barbie Girls once again served symbolically to affirm their group status. They were a team. They were the boys.

CONCLUSION

The overarching goal of this article has been to take one empirical observation from everyday life and demonstrate how a multilevel (interactionist, structural, cultural) analysis might reveal various layers of meaning that give insight into the everyday social construction of gender. This article builds on observations made by Thorne (1993) concerning ways to approach sociological analyses of children's worlds. The most fruitful approach is not to ask why boys and girls are so different but rather to ask how and under what conditions boys and girls constitute themselves as separate, oppositional groups. Sociologists need not debate whether gender is "there"— clearly, gender is always already there, built as it is into the structures, situations, culture, and consciousness of children and adults. The key issue is under what conditions gender is activated as a salient organizing principle in social life and under what conditions it may be less salient. These are important questions, especially since the social organization of categorical gender difference has always been so clearly tied to gender hierarchy (Acker 1990; Lorber 1994). In the Barbie Girls versus Sea Monsters moment, the performance of gendered boundaries and the construction of boys' and girls' groups as categorically different occurred in the context of a situation systematically structured by sex segregation, sparked by the imposing presence of a shared cultural symbol that is saturated with gendered meanings, and actively supported and applauded by adults who basked in the pleasure of difference, reaffirmed.[6]

I have suggested that a useful approach to the study of such "how" and "under what conditions" questions is to employ multiple levels of analysis. At the most general level, this project supports the following working propositions.

Interactionist theoretical frameworks that emphasize the ways that social agents "perform" or "do" gender are most useful in describing how groups of people actively create (or at times disrupt) the boundaries that delineate seemingly categorical differences between male persons and female persons. In this case, we saw how the children and the parents interactively performed gender in a way that constructed an apparently natural boundary between the two separate worlds of the girls and the boys.

Structural theoretical frameworks that emphasize the ways that gender is built into institutions through hierarchical sexual divisions of labor are most useful in explaining under what conditions social agents mobilize variously to disrupt or to affirm gender differences and inequalities. In this case, we saw how the sexual division of labor among parent volunteers (grounded in their own histories in the gender regime of sport), the formal sex segregation of the children's leagues, and the structured context of the opening ceremony created conditions for possible interactions between girls' teams and boys' teams.

Cultural theoretical perspectives that examine how popular symbols that are injected into circulation by the culture industry are variously taken up by differently situated people are most useful in analyzing how the meanings of cultural symbols, in a given institutional context, might trigger or be taken up by social agents and used as resources to reproduce, disrupt, or contest binary conceptions of sex difference and gendered relations of power. In this case, we saw how a girls' team appropriated a large Barbie around which to construct a pleasurable and empowering sense of group identity and how the boys' team responded with aggressive denunciations of Barbie and invasions.

Utilizing any one of the above theoretical perspectives by itself will lead to a limited, even distorted, analysis of the social construction of gender. Together, they can illuminate the complex, multileveled architecture of the social construction of gender in everyday life. For heuristic reasons, I have falsely separated structure, interaction, and culture. In fact, we need to explore their constant interrelationships, continuities, and contradictions. For instance, we cannot understand the boys' aggressive denunciations and invasions of the girls' space and the eventual clarification of categorical boundaries between the girls and the boys without first understanding how these boys and girls have already internalized four or five years of "gendering" experiences that have shaped their interactional tendencies and how they are already immersed in a culture of gendered symbols, including Barbie and sports media imagery. Although "only" preschoolers, they are already skilled in collectively taking up symbols from popular culture as resources to be used in their own group dynamics—building individual and group identities, sharing the pleasures of play, clarifying boundaries between in-group and out-group members, and constructing hierarchies in their worlds.

Furthermore, we cannot understand the reason that the girls first chose "Barbie Girls" as their team name without first understanding the fact that a particular institutional structure of AYSO soccer preexisted the girls' entrée into the league. The informal sexual division of labor among adults, and the formal sex segregation of children's teams, is a preexisting gender regime that constrains and enables the ways that the children enact gender relations and construct identities. One concrete manifestation of this constraining nature of sex segregated teams is the choice of team names. It is reasonable to speculate that if the four- and five-year-old children were still sex integrated, as in the pre-1995 era, no team would have chosen "Barbie Girls" as its team name, with Barbie as its symbol. In other words, the formal sex segregation created the conditions under which the girls were enabled—perhaps encouraged—to choose a "sweet" team name that is widely read as encoding feminine meanings. The eventual interactions between the boys and the girls were made possible—although by no means fully determined—by the structure of the gender regime and by the cultural resources that the children variously drew on.

On the other hand, the gendered division of labor in youth soccer is not seamless, static, or immune to resistance. One of the few woman head coaches, a very active athlete in her own right, told me that she is "challenging the sexism" in AYSO by becoming the head of her son's league. As post-Title IX women increasingly become mothers and as media images of competent, heroic female athletes become more a part of the cultural landscape for children, the gender regimes of children's sports may be increasingly challenged (Dworkin and Messner 1999). Put another way, the dramatically shifting opportunity structure and cultural imagery of post-Title IX sports have created opportunities for new kinds of interactions, which will inevitably challenge and further shift institutional structures. Social structures simultaneously constrain and enable, while agency is simultaneously reproductive and resistant.

NOTES

1. Most of the structural inventory presented here is from a content analysis of the 1998–99 regional American Youth Soccer League (AYSO) yearbook, which features photos and names of all of the teams, coaches, and managers. I counted the number of adult men and women occupying various positions. In the three cases where the sex category of a name was not immediately obvious (e.g., Rene or Terry), or in the five cases where simply a last name was listed, I did not count it. I also used the AYSO yearbook for my analysis of the children's team names. To check for reliability, another sociologist independently read and coded the list of team names. There was disagreement on how to categorize only 2 of the 156 team names.
2. The existence of some women coaches and some men team managers in this AYSO organization manifests a less extreme sexual division of labor than that of the same community's Little League baseball organization, in which there are proportionally far fewer women coaches. Similarly, Saltzman Chafetz and Kotarba's (1999, 52) study of parental labor in support of Little League baseball in a middle-class Houston community revealed an apparently absolute sexual division of labor, where nearly all of the supportive "activities off the field were conducted by the women in the total absence of men, while activities on the field were conducted by men and boys in the absence of women." Perhaps youth soccer, because of its more recent (mostly post-Title IX) history in the United States, is a more contested gender regime than the more patriarchally entrenched youth sports like Little League baseball or youth football.
3. The four- and five-year-old kids' games and practices were absolutely homosocial in terms of the kids, due to the formal structural sex segregation. However, 8 of the 12 girls' teams at this age level had male coaches, and 2 of the 14 boys' teams had female coaches.
4. By 1994, more than 800 million Barbies had been sold worldwide. More than $1 billion was spent on Barbies and accessories in 1992 alone. Two Barbie dolls were purchased every second in 1994, half of which were sold in the United States (DuCille 1994, 49).
5. Rogers (1999, 23) notes that if one extrapolates Barbie's bodily proportions to "real woman ones," she would be "33–18–31.5 and stand five feet nine inches tall, with fully half of her height accounted for by her 'shapely legs.'"
6. My trilevel analysis of structure, interaction, and culture may not be fully adequate to plumb the emotional depths of the magnified Barbie Girls versus Sea Monsters moment. Although it is beyond the purview of this article, an adequate rendering of the depths of pleasure and revulsion, attachment and separation, and commitment to ideologies of categorical sex difference may involve the integration of a fourth level of analysis: gender at the level of personality (Chodorow 1999). Object relations theory has fallen out of vogue in feminist sociology in recent years, but as Williams (1993) has argued, it might be most useful in revealing the mostly hidden social power of gender to shape people's unconscious predispositions to various structural contexts, cultural symbols, and interactional moments.

REFERENCES

Acker, Joan. 1990. Hierarchies, jobs, bodies: A theory of gendered organizations. *Gender & Society* 4:139–58.

Adler, Patricia A., and Peter Adler. 1998. *Peer power: Preadolescent culture and identity*. New Brunswick, NJ: Rutgers University Press.

Attfield, Judy. 1996. Barbie and Action Man: Adult toys for girls and boys, 1959–93. In *The gendered object*, edited by Pat Kirkham, 80–89. Manchester, UK, and New York: Manchester University Press.

Boyle, Maree, and Jim McKay. 1995. "You leave your troubles at the gate": A case study of the exploitation of older women's labor and "leisure" in sport. *Gender & Society* 9:556–76.

Bradbard, M. 1985. Sex differences in adults' gifts and children's toy requests. *Journal of Genetic Psychology* 145:283–84.

Butler, Judith. 1990. *Gender trouble: Feminism and the subversion of identity*. New York and London: Routledge.

Campenni, C. Estelle. 1999. Gender stereotyping of children's toys: A comparison of parents and nonparents. *Sex Roles* 40:121–38.

Chodorow, Nancy J. 1999. *The power of feelings: Personal meanings in psychoanalysis, gender, and culture*. New Haven, CT, and London: Yale University Press.

Connell, R.W. 1987. *Gender and power*. Stanford, CA: Stanford University Press.

———. 1989. Cool guys, swots and wimps: The interplay of masculinity and education. *Oxford Review of Education* 15:291–303.

DuCille, Anne. 1994. Dyes and dolls: Multicultural Barbie and the merchandising of difference. *Differences: A Journal of Cultural Studies* 6:46–68.

Dworkin, Shari L., and Michael A. Messner. 1999. Just do…what?: Sport, bodies, gender. In *Revisioning gender*, edited by Myra Marx Ferree, Judith Lorber, and Beth B. Hess, 341–61. Thousand Oaks, CA: Sage.

Etaugh, C., and M. B. Liss. 1992. Home, school, and playroom: Training grounds for adult gender roles. *Sex Roles* 26:129–47.

Heywood, Leslie, and Jennifer Drake, Eds. 1997. *Third wave agenda: Being feminist, doing feminism*. Minneapolis: University of Minnesota Press.

Hochschild, Arlie Russell. 1994. The commercial spirit of intimate life and the abduction of feminism: Signs from women's advice books. *Theory, Culture & Society* 11:1–24.

Jordan, Ellen, and Angela Cowan. 1995. Warrior narratives in the kindergarten classroom: Renogotiating the social contract? *Gender & Society* 9:727–43.

Kessler, Suzanne J., and Wendy McKenna. 1978. *Gender: An ethnomethodological approach*. New York: John Wiley.

Klein, Melissa. 1997. Duality and redefinition: Young feminism and the alternative music community. In *Third wave agenda: Being feminist, doing feminism*, edited by Leslie Heywood and Jennifer Drake, 207–25. Minneapolis: University of Minnesota Press.

Lorber, Judith. 1994. *Paradoxes of gender*. New Haven, CT, and London: Yale University Press.

McGuffy, C. Shawn, and B. Lindsay Rich. 1999. Playing in the gender transgression zone: Race, class and hegemonic masculinity in middle childhood. *Gender & Society* 13:608–27.

Messner, Michael A. 1992. *Power at play: Sports and the problem of masculinity*. Boston: Beacon.

Pope, Harrison G., Jr., Roberto Olivarda, Amanda Gruber, and John Borowiecki. 1999. Evolving ideals of male body image as seen through action toys. *International Journal of Eating Disorders* 26:65–72.

Raag, Tarja, and Christine L. Rackliff. 1998. Preschoolers' awareness of social expectations of gender: Relationships to toy choices. *Sex Roles* 38:685–700.

Rand, Erica. 1998. Older heads on younger bodies. In *The children's culture reader*, edited by Henry Jenkins, 382–93. New York: New York University Press.

Risman, Barbara. 1998. *Gender vertigo: American families in transition*. New Haven and London: Yale University Press.

Robinson, C. C., and J. T. Morris. 1986. The gender-stereotyped nature of Christmas toys received by 36-, 48-, and 60-month-old children: A comparison between nonrequested vs. requested toys. *Sex Roles* 15:21–32.

Rogers, Mary F. 1999. *Barbie culture*. Thousand Oaks, CA: Sage.

Saltzman Chafetz, Janet, and Joseph A. Kotarba. 1999. Little League mothers and the reproduction of gender. In *Inside sports*, edited by Jay Coakley and Peter Donnelly, 46–54. London and New York: Routledge.

Seiter, Ellen. 1995. *Sold separately: Parents and children in consumer culture*. New Brunswick, NJ: Rutgers University Press.

Spigel, Lynn. Forthcoming. Barbies without Ken: Femininity, feminism, and the art-culture system. In *Sitting room only: Television, consumer culture and the suburban home*, edited by Lynn Spigel. Durham, NC: Duke University Press.

Thorne, Barrie. 1993. *Gender play: Girls and boys in school*. New Brunswick, NJ: Rutgers University Press.

Walters, Suzanna Danuta. 1999. Sex, text, and context: (In) between feminism and cultural studies. In *Revisioning gender*, edited by Myra Marx Ferree, Judith Lorber, and Beth B. Hess, 222–57. Thousand Oaks, CA: Sage.

West, Candace, and Don Zimmerman. 1987. Doing gender. *Gender & Society* 1:125–51.

Williams, Christine. 1993. Psychoanalytic theory and the sociology of gender. In *Theory on gender, gender on theory*, edited by Paula England, 131–49. New York: Aldine.

QUESTIONS

? Messner emphasizes that parents of Barbie Girls *and* Sea Monsters seized upon the moment of conflict between the girls and boys to point out that there children were "so different." Are they right? Why or why not?

? Messner explains that cultural symbols like Barbie can be interpreted in different ways. Identify another cultural symbol that you think is gendered. Explain one typical and one non-typical way of interpreting this symbol.

? Societal lens question: Messner explores gender as an interaction, a cultural symbol, and a social structure. Select a moment in your life where "gender" became important. Describe the moment. Then, using each of Messner's levels, analyze what was going on during that moment.

Because She Looks like a Child

By KEVIN BALES

■ Siri, a fifteen-year old girl who lives in northeastern Thailand, looks like a child of eleven or twelve. But her life is far different than most fifteen year olds that most of us know. In the following account, author Kevin Bales, Director of Free the Slaves, an international agency dedicated to revealing and ending modern slavery, introduces an increasingly common fate of many poor young women (and young men) in the global economy—work in the global sex trade. While you are reading this article you should try to understand how industrialization, globalization, and class, gender, and race work together to put Siri and thousands like her in positions of modern day slavery.

When Siri wakes it is about noon.[1] In the instant of waking she knows exactly who and what she has become. As she explained to me, the soreness in her genitals reminds her of the fifteen men she had sex with the night before. Siri is fifteen years old. Sold by her parents a year ago, she finds that her resistance and her desire to escape the brothel are breaking down and acceptance and resignation are taking their place.

In the provincial city of Ubon Ratchathani, in northeastern Thailand, Siri works and lives in a brothel. About ten brothels and bars, dilapidated and dusty buildings, line the side street just around the corner from a new Western-style shopping mall. Food and noodle vendors are scattered between the brothels. The woman behind the noodle stall outside the brothel where Siri works is also a spy, warder, watchdog, procurer, and dinner lady to Siri and the other twenty-four girls and women in the brothel.

The brothel is surrounded by a wall, with iron gates that meet the street. Within the wall is a dusty yard, a concrete picnic table, and the ubiquitous spirit house, a small shrine that stands outside all Thai buildings. A low door leads into a windowless concrete room that is thick with the smell of cigarettes, stale beer, vomit, and sweat. This is the "selection" room (*hong du*). On one side of the room are stained and collapsing tables and booths; on the other side is a narrow elevated platform with a bench that runs the length of the room. Spotlights pick

---

Excerpts from "Thailand: Because She Looks Like a Child", pages 34–79 (excluding section on Burmese Prostitutes), Source: Chapter 2 of *Disposable People: New Slavery in the Global Economy*, Revised Edition, 2004, Berkely: University of California Press, author: Kevin Bales.

out this bench, and at night the girls and women sit here under the glare while the men at the tables drink and choose the one they want.

Passing through another door, at the far end of the bench, the man follows the girl past a window, where a bookkeeper takes his money and records which girl he has selected. From there he is led to the girl's room. Behind its concrete front room, the brothel degenerates even further, into a haphazard shanty warren of tiny cubicles where the girls live and work. A makeshift ladder leads up to what may have once been a barn. The upper level is now lined with doors about five feet apart, which open into rooms of about five by seven feet that hold a bed and little else.

Scraps of wood and cardboard separate one room from the next, and Siri has plastered her walls with pictures of teenage pop stars cut from magazines. Over her bed, as in most rooms, there also hangs a framed portrait of the king of Thailand; a single bare lightbulb dangles from the ceiling. Next to the bed a large tin can holds water; there is a hook nearby for rags and towels. At the foot of the bed, next to the door, some clothes are folded on a ledge. The walls are very thin, and everything can be heard from the surrounding rooms; a shout from the bookkeeper echoes through all of them, whether their doors are open or closed.

After rising at midday, Siri washes herself in cold water from the single concrete trough that serves the brothel's twenty-five women. Then, dressed in a T-shirt and skirt, she goes to the noodle stand for the hot soup that is a Thai breakfast. Through the afternoon, if she does not have any clients, she chats with the other girls and women as they drink beer and play cards or make decorative handicrafts together. If the pimp is away the girls will joke around, but if not they must be constantly deferential and aware of his presence, for he can harm them or use them as he pleases. Few men visit in the afternoon, but those who do tend to have more money and can buy a girl for several hours if they like. Some will even make appointments a few days in advance.

At about five, Siri and the other girls are told to dress, put on their makeup, and prepare for the night's work. By seven the men will be coming in, purchasing drinks, and choosing girls; Siri will be chosen by the first of the ten to eighteen men who will buy her that night. Many men choose Siri because she looks much younger than her fifteen years. Slight and round faced, dressed to accentuate her youth, she could pass for eleven or twelve. Because she looks like a child, she can be sold as a "new" girl at a higher price, about $15, which is more than twice that charged for the other girls.

Siri is very frightened that she will get AIDS. Long before she understood prostitution she knew about HIV, as many girls from her village returned home to die from AIDS after being sold into the brothels. Every day she prays to Buddha, trying to earn the merit that will preserve her from the disease. She also tries to insist that her clients use condoms, and in most cases she is successful, because the pimp backs her up. But when policemen use her, or the pimp himself, they will do as they please; if she tries to insist, she will be beaten and raped. She also fears pregnancy, but like the other girls she receives injections of the contraceptive drug Depo-Provera. Once a month she has an HIV test. So far it has been negative. She knows that if she tests positive she will be thrown out to starve.

Though she is only fifteen, Siri is now resigned to being a prostitute. The work is not what she had thought it would be. Her first client hurt her, and at the first opportunity she ran away. She was quickly caught, dragged back, beaten, and raped. That night she was forced to take on a chain of clients until the early morning. The beatings and the work continued night after night, until her will was broken. Now she is sure that she is a very bad person to have deserved what has happened to her. When I comment on how pretty she looks in a photograph, how like a pop star, she replies, "I'm no star; I'm just a whore, that's all." She copes as best she can. She takes a dark pride in her higher price and the large number of men who choose her. It is the adjustment of the concentration camp, an effort to make sense of horror.

In Thailand prostitution is illegal, yet girls like Siri are sold into sex slavery by the thousands. The brothels that hold these girls are but a small part of a much wider sex industry. How can this wholesale trade in girls continue? What keeps it working? The answer is more complicated than we might think. Thailand's economic boom and its social acceptance of prostitution contribute to the pressures that enslave girls like Siri.

RICE IN THE FIELD. FISH IN THE RIVER. DAUGHTERS IN THE BROTHEL.

Thailand is blessed with natural resources and sufficient food. The climate is mild to hot, there is dependable rain, and most of the country is a great plain, well watered and fertile. The reliable production of rice has for centuries made Thailand a large exporter of grains, as it is today. Starvation is exceedingly rare in its history, and social stability very much the norm. An old and often-repeated saying in Thai is "There is always rice in the fields and fish in the river." And anyone who has tried the imaginative Thai cuisine knows the remarkable things that can be done with those two ingredients and the local chili peppers.

One part of Thailand that is not so rich in necessities of life is the mountainous north. In fact, that area is not Thailand proper; originally the kingdom of Lanna, it was integrated into Thailand only in the late nineteenth century The influence of Burma here is very strong—as are the cultures of the seven main hill tribes, which are distinctly foreign to the dominant Thai society. Only about a tenth of the land of the north can be used for agriculture, though what can be used is the most fertile in the country. The result is that those who control good land are well-off; those who live in the higher elevations, in the forest, are not. In another part of the world this last group might be called hillbillies, and they share the hardscrabble life of mountain dwellers everywhere.

The harshness of this life stands in sharp contrast to that on the great plain of rice and fish. Customs and culture differ markedly as well, and one of those differences is a key to the sexual slavery practiced throughout Thailand today. For hundreds of years many people in the north, struggling for life, have been forced to view their own children as commodities. A failed harvest, the death of a key breadwinner, or any serious debt incurred by a family might lead to the sale of a daughter (never a son) as a slave or servant. In the culture of the north it was a life choice not preferred but acceptable, and one that was used regularly. In the past these sales fed a small, steady flow of servants, workers, and prostitutes south into Thai society.

ONE GIRL EQUALS ONE TELEVISION

The small number of children sold into slavery in the past has become a flood today. This increase reflects the enormous changes in Thailand over the past fifty years as the country has gone through the great transformation of industrialization—the same process that tore Europe apart over a century ago. If we are to understand slavery in Thailand, we must understand these changes as well, for like so many other parts of the world, Thailand has always had slavery, but never before on this scale.

The economic boom of 1977 to 1997 had a dramatic impact on the northern villages. While the center of the country, around Bangkok, rapidly industrialized, the north was left behind. Prices of food, land, and tools all increased as the economy grew, but the returns for rice and other agriculture were stagnant, held down by government policies guaranteeing cheap food for factory workers in Bangkok. Yet visible everywhere in the north is a flood of consumer goods—refrigerators, televisions, cars and trucks, rice cookers, air conditioners—all of which are extremely tempting. Demand for these goods is high as families try to join the ranks of the prosperous. As it happens, the cost of participating in this consumer boom can be met from an old source that has become much more profitable: the sale of children.

In the past, daughters were sold in response to serious family financial crises. Under threat of losing its mortgaged rice fields and facing destitution, a family might sell a daughter to redeem its debt, but for the most part daughters were worth about as much at home as workers as they would realize when sold. Modernization and economic growth have changed all that. Now parents feel a great pressure to buy consumer goods that were unknown even twenty years ago; the sale of a daughter might easily finance a new television set. A recent survey in the northern provinces found that of the families who sold their daughters, two-thirds could afford not to do so but "instead preferred to buy color televisions and video equipment."[2] And from the perspective of parents who are willing to sell their children, there has never been a better market.

The brothels' demand for prostitutes is rapidly increasing. The same economic boom that feeds consumer demand in the northern villages lines the pockets of laborers and workers in the central plain. Poor economic migrants from the rice fields now work on building sites or in new factories, earning many times what they did on the land. Possibly for the first time in their lives, these laborers can do what more well-off Thai men have always done: go to a brothel. The purchasing power of this increasing number of brothel users strengthens the call for northern girls and supports a growing business in their procurement and trafficking.

Siri's story was typical. A broker, a woman herself from a northern village, approached the families in Siri's village with assurances of well-paid work for their daughters. Siri's parents probably understood that the work would be as a prostitute, since they knew that other girls from their village had gone south to brothels. After some negotiation they were paid 50,000 baht (US$2,000) for Siri, a very significant sum for this family of rice farmers.[3] This exchange began the process of debt bondage that is used to enslave the girls. The contractual arrangement between the broker and the parents requires that this money be paid by the daughter's labor before she is free to leave or is allowed to send money home. Sometimes the money is treated as a loan to the parents, the girls being both the collateral and the means of repayment. In such cases the exorbitant interest charged on the loan means there is little chance that a girl's sexual slavery will ever repay the debt.

Siri's debt of 50,000 baht rapidly escalated. Taken south by the broker, Siri was sold for 100,000 baht to the brothel where she now works. After her rape and beating Siri was informed that the debt she must repay to the brothel equaled 200,000 baht. In addition, Siri learned of the other payments she would be required to make, including rent for her room, at 30,000 baht per month, as well as charges for food and drink, fees for medicine, and fines if she did not work hard enough or displeased a customer.

The total debt is virtually impossible to repay, even at Siri's higher rate of 400 baht. About 100 baht from each client is supposed to be credited to Siri to reduce her debt and pay her rent and other expenses; 200 goes to the pimp and the remaining 100 to the brothel. By this reckoning, Siri must have sex with three hundred men a month just to pay her rent, and what is left over after other expenses barely reduces her original debt. For girls who can charge only 100 to 200 baht per client, the debt grows even faster. This debt bondage keeps the girls under complete control as long as the brothel owner and the pimp believe they are worth having. Violence reinforces the control, and any resistance earns a beating as well as an increase in the debt. Over time, if the girl becomes a good and cooperative prostitute, the pimp may tell her she has paid off the debt and allow her to send small sums home. This "paying off" of the debt usually has nothing to do with an actual accounting of earnings but is declared at the discretion of the pimp, as a means to extend the brothel's profits by making the girl more pliable. Together with rare visits home, money sent back to the family operates to keep her at her job.

Most girls are purchased from their parents, as Siri was, but for others the enslavement is much more direct. Throughout Thailand agents travel to villages, offering work in factories or as domestics. Sometimes they bribe local officials to vouch for them, or they befriend the monks at the local temple to gain introductions. Lured by the promise of good jobs and the money that the daughters will send back to the village, the deceived families dispatch their girls with the agent, often paying for the privilege. Once they arrive in a city, the girls are sold to a brothel, where they are raped, beaten, and locked in. Still other girls are simply kidnapped. This is especially true of women and children who have come to visit relatives in Thailand from Burma or Laos. At bus and train stations, gangs watch for women and children who can be snatched or drugged for shipment to brothels.

Direct enslavement by trickery or kidnapping is not really in the economic interest of the brothel owners. The steadily growing market for prostitutes, the loss of girls to HIV infection, and the especially strong demand for younger and younger girls make it necessary for brokers and brothel owners to cultivate village families so that they can buy more daughters as they come of age. In Siri's case this means letting her maintain ties with her family and ensuring that after a year or so she send a monthly postal order for 10,000 baht to her parents. The monthly payment is a good investment, since it encourages Siri's parents to place their other daughters in the brothel as well. Moreover, the young girls themselves become willing to go when their older sisters and relatives returning for holidays bring stories of the rich life to be lived in the cities of the central plain. Village girls lead a sheltered life, and the appearance of women only a little older than themselves with money and nice clothes is tremendously appealing. They admire the results of this thing called prostitution with only the vaguest notion of what it is. Recent research found that young girls knew that their sisters and neighbors had become prostitutes, but when asked what it means to be a prostitute their most common answer was "wearing Western clothes in a restaurant."[4] Drawn by this glamorous life, they put up little opposition to being sent away with the brokers to swell an already booming sex industry.

By my own conservative estimate there are perhaps thirty-five thousand girls like Siri enslaved in Thailand. Remarkably, this is only a small proportion of the country's prostitutes. In the mid-1990s the government stated that there were 81,384 prostitutes in Thailand—but that official number is calculated from the number of registered (though still illegal) brothels, massage parlors, and sex establishments. One Thai researcher estimated the total number of prostitutes in 1997 to be around 200,000.[5] Every brothel, bar, and massage parlor we visited in Thailand was unregistered, and no one working with prostitutes believes the government figures. At the other end of the spectrum are the estimates put forward by activist organizations such as the Center for the Protection of Children's Rights. These groups assert that there are more than 2 million prostitutes. I suspect that this number is too high in a national population of 60 million. My own reckoning, based on information gathered by AIDS workers in different cities, is that there are between half a million and 1 million prostitutes.

Of this number, only about one in twenty is enslaved. Most become prostitutes voluntarily, through some start out in debt bondage. Sex is sold everywhere in Thailand: barbershops, massage parlors, coffee shops and cafés, bars and restaurants, nightclubs and karaoke bars, brothels, hotels, and even temples traffic in sex. Prostitutes range from the high-earning "professional" women who work with some autonomy, through the women working by choice as call girls or in massage parlors, to the enslaved rural girls like Siri. Many women work semi-independently in bars, restaurants, and nightclubs—paying a fee to the owner, working when they choose, and having the power to decide whom to take as a customer. Most bars and clubs cannot use an enslaved prostitute like Siri, as the women are often sent out on call and their clients expect a certain amount of cooperation and friendliness. Enslaved girls serve the lowest end of the market: the laborers, students, and workers who can afford only the 100 baht per half hour. It is low-cost sex in volume, and the demand is always there. For a Thai man, buying a woman is much like buying a round of drinks. But the reasons why such large numbers of Thai men use prostitutes are much more complicated and grow out of their culture, their history, and a rapidly changing economy.

"I DON'T WANT TO WASTE IT, SO I TAKE HER"

Until it was officially disbanded in 1910, the king of Thailand maintained a harem of hundreds of concubines, a few of whom might be elevated to the rank of "royal mother" or "minor wife." This form of polygamy was closely imitated by status-hungry nobles and emerging rich merchants of the nineteenth century. Virtually all men of any substance kept at least a mistress or a minor wife. For those with fewer resources, prostitution was a perfectly acceptable option, as renting took the place of out-and-out ownership.

Even today everyone in Thailand knows his or her place within a very elaborate and precise status system. Mistresses and minor wives continue to enhance any man's social standing, but the consumption of commercial sex has increased dramatically.[6] If an economic boom is a tide that raises all boats, then vast numbers of Thai men have now been raised to a financial position from which they can regularly buy sex. Nothing like the economic growth in Thailand was ever experienced in the West, but a few facts show its scale: in a country the size of Britain, one-tenth of the workforce moved from the land to industry in just the three years from 1993 to 1995; the number of factory workers doubled from less than 2 million to more than 4 million in the eight years from 1988 to 1995; and urban wages doubled from 1986 to 1996. Thailand is now the world's largest importer of motorcycles and the second-largest importer of pickup tricks, after the United States. Until the economic downturn of late 1997, money flooded Thailand, transforming poor rice farmers into wage laborers and fueling consumer demand.

With this newfound wealth, Thai men go to brothels in increasing numbers. Several recent studies show that between 80 and 87 percent of Thai men have had sex with a prostitute. Most report that their first sexual experience was with a prostitute. Somewhere between 10 and 40 percent of married men have paid for commercial sex within the past twelve months, as have up to 50 percent of single men. Though it is difficult to measure, these reports suggest something like 3 to 5 million regular customers for commercial sex. But it would be wrong to imagine millions of Thai men sneaking furtively on their own along dark streets lined with brothels; commercial sex is a social event, part of a good night out with friends. Ninety-five percent of men going to a brothel do so with their friends, usually at the end of a night spent drinking. Groups go out for recreation and entertainment, and especially to get drunk together. That is a strictly male pursuit, as Thai women usually abstain from alcohol. All-male groups out for a night on the town are considered normal in any Thai city, and whole neighborhoods are devoted to serving them. One man interviewed in a recent study explained, "When we arrive at the brothel, my friends take one and pay for me to take another. It costs them money; I don't want to waste it, so I take her."[7] Having one's prostitute paid for also brings an informal obligation to repay in kind at a later date. Most Thais, men and women, feel that commercial sex is an acceptable part of an ordinary outing for single men, and about two-thirds of men and one-third of women feel the same about married men.[8]

For most married women, having their husbands go to prostitutes is preferable to other forms of extramarital sex. Most wives accept that men naturally want multiple partners, and prostitutes are seen as less threatening to the stability of the family.[9] Prostitutes require no long-term commitment or emotional involvement. When a husband uses a prostitute he is thought to be fulfilling a male role, but when he takes a minor wife or mistress, his wife is thought to have failed. Minor wives are usually bigamous second wives, often married by law in a district different than that of the men's first marriage (easily done, since no national records are kept). As wives, they require upkeep, housing, and regular support, and their offspring have a claim on inheritance; so they present a significant danger to the well-being of the major wife and her children. The potential disaster for the first wife is a minor wife who convinces the man to leave his first family, and this happens often enough to keep first wives worried and watchful.

For many Thai men, commercial sex is a legitimate form of entertainment and sexual release. It is not just acceptable: it is a clear statement of status and economic power. Such attitudes reinforce the treatment of women as mere markers in a male game of status and prestige. Combined with the new economy's relentless drive for profits, the result for women can be horrific. Thousands more must be found to feed men's status needs, thousands more must be locked into sexual slavery to feed the profits of investors. And what are the police, government, and local authorities doing about slavery? Every case of sex slavery involves many crimes—fraud, kidnap, assault, rape, sometimes murder. These crimes are not rare or random; they are systematic and repeated in brothels thousands of times each month. Yet those with the power to stop this terror instead help it continue to grow and to line the pockets of the slaveholders.

MILLIONAIRE TIGER AND BILLIONAIRE GEESE

Who are these modern slaveholders? The answer is anyone and everyone—anyone, that is, with a little capital to invest. The people who *appear* to own the enslaved prostitutes—the pimps, madams, and brothel keepers—are usually just employees. As hired muscle, pimps and their helpers provide the brutality that controls women and makes possible their commercial exploitation. Although they are just employees, the pimps do rather well for themselves. Often living in the brothel, they receive a salary and add to that income by a number of scams; for example, food and drinks are sold to customers at inflated prices, and the pimps pocket the difference. Much more lucrative is their control of the price of sex. While each woman has a basic price, the pimps size up each customer and pitch the fee accordingly. In this way a client may pay two or three times more than the normal rate, and all of the surplus goes to the pimp. In league with the bookkeeper, the pimp systematically cheats the prostitutes of the little that is supposed to be credited against their debt. If they manage the sex slaves well and play all of the angles, pimps can easily make ten times their basic wage—a great income for an ex-peasant whose main skills are violence and intimidation, but nothing compared to the riches to be made by the brokers and the real slaveholders.

The brokers and agents who buy girls in the villages and sell them to brothels are only short-term slaveholders. Their business is part recruiting agency, part shipping company, part public relations, and part kidnapping gang. They aim to buy low and sell high while maintaining a good flow of girls from the villages. Brokers are equally likely to be men or women, and they usually come from the regions in which they recruit. Some are local people dealing in girls in addition to their jobs as police officers, government bureaucrats, or even schoolteachers. Positions of public trust are excellent starting points for buying young girls. In spite of the character of their work, they are well respected. Seen as job providers and sources of large cash payments to parents, they are well known in their communities. Many of the women brokers were once sold themselves; some spent years as prostitutes and now, in their middle age, make their living by supplying girls to the brothels. These women are walking advertisements for sexual slavery. Their lifestyle and income, their Western clothes and glamorous, sophisticated ways promise a rosy economic future for the girls they buy. That they have physically survived their years in the brothel may be the exception—many more young women come back to the village to die of AIDS—but the parents tend to be optimistic.

Whether these dealers are local people or traveling agents, they combine the business of procuring with other economic pursuits. A returned prostitute may live with her family, look after her parents, own a rice field or two, and buy and sell girls on the side. Like the pimps, they are in a good business, doubling their money on each girl within two or three weeks; but also like the pimps, their profits are small compared to those of the long-term slaveholders.

The real slaveholders tend to be middle-aged businessmen. They fit seamlessly into the community, and they suffer no social discrimination for what they do. If anything, they are admired as successful, diversified capitalists. Brothel ownership is normally only one of many business interests for the slaveholder. To be sure, a brothel owner may have some ties to organized crime, but in Thailand organized crime includes the police and much of the government. Indeed, the work of the modern slaveholder is best seen not as aberrant criminality but as a perfect example of disinterested capitalism. Owning the brothel that holds young girls in bondage is simply a business matter. The investors would say that they are creating jobs and wealth. There is no hypocrisy in their actions, for they obey an important social norm: earning a lot of money is good enough reason for anything.

The slaveholder may in fact be a partnership, company, or corporation. In the 1980s, Japanese investment poured into Thailand, in an enormous migration of capital that was called "Flying Geese."[10] The strong yen led to buying and building across the country, and while electronics firms built television factories, other investors found that there was much, much more to be made in the sex industry. Following the Japanese came investment from the so-called Four Tigers (South Korea, Hong Kong, Taiwan, and Singapore), which also found marvelous opportunities in commercial sex. (All five of these countries further proved to be strong import markets for enslaved Thai girls, as discussed below.) The Geese and the Tigers had the resources to buy the local criminals, police, administrators, and property needed to set up commercial sex businesses. Indigenous Thais also invested in brothels as the sex industry boomed; with less capital, they were more likely to open poorer, working-class outlets.

Whether they are individual Thais, partnerships, or foreign investors, the slaveholders share many characteristics. There is little or no racial or ethnic difference between them and the slaves they own (with the exception of the Japanese investors). They feel no need to rationalize their slaveholding on racial grounds. Nor are they linked in any sort of hereditary ownership of slaves or of the children of their slaves. They are not really interested in their slaves at all, just in the bottom line on then investment.

To understand the business of slavery today we have to know something about the economy in which it operates. Thailand's economic boom included a sharp increase in sex tourism tacitly backed by the government International tourist arrivals jumped from 2 million in. 1981 to 4 million in 1988 to over 7 million in 1996.[11] Two-thirds of tourists were unaccompanied men; in other words, nearly 5 million unaccompanied men visited Thailand in 1996. A significant proportion of these were sex tourists.

The recent downturn in both tourism and the economy may have slowed, but not dramatically altered, sex tourism. In 1997 the annual illegal income generated by sex workers in Thailand was roughly $10 billion, which is more than drug trafficking is estimated to generate.[12] According to ECPAT, an organization working against child prostitution, the economic crisis in Southeast Asia may have increased the exploitation of young people in sex tourism:

> *According to Professor Lae Dilokvidhayarat from Chulalongkorn University, there has been a 10 percent decrease in the school enrollment at primary school level in Thailand since 1996. Due to increased unemployment, children cannot find work in the formal sector, but instead are forced to "disappear" into the informal sector. This makes them especially vulnerable to sexual exploitation. Also, a great number of children are known to travel to tourist areas and to big cities hoping to find work.*
>
> *We cannot overlook the impact of the economic crisis on sex tourism, either. Even though travelling costs to Asian countries are approximately the same as before mid 1997, when the crisis began, the rates for sexual services in many places are lower due to increased competition in the business. Furthermore, since there are more children trying to earn money, there may also be more so called situational child sex tourists, i.e. those who do not necessarily prefer children as sexual partners, but who may well choose a child if the situation occurs and the price is low."*[13]

In spite of the economic boom, the average Thai's income is very low by Western standards. Within an industrializing country, millions still live in rural poverty. If a rural family owns its house and has a rice field, it might survive on as little as 500 baht ($20) per month. Such absolute poverty means a diet of rice supplemented with insects (crickets, grubs, and maggots are widely eaten), wild plants, and what fish the family can catch. If a family's standard of living drops below this level, which can be sustained only in the countryside, it faces hunger and the loss of its house or land. For most Thais, an income of 2,500 to 4,000 baht per month ($100 to $180) is normal. Government figures from December 1996 put two-thirds of the population at this level. There is no system of welfare or health care, and pinched budgets allow no space for saving. In these families, the 20,000 to 50,000 baht ($800 to $2,000) brought by selling a daughter provides a year's income. Such a vast sum is a powerful inducement that often blinds parents to the realities of sexual slavery.

DISPOSABLE BODIES

Girls are so cheap that there is little reason to take care of them over the long term. Expenditure on medical care or prevention is rare in the brothels, since the working life of girls in debt bondage is fairly short—two to five years. After that, most of the profit has been drained from the girl and it is more cost-effective to discard her and replace her with someone fresh. No brothel wants to take on the responsibility of a sick or dying girl.

Enslaved prostitutes in brothels face two major threats to their physical health and to their lives: violence and disease. Violence—their enslavement enforced through rape, beatings, or threats—is always present. It is a girl's typical introduction to her new status as a sex slave. Virtually every girl interviewed repeated the same story: after she was taken to the brothel or to her first client as a virgin, any resistance or refusal was met with beatings and rape. A few girls reported being drugged and then attacked; others reported being forced to submit at gunpoint. The immediate and forceful application of terror is the first step in successful enslavement. Within hours of being brought to the brothel, the girls are in pain and shock. Like other victims of torture they often go numb, paralyzed in their minds if not in their bodies. For the youngest girls, who understand little of what is happening to them, the trauma is overwhelming. Shattered and betrayed, they often have few clear memories of what occurred.

After the first attack, the girl has little resistance left, but the violence never ends. In the brothel, violence and terror are the final arbiters of all questions. There is no argument; there is no appeal. An unhappy customer brings a beating, a sadistic client brings more pain; in order to intimidate and cheat them more easily, the pimp rains down terror randomly on the prostitutes. The girls must do anything the pimp wants if they are to avoid being beaten. Escape is impossible. One girl reported that when she was caught trying to escape, the pimp beat her and then took her into the viewing room; with two helpers he then beat her again in front of all the girls in the brothel. Afterward she was locked into a room for three days and nights with no food or water. When she was released she was immediately put to work. Two other girls who attempted escape told of being stripped naked and whipped with steel coat hangers by pimps. The police serve as slave catchers whenever a girl escapes; once captured, girls are often beaten or abused at the police station before being sent back to the brothel. For most girls it soon becomes clear that they can never escape, that their only hope for release is to please the pimp and to somehow pay off their debt.

In time, confusion and disbelief fade, leaving dread, resignation, and a break in the conscious link between mind and body. Now the girl does whatever it takes to reduce the pain, to adjust mentally to a life that means being used by fifteen men a day. The reaction to this abuse takes many forms: lethargy, aggression, self-loathing, suicide attempts, confusion, self-abuse, depression, full-blown psychoses, and hallucinations. Girls who have been freed and taken into shelters exhibit all of these disorders. Rehabilitation workers report that the girls suffer emotional instability; they are unable to trust or to form relationships, to readjust to the world outside the brothel, or to learn and develop normally. Unfortunately, psychological counseling is virtually unknown in Thailand, as there is a strong cultural pressure to keep mental problems hidden. As a result, little therapeutic work is done with girls freed from brothels. The long-term impact of their experience is unknown.

The prostitute faces physical dangers as well as emotional ones. There are many sexually transmitted diseases, and prostitutes contract most of them. Multiple infections weaken the immune system and make it easier for other infections to take hold. If the illness affects a girl's ability to have sex, it may be dealt with, but serious chronic illnesses are often left untreated. Contraception often harms the girls as well. Some slaveholders administer contraceptive pills themselves, continuing them without any break and withholding the monthly placebo pills so that the girls can work more nights of the month. These girls stop menstruating altogether.

Not surprisingly, HIV/AIDS is epidemic in enslaved prostitutes. Thailand now has one of the highest rates of HIV infection in the world. Officially, the government admits to 800,000 cases, but health workers insist there are at least twice that many. Mechai Veravaidya, a birth-control campaigner and expert who has been so successful that *mechai* is now the Thai word for condom, predicts there will be 4.3 million people infected with HIV by 2001.[14] In some rural villages from which girls are regularly trafficked, the infection rate is over 60 percent. Recent research suggests that the younger the girl, the more susceptible she is to HIV, because her protective vaginal mucous membrane has not fully developed. Although the government distributes condoms, some brothels do not require their use.

TO JAPAN, SWITZERLAND, GERMANY, THE UNITED STATES

Women and girls flow in both directions over Thailand's borders.[18] The export of enslaved prostitutes is a robust business, supplying brothels in Japan, Europe, and America. Thailand's Ministry of Foreign Affairs estimated in 1994 that as many as 50,000 Thai women were living illegally in Japan and working in prostitution. Their situation in these countries parallels that of Burmese women held in Thailand. The enticement of Thai women follows a familiar pattern. Promised work as cleaners, domestics, dishwashers, or cooks, Thai girls and women pay large fees to employment agents to secure jobs in rich, developed countries. When they arrive, they are brutalized and enslaved. Their debt bonds are significantly larger than those of enslaved prostitutes in Thailand, since they include airfares, bribes to immigration officials, the costs of false passports, and sometimes the fees paid to foreign men to marry them and ease their entry.

Variations on sex slavery occur in different countries. In Switzerland girls are brought in on "artist" visas as exotic dancers. There, in addition to being prostitutes, they must work as striptease dancers in order to meet the carefully checked terms of their employment. The brochures of the European companies that have leaped into the sex-tourism business leave the customer no doubt about what is being sold:

Slim, sunburnt, and sweet, they love the white man in an erotic and devoted way. They are masters of the art of making love by nature, an art that we Europeans do not know. (Life Travel, Switzerland) [M]any girls from the sex world come from the poor north-eastern region of the country and from the slums of Bangkok. It has become a custom that one of the nice looking daughters goes into the business in order to earn money for the poor family...[Y]ou can get the feeling that taking a girl here is as easy as buying a package of cigarettes... little slaves who give real Thai warmth. (Kanita Kamha Travel, the Netherlands).[15]

In Germany they are usually bar girls, and they are sold to men by the bartender or bouncer. Some are simply placed in brothels or apartments controlled by pimps. After Japanese sex tours to Thailand began in the 1980s, Japan rapidly became the largest importer of Thai women. The fear of HIV in Japan has also increased the demand for virgins. Because of their large disposable incomes, Japanese men are able to pay considerable sums for young rural girls from Thailand. Japanese organized crime is involved throughout the importation process, sometimes shipping women via Malaysia or the Philippines. In the cities, the Japanese mob maintains bars and brothels that trade in Thai women. Bought and sold between brothels, these women are controlled with extreme violence. Resistance can bring murder. Because the girls are illegal aliens and often enter the country under false passports, Japanese gangs rarely hesitate to kill them if they have ceased to be profitable or if they have angered their slaveholders. Thai women deported from Japan also report that the gangs will addict girls to drugs in order to manage them more easily.

Criminal gangs, usually Chinese or Vietnamese, also control brothels in the United States that enslave Thai women. Police raids in New York, Seattle, San Diego, and Los Angeles have freed more than a hundred girls and women.[16] In New York, thirty Thai women were locked into the upper floors of a building used as a brothel. Iron bars sealed the windows and a series of buzzer-operated armored gates blocked exit to the street. During police raids, the women were herded into a secret basement room. At her trial, the brothel owner testified that she'd bought the women outright, paying between $6,000 and $15,000 for each. The women were charged $300 per week for room and board; they worked from 11:00 A.M. until 4:00 A.M. and were sold by the hour to clients. Chinese and Vietnamese gangsters were also involved in the brothel, collecting protection money and hunting down escaped prostitutes. The gangs owned chains of brothels and massage parlors, through which they rotated the Thai women in order to defeat law enforcement efforts. After being freed from the New York brothel, some of the women disappeared—only to turn up weeks later in similar circumstances three thousand miles away, in Seattle. One of the rescued Thai women, who had been promised restaurant work and then enslaved, testified that the brothel owners "bought something and wanted to use it to the full extent, and they didn't think those people were human beings."[17]

OFFICIAL INDIFFERENCE AND A GROWTH ECONOMY

In many ways, Thailand closely resembles another country, one that was going through rapid industrialization and economic boom one hundred years ago. Rapidly shifting its labor force off the farm, experiencing unprecedented economic growth, flooded with economic migrants, and run by corrupt politicians and a greedy and criminal police force, the United States then faced many of the problems confronting Thailand today. In the 1890s, political machines that brought together organized crime with politicians and police ran the prostitution and protection rackets, drug sales, and extortion in American cities. Opposing them were a weak and disorganized reform movement and a muckraking press. I make this comparison because it is important to explore why Thailand's government is so ineffective when faced with the enslavement of its own citizens, and also to remember that conditions *can* change over time. Discussions with Thais about the horrific nature of sex slavery often end with their assertion that "nothing will ever change this...the problem is just too big...and those with power will never allow change." Yet the social and economic underpinnings of slavery in Thailand are always changing, sometimes for the worse and sometimes for the better. No society can remain static, particularly one undergoing such upheavals as Thailand.

As the country takes on a new Western-style materialist morality, the ubiquitous sale of sex sends a clear message: women can be enslaved and exploited for profit. Sex tourism helped set the stage for the expansion of sexual slavery.

Sex tourism also generates some of the income that Thai men use to fund their own visits to brothels. No one knows how much money it pours into the Thai economy, but if we assume that just one-quarter of sex workers serve sex tourists and that their customers pay about the same as they would pay to use Siri, then 656 billion baht ($26.2 billion) a year would be about right. This is thirteen times more than the amount Thailand earns by building and exporting computers, one of the country's major industries, and it is money that floods into the country without any concomitant need to build factories or improve infrastructure. It is part of the boom raising the standard of living generally and allowing an even greater number of working-class men to purchase commercial sex.

Joining the world economy has done wonders for Thailand's income and terrible things to its society. According to Pasuk Phongpaichit and Chris Baker, economists who have analyzed Thailand's economic boom,

Government has let the businessmen ransack the nation's human and natural resources to achieve growth. It has not forced them to put much back. In many respects, the last generation of economic growth has been a disaster. The forests have been obliterated. The urban environment has deteriorated. Little has been done to combat the growth in industrial pollution and hazardous wastes. For many people whose labour has created the boom, the conditions of work, health, and safety are grim.

Neither law nor conscience has been very effective in limiting the social costs of growth. Business has reveled in the atmosphere of free-for-all. The machinery for social protection has proved very pliable. The legal framework is defective. The judiciary is suspect. The police are unreliable. The authorities have consistently tried to block popular organizations to defend popular rights.[18]

The situation in Thailand today is similar to that of the United States in the 1850s; with a significant part of the economy dependent on slavery, religious and cultural leaders are ready to explain why this is all for the best. But there is also an important difference: this is the new slavery, and the impermanence of modern slavery and the dedication of human-rights workers offer some hope.

---

[1] Siri is, of course, a pseudonym; the names of all respondents have been changed for their protection. I spoke with them in December 1996.

[2] "Caught in Modern Slavery: Tourism and Child Prostitution in Thailand," Country Report Summary prepared by Sudarat Sereewat-Srisang for the Ecumenical Consultation held in Chiang Mai in May 1990.

[3] Foreign exchange rates are in constant flux. Unless otherwise noted, dollar equivalences for all currencies reflect the rate at the time of the research.

[4] From interviews done by Human Rights Watch with freed child prostitutes in shelters in Thailand, reported in Jasmine Caye, *Preliminary Survey on Regional Child Trafficking for Prostitution in Thailand* (Bangkok: Center for the Protection of Children's Rights, 1996), p. 25.

[5] Kulachada Chaipipat, "New Law Targets Human Trafficking," Bangkok *Nation*, November 30, 1997.

[6] Thais told me that it would be very surprising if a well-off man or a politician did not have at least one mistress. When I was last in Thailand there was much public mirth over the clash of wife and mistress outside the hospital room of a high government official who had suffered a heart attack, as each in turn barricaded the door.

[7] Quoted in Mark Van Landingham, Chanpen Saengtienchai, John Knodel, and Anthony Pramualratana, *Friends, Wives, and Extramarital Sex in Thailand* (Bangkok: Institute of Population Studies, Chulalongkorn University, 1995), p. 18.

[8] Van Landingham et al., 1995, pp. 9–25.

[9] Van Landingham et al., 1995, p. 53.

[10] Pasuk Phongpaichit and Chris Baker, *Thailand's Boom* (Chiang Mai: Silkworm Books, 1996), pp. 51–54.

[11] Center for the Protection of Children's Rights, *Case Study Report on Commercial Sexual Exploitation of Children in Thailand* (Bangkok, October 1996), p. 37.

[12] David Kyle and John Dale, "Smuggling the State Back In: Agents of Human Smuggling Reconsidered," in *Global Human Smuggling: Comparative Perspectives*, ed. David Kyle and Rey Koslowski (Baltimore: Johns Hopkins University Press, 2001).

[13] "Impact of the Asian Economic Crisis on Child Prostitution," *ECPAT International Newsletter* 27 (May 1, 1999), found at http://www.ecpat.net/eng/Ecpat_inter/IRC/articles.asp?articleID=1438&NewsID=21.

[14] Mechai Veravaidya, address to the International Conference on HIV/AIDS, Chiang Mai, September 1995. See also Gordon Fairdough, "Gathering Storm," *Far Eastern Review*, September 21, 1995, pp. 26–30.

[15] The brochures are quoted in Truong, *Sex, Money, and Morality: Prostitution and Tourism in Southeast Asia* (London: Zed Books, 1990), p. 178.

[16] Carey Goldberg, "Sex Slavery, Thailand to New York," *New York Times* (September 11, 1995), p. 81.

[17] Quoted in Goldberg.

[18] Phongpaichit and Baker, 1996, p. 237.

QUESTIONS

? Kevin Bales states that prostitution is illegal in Thailand. If this is the case, then why is Siri's story an increasingly common fate for young girls in Thailand?

? What problems do enslaved prostitutes like Siri face in their daily life?

? Societal lens question: You are following-up on Siri's story 10 years later. What has become of her? Using your sociological skills, explain two possible outcomes of her story. Make sure these are likely outcomes based on the evidence in the article.

Chapter 7

Racism and Research: The Case of the Tuskegee Syphillis Experiment

By ALLAN M. BRANDT

■ Imagine that you and your friends were selected to be in a government funded medical study that would dispense free medication to treat the potentially fatal disease that you had contracted. For years everyone was given medication, but no one seemed to get better—in fact everyone in the study developed illness-related problems or died. Suppose, many years later, you find to your surprise and horror, that you were deliberately *not* given the proper medication because of your social class and racial background. Furthermore, you discover that doctors, nurses, the military, and the federal government all colluded to withhold treatment for your friends and you. Could it happen? It could, and did. In this article, historian Allan M. Brandt provides the details regarding the Tuskegee Experiment, a medical research project that, beginning in 1932, spanned forty years and, as Brandt puts it "revealed more about the pathology of racism than about the pathology of the subjects." Read carefully to understand the history of this experiment, the ethical problems with such an undertaking, and the racist cultural norms that made such an experiment possible.

In 1932 the U.S. Public Health Service (USPHS) initiated an experiment in Macon County, Alabama, to determine the natural course of untreated, latent syphilis in black males. The test comprised 400 syphilitic men, as well as 200 uninfected men who served as controls. The first published report of the study appeared in 1936 with subsequent papers issued every four to six years, through the 1960s. When penicillin became widely available by the early 1950s as the preferred treatment for syphilis, the men did not receive therapy. In fact on several occasions, the USPHS actually sought to prevent treatment. Moreover, a committee at the federally operated Center for Disease Control decided in 1969 that the study should be continued. Only in 1972, when accounts

---

From *The Hastings Center Report*, Vol. 8, December 1978 by Allan M. Brandt. Copyright © 1978 by The Hastings Center. Reprinted by permission.

of the study first appeared in the national press, did the Department of Health, Education and Welfare halt the experiment. At that time seventy-four of the test subjects were still alive; at least twenty-eight, but perhaps more than 100, had died directly from advanced syphilitic lesions.[1] In August 1972, HEW appointed an investigatory panel which issued a report the following year. The panel found the study to have been "ethically unjustified," and argued that penicillin should have been provided to the men.[2]

This article attempts to place the Tuskegee Study in a historical context and to assess its ethical implications. Despite the media attention which the study received, the HEW *Final Report*, and the criticism expressed by several professional organizations, the experiment has been largely misunderstood. The most basic questions of *how* the study was undertaken in the first place and *why* it continued for forty years were never addressed by the HEW investigation. Moreover, the panel misconstrued the nature of the experiment, failing to consult important documents available at the National Archives which bear significantly on its ethical assessment. Only by examining the specific ways in which values are engaged in scientific research can the study be understood.

RACISM AND MEDICAL OPINION

A brief review of the prevailing scientific thought regarding race and heredity in the early twentieth century is fundamental for an understanding of the Tuskegee Study. By the turn of the century, Darwinism had provided a new rationale for American racism.[3] Essentially primitive peoples, it was argued, could not be assimilated into a complex, white civilization. Scientists speculated that in the struggle for survival the Negro in America was doomed. Particularly prone to disease, vice, and crime, black Americans could not be helped by education or philanthropy. Social Darwinists analyzed census data to predict the virtual extinction of the Negro in the twentieth century, for they believed the Negro race in America was in the throes of a degenerative evolutionary process.[4]

The medical profession supported these findings of late nineteenth- and early twentieth-century anthropologists, ethnologists, and biologists. Physicians studying the effects of emancipation on health concluded almost universally that freedom had caused the mental, moral, and physical deterioration of the black population.[5] They substantiated this argument by citing examples in the comparative anatomy of the black and white races. As Dr. W. T. English wrote: "A careful inspection reveals the body of the negro a mass of minor defects and imperfections from the crown of the head to the soles of the feet…"[6] Cranial structures, wide nasal apertures, receding chins, projecting jaws, all typed the Negro as the lowest species in the Darwinian hierarchy.[7]

Interest in racial differences centered on the sexual nature of blacks. The Negro, doctors explained, possessed an excessive sexual desire, which threatened the very foundations of white society. As one physician noted in the *Journal of the American Medical Association*, "The negro springs from a southern race, and as such his sexual appetite is strong; all of his environments stimulate this appetite, and as a general rule his emotional type of religion certainly does not decrease it."[8] Doctors reported a complete lack of morality on the part of blacks:

> *Virtue in the negro race is like angels' visits—few and far between. In a practice of sixteen years I have never examined a virgin negro over fourteen years of age.*[9]

A particularly ominous feature of this overzealous sexuality, doctors argued, was the black males' desire for white women. "A perversion from which most races are exempt," wrote Dr. English, "prompts the negro's inclination towards white women, whereas other races incline towards females of their own."[10] Though English estimated the "gray matter of the negro brain" to be at least a thousand years behind that of the white races, his genital organs were overdeveloped. As Dr. William Lee Howard noted:

> *The attacks on defenseless white women are evidences of racial instincts that are about as amenable to ethical culture as is the inherent odor of the race.… When education will reduce the size of the negro's penis as well as bring about the sensitiveness of the terminal fibers which exist in the Caucasian, then will it also be able to prevent the African's birthright to sexual madness and excess.*[11]

One southern medical journal proposed "Castration Instead of Lynching," as retribution for black sexual crimes. "An impressive trial by a ghost-like kuklux klan [sic] and a 'ghost' physician or surgeon to perform the operation would make it an event the 'patient' would never forget," noted the editorial.[12]

According to these physicians, lust and immorality, unstable families, and reversion to barbaric tendencies made blacks especially prone to venereal diseases. One doctor estimated that over 50 percent of all Negroes over the age of twenty-five were syphilitic.[13] Virtually free of disease as slaves, they were now overwhelmed by it, according to informed medical opinion. Moreover, doctors believed that treatment for venereal disease among blacks was impossible, particularly because in its latent stage the symptoms of syphilis become quiescent. As Dr. Thomas W. Murrell wrote:

They come for treatment at the beginning and at the end. When there are visible manifestations or when harried by pain, they readily come, for as a race they are not averse to physic; but tell them not, though they look well and feel well, that they are still diseased. Here ignorance rates science a fool...[14]

Even the best educated black, according to Murrell, could not be convinced to seek treatment for syphilis.[15] Venereal disease, according to some doctors, threatened the future of the race. The medical profession attributed the low birth rate among blacks to the high prevalence of venereal disease which caused stillbirths and miscarriages. Moreover, the high rates of syphilis were thought to lead to increased insanity and crime. One doctor writing at the turn of the century estimated that the number of insane Negroes had increased thirteen-fold since the end of the Civil War.[16] Dr. Murrell's conclusion echoed the most informed anthropological and ethnological data:

So the scourge sweeps among them. Those that are treated are only half cured, and the effort to assimilate a complex civilization driving their diseased minds until the results are criminal records. Perhaps here, in conjunction with tuberculosis, will be the end of the negro problem. Disease will accomplish what man cannot do.[17]

This particular configuration of ideas formed the core of medical opinion concerning blacks, sex, and disease in the early twentieth century. Doctors generally discounted socio-economic explanations of the state of black health, arguing that better medical care could not alter the evolutionary scheme.[18] These assumptions provide the backdrop for examining the Tuskegee Syphilis Study.

THE ORIGINS OF THE EXPERIMENT

In 1929, under a grant from the Julius Rosenwald Fund, the USPHS conducted studies in the rural South to determine the prevalence of syphilis among blacks and explore the possibilities for mass treatment. The USPHS found Macon County, Alabama, in which the town of Tuskegee is located, to have the highest syphilis rate of the six counties surveyed. The Rosenwald Study concluded that mass treatment could be successfully implemented among rural blacks.[19] Although it is doubtful that the necessary funds would have been allocated even in the best economic conditions, after the economy collapsed in 1929, the findings were ignored. It is, however, ironic that the Tuskegee Study came to be based on findings of the Rosenwald Study that demonstrated the possibilities of mass treatment.

Three years later, in 1932, Dr. Taliaferro Clark, Chief of the USPHS Venereal Disease Division and author of the Rosenwald Study report, decided that conditions in Macon County merited renewed attention. Clark believed the high prevalence of syphilis offered an "unusual opportunity" for observation. From its inception, the USPHS regarded the Tuskegee Study as a classic "study in nature,"* rather than an experiment.[20] As long as syphilis was so prevalent in Macon and most of the blacks went untreated throughout life, it seemed only natural to Clark that it would be valuable to observe the consequences. He described it as a "ready-made situation."[21] Surgeon General H. S. Cumming wrote to R. R. Moton, Director of the Tuskegee Institute:

> *The recent syphilis control demonstration carried out in Macon County, with the financial assistance of the Julius Rosenwald Fund, revealed the presence of an unusually high rate in this county and, what is more remarkable, the fact that 99 per cent of this group was entirely without previous treatment. This combination, together with the expected cooperation of your hospital, offers an unparalleled opportunity for carrying on this piece of scientific research which probably cannot be duplicated anywhere else in the world.*[22]

Although no formal protocol appears to have been written, several letters of Clark and Cumming suggest what the USPHS hoped to find. Clark indicated that it would be important to see how disease affected the daily lives of the men:

> *The results of these studies of case records suggest the desirability of making a further study of the effect of untreated syphilis on the human economy among people now living and engaged in their daily pursuits.*[23]

It also seems that the USPHS believed the experiment might demonstrate that antisyphilitic treatment was unnecessary. As Cumming noted: "It is expected the results of this study may have a marked bearing on the treatment, or conversely the non-necessity of treatment, of cases of latent syphilis."[24]

The immediate source of Cumming's hypothesis appears to have been the famous Oslo Study of untreated syphilis. Between 1890 and 1910, Professor C. Boeck, the chief of the Oslo Venereal Clinic, withheld treatment from almost two thousand patients infected with syphilis. He was convinced that therapies then available, primarily mercurial ointment, were of no value. When arsenic therapy became widely available by 1910, after Paul Ehrlich's historic discovery of "606," the study was abandoned. E. Bruusgaard, Boeck's successor, conducted a follow-up study of 473 of the untreated patients from 1925 to 1927. He found that 27.9 percent of these patients had undergone a "spontaneous cure," and now manifested no symptoms of the disease. Moreover, he estimated that as many as 70 percent of all syphilitics went through life without inconvenience from the disease.[25] His study, however, clearly acknowledged the dangers of untreated syphilis for the remaining 30 percent.

Thus every major textbook of syphilis at the time of the Tuskegee Study's inception strongly advocated treating syphilis even in its latent stages, which follow the initial inflammatory reaction. In discussing the Oslo Study, Dr. J. E. Moore, one of the nation's leading venereologists wrote, "This summary of Bruusgaard's study is by no means intended to suggest that syphilis be allowed to pass untreated."[26] If a complete cure could not be effected, at least the most devastating effects of the disease could be avoided. Although the standard therapies of the time, arsenical compounds and bismuth injection, involved certain dangers because of their toxicity, the alternatives were much worse. As the Oslo Study had shown, untreated syphilis could lead to cardiovascular disease, insanity, and premature death.[27] Moore wrote in his 1933 textbook:

> *Though it imposes a slight though measurable risk of its own, treatment markedly diminishes the risk from syphilis. In latent syphilis, as I shall show, the probability of progression, relapse, or death is reduced from a probable 25–30 percent without treatment to about 5 percent with it; and the gravity of the relapse if it occurs, is markedly diminished."*[28]

"Another compelling reason for treatment," noted Moore, "exists in the fact that every patient with latent syphilis may be, and perhaps is, infectious for others."[29] In 1932, the year in which the Tuskegee Study began, the USPHS sponsored and published a paper by Moore and six other syphilis experts that strongly argued for treating latent syphilis.[30]

The Oslo Study, therefore, could not have provided justification for the USPHS to undertake a study that did not entail treatment. Rather, the suppositions that conditions in Tuskegee existed "naturally" and that the men would not be treated anyway provided the experiment's rationale. In turn, these two assumptions rested on the prevailing medical attitudes concerning blacks, sex, and disease. For example, Clark explained the prevalence of venereal disease in Macon County by emphasizing promiscuity among blacks:

This state of affairs is due to the paucity of doctors, rather low intelligence of the Negro population in this section, depressed economic conditions, and the very common promiscuous sex relations of this population group which not only contribute to the spread of syphilis but also contribute to the prevailing indifference with regard to treatment.[31]

In fact, Moore, who had written so persuasively in favor of treating latent syphilis, suggested that existing knowledge did not apply to Negroes. Although he had called the Oslo Study "a never-to-be-repeated human experiment,"[32] he served as an expert consultant to the Tuskegee Study:

I think that such a study as you have contemplated would be of immense value. It will be necessary of course in the consideration of the results to evaluate the special factors introduced by a selection of the material from negro males. Syphilis in the negro is in many respects almost a different disease from syphilis in the white.[33]

Dr. O. C. Wenger, chief of the federally operated venereal disease clinic at Hot Springs, Arkansas, praised Moore's judgment, adding, "This study will emphasize those differences."[34] On another occasion he advised Clark, "We must remember we are dealing with a group of people who are illiterate, have no conception of time, and whose personal history is always indefinite."[35]

The doctors who devised and directed the Tuskegee Study accepted the mainstream assumptions regarding blacks and venereal disease. The premise that blacks, promiscuous and lustful, would not seek or continue treatment, shaped the study. A test of untreated syphilis seemed "natural" because the USPHS presumed the men would never be treated; the Tuskegee Study made that a self-fulfilling prophecy.

SELECTING THE SUBJECTS

Clark sent Dr. Raymond Vonderlehr to Tuskegee in September 1932 to assemble a sample of men with latent syphilis for the experiment. The basic design of the study called for the selection of syphilitic black males between the ages of twenty-five and sixty, a thorough physical examination including x-rays, and finally, a spinal tap to determine the incidence of neuro-syphilis.[36] They had no intention of providing any treatment for the infected men.[37] The USPHS originally scheduled the whole experiment to last six months; it seemed to be both a simple and inexpensive project.

The task of collecting the sample, however, proved to be more difficult than the USPHS had supposed. Vonderlehr canvassed the largely illiterate, poverty-stricken population of sharecroppers and tenant farmers in search of test subjects. If his circulars requested only men over twenty-five to attend his clinics, none would appear, suspecting he was conducting draft physicals. Therefore, he was forced to test large numbers of women and men who did not fit the experiment's specifications. This involved considerable expense since the USPHS had promised the Macon County Board of Health that it would treat those who were infected, but not included in the study.[38] Clark wrote to Vonderlehr about the situation: "It never once occured to me that we would be called upon to treat a large part of the county as return for the privilege of making this study. ... I am anxious to keep the expenditures for treatment down to the lowest possible point because it is the one item of expenditure in connection with the study most difficult to defend despite our knowledge of the need therefor."[39] Vonderlehr responded: "If we could find from 100 to 200 cases…we would not have to do another Wassermann on useless individuals…"[40]

Significantly, the attempt to develop the sample contradicted the prediction the USPHS had made initially regarding the prevalence of the disease in Macon County. Overall rates of syphilis fell well below expectations; as opposed to the USPHS projection of 35 percent, 20 percent of those tested were actually diseased.[41] Moreover, those who had sought and received previous treatment far exceeded the expectations of the USPHS. Clark noted in a letter to Vonderlehr:

> *I find your report of March 6th quite interesting but regret the necessity for Wassermanning [sic]...such a large number of individuals in order to uncover this relatively limited number of untreated cases.*[42]

Further difficulties arose in enlisting the subjects to participate in the experiment, to be "Wassermanned," and to return for a subsequent series of examinations. Vonderlehr found that only the offer of treatment elicited the cooperation of the men. They were told they were ill and were promised free care. Offered therapy, they became willing subjects.[43] The USPHS did not tell the men that they were participants in an experiment; on the contrary, the subjects believed they were being treated for "bad blood"—the rural South's colloquialism for syphilis. They thought they were participating in a public health demonstration similar to the one that had been conducted by the Julius Rosenwald Fund in Tuskegee several years earlier. In the end, the men were so eager for medical care that the number of defaulters in the experiment proved to be insignificant.[44]

To preserve the subjects' interest, Vonderlehr gave most of the men mercurial ointment, a noneffective drug, while some of the younger men apparently received inadequate dosages of neoarsphenamine.[45] This required Vonderlehr to write frequently to Clark requesting supplies. He feared the experiment would fail if the men were not offered treatment.

> *It is desirable and essential if the study is to be a success to maintain the interest of each of the cases examined by me through to the time when the spinal puncture can be completed. Expenditure of several hundred dollars for drugs for these men would be well worth while if their interest and cooperation would be maintained in so doing. ... It is my desire to keep the main purpose of the work from the negroes in the county and continue their interest in treatment. That is what the vast majority wants and the examination seems relatively unimportant to them in comparison. It would probably cause the entire experiment to collapse if the clinics were stopped before the work is completed.*[46]

On another occasion he explained:

> *Dozens of patients have been sent away without treatment during the past two weeks and it would have been impossible to continue without the free distribution of drugs because of the unfavorable impression made on the negro.*[47]

The readiness of the test subjects to participate of course contradicted the notion that blacks would not seek or continue therapy.

The final procedure of the experiment was to be a spinal tap to test for evidence of neuro-syphilis. The USPHS presented this purely diagnostic exam, which often entails considerable pain and complications, to the men as a "special treatment." Clark explained to Moore:

> *We have not yet commenced the spinal punctures. This operation will be deferred to the last in order not to unduly disturb our field work by any adverse reports by the patients subjected to spinal puncture because of some disagreeable sensations following this procedure. These negroes are very ignorant and easily influenced by things that would be of minor significance in a more intelligent group.*[48]

The letter to the subjects announcing the spinal tap read:

> *Some time ago you were given a thorough examination and since that time we hope you have gotten a great deal of treatment for bad blood. You will now be given your last chance to get a second examination. This examination is a very special one and after it is finished you will be given a special treatment if it is believed you are in a condition to stand it....*
>
> *Remember This Is Your Last Chance For Special Free Treatment. Be Sure To Meet The Nurse.*[49]

The HEW investigation did not uncover this crucial fact: the men participated in the study under the guise of treatment.

Despite the fact that their assumption regarding prevalence and black attitudes toward treatment had proved wrong, the USPHS decided in the summer of 1933 to continue the study. Once again, it seemed only "natural" to pursue the research since the sample already existed, and with a depressed economy, the cost of treatment appeared prohibitive—although there is no indication it was ever considered. Vonderlehr first suggested extending the study in letters to Clark and Wenger:

> At the end of this project we shall have a considerable number of cases presenting various complications of syphilis, who have received only mercury and may still be considered untreated in the modern sense of therapy. Should these cases be followed over a period of from five to ten years many interesting facts could be learned regarding the course and complications of untreated syphilis.[50]

"As I see it," responded Wenger, "we have no further interest in these patients *until they die.*"[51] Apparently, the physicians engaged in the experiment believed that only autopsies could scientifically confirm the findings of the study. Surgeon General Cumming explained this in a letter to R. R. Moton, requesting the continued cooperation of the Tuskegee Institute Hospital:

> This study which was predominantly clinical in character points to the frequent occurrence of severe complications involving the various vital organs of the body and indicates that syphilis as a disease does a great deal of damage. Since clinical observations are not considered final in the medical world, it is our desire to continue observation on the cases selected for the recent study and if possible to bring a percentage of these cases to autopsy so that pathological confirmation may be made of the disease processes.[52]

Bringing the men to autopsy required the USPHS to devise a further series of deceptions and inducements. Wenger warned Vonderlehr that the men must not realize that they would be autopsied:

> There is one danger in the latter plan and that is if the colored population become aware that accepting free hospital care means a post-mortem, every darkey will leave Macon County and it will hurt [Dr. Eugene] Dibble's hospital.[53]

"Naturally," responded Vonderlehr, "it is not my intention to let it be generally known that the main object of the present activities is the bringing of the men to necropsy."[54] The subjects' trust in the USPHS made the plan viable. The USPHS gave Dr. Dibble, the Director of the Tuskegee Institute Hospital, an interim appointment to the Public Health Service. As Wenger noted:

> One thing is certain. The only way we are going to get postmortems is to have the demise take place in Dibble's hospital and when these colored folks are told that Doctor Dibble is now a Government doctor too they will have more confidence.[55]

After the USPHS approved the continuation of the experiment in 1933, Vonderlehr decided that it would be necessary to select a group of healthy, uninfected men to serve as controls. Vonderlehr, who had succeeded Clark as Chief of the Venereal Disease Division, sent Dr. J. R. Heller to Tuskegee to gather the control group. Heller distributed drugs (noneffective) to these men, which suggests that they also believed they were undergoing treatments.[56] Control subjects who became syphilitic were simply transferred to the test group—a strikingly inept violation of standard research procedure.[57]

The USPHS offered several inducements to maintain contact and to procure the continued cooperation of the men. Eunice Rivers, a black nurse, was hired to follow their health and to secure approval for autopsies. She gave the men non-effective medicines—"spring tonic" and aspirin—as well as transportation and hot meals on the days of their examinations.[58] More important, Nurse Rivers provided continuity to the project over the entire forty-year period. By supplying "medicinals," the USPHS was able to continue to deceive the participants, who believed that they were receiving therapy from the government doctors. Deceit was integral to the study. When the test subjects complained about spinal taps one doctor wrote:

They simply do not like spinal punctures. A few of those who were tapped are enthusiastic over the results but to most, the suggestion causes violent shaking of the head; others claim they were robbed of their procreative powers (regardless of the fact that I claim it stimulates them).[59]

Letters to the subjects announcing an impending USPHS visit to Tuskegee explained: "[The doctor] wants to make a special examination to find out how you have been feeling and whether the treatment has improved your health."[60] In fact, after the first six months of the study, the USPHS had furnished no treatment whatsoever.

Finally, because it proved difficult to persuade the men to come to the hospital when they became severely ill, the USPHS promised to cover their burial expenses. The Milbank Memorial Fund provided approximately $50 per man for this purpose beginning in 1935. This was a particularly strong inducement as funeral rites constituted an important component of the cultural life of rural blacks.[61] One report of the study concluded, "Without this suasion it would, we believe, have been impossible to secure the cooperation of the group and their families."[62]

Reports of the study's findings, which appeared regularly in the medical press beginning in 1936, consistently cited the ravages of untreated syphilis. The first paper, read at the 1936 American Medical Association annual meeting, found "that syphilis in this period [latency] tends to greatly increase the frequency of manifestations of cardiovascular disease."[63] Only 16 percent of the subjects gave no sign of morbidity as opposed to 61 percent of the controls. Ten years later, a report noted coldly, "The fact that nearly twice as large a proportion of the syphilitic individuals as of the control group has died is a very striking one." Life expectancy, concluded the doctors, is reduced by about 20 percent.[64]

A 1955 article found that slightly more than 30 percent of the test group autopsied had died *directly* from advanced syphilitic lesions of either the cardiovascular or the central nervous system.[65] Another published account stated, "Review of those still living reveals that an appreciable number have late complications of syphilis which probably will result, for some at least, in contributing materially to the ultimate cause of death."[66] In 1950, Dr. Wenger had concluded, "We now know, where we could only surmise before, that we have contributed to their ailments and shortened their lives."[67] As black physician Vernal Cave, a member of the HEW panel, later wrote, "They proved a point, then proved a point, then proved a point."[68]

During the forty years of the experiment the USPHS had sought on several occasions to ensure that the subjects did not receive treatment from other sources. To this end, Vonderlehr met with groups of local black doctors in 1934, to ask their cooperation in not treating the men. Lists of subjects were distributed to Macon County physicians along with letters requesting them to refer these men back to the USPHS if they sought care.[69] The USPHS warned the Alabama Health Department not to treat the test subjects when they took a mobile VD unit into Tuskegee in the early 1940s.[70] In 1941, the Army drafted several subjects and told them to begin antisyphilitic treatment immediately. The USPHS supplied the draft board with a list of 256 names they desired to have excluded from treatment, and the board complied.[71]

In spite of these efforts, by the early 1950s many of the men had secured some treatment on their own. By 1952, almost 30 percent of the test subjects had received some penicillin, although only 7.5 percent had received what could be considered adequate doses.[72] Vonderlehr wrote to one of the participating physicians, "I hope that the availability of antibiotics has not interfered too much with this project."[73] A report published in 1955 considered whether the treatment that some of the men had obtained had "defeated" the study. The article attempted to explain the relatively low exposure to penicillin in an age of antibiotics, suggesting as a reason: "the stoicism of these men as a group; they still regard hospitals and medicines with suspicion and prefer an occasional dose of time-honored herbs or tonics to modern drugs."[74] The authors failed to note that the men believed they already were under the care of the government doctors and thus saw no need to seek treatment elsewhere. Any treatment which the men might have received, concluded the report, had been insufficient to compromise the experiment.

When the USPHS evaluated the status of the study in the 1960s they continued to rationalize the racial aspects of the experiment. For example, the minutes of a 1965 meeting at the Center for Disease Control recorded:

Racial issue was mentioned briefly. Will not affect the study. Any questions can be handled by saying these people were at the point that therapy would no longer help them. They are getting better medical care than they would under any other circumstances.[75]

A group of physicians met again at the CDC in 1969 to decide whether or not to terminate the study. Although one doctor argued that the study should be stopped and the men treated, the consensus was to continue. Dr. J. Lawton Smith remarked, "You will never have another study like this; take advantage of it."[76] A memo prepared by Dr. James B. Lucas, Assistant Chief of the Venereal Disease Branch, stated: "Nothing learned will prevent, find, or cure a single case of infectious syphilis or bring us closer to our basic mission of controlling venereal disease in the United States."[77] He concluded, however, that the study should be continued "along its present lines." When the first accounts of the experiment appeared in the national press in July 1972, data were still being collected and autopsies performed.[78]

THE HEW FINAL REPORT

HEW finally formed the Tuskegee Syphilis Study Ad Hoc Advisory Panel on August 28, 1972, in response to criticism that the press descriptions of the experiment had triggered. The panel, composed of nine members, five of them black, concentrated on two issues. First, was the study justified in 1932 and had the men given their informed consent? Second, should penicillin have been provided when it became available in the early 1950s? The panel was also charged with determining if the study should be terminated and assessing current policies regarding experimentation with human subjects.[79] The group issued their report in June 1973.

By focusing on the issues of penicillin therapy and informed consent, the *Final Report* and the investigation betrayed a basic misunderstanding of the experiment's purposes and design. The HEW report implied that the failure to provide penicillin constituted the study's major ethical misjudgment; implicit was the assumption that no adequate therapy existed prior to penicillin. Nonetheless medical authorities firmly believed in the efficacy of arsenotherapy for treating syphilis at the time of the experiment's inception in 1932. The panel further failed to recognize that the entire study had been predicated on nontreatment. Provision of effective medication would have violated the rationale of the experiment—to study the natural course of the disease until death. On several occasions, in fact, the USPHS had prevented the men from receiving proper treatment. Indeed, there is no evidence that the USPHS ever considered providing penicillin.

The other focus of the *Final Report*—informed consent—also served to obscure the historical facts of the experiment. In light of the deceptions and exploitations which the experiment perpetrated, it is an understatement to declare, as the *Report* did, that the experiment was "ethically unjustified," because it failed to obtain informed consent from the subjects. The *Final Report's* statement, "Submitting voluntarily is not informed consent," indicated that the panel believed that the men had volunteered *for the experiment.*[80] The records in the National Archives make clear that the men did not submit voluntarily to an experiment; they were told and they believed that they were getting free treatment from expert government doctors for a serious disease. The failure of the HEW *Final Report* to expose this critical fact—that the USPHS lied to the subjects—calls into question the thoroughness and credibility of their investigation.

Failure to place the study in a historical context also made it impossible for the investigation to deal with the essentially racist nature of the experiment. The panel treated the study as an aberration, well-intentioned but misguided.[81] Moreover, concern that the *Final Report* might be viewed as a critique of human experimentation in general seems to have severely limited the scope of the inquiry. The *Final Report* is quick to remind the reader on two occasions: "The position of the Panel must not be construed to be a general repudiation of scientific research with human subjects."[82] The *Report* assures us that a better designed experiment could have been justified:

It is possible that a scientific study in 1932 of untreated syphilis, properly conceived with a clear protocol and conducted with suitable subjects who fully understood the implications of their involvement, might have been justified in the pre-penicillin era. This is especially true when one considers the uncertain nature of the results of treatment of late latent syphilis and the highly toxic nature of therapeutic agents then available.[83]

This statement is questionable in view of the proven dangers of untreated syphilis known in 1932.

Since the publication of the HEW *Final Report*, a defense of the Tuskegee Study has emerged. These arguments, most clearly articulated by Dr. R. H. Kampmeier in the *Southern Medical Journal*, center on the limited knowledge of effective therapy for latent syphilis when the experiment began. Kampmeier argues that by 1950, penicillin would have been of no value for these men.[84] Others have suggested that the men were fortunate to have been spared the highly toxic treatments of the earlier period.[85] Moreover, even these contemporary defenses assume that the men never would have been treated anyway. As Dr. Charles Barnett of Stanford University wrote in 1974, "The lack of treatment was not contrived by the USPHS but was an established fact of which they proposed to take advantage."[86] Several doctors who participated in the study continued to justify the experiment. Dr. J. R. Heller, who on one occasion had referred to the test subjects as the "Ethiopian population," told reporters in 1972:

I don't see why they should be shocked or horrified. There was no racial side to this. It just happened to be in a black community. I feel this was a perfectly straightforward study, perfectly ethical, with controls. Part of our mission as physicians is to find out what happens to individuals with disease and without disease.[87]

These apologies, as well as the HEW *Final Report*, ignore many of the essential ethical issues which the study poses. The Tuskegee Study reveals the persistence of beliefs within the medical profession about the nature of blacks, sex, and disease—beliefs that had tragic repercussions long after their alleged "scientific" bases were known to be incorrect. Most strikingly, the entire health of a community was jeopardized by leaving a communicable disease untreated.[88] There can be little doubt that the Tuskegee researchers regarded their subjects as less than human.[89] As a result, the ethical canons of experimenting on human subjects were completely disregarded.

The study also raises significant questions about professional self-regulation and scientific bureaucracy. Once the USPHS decided to extend the experiment in the summer of 1933, it was unlikely that the test would be halted short of the men's deaths. The experiment was widely reported for forty years without evoking any significant protest within the medical community. Nor did any bureaucratic mechanism exist within the government for the periodic reassessment of the Tuskegee experiment's ethics and scientific value. The USPHS sent physicians to Tuskegee every several years to check on the study's progress, but never subjected the morality or usefulness of the experiment to serious scrutiny. Only the press accounts of 1972 finally punctured the continued rationalizations of the USPHS and brought the study to an end. Even the HEW investigation was compromised by fear that it would be considered a threat to future human experimentation.

In retrospect the Tuskegee Study revealed more about the pathology of racism than it did about the pathology of syphilis; more about the nature of scientific inquiry than the nature of the disease process. The injustice committed by the experiment went well beyond the facts outlined in the press and the HEW *Final Report*. The degree of deception and damages have been seriously underestimated. As this history of the study suggests, the notion that science is a value-free discipline must be rejected. The need for greater vigilance in assessing the specific ways in which social values and attitudes affect professional behavior is clearly indicated.

Claude Bernard on Human Experimentation (1865)

Experiments, then, may be performed on man, but within what limits? It is our duty and our right to perform an experiment on man whenever it can save his life, cure him or gain him some personal benefit. The principle of medical and surgical morality, therefore, consists in never performing on man an experiment which might be harmful to him to any extent, even though the result might be highly advantageous to science, i.e., to the health of others. But performing experiments and operations exclusively from the point of view of the patient's own advantage does not prevent their turning out profitably to science.... For we must not deceive ourselves, morals do not forbid making experiments on one's neighbor or on one's self. Christian morals forbid only one thing, doing ill to one's neighbor. So, among the experiments that may be tried on man, those that can only harm are forbidden, those that are innocent are permissible, and those that may do good are obligatory. *Claude Bernard, An Introduction to the Study of Experimental Medicine (1865). Trans, by Henry C. Green (New York: Dover Publications, 1957).*

From the HEW Final Report (1973)

1. In retrospect, the Public Health Service Study of Untreated Syphilis in the Male Negro in Macon County, Alabama, was ethically unjustified in 1932. This judgement made in 1973 about the conduct of the study in 1932 is made with the advantage of hindsight acutely sharpened over some forty years, concerning an activity in a different age with different social standards. Nevertheless, orle fundamental ethical rule is that a person should not be subjected to avoidable risk of death or physical harm unless he freely and intelligently consents. There is no evidence that such consent was obtained from the participants in this study.

2. Because of the paucity of information available today on the manner in which the study was conceived, designed and sustained, a scientific justification for a short term demonstration study cannot be ruled out. However, the conduct of the longitudinal study as initially reported in 1936 and through the years is judged to be scientifically unsound and its results are disproportionately meager compared with known risks to human subjects involved....

NOTES

1. The best general accounts of the study are "The 40-Year Death Watch," *Medical World News* (August 18, 1972), pp. 15–17; and Dolores Katz, "Why 430 Blacks with Syphilis Went Uncured for 40 Years," Detroit *Free Press* (November 5, 1972). The mortality figure is based on a published report of the study which appeared in 1955. See Jesse J. Peters, James H. Peers, Sidney Olansky, John C. Cutler, and Geraldine Gleeson, "Untreated Syphilis in the Male Negro: Pathologic Findings in Syphilitic and Nonsyphilitic Patients," *Journal of Chronic Diseases* 1 (February 1955), 127–48. The article estimated that 30.4 percent of the untreated men would die from syphilitic lesions.

2. *Final Report* of the Tuskegee Syphilis Study Ad Hoc Advisory Panel, Department of Health, Education, and Welfare (Washington. D.C.: GPO, 1973). (Hereafter, HEW *Final Report*).

3. See George M. Frederickson, *The Black Image in the White Mind* (New York: Harper and Row, 1971), pp. 228–55. Also, John H. Haller, *Outcasts From Evolution* (Urbana, III.: University of Illinois Press, 1971), pp. 40–68.

4. Frederickson, pp. 247–49.

5. "Deterioration of the American Negro," *Atlanta Journal-Record of Medicine* 5 (July 1903), 287–88. See also J. A. Rodgers, 'The Effect of Freedom upon the Psychological Development of the Negro," *Proceedings* of the American Medico-Psychological Association 7 (1900), 88–99. "From the most healthy race in the country forty years ago," concluded Dr. Henry McHatton, "he is today the most diseased." "The Sexual Status of the Negro—Past and Present," *American Journal of Dermatology and Genito-Urinary Diseases* 10 (January 1906), 7–9.

6. W. T. English, "The Negro Problem from the Physician's Point of View," *Atlanta Journal-Record of Medicine* 5 (October 1903), 461. See also, "Racial Anatomical Peculiarities," *New York Medical Journal* 63 (April 1896), 500–01.

7. "Racial Anatomical Peculiarities," p. 501. Also, Charles S. Bacon, "The Race Problem," *Medicine* (Detroit) 9 (May 1903), 338–43.

8. H. H. Hazen, "Syphilis in the American Negro," *Journal of the American Medical Association* 63 (August 8, 1914), 463. For deeper background into the historical relationship of racism and sexuality see Winthrop D. Jordan, *White Over Black* (Chapel Hill: University of North Carolina Press, 1968; Pelican Books, 1969), pp. 32–40.

9. Daniel David Quillian, "Racial Peculiarities: A Cause of the Prevalence of Syphilis in Negroes," *American Journal of Dermatology and Genito-Urinary Diseases* 10 (July 1906), p. 277.

10. English, p. 463.

11. William Lee Howard, "The Negro as a Distinct Ethnic Factor in Civilization," *Medicine* (Detroit) 9 (June 1903), 424. See also, Thomas W. Murrell, "Syphilis in the American Negro," *Journal of the American Medical Association* 54 (March 12, 1910), 848.

12. "Castration Instead of Lynching," *Atlanta Journal-Record of Medicine* 8 (October 1906), 457. The editorial added: "The badge of disgrace and emasculation might be branded upon the face or forehead, as a warning, in the form of an 'R,' emblematic of the crime for which this punishment was and will be inflicted."

13. Searle Harris, "The Future of the Negro from the Standpoint of the Southern Physician," *Alabama Medical Journal* 14 (January 1902), 62. Other articles on the prevalence of venereal disease among blacks are: H. L. McNeil, "Syphilis in the Southern Negro," *Journal of the American Medical Association* 67 (September 30, 1916), 1001–04; Ernest Philip Boas, "The Relative Prevalence of Syphilis Among Negroes and Whites," *Social Hygiene* 1 (September 1915), 610–16. Doctors went to considerable trouble to distinguish the morbidity and mortality of various diseases among blacks and whites. See, for example, Marion M. Torchia, "Tuberculosis Among American Negroes: Medical Research on a Racial Disease, 1830–1950," *Journal of the History of Medicine and Allied Sciences* 32 (July 1977), 252–79.

14. Thomas W. Murrell, "Syphilis in the Negro: Its Bearing on the Race Problem," *American Journal of Dermatology and Genito-Urinary Diseases* 10 (August 1906), 307.

15. "Even among the educated, only a very few will carry out the most elementary instructions as to personal hygiene. One thing you cannot do, and that is to convince the negro that he has a disease that he cannot see or feel. This is due to lack of concentration rather than lack of faith; even if he does believe, he does not care; a child of fancy, the sensations of the passing hour are his only guides to the future." Murrell, "Syphilis in the American Negro," p. 847.

16. "Deterioration of the American Negro," *Atlanta Journal-Record of Medicine* 5 (July 1903), 288.

17. Murrell, "Syphilis in the Negro; Its Bearing on the Race Problem," p. 307.

18. "The anatomical and physiological conditions of the African must be understood, his place in the anthropological scale realized, and his biological basis accepted as being unchangeable by man, before we shall be able to govern his natural uncontrollable sexual passions." See, "As Ye Sow That Shall Ye Also Reap," *Atlanta Journal-Record of Medicine* 1 (June 1899), 266.

19. Taliaferro Clark, *The Control of Syphilis in Southern Rural Areas* (Chicago: Julius Rosenwald Fund, 1932), 53–58. Approximately 35 percent of the inhabitants of Macon County who were examined were found to be syphilitic.

20. See Claude Bernard, *An Introduction to the Study of Experimental Medicine* (New York: Dover, 1865, 1957), pp. 5–26.

21. Taliaferro Clark to M. M. Davis, October 29, 1932. Records of the USPHS Venereal Disease Division, Record Group 90, Box 239, National Archives, Washington National Record Center, Suitland, Maryland. (Hereafter, NA-WNRC). Materials in this collection which relate to the early history of the study were apparently never consulted by the HEW investigation. Included are letters, reports, and memoranda written by the physicians engaged in the study.

22. H. S. Cumming to R. R. Moton, September 20, 1932, NAWNRC.

23. Clark to Davis, October 29, 1932, NA-WNRC.

24. Cumming to Moton, September 20, 1932, NA-WNRC.

25. Bruusgaard was able to locate 309 living patients, as well as records from 164 who were diseased. His findings were published as "*Ueber das Schicksal der nicht specifizch behandelten Luetiken,*" *Archives of Dermatology and Syphilis* 157 (1929), 309–32. The best discussion of the Boeck-Bruusgaard data is E. Gurney Clark and Niels Danbolt, "The Oslo Study of the Natural History of Untreated Syphilis," *Journal of Chronic Diseases* 2 (September 1955), 311–44.

26. Joseph Earle Moore, *The Modern Treatment of Syphilis* (Baltimore: Charles C. Thomas, 1933), p. 24.

27. Moore, pp. 231–47; see also John H. Stokes, *Modern Clinical Syphilology* (Philadelphia: W. B. Saunders, 1928), pp. 231–39.

28. Moore, p. 237.

29. Moore, p. 236.

30. J. E. Moore, H. N. Cole, P. A. O'Leary, J. H. Stokes, U. J. Wile, T. Clark, T. Parran, J. H. Usilton, "Cooperative Clinical Studies in the Treatment of Syphilis: Latent Syphilis," *Venereal Disease Information* 13 (September 20, 1932), 351. The authors also concluded that the latently syphilitic were potential carriers of the disease, thus meriting treatment.

31. Clark to Paul A. O'Leary, September 27, 1932, NA-WNRC. O'Leary, of the Mayo Clinic, misunderstood the design of the study, replying: "The investigation which you are planning in Alabama is indeed an intriguing one, particularly because of the opportunity it affords of observing treatment in a previously untreated group. I assure you such a study is of interest to me, and I shall look forward to its report in the future." O'Leary to Clark, October 3, 1932, NA-WNRC.

32. Joseph Earle Moore, "Latent Syphilis," unpublished typescript (n.d.), p. 7. American Social Hygiene Association Papers, Social Welfare History Archives Center, University of Minnesota, Minneapolis, Minnesota.

33. Moore to Clark, September 28, 1932, NA-WNRC. Moore had written in his textbook, "In late syphilis the negro is particularly prone to the development of bone or cardiovascular lesions." See Moore, *The Modern Treatment of Syphilis*, p. 35.

34. O. C. Wenger to Clark, October 3, 1932, NA-WNRC.

35. Wenger to Clark, September 29, 1932, NA-WNRC.

36. Clark Memorandum, September 26, 1932, NA-WNRC. See also, Clark to Davis, October 29, 1932, NA-WNRC.

37. As Clark wrote: "You will observe that our plan has nothing to do with treatment. It is purely a diagnostic procedure carried out to determine what has happened to the syphilitic Negro who has had no treatment." Clark to Paul A. O'Leary, September 27, 1932, NA-WNRC.

38. D. G. Gill to O. C. Wenger, October 10, 1932, NA-WNRC.

39. Clark to Vonderlehr, January 25, 1933, NA-WNRC.

40. Vonderlehr to Clark, February 28, 1933, NA-WNRC.
41. Vonderlehr to Clark, November 2, 1932, NA-WNRC. Also, Vonderlehr to Clark, February 6, 1933, NA-WNRC.
42. Clark to Vonderlehr, March 9, 1933, NA-WNRC.
43. Vonderlehr later explained: "The reason treatment was given to many of these men was twofold: First, when the study was started in the fall of 1932, no plans had been made for its continuation and a few of the patients were treated before we fully realized the need for continuing the project on a permanent basis. Second it was difficult to hold the interest of the group of Negroes in Macon County unless some treatment was given." Vonderlehr to Austin V. Diebert, December 5, 1938, Tuskegee Syphilis Study Ad Hoc Advisory Panel Papers, Box 1, National Library of Medicine, Bethesda, Maryland. (Hereafter, TSS-NLM). This collection contains the materials assembled by the HEW investigation in 1972.
44. Vonderlehr to Clark, February 6, 1933, NA-WNRC.
45. H. S. Cumming to J. N. Baker, August 5, 1933, NA-WNRC.
46. January 22, 1933; January 12, 1933, NA-WNRC.
47. Vonderlehr to Clark, January 28, 1933, NA-WNRC.
48. Clark to Moore, March 25, 1933, NA-WNRC.
49. Macon County Health Department, "Letter to Subjects," n.d., NA-WNRC.
50. Vonderlehr to Clark, April 8, 1933, NA-WNRC. See also, Vonderlehr to Wenger, July 18, 1933, NA-WNRC.
51. Wenger to Vonderlehr, July 21, 1933, NA-WNRC. The italics are Wenger's.
52. Cumming to Moton, July 27, 1933, NA-WNRC.
53. Wenger to Vonderlehr, July 21, 1933, NA-WNRC.
54. Vonderlehr to Murray Smith, July 27, 1933, NA-WNRC.
55. Wenger to Vonderlehr, August 5, 1933, NA-WNRC.
56. Vonderlehr to Wenger, October 24, 1933, NA-WNRC. Controls were given salicylates.
57. Austin V. Diebert and Martha C. Bruyere, "Untreated Syphilis in the Male Negro, III," *Venereal Disease Information* 27 (December 1946), 301–14.
58. Eunice Rivers, Stanley Schuman, Lloyd Simpson, Sidney Olansky, "Twenty-Years of Followup Experience In a Long-Range Medical Study," *Public Health Reports* 68 (April 1953), 391–95. In this article Nurse Rivers explains her role in the experiment. She wrote: "Because of the low educational status of the majority of the patients, it was impossible to appeal to them from a purely scientific approach. Therefore, various methods were used to maintain their interest. Free medicines, burial assistance or insurance (the project being referred to as 'Miss Rivers' Lodge'), free hot meals on the days of examination, transportation to and from the hospital, and an opportunity to stop in town on the return trip to shop or visit with their friends on the streets all helped. In spite of these attractions, there were some who refused their examinations because they were not sick and did not see that they were being benefitted." (p. 393).
59. Austin V. Diebert to Raymond Vonderlehr, March 20, 1939, TSS-NLM, Box 1.
60. Murray Smith to Subjects, (1938), TSS-NLM, Box 1. See also, Sidney Olansky to John C. Cutler, November 6, 1951, TSS-NLM, Box 2.
61. The USPHS originally requested that the Julius Rosenwald Fund meet this expense. See Cumming to Davis, October 4, 1934, NA-WNRC. This money was usually divided between the undertaker, pathologist, and hospital. Lloyd Isaacs to Raymond Vonderlehr, April 23, 1940, TSS-NLM, Box 1.
62. Stanley H. Schuman, Sidney Olansky, Eunice Rivers, C. A. Smith, Dorothy S. Rambo, "Untreated Syphilis in the Male Negro: Background and Current Status of Patients in the Tuskegee Study," *Journal of Chronic Diseases* 2 (November 1955), 555.
63. R. A. Vonderlehr and Taliaferro Clark, "Untreated Syphilis in the Male Negro," Venereal Disease Information 17 (September 1936), 262.
64. J. R. Heller and P. T. Bruyere, "Untreated Syphilis in the Male Negro: II. Mortality During 12 Years of Observation," *Venereal Disease Information* 27 (February 1946), 34–38.
65. Jesse J. Peters, James H. Peers, Sidney Olansky, John C. Cutler, and Geraldine Gleeson, "Untreated Syphilis in the Male Negro: Pathologic Findings in Syphilitic and Non-Syphilitic Patients," *Journal of Chronic Diseases* 1 (February 1955), 127–48.
66. Sidney Olansky, Stanley H. Schuman, Jesse J. Peters, C. A. Smith, and Dorothy S. Rambo, "Untreated Syphilis in the Male Negro, X. Twenty Years of Clinical Observation of Untreated Syphilitic and Presumably Nonsyphilitic Groups," *Journal of Chronic Diseases* 4 (August 1956), 184.
67. O. C. Wenger, "Untreated Syphilis in Male Negro," unpublished typescript, 1950, p. 3. Tuskegee Files, Center for Disease Control, Atlanta, Georgia. (Hereafter TF-CDC).
68. Vernal G. Cave, "Proper Uses and Abuses of the Health Care Delivery System for Minorities with Special Reference to the Tuskegee Syphilis Study," *Journal of the National Medical Association* 67 (January 1975), 83.
69. See for example, Vonderlehr to B. W. Booth, April 18, 1934; Vonderlehr to E. R. Lett, November 20, 1933, NA-WNRC.
70. "Transcript of Proceedings—Tuskegee Syphilis Ad Hoc Advisory Panel," February 23, 1973, unpublished typescript, TSS-NLM, Box 1.
71. Raymond Vonderlehr to Murray Smith, April 30, 1942; and Smith to Vonderlehr, June 8, 1942, TSS-NLM, Box 1.

72. Stanley H. Schuman, Sidney Olansky, Eunice Rivers, C. A. Smith, and Dorothy S. Rambo, "Untreated Syphilis in the Male Negro: Background and Current Status of Patients in the Tuskegee Study," *Journal of Chronic Diseases* 2 (November 1955), 550–53.
73. Raymond Vonderlehr to Stanley H. Schuman, February 5, 1952. TSS-NLM, Box 2.
74. Schuman et al., p. 550.
75. "Minutes, April 5, 1965" unpublished typescript, TSS-NLM, Box 1.
76. "Tuskegee Ad Hoc Committee Meeting—Minutes, February 6, 1969," TF-CDC.
77. James B. Lucas to William J. Brown, September 10, 1970, TF-CDC.
78. Elizabeth M. Kennebrew to Arnold C. Schroeter, February 24, 1971, TSS-NLM, Box 1.
79. See Medical Tribune (September 13, 1972), pp. 1, 20; and Report on HEW's Tuskegee Report," *Medical World News* (September 14, 1973), pp. 57–58.
80. HEW *Final Report*, p. 7.
81. The notable exception is Jay Katz's eloquent "Reservations About the Panel Report on Charge 1," HEW *Final Report*, pp. 14–15.
82. HEW *Final Report*, pp. 8, 12.
83. HEW *Final Report*, pp. 8, 12.
84. See R. H. Kampmeier, "The Tuskegee Study of Untreated Syphilis," *Southern Medical Journal* 65 (October 1972), 1247–51; and "Final Report on the 'Tuskegee Syphilis Study,'" *Southern Medical Journal* 67 (November 1974), 1349–53.
85. Leonard J. Goldwater, "The Tuskegee Study in Historical Perspective," unpublished typescript, TSS-NLM; see also "Treponemes and Tuskegee," *Lancet* (June 23, 1973), p. 1438; and Louis Lasagna, *The VD Epidemic* (Philadelphia: Temple University Press, 1975), pp. 64–66.
86. Quoted in "Debate Revives on the PHS Study," *Medical World News* (April 19, 1974), p. 37.
87. Heller to Vonderlehr, November 28, 1933, NA-WNRC; quoted in *Medical Tribune* (August 23, 1972), p. 14.
88. Although it is now known that syphilis is rarely infectious after its early phase, at the time of the study's inception latent syphilis was thought to be communicable. The fact that members of the control group were placed in the test group when they became syphilitic proves that at least some infectious men were denied treatment.
89. When the subjects are drawn from minority groups, especially those with which the researcher cannot identify, basic human rights may be compromised. Hans Jonas has clearly explicated the problem in his "Philosophical Reflections on Experimentation," *Daedalus* 98 (Spring 1969), 234–37. As Jonas writes: "If the properties we adduced as the particular qualifications of the members of the scientific fraternity itself are taken as general criteria of selection, then one should look for additional subjects where a maximum of identification, understanding, and spontaneity can be expected—that is, among the most highly motivated, the most highly educated, and the least 'captive' members of the community."

---

* In 1865, Claude Bernard, the famous French physiologist, outlined the distinction between a "study in nature" and experimentation. A study in nature required simple observation, an essentially passive act, while experimentation demanded intervention which altered the original condition. The Tuskegee Study was thus clearly not a study in nature. The very act of diagnosis altered the original conditions. "It is on this very possibility of acting or not acting on a body," wrote Bernard, "that the distinction will exclusively rest between sciences called sciences of observation and sciences called experimental."

* The degree of black cooperation in conducting the study remains unclear and would be impossible to properly assess in an article of this length. It seems certain that some members of the Tuskegee Institute staff such as R. R. Moton and Eugene Dibble understood the nature of the experiment and gave their support to it. There is, however, evidence that some blacks who assisted the USPHS physicians were not aware of the deceptive nature of the experiment. Dr. Joshua Williams, an intern at the John A. Andrew Memorial Hospital (Tuskegee Institute) in 1932, assisted Vonderlehr in taking blood samples of the test subjects. In 1973 he told the HEW panel: "I know we thought it was merely a service group organized to help the people in the area. We didn't know it was a research project at all at the time." (See, 'Transcript of Proceedings," Tuskegee Syphilis Study Ad Hoc Advisory Panel, February 23, 1973, Unpublished typescript. National Library of Medicine, Bethesda, Maryland.) It is also apparent that Eunice Rivers, the black nurse who had primary responsibility for maintaining contact with the men over the forty years, did not fully understand the dangers of the experiment. In any event, black involvement in the study in no way mitigates the racial assumptions of the experiment, but rather, demonstrates their power.

QUESTIONS

? What was the purpose of the Tuskegee Experiment? Who was selected to be in the original sample? How and why were they selected for this study?

? How did racism play a role in the selection and continued enrollment of men in this study? How and why was racism ignored in the 1972 HEW panel findings?

? Societal lens question: You are a researcher with the National Institutes of Health. You have just begun your career and hope to become famous. You have recently discovered that a new sexually transmitted disease is spreading rapidly. You have noticed that it can be contracted by anyone, but it is most likely to occur in young, poor, undocumented immigrant women. You believe that you might have a medication that will work on the horizon, but you will first need to understand how the disease plays out at different stages. Can such a study be done? What ethical issues will you need to be wary of? What prejudices of modern society will you need to avoid?

Experiences of Discrimination Among African American, Asian American, and Latino Adolescents in an Urban High School

By SUSAN RAKOSI ROSENBLOOM & NIOBE WAY

■ Have you ever experienced discrimination in school? Researchers Susan Rakosi Rosenbloom and Niobe Way pose this and other questions about discrimination and prejudice to a sample of Asian American, Latino/a, and African American ninth grade students in an American urban high school. The students' respond that prejudice and discrimination are common experiences for them. But they also reveal that the students experienced prejudice and discrimination very differently depending on what racial group they belong to. While you are reading this article, pay close attention to how the student's experiences are similar and how they differ.

Keywords: discrimination; adolescents; school

Interviewer: Have you ever experienced discrimination in school?
Sheerah (African American): The teachers think that the Chinese kids can do everything. ... Kids bother the Chinese kids in the hallway.... You know Chinese kids are quiet in my class so, it's like, they get a better grade.
Interviewer: So you think the teachers discriminate in favor of the Chinese kids?
Sheerah: I don't think they (are) racist.... It's just that they give Chinese kids a better grade.
Interviewer: Why do you think that is?
Sheerah: Cause they (are) quiet...and we (are) loud.

Sheerah's response is typical of African American and Latino students attending urban high schools that include Asian American students (see Conchas & Noguero, 2004). Experiences of discrimination in these schools are often subtle so that it is unclear to the students whether their experiences are, in fact, examples of discrimination. Furthermore, experiences of discrimination are frequently not based on Black/White relations but on relations among and between ethnic minority groups. In addition, the source of the discrimination is not simply from adults toward students but between peers as well. Finally, racial/ethnic discrimination is not necessarily based entirely on racial/ethnic categories. Differences, for example, in language and immigration status are also an important component of ethnic/racial discrimination in school. These nuances in the experiences of discrimination among urban ethnic minority adolescents, however, have not been explored in social science research. The majority of research about racial and ethnic discrimination focuses on Black/White relations and does not address the more subtle forms of racism and discrimination that often occur in urban high schools. The purpose of this article is to explore, using qualitative methods, the ways in which African American, Latino, and Asian American high school students experience discrimination in an urban high school context. We explore how racial/ethnic categories (e.g., being African American) contribute to experiences of discrimination as well as how other components of experience (e.g., recentness of immigration) contribute to racial/ethnic discrimination in school.

When thinking about discrimination in schools, a common reference is to September 1957, when the young, African American high school students, "the Little Rock Nine," walked through a jeering crowd of White students and parents in Alabama. The powerful images of Army troops enforcing the court order for desegregation conjures the ongoing struggles of African Americans to integrate the public schools and the fierce rejection by Whites. A more current image of discrimination in schools, however, requires a different conceptual framework.

Adolescents who attend urban public schools are increasingly experiencing what has been popularly called the "browning of America." In comparison with previous waves of immigration, the post-1965 wave of immigration (the "new second generation") is more diverse consisting of people from a larger variety of countries (Portes & Rumbaut, 1996). Therefore, adolescents, particularly those in large urban centers, are typically not attending schools that are either segregated or integrated along Black/White lines but have a culturally diverse student body that includes students from Latin America, Central America, Central Asia, South East Asia, West Indies, and the Caribbean Islands. Furthermore, recent immigrant students from these countries also attend school with first-, second-, and third-generation Americans who share their country of origin. Given the rich diversity of the student body and the tensions that are emerging in these schools regarding race and ethnicity (Conchas & Noguero, 2004), researchers should begin examining the inter- and intragroup relations among students who attend such ethnically and racially diverse schools.

PURPOSE OF STUDY

Research in education has only begun to explore the relationships among and between racial and ethnic minorities of Latino, African, and Asian descent (Goto, 1997; Hamm, 1998; Kiang & Kaplan, 1994; Lee, 1994; Olsen, 1997; Sellar & Weis, 1997), and has generally not explored students' experiences of discrimination in multiracial/ethnic urban high schools. Based on this gap in the literature as well as the need to understand adolescents' own perspectives on discrimination, the current study examined how adolescents' describe their experiences of racial and/or ethnic discrimination in school. Given the general lack of research on this topic, we had no specific hypotheses. We aimed to generate rather than test hypotheses (Way, 1998) to aid future research on discriminatory practices and experiences in urban high school settings.

METHOD

Participants

The sample during the first wave of data collection consisted of 20 Asian American, 20 Latinos, and 20 African American, ninth-grade high school students (50% girls, mean age is 14.2). The data were collected during the academic year 1996 and 1997.[1] A second wave of interviews (Time 2) was conducted during the 1997 and 1998 academic year with the same students who were interviewed the previous year. A sample of students attending school was chosen through approaching every mainstream English class and encouraging students to obtain parental permissions.[2] Choosing the sample from mainstream English classes, a requirement for all ninth-grade English-speaking students, resulted in a sample of students that represented the student body as a whole in terms of race, class, and gender and also limited the sample to those who were proficient in the English language.

The most prominent racial/ethnic groups at Neighborhood High School (NHS) were Latino (48%), Asian American (36%), and African American (15%).[3] More than 90% of the students in the school were eligible for free lunch. Asian American students were mostly Chinese American, and most of the Latino students were of Puerto Rican or Dominican descent. Many Puerto Ricans students were second-or third-generation Americans while Dominican students were more recent immigrants. The African American sample was primarily American born although some were the children or grandchildren of Caribbean or West Indian immigrants. More than 90% of the Chinese American–born sample were foreign born, while the Latino population included foreign and native born. We chose to use the racial and ethnic categories of African American, Latino, and Asian American because they were understood and used by students themselves. In their interviews, they were asked how they identified themselves ethnically, and they often referred to one of these categories or, for the Latino adolescents, to a similar category (e.g., "Spanish").[4]

Setting

NHS is a comprehensive, historically immigrant school located in a neighborhood known for its succession of immigrant groups in New York City. New York City public schools are stratified into three tiers with the most prestigious specialized high schools at the top, followed by "educational option" and then "lower tier." NHS is a typical, lower-tier, comprehensive or neighborhood high school, most of which are the largest and least academically successful schools in the city. Neighborhood schools are, for the most part, where students are sent when they are not accepted at the schools that they would prefer to attend. During the time of the students' attendance at NHS, the school was placed on a state-wide list for failing schools based on state test scores, attendance rates, graduation rates, and several other indicators of academic failure.

Analyzing the race and/or ethnicity of the graduating class, an observer would assume that most of the students in the school are Asian Americans as opposed to only 36% of the school. Although African American and Latinos made up 15% and 48%, respectively, of the school population, only 7% African Americans and 22% Latinos were found in the graduating class of 2000. Of the 348 awards given out to this senior class, 6.6% went to African Americans, 18.10% went to Latinos, and 70% went to Asian Americans (5.7% went to students from diverse racial and ethnic backgrounds). After calculating who graduated in 4 years, who won awards, and who attended 4-year colleges or universities as opposed to community college, the military, or employment, it was clear that the Asian American students graduated at higher rates, received more honors, and attended more prestigious colleges than Latino and African American students.

Data Analysis

The interviews with the adolescents were content analyzed (Miles & Huberman, 1984). The content analysis revealed thematic variations and similarities across ethnic and racial groups in the type and source of discrimination. Asian American students reported that their experiences of discrimination were primarily with their non-Asian peers. They frequently discussed the ways in which African American and Latino peers harassed and discriminated against them. They also discussed the discrimination that took place between the American-born Asians and foreign-born Asians. The experiences of discrimination among the African Americans and the Latino students were with adults, such as teachers, police, and shopkeepers. Their direct or overt experiences of discrimination often took place outside the school. However, many of their more subtle experiences of discrimination were in the school with teachers. The Latino students also reported discrimination between the Puerto Ricans and the Dominicans. In sum, there appeared to be intergroup and intragroup experiences of discrimination in the school. Finally, a theme that was evident among all the students was that they strongly believed in American egalitarianism. At the same time, however, they reported numerous examples of unequal treatment and racism. We used Atlas Ti, a qualitative data analysis computer program, to determine the frequency of these themes within and across each ethnic group.[5] A description of these themes and the nuances in these themes is the focus of the remainder of this article.

RESULTS

Intergroup Discrimination

Discrimination by peers. When Asian American students were asked in their interviews to discuss discrimination, they described stories of harassment and discrimination from their non-Asian American peers in school.

When the interviewer asked Cindy about discrimination, she responded,

TABLE 1: SOURCE, TYPE, AND FREQUENCY OF DISCRIMINATION AS PERCEIVED BY AFRICAN AMERICAN, LATINO, AND ASIAN AMERICAN HIGH SCHOOL STUDENTS

	Peers		Adults		
	Intergroup Physical and Verbal Attacks	Intragroup Verbal Attacks, Teasing, Name Calling	Teachers' Low Expectations, Negative Comments, Not Caring	Police Suspicion of Guilt, Harassment	Shopkeepers' Suspicion of Stealing, Extreme Surveillance
African American (includes Caribbean and West Indians)	1	0	6	4	4
Latino (mostly Puerto Rican and Dominicans)	3[a]	11	6	5	5
Chinese American (mostly Chinese)	26	3	0	0	0

a. Two of the three reported incidents of intergroup tensions from Latinos occurred to light-skinned Puerto Rican students who were mistaken as Whites.

> *The people in the school, they call me chino, stupid, or geek, or anything like that because I'm Chinese. But it really doesn't bother me or my friends. Just that some of us then we'll get really angry and want to beat them up, but I don't care.*

Participant observation and the interviews revealed numerous incidences of physical harassment of the Asian American students by the non-Asian American students in school. Students reported random "slappings" by male and female peers as they walked through the hallways. Slappings are quick, pop shots often to the head or body as students passed one another in the hall or anywhere else. Asian American students described them as unnerving, randomly occurring, and humiliating violations that are particularly harrowing for the boys when girls slap them.

Stemming from being physically harassed, many of the Asian American males in ninth grade reported wanting to grow taller, to be larger, or to work out so as to prevent attacks, or be ready to physically defend themselves in school. An Asian American boy explained that being bigger would prevent physical harassment. Along with slappings, Asian American students were observed and reported being pushed, punched, teased, and mocked by their non-Asian American peers. The racial slur "chino" or "geek" was often heard as Asian American students passed by. The physical and verbal harassment of the Asian American students occurred when adults were present and when they were not.

Kit Wah told the interviewer that a male Asian American friend was held up with a knife in the gym locker by a student in his class. His friend was robbed of several items. All their Asian American friends knew about the robbery, however the student himself was too afraid to tell the authorities in school about the incident. Kit Wah felt that if his friend told the school authorities he would appear weak to his peers and his assailant, and the school authorities would not be able to protect him from being attacked again.[6]

Incidents such as these that included having money, jewelry, and jackets stolen are typical events that Asian American students described when discussing how they were victimized for being Asian American in school. African American and Latino students also described having possessions stolen. However, Asian American students appeared to be more frequently targeted for robbery.[7] These events seemed to be a part of the normalized landscape of behaviors that Asian American students endured in this school.

Students from all racial and ethnic groups at NHS noted segregation and discrimination against Asian American students. In their interviews, African American and Latino students pointed to a social hierarchy in school based on valuing the ability to interact with people from many racial and ethnic backgrounds, defending oneself if necessary, and knowledge about how to get along. Low status was relegated to Asian Americans even though Asian Americans were the second largest ethnic group in the school. When Asian American students did not fight back, they lost face among their peers because they appeared weak, scared, and unwilling to defend themselves. According to the African American and Latino students, when Asian Americans show that they are scared of their peers and/or cannot differentiate between people who will or will not victimize them, they further displayed their vulnerability and inability to know how to get along with people from a variety of racial and ethnic backgrounds.

Discrimination by adults. When African American and Latino students were asked about their experiences with discrimination, they described hostile relationships with adults in positions of authority such as police officers, shopkeepers, and teachers in school. Many of the African American and Latino students reported being followed by shopkeepers in stores with friends and sometimes when they were with their parents. Stories were told repeatedly about being harassed by police officers while walking through their neighborhood, and hanging out with friends in and around school. The frequency of these hostile encounters sends a clear message of distrust by adults, most of whom are White but some of whom are Asian American, Black, or Latino, to African American and Latino students. These stories were not isolated or singular events. They were experienced repeatedly over the years and in different locations. It is important to note that none of the Asian American students reported experiencing racial and ethnic discrimination by teachers, shopkeepers, or police officers.

Benjamin described an encounter with the police who patrol the school. He described a situation in which the police harassed him on two occasions as he was on his way to school. When Benjamin responded to the officers' questions, they picked him up for disrespecting their authority and searched through his belongings. Benjamin, a Dominican student who also identified as Black, explained candidly how being a Black teenager feels:

> *Interviewer:* And what do you think, what do you feel about being Black?
>
> *Benjamin:* It's alright. It's just that there's a lot of flaws…. There's so much stuff that…happens to Black people and like it may be just because I'm a Black teen now…when people seem to think of me in one way…as like the other Black teens…a lot of Black teens do bad stuff…and *I'm like in a stereotype* (emphasis added) and even a lot of stuff that happens you know they just see me as that Black teen and stuff's a lot of trouble…and I'm not (a lot of trouble).

Encounters, such as those with the police, were examples of how "controlling images" (Collins, 1991) of Black teenagers as guilty until proven innocent or as threatening and violent (Gardner, 1980) have a negative emotional impact on an adolescent's life. Benjamin's poignant feelings about being trapped in a stereotype was similar to the stories told by his Black and Latino peers.

Anton, an African American student also of Caribbean descent was asked what it means to be African American. He replied,

Anton: I feel it's a struggle.... It is a struggle because...if you're not dressed...appropriate, and you go into a store...they feel like if you're Dominican, or you're Black, or Puerto Rican, with your hat backwards, they think you're gonna steal something.... That's the...thing, I'm...really worried about.

Interviewer: How do you worry about it?

Anton: I'm going to the store...I'm just looking at stuff, I don't buy something...I just feel guilty, even though I didn't steal nothing...People looking at me, look at my friends. But if you go to a store...you know, dressed nice, slacks, shoes, you know, they think you ain't gonna steal nothing...they just...too quick to judge.

Interviewer: And who is...too quick to judge?

Anton: Like, anyone, people in general, people who are in control of the store.

Interviewer: Yeah. And does it happen in other places like school?

Anton: Yeah. It happens everywhere in the world.

Benjamin and Anton's statement referred not just to one incident with the police or shopkeepers but to many incidents of being caught in a stereotype. They referred to experiences of discrimination that accumulated over time and in different locations.

The Latino and African American students also perceived their teachers as implicitly or explicitly racist or discriminatory. Although students did not necessarily perceive their conflicts with teachers as examples of discrimination, they perceived them as unjust and as implicit examples of racism. They described their teachers' low academic expectations and stereotypes about "bad kids" or kids who "start trouble." They felt that no matter what their actual behavior was in the classroom, they were typically stereotyped by their teachers as bad kids. The teachers were generally, in the eyes of the Latino and Black students, uncaring and ineffective. Valeria described her experiences with teachers:

Valeria: I don't know, some of the teachers don't care, they don't teach you. I had some problems with teachers, they just passed me, but they did not teach me anything, and that's bad for me, for the state exams.

Interviewer: How would you define a good teacher?

Valeria: I don't know. I guess the ones that are stricter and that give you more work. I think that those are good teachers' cause they care. But the ones that don't...give you work...and its' cause they don't care, they still gonna get paid...so they [are] not teaching us anything. And that's harder for us, not them, because they already been through it.... They already working in their careers, but we're the ones that are trying to get up there [become successful].

Students felt that a caring teacher should help students when they did not understand the material, control the students in the classroom, and maintain high expectations by encouraging students to study and achieve academically. Yet teachers were perceived by Black and Latino students as emotionally distant and not committed to education.

Participant observation also suggested that some teachers seemed generally unconcerned with the academic or emotional well-being of their Black and Latino students. For example, Ms. Schwartz showed minimal understanding about respecting the diversity of cultures in her classroom. After complimenting Latoya, an African American student, on the attractiveness of her new braids, the teacher asked Latoya how she would wash her head if she kept the braids. Latoya, looking vulnerable, said that she would keep the braids in for several months and wash her head in the shower. Ms. Schwartz, looking surprised exclaimed loudly, "Oh that is so dirty, you will have bugs in your hair." The student appeared alarmed. Latoya and her peers were angered by such a culturally insensitive remark. The consequence of their interactions was that the teacher repeatedly reprimanded Latoya during the same class for being a troublemaker.

A Chinese American student, Allen, told a story about teachers that he did not like because they discriminated against African American and Latino students. He said that Mr. Lowe was reviewing a list of materials for a final exam and came to the section on African American history. A student asked a question about an aspect of African American history that was confusing, and the teacher responded by saying that knowing about African American history was unimportant and it would not help the students in their knowledge of history. Allen understood that not only was the teacher's statement untrue but also was racist.

In contrast to the African American and Latino students, most Asian American students reported that the teachers were caring and fair to the Asian American students. The disparity in relationships with teachers between Asian American students and the rest of the students was readily apparent. Mai, a particularly outspoken Asian American girl, captured the feelings of many of the Asian American students toward the teacher.

Interviewer: How do you think that you are treated in school by the teachers and other staff here?

Mai: Well I think they like me cause like I'm always there raising my hand or something. And I know my math teacher she love(s) me. … I always go…up to the board. I'm like her number one student right now. Cause I'm getting like all 100's on the tests.… And she loves that…Someone she can get through to. Everybody else is like dead.… Teachers like me because I listen. I pay attention. I understand.… They want you to understand quicker so they can get through a different lesson.… They don't wanna go slow.

Viewing her peers like her teachers do ("everybody else is like dead"), Mai justifies to herself as well as to the interviewer the teacher's clear preference for her. Mai's feelings of confidence in her academic skills and consequently positive relationship with teachers may stem from the teachers' general preference for teaching "immigrant students"—a view that was openly expressed in the faculty lounge and departmental offices. Immigrant students generally meant Asian American students who formed the vast majority of immigrant students in this school. It included those Asian American students who were recent immigrants as well as those who were not and referred to "well-behaved and hard working" students. This description implicitly contrasted the "lazy" behavior of "other" students. These code words for Asian versus Black and Latino appeared to be attempts by the teachers to avoid any suggestion of racism—preferring immigrant students over nonimmigrant students did not seem to be as racist as preferring Asian students over Black and Latino students.

Intragroup Discrimination

When students of Dominican, Puerto Rican, and Chinese descent were asked to discuss the different cliques in school (i.e., the jocks, nerds, etc.), they interpreted this question as referring to within-ethnic-group tensions, such as tensions between Puerto Rican and Dominicans, or between Chinese born in the United States and recently emigrated Chinese. The within-ethnic-group tensions appeared more germane to minority urban adolescents' lives than were the categories of cliques or peer groups based on research in White, middle-class, suburban high schools (Coleman, 1960; Eckert, 1989). Because Dominicans and Puerto Ricans are from different countries, and most Puerto Rican Americans came to New York City before the Dominicans, it was not surprising that they found differences among themselves. The Puerto Ricans often felt discriminated against by the Dominicans, and the Dominicans often felt discriminated against by the Puerto Ricans based on the other groups' overt display of ethnic pride and/or differences in speaking Spanish too quickly or too loudly.

When Tanya, a Chilean American, is asked to describe where she fits in with the segregated groups of Dominicans and Puerto Ricans in school she said,

I hang out with both.… The group I hang out with is like, mix. It's Puerto Ricans and Dominicans.… But like, you know, you shouldn't say something about one heritage that would hurt somebody else's feelings.… Cause that's how fights start.… Cause last year there was a problem. This girl…was proud of being Dominican, there' nothing wrong with that, you should be proud. So then, this Puerto Rican girl said (to Dominicans)… not to get too happy because they were immigrants. That's how the fight started. She shouldn't say that…just cause you're Puerto Rican and you (are) part of the United States, doesn't mean…you (are a) big thing.… That really hurt that person's feeling, as well as, for the other Dominican kids. So that started a big fight. It's usually like…they would dis(respect) you, or…if you're an immigrant…usually Puerto Ricans, they be saying that to other (people), from other countries.

Throughout her interview, Tanya struggled to reconcile her position as a Chilean American whose friends are Puerto Rican and Dominican. Although she professed in her interviews that everyone gets along, her interviews were also replete with stories of fights that created rifts between Dominicans and Puerto Ricans. Tanya struggled with her desire to believe that race and ethnicity is not important for her friends, while conceding that for some friends and peers in school it does matter. Tanya and others suggested that some of the problems stemmed from varying degrees of feeling more American and recentness of immigration. Puerto Rican students often felt more American and saw Dominicans as less American.

Ethnographic and interview data also revealed strain among the Chinese American students. At NHS, there was a large population of Chinese American English Language Learners (ELL) and a smaller population of English-speaking Asian American students. "Mainstream" (i.e., raised predominantly in the United States) Chinese American students, most of whom emigrated when they were very young, considered themselves "ABCs" (American Born Chinese) and felt embarrassment, discomfort, and sometimes outrage when they were confused with "FOBs" which stands for "fresh off the boat" or very recent immigrants. The mainstream Chinese American students, using their knowledge of the differences between ABCs and FOB's, were acutely aware of the subtle clues of dress, style, and manner that distinguished them from recently emigrated Chinese American.[8]

Mainstream Chinese Americans voiced anger by the inability of others in the school to distinguish among groups of Chinese Americans.

Chinese American students in the sample described tensions that related directly to being more Americanized or assimilated than more recently immigrated Chinese American peers. Lena, a recent Chinese immigrant, described the differences between her and mainstream Chinese American students in school.

Interviewer: So how do you describe yourself?

Lena: I grew up in China so…I think the way Chinese does.… I compare myself…to people that were my friends. (Refers to Chinese American students) And they grew up here, they just have different things, they might be high confidence, they will do stuff that I won't do…because I grew up in China.… I have that kind of personality of old-fashioned people.… Because they grew up here and they use a lot of money…and their parents might have money. And they will think that $50 is not that much for clothes.… For me it's a lot.… I think that $50 could buy a lot of things.

Lena articulated the differences between Chinese American students in school who shared similar aspects of her ethnicity, but from whom she felt different psychologically. When talking about herself and friends in school, Lena drew distinctions based on degrees of acculturation by referring to their consumerism. Although research has focused on students' preferences for same-race or ethnic friends (Kandel, 1978; MacLeod, 1987), Lena focused on critical differences among Chinese Americans. These differences were important to adolescents' understanding of how it felt to share the same race and ethnicity with friends while simultaneously experiencing differences based on degrees of acculturation. At NHS, it was unlikely that Lena will become friends with students who are not of Chinese descent. Yet she also felt isolated from those she was "supposed" to feel close to. Limited to choosing friends based on ethnicity, as opposed to shared interests, many students appeared to find themselves even more isolated when they felt distanced not only from the mainstream culture but also from same ethnic peers.

When listening to students' stories it was clear that tensions and divisions within racial or ethnic groups were important aspects of many students everyday lived experiences. A theme in students' discussion about race and ethnicity was the need for others to acknowledge differences between themselves and others in the same racial or ethnic category. Our interviews and participant observations suggested that experiences of race and ethnicity differed by racial and ethnic group in the same locale and may be as much about defining individual and collective identity and differences among the in-group as it was about defining the identity of those outside of the group.

American Egalitarianism

In *An American Dilemma*, Gunnar Myrdal (1944) named a fundamental disjunction between the American belief in egalitarian ideas of freedom and equality and the persistence of segregation that caused discrimination. The American voice of equality references a dominant belief in American culture that downplays the differences among racial and ethnic groups, often ignores the significance of racism, and fosters the perception of equality among the races. This contradiction described by Myrdal (1944) was heard in many of the students' interviews.

When responding to our questions about race and ethnicity and/or experiences of racism or discrimination, students spoke initially in a language or "voice" of American equality saying comments such as "I have friends of all colors," and "Everyone gets along here." When Nikki, an African American girl, was asked if it is important being African American she said "not really." When probed about her answer Nikki said,

Nikki: It's just that you don't think about it, it don't matter to me. If I was Black, Puerto Rican, it won't matter to me.
Interviewer: Why not?
Nikki: I just feel that everybody's the same no matter what they are.

These adolescents wanted to believe in the American ideals of equality and opportunity for all. However, when probed about the realness of equality in relation to their own experiences, students often recalled poignant examples of discrimination. Some students struggled moving back and forth between professing their desire to exist in a world free of discrimination while using their everyday experiences to challenge American egalitarianism. Students expressed this contradiction by claiming that race and ethnicity does not and does matter.

Tanya, who in the previous section discussed tensions between Puerto Ricans and Dominicans, was asked to describe her personality. Tanya responded,

Well, I get along with everybody, you know. It's like, the friends I have, they don't have to be a certain color. You know, I get along with everybody. It don't...matter how they are...Its like...they (peers) don't get you (like you) because of your color, they way you speak, or like what you are, where you're from.... But, you know, I just get along with everybody, I don't care where they're from.

In several sections of her interview, whether she described her personality, her friends, or the relationship between friendship and her Chilean heritage, Tanya believed and relied on a value of American egalitarianism. Simultaneously, she struggled with knowing that some of her friends and peers in school did not want to be friends with people from other racial and/or ethnic groups. For instance, when she was asked to describe herself, Tanya articulated this struggle:

I think I'm a good friend to...know cause...I give everybody a chance...not just because you're Black or you're Chinese, I'm not gonna talk to you...cause I have Chinese friends...but you hear..."oh they're stupid, they're nerds." I go, no, I'll...give everybody a chance not by the way they look...Some of them are...nice...You never know, they could be your best friend.

Repeatedly saying that it was important not to be ashamed of her heritage, Tanya was also careful not to show excessive pride that may insult her peers. As such, Tanya demonstrated her knowledge of how to behave by claiming her ethnicity without denigrating others' ethnicity or being too assertive about her own ethnicity. Other students responded to this implicit and explicit set of behavioral guidelines by assuming that talking about one's own race or ethnicity or expressing feelings of pride could have negative consequences. For some students in the sample, discussing race and ethnicity could be misunderstood as being racist. These students prefaced their statements about their experiences of race and ethnicity by saying, "I'm not racist." Following such proclamations, however, they were willing to discuss their views on race, ethnicity, and discrimination.

DISCUSSION

The current study suggested that variations in the experience of discrimination differed depending on the racial and/or ethnic background of the students involved. African American and Latino students experienced discrimination from adults in positions of authority including teachers, police officers, and shopkeepers, whereas Asian Americans struggled with discrimination from their peers. The public nature of the discrimination, in the hallways, on the stairways, and the frequency with which all students reported seeing and experiencing these acts from peers and from adults were striking. The observation of discrimination by peers and by teachers created a hostile school climate where everyone observed and knew students were discriminated against either from adults or peers. The minimal intervention and the lack of a response by adults in school, furthermore, appeared to condone the behavior.

Peer discrimination may have less dire consequences on academic and career outcomes than adult discrimination and may begin to explain why Asian American students often seem more resilient to the effects of discrimination than Black or Latino students. Peer discrimination, however, may have very serious effects on peer relations and on psychological adjustment. For example, all students, Asian American, African American, and Latino, valued and wanted to have friends from different racial and ethnic backgrounds. However, the interviews suggested that only the Black and Latino students felt confident and comfortable in their abilities to maintain racially and ethnically diverse friendships (although these friendships rarely included Asian Americans). The Asian American students seemed more clannish and afraid to interact with African American and Latino students. The lack of racial/ethnic diversity in their friendships may be due to the harassment by their non-Asian peers, and, perhaps, to their own negative stereotypes of Black and Latino students. In addition, previous analysis of the survey-based data from the current study (Way & Chen, 2000) suggested that the Asian American students were more likely to report depression, low self-esteem, and poor friendship quality than were the African American and Latino students. Peer discrimination experienced by the Asian American students may have a negative influence on their psychological and social well-being. Efforts to address problems of discrimination in schools need to recognize the variety of forms of discrimination and how each form may have consequences on the academic, social, and emotional well-being of students.

Discussions with teachers, observational data, and interviews suggested that many of the teachers at NHS implicitly or explicitly believed in the model minority myth regarding Asian students and, thus, had contentious relationships with Latinos and African Americans. From the African American and Latino students' perspective, teachers favored and had high academic expectations for Asian American students but not for them. Teachers' low expectations for African American and Latino students' achievement and behavior has been previously noted (Farkas et al., 1990; Ladson-Billings, 1994; Lipman, 1998; Rist, 1970) and teachers' high expectations for Asian American students' achievement and behavior has also been documented (Goto, 1997; Lee, 1994). However, it is the interaction between these two expectations that has rarely been addressed. The stereotypes about one group relied and were built on the stereotypes about the other group. When students' perceive teachers have high expectations for some students and low expectations for others, they perpetuate a zero-sum game where only some students can succeed. Consequently racial and ethnic groups are pitted against each other. The prevailing logic is, if Asian Americans are hardworking and successful then African American and Latino students are lazy and unsuccessful.

Research about the implications of the Asian American model minority stereotype has underscored how the stereotype prevented teachers from identifying Asian American students who are not doing well in school and or performed poorly in math and science (Lee, 1994). Less research has emphasized the social consequences of the myth of the model minority for Asian American peer relations, for African American and Latino academic success, and for the interracial school climate. The implications of the myth of the model minority are the messages it sends to less academically successful minority groups. Inherent in the model minority myth is the argument to Blacks and Latinos: "They overcame discrimination-why can't you?" (Tatum, 1997, p. 160). These messages penetrated the social relations among the students and fostered a hostile school climate.

The faculty at the school rarely acknowledged these poor teacher/student and student/student relationships or recognized the differences in experiences among racial and ethnic minority groups. The lack of attention to social relationships in the school appeared to adversely affect not only the relations between the teachers and the African American and Latino students but also the Asian American students' interactions with their peers including their feelings of safety and ability to build friendships with students outside of their own racial and ethnic group.

According to Allport (1954), to promote positive interracial interactions, people need to have contact under specific conditions that include equal status. Because of tracking in the school, which separated the many Asian students from the rest of the students, students from Asian backgrounds had minimal contact with African American and Latino students in the classroom and not under conditions of equal status. School programs also reinforced this segregation through such programs as English Language Learners, Special Education, honors track, and GED. Most extracurricular activities were also segregated by race and ethnicity including the most prominent activities, such as the African American club, the Latino club, and the Asian American club. By far the most significant school events were the cultural performances by each of these groups that included only members of one racial and ethnic group. Although racially and ethnically based clubs are not in and of themselves problematic, when students have few other opportunities in the classroom to interact with students from other cultures and little interest in other clubs besides those based on racial and ethnic identity, these clubs reinforce the segregation permeating the rest of the interactions in school. Hostile intergroup interactions made the school unsafe and harmful for Asian American, Latino, and African American students.

Although the term *minority* is useful to organize a diverse group of people with some of the same social and political needs, the term can also obscure differences such as treatment by those in positions of power. As such, comparisons between the relative successes and failures of minority groups often do not account for tangible variation in barriers. Minority group comparisons are often unfair, and the success or failure of one group is attributed to the particularities of cultural practices or individual merit, again disregarding concrete and systemic differences in treatment by the wider society. Furthermore assuming coherence or uniformity within a minority group overlooks glaring tensions within the group that often defined social relations from the perspective of those who experienced them. In particular, intragroup differences, such as language use, recentness of immigration, degree of acculturation, and attitudes toward consumerism, were just some of the differences students described about members of their same racial and ethnic group.

Our research also suggested that although adolescents make distinctions based on racial and ethnic group membership, they are determined to resist the stereotypes that are associated with these racial and ethnic categories. For example, the African American and Latino students reported that teachers assumed Asian American students were good in math and that African American or Latino students were not good at math. Some Asian American students reported they were not good at math and recognized that others expected them to excel. These students were upset by these stereotypes and thought they were an unfair representation of their potential. Yet they made use of numerous ethnic/racial stereotypes to foster their own beliefs about other groups (e.g., that Asian Americans don't fight back). Students defined themselves in opposition to particular stereotypes about their own groups and used stereotypes to shape their understanding of different ethnic/ racial groups within the school.

Students also made it clear that the racial and ethnic categories used by the institution of school and by their peers (and by themselves) to describe them did not adequately capture their full identities (e.g., "I am Dominican but I only listen to rap" or "I am Chinese American but I do not speak Cantonese"). Students described differences based on immigration status, language use, music preferences, and/or style preferences. These distinctions were considered, at times, much more relevant to their experiences of discrimination than global ethnic/racial categories. However, these distinctions were often embedded in ethnic/racial categories, such as the recent Chinese immigrants being referred to as fresh off the boat. Although the global categories of race/ethnicity did not adequately describe the distinctions that the students made to describe themselves and others, they were often implicated in these distinctions.

Finally, our findings suggest that urban high school students struggle to live with the contradiction of American egalitarianism and the stereotypes, harassment, and discrimination they experienced in their lives. They spoke passionately about the ways in which the assumption of uniformity is harmful and how the interaction between positive and negative stereotypes shapes their daily interactions. They revealed patterns of discriminatory processes that have yet to be noted in the social science literature. Listening to their stories allowed us to begin to understand the ways in which symbolic, traditional, institutional, and individual forms of discrimination worked in an urban high school setting that is more diverse and complex, nationally and locally, than ever before.

In a school, where Asian American students were academically more successful than Latino and African American students, the inequalities within one school can seem as significant as those between wealthy suburban schools and poor urban schools. Future research should continue to explore the diverse experiences of urban, ethnic minority students in multicultural schools, particularly where White students are not the dominant population. Research in other contexts, such as employment or housing, can further elaborate how different forms of discrimination work in other sectors of social life. Analysis within and between racial and ethnic groups in various contexts is an important direction for future research, not as a way of denigrating one group while lauding the accomplishments of another group, but rather as a way of understanding how social processes shape life opportunities.

NOTES

1. The sample was chosen from a larger population of 133 students. During the fall of 1996, 133 ninth–grade students (52.6% girls, 43% Latino, 28.3% African American or Black, 19% Asian-American, and 9% biracial).
2. "Mainstream English Classes" are distinguished from English classes for students learning English as a second language.
3. These statistics are the racial and ethnic population of the school as reported by the Board of Education. The racial and ethnic population of the school greatly differs from the population of the graduating class. See the Setting section for a comparison of the racial and ethnic makeup of the graduating class and the whole school.
4. The one exception to this pattern was that the Asian American students often referred to themselves as Chinese rather than Asian Americans. However, we selected the category of Asian American to include those few students who were not Chinese but who were Asian American (Burmese, Vietnamese, Taiwanese).
5. Using AtlasTi, we could easily divide students by race and ethnicity and then retrieve examples of discrimination based on the codes given to each example of discrimination. For instance, codes such as discrimination by adult, discrimination by peers, intragroup discrimination, and egalitarianism were all used to count the number of times students discussed these experiences.
6. After the interview, the interviewer consulted several other members of the research team to decide how to handle this situation. The interviewee was contacted again and asked if he would be willing to talk to school officials about the robbery. Together the student and the interviewer spoke with school authorities who immediately responded.
7. For example, during their first 2 years of high school, Asian American students were targeted for robberies walking to and from the school. School officials responded by suggesting that Asian American students walk in groups and encouraging students not to wear jewelry to school. In another case, a male student was prosecuted for pulling a necklace off of a Chinese American student in the hallway.
8. Shih (1998) wrote that according to the immigrant Chinese students she studied, the term *ABC* is more complex than just having been born in the United States. ABC can also refer to limited Chinese language ability, cultural identification with Americans, and a dislike for spending time with other Chinese people. Although the term is not necessarily derogatory, immigrant Chinese students can use it negatively when discussing their more Americanized peers.

REFERENCES

Adler, P. A., & Adler, P. (1987). *Membership roles in field research*. Newbury Park, CA: Sage.

Allport, G. W. (1954). *The nature of prejudice*. Cambridge, MA: Addison-Wesley.

Anyon, J. (1997). *Ghetto schooling: A political economy of urban educational reform*. New York: Teachers College Press.

Coleman, J. S. (1960). *The adolescent society: The social life of the teenager and its impact on education*. New York: Free Press.

Collins, P. H. (1991). *Black feminist thought: Knowledge, consciousness, and the politics of empowerment*. New York: Routledge.

Conchas, G., & Noguero, P. (2004) Explaining the academic success of African American males. In N. Way & J. Chu (Eds.), *Adolescent boys in context* (pp. 245–280). New York: New York University Press.

Damico, S. B., & Sparks, C. (1986, April). Cross-group contact opportunities: Impact on interpersonal relationships in desegregated middle schools. *Sociology of Education*, 59, 113–123.

Eckert, P. (1989). *Jocks and burnouts: Social categories and identity in the high school*. New York: Teachers College Press.

Farkas, G., Grobe, R. P., Sheehan, D., & Shuan, Y. (1990, February). Cultural resources and school success: Gender, ethnicity, and poverty groups within an urban school district. *American Sociological Review*, 55, 127–142.

Feagin, J., Hernan, V., & Imani, N. (1996). *The agony of education: Black students at White colleges and universities*. New York: Routledge.

Feagin, J. R. (1977, April). Indirect institutional discrimination. *American Politics Quarterly*, 5, 177–200.

Feagin, J. R. (1992, June). The continuing significance of racism. *Journal of Black Studies*, 22, 546–578.

Feagin, J. R., & Eckberg, D. (1980). Prejudice and discrimination. *Annual Review of Sociology*, 6, 1–20.

Feagin, J. R., & Feagin, C. B. (1996). *Racial and ethnic relations* (5th ed.). Upper Saddle River, NJ: Prentice Hall.

Feagin, J. R., & Sikes, M. P. (1994). *Living with racism*: The Black middle class. Boston: Beacon.

Felice, L. G. (1981). Black student dropout behavior: Disengagement from school rejection and racial discrimination. *Journal of Negro Education*, 50(4), 415–424.

Fine, M. (1991). *Framing dropouts: Notes on the politics of an urban high school*. Albany: State University of New York Press.

Gardner. C. B. (1980). Access information: Public lies and private peril. *Social Problems*, 35, 384–397.

Goto, S. T. (1997). Nerds, normal people, and homeboys: Accommodation and resistance among Chinese American students. *Anthropology and Education Quarterly*, 28(1), 70–84.

Grant, L. (1984). Black females "place" in desegregated classrooms. *Sociology of Education*, 57, 98–111.

Hamilton, C., & Carmichael, S. (1967). *Black power*. New York: Random House.

Hamm, J. V. (1998). Negotiating the maze: Adolescents' cross-ethnic peer relations in ethnically diverse school. In L. H. Meyer, H.-S. Park, M. Grenot-Scheyer, I. S. Schwartz, & B. Harry (Eds.), *Making friends: The influences of culture and development* (pp. 243–261). Baltimore: Paul H. Brooks.

Hamm, J. V. (2001). Barriers and bridges to positive cross-ethnic relations: African American and White parent socialization beliefs and practices. *Youth & Society*, 33(1), 62–98.

Hochschild, J. L. (1984). *The new American dilemma: Liberal democracy and school desegregation*. New Haven, CT: Yale University Press.

Kandel, D. (1978). Homophily, selection, and socialization in adolescent friendships. *American Journal of Sociology*, 84, 427–436.

Kasinitz, P. (1982). *Caribbean New York: Black immigrants and the politics of race*. Ithaca, NY: Cornell University Press.

Kiang, P. N., & Kaplan, J. (1994). Where do we stand? Views of racial conflict by Vietnamese American high-school students in a Black and White context. *Urban Review*, 26(2), 95–119.

Kinder, D. R. (1986). The continuing American dilemma: White resistance to racial change 40 years after Myrdal. *Journal of Social Issues*, 42, 151–171.

Kinder, D. R., & Sears, D. O. (1981). Prejudice and politics: Symbolic racism versus racial threats to the good life. *Journal of Personality and Social Psychology*, 48, 414–431.

Kozol, J. (1991). *Savage inequalities*. New York: Crown.

Ladson-Billings, G. (1994). *The dreamkeepers: Successful teachers of African American children*. San Francisco: Jossey-Bass.

Lee, S. J. (1994). Behind the model-minority stereotype: Voices of high-and low-achieving Asian American students. *Anthropology and Educational Quarterly*, 25(4), 413–429.

Lee, S. J. (1996). *Unraveling the "model minority" stereotype: Listening to Asian American youth*. New York: Teachers College Press.

Lipman, P. (1998). *Race, class, and power in school restructuring*. Albany: State University of New York Press.

Lofland, J., & Lofland, L. H. (1995). *Analyzing social settings: A guide to qualitative observation and analysis* (3rd ed.). New York: Wadsworth.

MacLeod, J. (1987). *Ain't no makin' it*. Boulder, CO: Westview.

McClelland, K. E., & Auster, C. J. (1990, November/December). Public platitudes and hidden tensions: Racial climates at predominantly White liberal arts colleges. *Journal of Higher Education*, 61(6), 607–642.

McConahay, J. B., & Hough, J. C., Jr. (1976). Symbolic racism. *Journal of Social Issues*, 32, 23–45.

Miles, M., & Huberman, A. M. (1984). *Qualitative data analysis: A sourcebook of new methods*. Beverly Hills, CA: Sage.

Myrdal, G. (1944). *American dilemma: The Negro problem and modern democracy*. New York: Harper and Brothers.

O'Connor, C. (1999). Race, class, and gender in America: Narratives of opportunity among low-income African American youths. *Sociology of Education*, 72(3), 137–157.

Ogbu, J. U. (1987). Variability in minority school performance: A problem in search of an explanation. *Anthropology and Education Quarterly*, 18, 312–334.

Olsen, L. (1997). *Made in America: Immigrant students in our public high school*. New York: New Press.

Plank, S. B. (2000). *Finding one's place: Teaching styles and peer relations in diverse classrooms*. New York: Teachers College Press.

Portes, A., & Rumbaut, R. G. (1996). *Immigrant America: A portrait*. Berkeley: University of California Press.

Rist, R. (1970). The self-fulfilling prophecy of the ghetto school. *Harvard Educational Review*, 40, 411–451.

Schofield, J. W. (1989). *Black and White in schools: Trust, tensions, or tolerance?* New York: Praeger.

Schofield, J. W., & McGivern, E. P. (1979). Creating interracial bonds in a desegregated school. In R. G. Blumberg & W. J. Roye (Eds.), *Interracial bonds* (pp. 106–119). Bayside, NY: General Hall.

Sellar, M., & Weis, L. (Eds.). (1997). *Beyond Black and White: New faces and voices in US school*. Albany: State University of New York Press.

Shih, T. A. (1998). Finding the niche: Friendship formation of immigrant adolescents. *Youth & Society*, 30(2). 209–240.

Smith, S. S., & Moore, M. R. (2000). Intraracial diversity and relations among African-Americans: Closeness among Black students at a predominantly White university. *American Journal of Sociology*, 106(1), 1–39.

Tatum, B. D. (1997). *Why are all the Black kids sitting together in the cafeteria? And other conversations about race.* New York: Basic Books.

Waters, M. C. (1996). Second-generation Black immigrants in New York City. In A. Portes (Ed.), *The new second generation* (pp. 171–196). New York: Russell Sage Foundation.

Way, N. (1998). *Everyday courage: The lives and stories of urban teenagers.* New York: New York University Press.

Way, N., & Chen, L. (2000). Close and general friendships among African American, Latino, and Asian American adolescents from low–income families. *Journal of Adolescent Research*, 15(2), 274–301.

Yoshino, R. (1961). Children, teachers and ethnic discrimination. *Journal of Educational Sociology*, 34(9), 391–397.

QUESTIONS

? How did the researchers collect their data? What are the benefits to this type of data collection? What are some of the potential problems with this type of data collection?

? Asian American students report being labeled as "model minority" students. What does this label mean? Does it benefit the student in this study? Why or why not?

? Societal lens question: You have been asked to sociologically research prejudice and discrimination at your school. How will you do it? Describe what you will do and what you think you will find. What will you do with the information?

Section III

*The Sociological Map:
Locating Sources of Societal Stability, Conflict, Change*

Chapter 8

Nickel-and-Dimed
On (not) getting by in America

By BARBARA EHRENREICH

■ Have you ever worked a low-wage job? If so, were you able to make ends meet? Upon discovering that an astounding thirty percent of the American workforce labors for less than $8 an hour, essayist Barbara Ehrenreich conducted the following experiment. She went to work in the service sector (the sector of the economy that provides services, e.g., restaurant, retail, entertainment, etc.) trying to support herself on a $7 hourly wage. In the account that follows, Ehrenreich finds that survival on such low pay is only *one* of the many pitfalls that low-wage laborers encounter.

At the beginning of June 1998 I leave behind everything that normally soothes the ego and sustains the body—home, career, companion, reputation, ATM card—for a plunge into the low-wage workforce. There, I become another, occupationally much diminished "Barbara Ehrenreich"—depicted on job-application forms as a divorced homemaker whose sole work experience consists of housekeeping in a few private homes. I am terrified, at the beginning, of being unmasked for what I am: a middle-class journalist setting out to explore the world that welfare mothers are entering, at the rate of approximately 50,000 a month, as welfare reform kicks in. Happily, though, my fears turn out to be entirely unwarranted: during a month of poverty and toil, my name goes unnoticed and for the most part unuttered. In this parallel universe where my father never got out of the mines and I never got through college, I am "baby," "honey," "blondie," and, most commonly, "girl."

My first task is to find a place to live. I figure that if I can earn $7 an hour—which, from the want ads, seems doable—I can afford to spend $500 on rent, or maybe, with severe economies, $600. In the Key West area, where I live, this pretty much confines me to flophouses and trailer homes—like the one, a pleasing fifteen-minute drive from town, that has no air-conditioning, no screens, no fans, no television, and, by way of diversion, only the challenge of evading the landlord's Doberman pinscher. The big problem with this place, though, is the rent, which at $675 a month is well beyond my reach. All right, Key West is expensive. But so is New York City, or the

---

Reprinted by permission of International Creative Management, Inc. Copyright © 1999 by Barbara Ehrenreich.

Bay Area, or Jackson Hole, or Telluride, or Boston, or any other place where tourists and the wealthy compete for living space with the people who clean their toilets and fry their hash browns.[1] Still, it is a shock to realize that "trailer trash" has become, for me, a demographic category to aspire to.

So I decide to make the common trade-off between affordability and convenience, and go for a $500-a-month efficiency thirty miles up a two-lane highway from the employment opportunities of Key West, meaning forty-five minutes if there's no road construction and I don't get caught behind some sun-dazed Canadian tourists. I hate the drive, along a roadside studded with white crosses commemorating the more effective head-on collisions, but it's a sweet little place—a cabin, more or less, set in the swampy back yard of the converted mobile home where my landlord, an affable TV repairman, lives with his bartender girlfriend. Anthropologically speaking, a bustling trailer park would be preferable, but here I have a gleaming white floor and a firm mattress, and the few resident bugs are easily vanquished.

Besides, I am not doing this for the anthropology. My aim is nothing so mistily subjective as to "experience poverty" or find out how it "really feels" to be a long-term low-wage worker. I've had enough unchosen encounters with poverty and the world of low-wage work to know it's not a place you want to visit for touristic purposes; it just smells too much like fear. And with all my real-life assets—bank account, IRA, health insurance, multiroom home—waiting indulgently in the background, I am, of course, thoroughly insulated from the terrors that afflict the genuinely poor.

No, this is a purely objective, scientific sort of mission. The humanitarian rationale for welfare reform—as opposed to the more punitive and stingy impulses that may actually have motivated it—is that work will lift poor women out of poverty while simultaneously inflating their self-esteem and hence their future value in the labor market. Thus, whatever the hassles involved in finding child care, transportation, etc., the transition from welfare to work will end happily, in greater prosperity for all. Now there are many problems with this comforting prediction, such as the fact that the economy will inevitably undergo a downturn, eliminating many jobs. Even without a downturn, the influx of a million former welfare recipients into the low-wage labor market could depress wages by as much as 11.9 percent, according to the Economic Policy Institute (EPI) in Washington, D.C.

But is it really possible to make a living on the kinds of jobs currently available to unskilled people? Mathematically, the answer is no, as can be shown by taking $6 to $7 an hour, perhaps subtracting a dollar or two an hour for child care, multiplying by 160 hours a month, and comparing the result to the prevailing rents. According to the National Coalition for the Homeless, for example, in 1998 it took, on average nationwide, an hourly wage of $8.89 to afford a one-bedroom apartment, and the Preamble Center for Public Policy estimates that the odds against a typical welfare recipient's landing a job at such a "living wage" are about 97 to 1. If these numbers are right, low-wage work is not a solution to poverty and possibly not even to homelessness.

It may seem excessive to put this proposition to an experimental test. As certain family members keep unhelpfully reminding me, the viability of low-wage work could be tested, after a fashion, without ever leaving my study. I could just pay myself $7 an hour for eight hours a day, charge myself for room and board, and total up the numbers after a month. Why leave the people and work that I love? But I am an experimental scientist by training. In that business, you don't just sit at a desk and theorize; you plunge into the everyday chaos of nature, where surprises lurk in the most mundane measurements. Maybe, when I got into it, I would discover some hidden economies in the world of the low-wage worker. After all, if 30 percent of the workforce toils for less than $8 an hour, according to the EPI, they may have found some tricks as yet unknown to me. Maybe—who knows?—I would even be able to detect in myself the bracing psychological effects of getting out of the house, as promised by the welfare wonks at places like the Heritage Foundation. Or, on the other hand, maybe there would be unexpected costs—physical, mental, or financial—to throw off all my calculations. Ideally, I should do this with two small children in tow, that being the welfare average, but mine are grown and no one is willing to lend me theirs for a month-long vacation in penury. So this is not the perfect experiment, just a test of the best, possible case: an unencumbered woman, smart and even strong, attempting to live more or less off the land.

On the morning of my first full day of job searching, I take a red pen to the want ads, which are auspiciously numerous. Everyone in Key West's booming "hospitality industry" seems to be looking for someone like me—trainable, flexible, and with suitably humble expectations as to pay. I know I possess certain traits that might be advantageous—I'm white and, I like to think, well-spoken and poised—but I decide on two rules: One, I cannot use any skills derived from my education or usual work—not that there are a lot of want ads for satirical essayists anyway. Two, I have to take the best-paid job that is offered me and of course do my best to hold it; no Marxist rants or sneaking off to read novels in the ladies' room. In addition, I rule out various occupations for one reason or another: Hotel front-desk clerk, for example, which to my surprise is regarded as unskilled and pays around $7 an hour, gets eliminated because it involves standing in one spot for eight hours a day. Waitressing is similarly something I'd like to avoid, because I remember it leaving me bone tired when I was eighteen, and I'm decades of varicosities and back pain beyond that now. Telemarketing, one of the first refuges of the suddenly indigent, can be dismissed on grounds of personality. This leaves certain supermarket jobs, such as deli clerk, or housekeeping in Key West's thousands of hotel and guest rooms. Housekeeping is especially appealing, for reasons both atavistic and practical: it's what my mother did before I came along, and it can't be too different from what I've been doing part-time, in my own home, all my life.

So I put on what I take to be a respectful-looking outfit of ironed Bermuda shorts and scooped-neck T-shirt and set out for a tour of the local hotels and supermarkets. Best Western, Econo Lodge, and HoJo's all let me fill out application forms, and these are, to my relief, interested in little more than whether I am a legal resident of the United States and have committed any felonies. My next stop is Winn-Dixie, the supermarket, which turns out to have a particularly onerous application process, featuring a fifteen-minute "interview" by computer since, apparently, no human on the premises is deemed capable of representing the corporate point of view. I am conducted to a large room decorated with posters illustrating how to look "professional" (it helps to be white and, if female, permed) and warning of the slick promises that union organizers might try to tempt me with. The interview is multiple choice: Do I have anything, such as child-care problems, that might make it hard for me to get to work on time? Do I think safety on the job is the responsibility of management? Then, popping up cunningly out of the blue: How many dollars' worth of stolen goods have I purchased in the last year? Would I turn in a fellow employee if I caught him stealing? Finally, "Are you an honest person?"

Apparently, I ace the interview, because I am told that all I have to do is show up in some doctor's office tomorrow for a urine test. This seems to be a fairly general rule: if you want to stack Cheerio boxes or vacuum hotel rooms in chemically fascist America, you have to be willing to squat down and pee in front of some health worker (who has no doubt had to do the same thing herself). The wages Winn-Dixie is offering—$6 and a couple of dimes to start with—are not enough, I decide, to compensate for this indignity.[2]

I lunch at Wendy's, where $4.99 gets you unlimited refills at the Mexican part of the Super-bar, a comforting surfeit of refried beans and "cheese sauce." A teenage employee, seeing me studying the want ads, kindly offers me an application form, which I fill out, though here, too, the pay is just $6 and change an hour. Then it's off for a round of the locally owned inns and guesthouses. At "The Palms," let's call it, a bouncy manager actually takes me around to see the rooms and meet the existing housekeepers, who, I note with satisfaction, look pretty much like me—faded ex-hippie types in shorts with long hair pulled back in braids. Mostly, though, no one speaks to me or even looks at me except to proffer an application form. At my last stop, a palatial B&B, I wait twenty minutes to meet "Max," only to be told that there are no jobs now but there should be one soon, since "nobody lasts more than a couple weeks." (Because none of the people I talked to knew I was a reporter, I have changed their names to protect their privacy and, in some cases perhaps, their jobs.)

Three days go by like this, and, to my chagrin, no one out of the approximately twenty places I've applied calls me for an interview. I had been vain enough to worry about coming across as too educated for the jobs I sought, but no one even seems interested in finding out how overqualified I am. Only later will I realize that the want ads are not a reliable measure of the actual jobs available at any particular time. They are, as I should have guessed from Max's comment, the employers' insurance policy against the relentless turnover of the low-wage workforce. Most of the big hotels run ads almost continually, just to build a supply of applicants to replace the current workers as they drift away or are fired, so finding a job is just a matter of being at the right place at the right time and flexible enough to take whatever is being offered that day. This finally happens to me at a one of the big discount hotel chains, where I go, as usual, for housekeeping and am sent, instead, to try out as a waitress at the attached "family restaurant," a dismal spot with a counter and about thirty tables that looks out on a parking garage and features such tempting fare as "Pollish [sic] sausage and BBQ sauce" on 95-degree days. Phillip, the dapper young West Indian who introduces himself as the manager, interviews me with about as much enthusiasm as if he were a clerk processing me for Medicare, the principal questions being what shifts can I work and when can I start. I mutter something about being woefully out of practice as a waitress, but he's already on to the uniform: I'm to show up tomorrow wearing black slacks and black shoes; he'll provide the rust-colored polo shirt with HEARTHSIDE embroidered on it, though I might want to wear my own shirt to get to work, ha ha. At the word "tomorrow," something between fear and indignation rises in my chest. I want to say, "Thank you for your time, sir, but this is just an experiment, you know, not my actual life."

So begins my career at the Hearthside, I shall call it, one small profit center within a global discount hotel chain, where for two weeks I work from 2:00 till 10:00 P.M. for $2.43 an hour plus tips.[3] In some futile bid for gentility, the management has barred employees from using the front door, so my first day I enter through the kitchen, where a red-faced man with shoulder-length blond hair is throwing frozen steaks against the wall and yelling, "Fuck this shit!" "That's just Jack," explains Gail, the wiry middle-aged waitress who is assigned to train me. "He's on the rag again"—a condition occasioned, in this instance, by the fact that the cook, on the morning shift had forgotten to thaw out the steaks. For the next eight hours, I run after the agile Gail, absorbing bits of instruction along with fragments of personal tragedy. All food must be trayed, and the reason she's so tired today is that she woke up in a cold sweat thinking of her boyfriend, who killed himself recently in an upstate prison. No refills on lemonade. And the reason he was in prison is that a few DUIs caught up with him, that's all, could have happened to anyone. Carry the creamers to the table in a monkey bowl, never in your hand. And after he was gone she spent several months living in her truck, peeing in a plastic pee bottle and reading by candlelight at night, but you can't live in a truck in the summer, since you need to have the windows down, which means anything can get in, from mosquitoes on up.

At least Gail puts to rest any fears I had of appearing overqualified. From the first day on, I find that of all the things I have left behind, such as home and identity, what I miss the most is competence. Not that I have ever felt utterly competent in the writing business, in which one day's success augurs nothing at all for the next. But in my writing life, I at least have some notion of procedure: do the research, make the outline, rough out a draft, etc. As a server, though, I am beset by requests like bees: more iced tea here, ketchup over there, a to-go box for table fourteen, and where are the high chairs, anyway? Of the twenty-seven tables, up to six are usually mine at any time, though on slow afternoons or if Gail is off, I sometimes have the whole place to myself. There is the touch-screen computer-ordering system to master, which is, I suppose, meant to minimize server-cook contact, but in practice requires constant verbal fine-tuning: "That's gravy on the mashed, okay? None on the meatloaf," and so forth—while the cook scowls as if I were inventing these refinements just to torment him. Plus, something I had forgotten in the years since I was eighteen: about a third of a server's job is "side work" that's invisible to customers—sweeping, scrubbing, slicing, refilling, and restocking. If it isn't all done, every little bit of it, you're going to face the 6:00 P.M. dinner rush defenseless and probably go down in flames. I screw up dozens of times at the beginning, sustained in my shame entirely by Gail's support—"It's okay, baby, everyone does that sometime"—because, to my total surprise and despite the scientific detachment I am doing my best to maintain, I care.

The whole thing would be a lot easier if I could just skate through it as Lily Tomlin in one of her waitress skins, but I was raised by the absurd Booker T. Washingtonian precept that says: If you're going to do something, do it well. In fact, "well" isn't good enough by half. Do it better than anyone has ever done it before. Or so said my father, who must have known what he was talking about because he managed to pull himself, and us with him, up from the mile-deep copper mines of Butte to the leafy suburbs of the Northeast, ascending from boilermakers to martinis before booze beat out ambition. As in most endeavors I have encountered in my life, doing it "better than anyone" is not a reasonable goal. Still, when I wake up at 4:00 A.M. in my own cold sweat, I am not thinking about the writing deadlines I'm neglecting; I'm thinking about the table whose order I screwed up so that one of the boys didn't get his kiddie meal until the rest of the family had moved on to their Key Lime pies. That's the other powerful motivation I hadn't expected—the customers, or "patients," as I can't help thinking of them on account of the mysterious vulnerability that seems to have left them temporarily unable to feed themselves. After a few days at the Hearthside, I feel the service ethic kick in like a shot of oxytocin, the nurturance hormone. The plurality of my customers are hard-working locals—truck drivers, construction workers, even housekeepers from the attached hotel—and I want them to have the closest to a "fine dining" experience that the grubby circumstances will allow. No "you guys" for me; everyone over twelve is "sir" or "ma'am." I ply them with iced tea and coffee refills; I return, mid-meal, to inquire how everything is; I doll up their salads with chopped raw mushrooms, summer squash slices, or whatever bits of produce I can find that have survived their sojourn in the cold-storage room mold-free.

There is Benny, for example, a short, tight-muscled sewer repairman, who cannot even think of eating until he has absorbed a half hour of air-conditioning and ice water. We chat about hyperthermia and electrolytes until he is ready to order some finicky combination like soup of the day, garden salad, and a side of grits. There are the German tourists who are so touched by my pidgin "Willkommen" and "Ist alles gut?" that they actually tip. (Europeans, spoiled by their trade-union-ridden, high-wage welfare states, generally do not know that they are supposed to tip. Some restaurants, the Hearthside included, allow servers to "grat" their foreign customers, or add a tip to the bill. Since this amount is added before the customers have a chance to tip or not tip, the practice amounts to an automatic penalty for imperfect English.) There are the two dirt-smudged lesbians, just off their construction shift, who are impressed enough by my suave handling of the fly in the piña colada that they take the time to praise me to Stu, the assistant manager. There's Sam, the kindly retired cop, who has to plug up his tracheotomy hole with one finger in order to force the cigarette smoke into his lungs.

Sometimes I play with the fantasy that I am a princess who, in penance for some tiny transgression, has undertaken to feed each of her subjects by hand. But the non-princesses working with me are just as indulgent, even when this means flouting management rules—concerning, for example, the number of croutons that can go on a salad (six). "Put on all you want," Gail whispers, "as long as Stu isn't looking." She dips into her own tip money to buy biscuits and gravy for an out-of-work mechanic who's used up all his money on dental surgery, inspiring me to pick up the tab for his milk and pie. Maybe the same high levels of agape can be found throughout the "hospitality industry." I remember the poster decorating one of the apartments I looked at, which said "If you seek happiness for yourself you will never find it. Only when you seek happiness for others will it come to you," or words to that effect—an odd sentiment, it seemed to me at the time, to find in the dank one-room basement apartment of a bellhop at the Best Western. At the Hearthside, we utilize whatever bits of autonomy we have to ply our customers with the illicit calories that signal our love. It is our job as servers to assemble the salads and desserts, pouring the dressings and squirting the whipped cream. We also control the number of butter patties our customers get and the amount of sour cream on their baked potatoes. So if you wonder why Americans are so obese, consider the fact that waitresses both express their humanity and earn their tips through the covert distribution of fats.

Ten days into it, this is beginning to look like a livable lifestyle. I like Gail, who is "looking at fifty" but moves so fast she can alight in one place and then another without apparently being anywhere between them. I clown around with Lionel, the teenage Haitian busboy, and catch a few fragments of conversation with Joan, the svelte fortyish hostess and militant feminist who is the only one of us who dares to tell Jack to shut the fuck up. I even warm up to Jack when, on a slow night and to make up for a particularly unwarranted attack on my abilities, or so I imagine, he tells me about his glory days as a young man at "coronary school"—or do you say "culinary"?—in Brooklyn, where he dated a knock-out Puerto Rican chick and learned everything there is to know about food. I finish up at 10:00 or 10:30, depending on how much side work I've been able to get done during the shift, and cruise home to the capes I snatched up at random when I left my real home—Marianne Faithfull, Tracy

Chapman, Enigma, King Sunny Ade, the Violent Femmes—just drained enough for the music to set my cranium resonating but hardly dead. Midnight snack is Wheat Thins and Monterey Jack, accompanied by cheap white wine on ice and whatever AMC has to offer. To bed by 1:30 or 2:00, up at 9:00 or 10:00, read for an hour while my uniform whirls around in the landlord's washing machine, and then it's another eight hours spent following Mao's central instruction, as laid out in the Little Red Book, which was: Serve the people.

I could drift along like this, in some dreamy proletarian idyll, except for two things. One is management. If I have kept this subject on the margins thus far it is because I still flinch to think that I spent all those weeks under the surveillance of men (and later women) whose job it was to monitor my behavior for signs of sloth, theft, drug abuse, or worse. Not that managers and especially "assistant managers" in low-wage settings like this are exactly the class enemy. In the restaurant business, they are mostly former cooks or servers, still capable of pinch-hitting in the kitchen or on the floor, just as in hotels they are likely to be former clerks, and paid a salary of only about $400 a week. But everyone knows they have crossed over to the other side, which is, crudely put, corporate as opposed to human. Cooks want to prepare tasty meals; servers want to serve them graciously; but managers are there for only one reason—to make sure that money is made for some theoretical entity that exists far away in Chicago or New York, if a corporation can be said to have a physical existence at all. Reflecting on her career, Gail tells me ruefully that she had sworn, years ago, never to work for a corporation again. "They don't cut you no slack. You give and you give, and they take."

Managers can sit—for hours at a time if they want—but it's their job to see that no one else ever does, even when there's nothing to do, and this is why, for servers, slow times can be as exhausting as rushes. You start dragging out each little chore, because if the manager on duty catches you in an idle moment, he will give you something far nastier to do. So I wipe, I clean, I consolidate ketchup bottles and recheck the cheesecake supply, even tour the tables to make sure the customer evaluation forms are all standing perkily in their places—wondering all the time how many calories I burn in these strictly theatrical exercises. When, on a particularly dead afternoon, Stu finds me glancing at a *USA Today* a customer has left behind, he assigns me to vacuum the entire floor with the broken vacuum cleaner that has a handle only two feet long, and the only way to do that without incurring orthopedic damage is to proceed from spot to spot on your knees.

On my first Friday at the Hearthside there is a "mandatory meeting for all restaurant employees," which I attend, eager for insight into our overall marketing strategy and the niche (your basic Ohio cuisine with a tropical twist?) we aim to inhabit. But there is no "we" at this meeting. Phillip, our top manager except for an occasional "consultant" sent out by corporate headquarters, opens it with a sneer: "The break room—it's disgusting. Butts in the ashtrays, newspapers lying around, crumbs." This windowless little room, which also houses the time clock for the entire hotel, is where we stash our bags and civilian clothes and take our half-hour meal breaks. But a break room is not a right, he tells us. It can be taken away. We should also know that the lockers in the break room and whatever is in them can be searched at any time. Then comes gossip; there has been gossip; gossip (which seems to mean employees talking among themselves) must stop. Off-duty employees are henceforth barred from eating at the restaurant, because "other servers gather around them and gossip." When Phillip has exhausted his agenda of rebukes, Joan complains about the condition of the ladies' room and I throw in my two bits about the vacuum cleaner. But I don't see any backup coming from my fellow servers, each of whom has subsided into her own personal funk; Gail, my role model, stares sorrowfully at a point six inches from her nose. The meeting ends when Andy, one of the cooks, gets up, muttering about breaking up his day off for this almighty bullshit.

Just four days later we are suddenly summoned into the kitchen at 3:30 P.M., even though there are live tables on the floor. We all—about ten of us—stand around Phillip, who announces grimly that there has been a report of some "drug activity" on the night shift and that, as a result, we are now to be a "drug-free" workplace, meaning that all new hires will be tested, as will possibly current employees on a random basis. I am glad that this part of the kitchen is so dark, because I find myself blushing as hard as if I had been caught toking up in the ladies' room myself: I haven't been treated this way—lined up in the corridor, threatened with locker searches, peppered with carelessly aimed accusations—since junior high school. Back on the floor, Joan cracks, "Next they'll be telling us we can't have sex on the job." When I ask Stu what happened to inspire the crackdown, he just mutters about "management decisions" and takes the opportunity to upbraid Gail and me for being too generous with the rolls. From now on there's to be only one per customer, and it goes out with the dinner, not with the salad. He's also been riding the cooks, prompting Andy to come out of the kitchen and observe—with the serenity of a man whose customary implement is a butcher knife—that "Stu has a death wish today."

Later in the evening, the gossip crystallizes around the theory that Stu is himself the drug culprit, that he uses the restaurant phone to order up marijuana and sends one of the late servers out to fetch it for him. The server was caught, and she may have ratted Stu out or at least said enough to cast some suspicion on him, thus accounting for his pissy behavior. Who knows? Lionel, the busboy, entertains us for the rest of the shift by standing just behind Stu's back and sucking deliriously on an imaginary joint.

The other problem, in addition to the less-than-nurturing management style, is that this job shows no sign of being financially viable. You might imagine, from a comfortable distance, that people who live, year in and year out, on $6 to $10 an hour have discovered some survival stratagems unknown to the middle class. But no. It's not hard to get my co-workers to talk about their living situations, because housing, in almost every case, is the principal source of disruption in their lives, the first thing they fill you in on when they arrive for their shifts. After a week, I have compiled the following survey:

- Gail is sharing a room in a well-known downtown flophouse for which she and a roommate pay about $250 a week. Her roommate, a male friend, has begun hitting on her, driving her nuts, but the rent would be impossible alone.
- Claude, the Haitian cook, is desperate to get out of the two-room apartment he shares with his girlfriend and two other, unrelated, people. As far as I can determine, the other Haitian men (most of whom only speak Creole) live in similarly crowded situations.
- Annette, a twenty-year-old server who is six months pregnant and has been abandoned by her boyfriend, lives with her mother, a postal clerk.
- Marianne and her boyfriend are paying $170 a week for a one-person trailer.
- Jack, who is, at $10 an hour, the wealthiest of us, lives in the trailer he owns, paying only the $400-a-month lot fee.
- The other white cook, Andy, lives on his dry-docked boat, which, as far as I can tell from his loving descriptions, can't be more than twenty feet long. He offers to take me out on it, once it's repaired, but the offer comes with inquiries as to my marital status, so I do not follow up on it.
- Tina and her husband are paying $60 a night for a double room in a Days Inn. This is because they have no car and the Days Inn is within walking distance of the Hearthside. When Marianne, one of the breakfast servers, is tossed out of her trailer for subletting (which is against the trailer-park rules), she leaves her boyfriend and moves in with Tina and her husband.
- Joan, who had fooled me with her numerous and tasteful outfits (hostesses wear their own clothes), lives in a van she parks behind a shopping center at night and showers in Tina's motel room. The clothes are from thrift shops.[4]

It strikes me, in my middle-class solipsism, that there is gross improvidence in some of these arrangements. When Gail and I are wrapping silverware in napkins—the only task for which we are permitted to sit—she tells me she is thinking of escaping from her roommate by moving into the Days Inn herself. I am astounded: How can she even think of paying between $40 and $60 a day? But if I was afraid of sounding like a social worker, I come out just sounding like a fool. She squints at me in disbelief, "And where am I supposed to get a month's rent and a month's deposit for an apartment?" I'd been feeling pretty smug about my $500 efficiency, but of course it was made possible only by the $1,300 I had allotted myself for start-up costs when I began my low-wage life: $1,000 for the first month's rent and deposit, $100 for initial groceries and cash in my pocket, $200 stuffed away for emergencies. In poverty, as in certain propositions in physics, starting conditions are everything.

There are no secret economies that nourish the poor; on the contrary, there are a host of special costs. If you can't put up the two months' rent you need to secure an apartment, you end up paying through the nose for a room by the week. If you have only a room, with a hot plate at best, you can't save by cooking up huge lentil stews that can be frozen for the week ahead. You eat fast food, or the hot dogs and styrofoam cups of soup that can be microwaved in a convenience store. If you have no money for health insurance—and the Hearthside's niggardly plan kicks in only after three months—you go without routine care or prescription drugs and end up paying the price. Gail, for example, was fine until she ran out of money for estrogen pills. She is supposed to be on the company plan by now, but they claim to have lost her application form and need to begin the paperwork all over again. So she spends $9 per migraine pill to control the headaches she wouldn't have, she insists, if her estrogen supplements were covered. Similarly, Marianne's boyfriend lost his job as a roofer because he missed so much time after getting a cut on his foot for which he couldn't afford the prescribed antibiotic.

My own situation, when I sit down to assess it after two weeks of work, would not be much better if this were my actual life. The seductive thing about waitressing is that you don't have to wait for payday to feel a few bills in your pocket, and my tips usually cover meals and gas, plus something left over to stuff into the kitchen drawer I use as a bank. But as the tourist business slows in the summer heat, I sometimes leave work with only $20 in tips (the gross is higher, but servers share about 15 percent of their tips with the busboys and bartenders). With wages included, this amounts to about the minimum wage of $5.15 an hour. Although the sum in the drawer is piling up, at the present rate of accumulation it will be more than a hundred dollars short of my rent when the end of the month comes around. Nor can I see any expenses to cut. True, I haven't gone the lentil-stew route yet, but that's because I don't have a large cooking pot, pot holders, or a ladle to stir with (which cost about $30 at Kmart, less at thrift stores), not to mention onions, carrots, and the indispensable bay leaf. I do make my lunch almost every day—usually some slow-burning, high-protein combo like frozen chicken patties with melted cheese on top and canned pinto beans on the side. Dinner is at the Hearthside, which offers its employees a choice of BLT, fish sandwich, or hamburger for only $2. The burger lasts longest, especially if it's heaped with gut-puckering jalapeños, but by midnight my stomach is growling again.

So unless I want to start using my car as a residence, I have to find a second, or alternative, job. I call all the hotels where I filled out housekeeping applications weeks ago—the Hyatt, Holiday Inn, Econo Lodge, HoJo's, Best Western, plus a half dozen or so locally run guesthouses. Nothing. Then I start making the rounds again, wasting whole mornings waiting for some assistant manager to show up, even dipping into places so creepy that the front-desk clerk greets you from behind bulletproof glass and sells pints of liquor over the counter. But either someone has exposed my real-life housekeeping habits—which are, shall we say, mellow—or I am at the wrong end of some infallible ethnic equation: most, but by no means all, of the working housekeepers I see on my job searches are African Americans, Spanish-speaking, or immigrants from the Central European post-Communist world, whereas servers are almost invariably white and monolingually English-speaking. When I finally get a positive response, I have been identified once again as server material. Jerry's, which is part of a well-known national family restaurant chain and physically attached here to another budget hotel chain, is ready to use me at once. The prospect is both exciting and terrifying, because, with about the same number of tables and counter seats, Jerry's attracts three or four times the volume of customers as the gloomy old Hearthside.

Picture a fat person's hell, and I don't mean a place with no food. Instead there is everything you might eat if eating had no bodily consequences—cheese fries, chicken-fried steaks, fudge-laden desserts—only here every bite must be paid for, one way or another, in human discomfort. The kitchen is a cavern, a stomach leading to the lower intestine that is the garbage and dishwashing area, from which issue bizarre smells combining the edible and the offal: creamy carrion, pizza barf, and that unique and enigmatic Jerry's scent—citrus fart. The floor is slick with spills, forcing us to walk through the kitchen with tiny steps, like Susan McDougal in leg irons. Sinks everywhere are clogged with scraps of lettuce, decomposing lemon wedges, waterlogged toast crusts. Put your hand down on any counter and you risk being stuck to it by the film of ancient syrup spills, and this is unfortunate, because hands are utensils here, used for scooping up lettuce onto salad plates, lifting out pie slices, and even moving hash browns from one plate to another. The regulation poster in the single unisex restroom admonishes us to wash our hands thoroughly and even offers instructions for doing so, but there is always some vital substance missing—soap, paper towels, toilet paper—and I never find all three at once. You learn to stuff your pockets with napkins before going in there, and too bad about the customers, who must eat, though they don't realize this, almost literally out of our hands.

The break room typifies the whole situation: there is none, because there are no breaks at Jerry's. For six to eight hours in a row, you never sit except to pee. Actually, there are three folding chairs at a table immediately adjacent to the bathroom, but hardly anyone ever sits here, in the very rectum of the gastro-architectural system. Rather, the function of the peritoilet area is to house the ashtrays in which servers and dishwashers leave their cigarettes burning at all times, like votive candles, so that they don't have to waste time lighting up again when they dash back for a puff. Almost everyone smokes as if his or her pulmonary well-being depended on it—the multinational mélange of cooks, the Czech dishwashers, the servers, who are all American natives—creating an atmosphere in which oxygen is only an occasional pollutant. My first morning at Jerry's, when the hypoglycemic shakes set in, I complain to one of my fellow servers that I don't understand how she can go so long without food. "Well, I don't understand how you can go so long without a cigarette," she responds in a tone of reproach—because work is what you do for others; smoking is what you do for yourself. I don't know why the antismoking crusaders have never grasped the element of defiant self-nurturance that makes the habit so endearing to its victims—as if, in the American workplace, the only thing people have to call their own is the tumors they are nourishing and the spare moments they devote to feeding them.

Now, the Industrial Revolution is not an easy transition, especially when you have to zip through it in just a couple of days. I have gone from craft work straight into the factory, from the air-conditioned morgue of the Hearthside directly into the flames. Customers arrive in human waves, sometimes disgorged fifty at a time from their tour buses, peckish and whiny. Instead of two "girls" on the floor at once, there can be as many as six of us running around in our brilliant pink-and-orange Hawaiian shirts. Conversations, either with customers or fellow employees, seldom last more than twenty seconds at a time. On my first day, in fact, I am hurt by my sister servers' coldness. My mentor for the day is an emotionally uninflected twenty-three-year-old, and the others, who gossip a little among themselves about the real reason someone is out sick today and the size of the bail bond someone else has had to pay, ignore me completely. On my second day, I find out why. "Weil, it's good to see you again," one of them says in greeting. "Hardly anyone comes back after the first day." I feel powerfully vindicated—a survivor—but it would take a long time, probably months, before I could hope to be accepted into this sorority.

I start out with the beautiful, heroic idea of handling the two jobs at once, and for two days I almost do it: the breakfast/lunch shift at Jerry's, which goes till 2:00, arriving at the Hearthside at 2:10, and attempting to hold out until 10:00. In the ten minutes between jobs, I pick up a spicy chicken sandwich at the Wendy's drive-through window, gobble it down in the car, and change from khaki slacks to black, from Hawaiian to rust polo. There is a problem, though. When during the 3:00 to 4:00 P.M. dead time I finally sit down to wrap silver, my flesh seems to bond to the seat. I try to refuel with a purloined cup of soup, as I've seen Gail and Joan do dozens of times, but a manager catches me and hisses "No eating!" though there's not a customer around to be offended by the sight of food making contact with a server's lips. So I tell Gail I'm going to quit, and she hugs me and says she might just follow me to Jerry's herself.

But the chances of this are minuscule. She has left the flophouse and her annoying roommate and is back to living in her beat-up old truck. But guess what? she reports to me excitedly later that evening: Phillip has given her permission to park overnight in the hotel parking lot, as long as she keeps out of sight, and the parking lot should be totally safe, since it's patrolled by a hotel security guard! With the Hearthside offering benefits like that, how could anyone think of leaving?

Gail would have triumphed at Jerry's, I'm sure, but for me it's a crash course in exhaustion management. Years ago, the kindly fry cook who trained me to waitress at a Los Angeles truck stop used to say: Never make an unnecessary trip; if you don't have to walk fast, walk slow; if you don't have to walk, stand. But at Jerry's the effort of distinguishing necessary from unnecessary and urgent from whenever would itself be too much of an energy drain. The only thing to do is to treat each shift as a one-time-only emergency: you've got fifty starving people out there, lying scattered on the battlefield, so get out there and feed them! Forget that you will have to do this again tomorrow, forget that you will have to be alert enough to dodge the drunks on the drive home tonight—just burn, burn, burn! Ideally, at some point you enter what servers call "a rhythm" and psychologists term a "flow state," in which signals pass from the sense organs directly to the muscles, bypassing the cerebral cortex, and a Zen-like emptiness sets in. A male server from the Hearthside's morning shift tells me about the time he "pulled a triple"—three shifts in a row, all the way around the clock—and then got off and had a drink and met this girl, and maybe he shouldn't tell me this, but they had sex right then and there, and it was like, beautiful.

But there's another capacity of the neuromuscular system, which is pain. I start tossing back drugstore-brand ibuprofen pills as if they were vitamin C, four before each shift, because an old mouse-related repetitive-stress injury in my upper back has come back to full-spasm strength, thanks to the tray carrying. In my ordinary life, this level of disability might justify a day of ice packs and stretching. Here I comfort myself with the Aleve commercial in which the cute blue-collar guy asks: If you quit after working four hours, what would your boss say? And the not-so-cute blue-collar guy, who's lugging a metal beam on his back, answers: He'd fire me, that's what. But fortunately, the commercial tells us, we workers can exert the same kind of authority over our painkillers that our bosses exert over us. If Tylenol doesn't want to work for more than four hours, you just fire its ass and switch to Aleve.

True, I take occasional breaks from this life, going home now and then to catch up on e-mail and for conjugal visits (though I am careful to "pay" for anything I eat there), seeing *The Truman Show* with friends and letting them buy my ticket. And I still have those what-am-I-doing-here moments at work, when I get so homesick for the printed word that I obsessively reread the six-page menu. But as the days go by, my old life is beginning to look exceedingly strange. The e-mails and phone messages addressed to my former self come from a distant race of people with exotic concerns and far too much time on their hands. The neighborly market I used to cruise for produce now looks forbiddingly like a Manhattan yuppie emporium. And when I sit down one morning in my real home to pay bills from my past life. I am dazzled at the two- and three-figure sums owed to outfits like Club Body Tech and Amazon.com.

Management at Jerry's is generally Calmer and more "professional" than at the Hearthside, with two exceptions. One is joy, a plump, blowsy woman in her early thirties, who once kindly devoted several minutes to instructing me in the correct one-handed method of carrying trays but whose moods change disconcertingly from shift to shift and even within one. Then there's B.J., a.k.a. B.J.-the-bitch, whose contribution is to stand by the kitchen counter and yell, "Nita, your order's up, move it!" or, "Barbara, didn't you see you've got another table out there? Come on, girl!" Among other things, she is hated for having replaced the whipped-cream squirt cans with big plastic whipped-cream-filled baggies that have to be squeezed with both hands—because, reportedly, she saw or thought she saw employees trying to inhale the propellant gas from the squirt cans, in the hope that it might be nitrous oxide. On my third night, she pulls me aside abruptly and brings her face so close that it looks as if she's planning to butt me with her forehead. But instead of saying, "You're fired," she says, "You're doing fine." The only trouble is I'm spending time chatting with customers: "That's how they're getting you." Furthermore I am letting them "run me," which means harassment by sequential demands: you bring the ketchup and they decide they want extra Thousand Island; you bring that and they announce they now need a side of fries; and so on into distraction. Finally she tells me not to take her wrong. She tries to say things in a nice way, but you get into a mode, you know, because everything has to move so fast.[5]

I mumble thanks for the advice, feeling like I've just been stripped naked by the crazed enforcer of some ancient sumptuary law: No chatting for you, girl. No fancy service ethic allowed for the serfs. Chatting with customers is for the beautiful young college-educated servers in the downtown carpaccio joints, the kids who can make $70 to $100 a night. What had I been thinking? My job is to move orders from tables to kitchen and then trays from kitchen to tables. Customers are, in fact, the major obstacle to the smooth transformation of information into food and food into money—they are, in short, the enemy. And the painful thing is that I'm beginning to see it this way myself. There are the traditional asshole types— frat boys who down multiple Buds and then make a fuss because the steaks are so emaciated and the fries so sparse—as well as the variously impaired—due to age, diabetes, or literacy issues—who require patient nutritional counseling. The worst, for some reason, are the Visible Christians—like the ten-person table, all jolly and sanctified after Sunday-night service, who run me mercilessly and then leave me $1 on a $92 bill. Or the guy with the crucifixion T-shirt (SOMEONE TO LOOK UP TO) who complains that his baked potato is too hard and his iced tea too icy (I cheerfully fix both) and leaves no tip. As a general rule, people wearing crosses or WWJD? (What Would Jesus Do?) buttons look at us disapprovingly no matter what we do, as if they were confusing waitressing with Mary Magdalene's original profession.

I make friends, over time, with the other "girls" who work my shift: Nita, the tattooed twenty-something who taunts us by going around saying brightly, "Have we started making money yet?" Ellen, whose teenage son cooks on the graveyard shift and who once managed a restaurant in Massachusetts but won't try out for management here because she prefers being a "common worker" and not "ordering people around." Easy-going fiftyish Lucy, with the raucous laugh, who limps toward the end of the shift because of something that has gone wrong with her leg, the exact nature of which cannot be determined without health insurance. We talk about the usual girl things—men, children, and the sinister allure of Jerry's chocolate peanut-butter cream pie—though no one, I notice, ever brings up anything potentially expensive, like shopping or movies. As at the Hearthside, the only recreation ever referred to is partying, which requires little more than some beer, a joint, and a few close friends. Still, no one here is homeless, or cops to it anyway, thanks usually to a working husband or boyfriend. All in all, we form a reliable mutual-support group: If one of us is feeling sick or overwhelmed, another one will "bev" a table or even carry trays for her. If one of us is off sneaking a cigarette or a pee,[6] the others will do their best to conceal her absence from the enforcers of corporate rationality.

But my saving human connection—my oxytocin receptor, as it were—is George, the nineteen-year-old, fresh-off-the-boat Czech dishwasher. We get to talking when he asks me, tortuously, how much cigarettes cost at Jerry's. I do my best to explain that they cost over a dollar more here than at a regular store and suggest that he just take one from the half-filled packs that are always lying around on the break table. But that would be unthinkable. Except for the one tiny earring signaling his allegiance to some vaguely alternative point of view, George is a perfect straight arrow—crew-cut, hardworking, and hungry for eye contact. "Czech Republic," I ask, "or Slovakia?" and he seems delighted that I know the difference. "Václav Havel," I try. "Velvet Revolution, Frank Zappa?" "Yes, yes, 1989," he says, and I realize we are talking about history.

My project is to teach George English. "How are you today, George?" I say at the start of each shift. "I am good, and how are you today, Barbara?" I learn that he is not paid by Jerry's but by the "agent" who shipped him over—$5 an hour, with the agent getting the dollar or so difference between that and what Jerry's pays dishwashers. I learn also that he shares an apartment with a crowd of other Czech "dishers," as he calls them, and that he cannot sleep until one of them goes off for his shift, leaving a vacant bed. We are having one of our ESL sessions late one afternoon when B.J. catches us at it and orders "Joseph" to take up the rubber mats on the floor near the dishwashing sinks and mop underneath. "I thought your name was George," I say loud enough for B.J. to hear as she strides off back to the counter. Is she embarrassed? Maybe a little, because she greets me back at the counter with "George, Joseph—there are so many of them!" I say nothing, neither nodding nor smiling, and for this I am punished later when I think I am ready to go and she announces that I need to roll fifty more sets of silverware and isn't it time I mixed up a fresh four-gallon batch of blue-cheese dressing? May you grow old in this place, B.J., is the curse I beam out at her when I am finally permitted to leave. May the syrup spills glue your feet to the floor.

I make the decision to move closer to Key West. First, because of the drive. Second and third, also because of the drive: gas is eating up $4 to $5 a day, and although Jerry's is as high-volume as you can get, the tips average only 10 percent, and not just for a newbie like me. Between the base pay of $2.15 an hour and the obligation to share tips with the busboys and dishwashers, we're averaging only about $7.50 an hour. Then there is the $30 I had to spend on the regulation tan slacks worn by Jerry's servers—a setback it could take weeks to absorb.

(I had combed the town's two downscale department stores hoping for something cheaper but decided in the end that these marked-down Dockers, originally $49, were more likely to survive a daily washing.) Of my fellow servers, everyone who lacks a working husband or boyfriend seems to have a second job: Nita does something at a computer eight hours a day; another welds. Without the forty-five-minute commute, I can picture myself working two jobs and having the time to shower between them.

So I take the $500 deposit. I have coming from my landlord, the $400 I have earned toward the next month's rent, plus the $200 reserved for emergencies, and use the $1,100 to pay the rent and deposit on trailer number 46 in the Overseas Trailer Park, a mile from the cluster of budget hotels that constitute Key West's version of an industrial park. Number 46 is about eight feet in width and shaped like a barbell inside, with a narrow region—because of the sink and the stove—separating the bedroom from what might optimistically be called the "living" area, with its two-person table and half-sized couch. The bathroom is so small my knees rub against the shower stall when I sit on the toilet, and you can't just leap out of the bed, you have to climb down to the foot of it in order to find a patch of floor space to stand on. Outside, I am within a few yards of a liquor store, a bar that advertises "free beer tomorrow," a convenience store, and a Burger King—but no supermarket or, alas, laundromat. By reputation, the Overseas park is a nest of crime and crack, and I am hoping at least for some vibrant, multicultural street life. But desolation rules night and day, except for a thin stream of pedestrian traffic heading for their jobs at the Sheraton or 7-Eleven. There are not exactly people here but what amounts to canned labor, being preserved from the heat between shifts.

In line with my reduced living conditions, a new form of ugliness arises at Jerry's. First we are confronted—via an announcement on the computers through which we input orders—with the new rule that the hotel bar is henceforth off-limits to restaurant employees. The culprit, I learn through the grapevine, is the ultra-efficient gal who trained me—another trailer-home dweller and a mother of three. Something had set her off one morning, so she slipped out for a nip and returned to the floor impaired. This mostly hurts Ellen, whose habit it is to free her hair from its rubber band and drop by the bar for a couple of Zins before heading home at the end of the shift, but all of us feel the chill. Then the next day, when I go for straws, for the first time I find the dry-storage room locked. Ted, the portly assistant manager who opens it for me, explains that he caught one of the dishwashers attempting to steal something, and, unfortunately, the miscreant will be with us until a replacement can be found—hence the locked door. I neglect to ask what he had been trying to steal, but Ted tells me who he is—the kid with the buzz cut and the earring. You know, he's back there right now.

I wish I could say I rushed back and confronted George to get his side of the story. I wish I could say I stood up to Ted and insisted that George be given a translator and allowed to defend himself, or announced that I'd find a lawyer who'd handle the case pro bono. The mystery to me is that there's not much worth stealing in the dry-storage room, at least not in any fenceable quantity: "Is Gyorgi here, and am having 200—maybe 250—ketchup packets. What do you say?" My guess is that he had taken—if he had taken anything at all—some Saltines or a can of cherry-pie mix, and that the motive for taking it was hunger.

So why didn't I intervene? Certainly not because I was held back by the kind of moral paralysis that can pass as journalistic objectivity. On the contrary, something new—something loathsome and servile—had infected me, along with the kitchen odors that I could still sniff on my bra when I finally undressed at night. In real life I am moderately brave, but plenty of brave people shed their courage in concentration camps, and maybe something similar goes on in the infinitely more congenial milieu of the low-wage American workplace. Maybe, in a month or two more at Jerry's, I might have regained my crusading spirit. Then again, in a month or two I might have turned into a different person altogether—say, the kind of person who would have turned George in.

But this is not something I am slated to find out. When my month-long plunge into poverty is almost over, I finally land my dream job— housekeeping. I do this by walking into the personnel office of the only place I figure I might have some credibility, the hotel attached to Jerry's, and confiding urgently that I have to have a second job if I am to pay my rent and, no, it couldn't be front-desk clerk. "All right," the personnel lady fairly spits, "So it's housekeeping," and she marches me back to meet Maria, the housekeeping manager, a tiny, frenetic Hispanic woman who greets me as "babe" and hands me a pamphlet emphasizing the need for a positive attitude. The hours are nine in the morning till whenever, the pay is $6.10 an hour, and there's one week of vacation a year. I don't have to ask about health insurance once I meet Carlotta; the middle-aged African-American woman who will be training me. Carla, as she tells me to call her, is missing all of her top front teeth.

On that first day of housekeeping and last day of my entire project—although I don't yet know it's the last—Carla is in a foul mood. We have been given nineteen rooms to clean, most of them "checkouts," as opposed to "stay-overs," that require the whole enchilada of bed-stripping, vacuuming, and bathroom-scrubbing. When one of the rooms that had been listed as a stay-over turns out to be a checkout, Carla calls Maria to complain, but of course to no avail. "So make up the motherfucker," Carla orders me, and I do the beds while she sloshes around the bathroom. For four hours without a break I strip and remake beds, taking about four and a half minutes per queen-sized bed, which I could get down to three if there were any reason to. We try to avoid vacuuming by picking up the larger specks by hand, but often there is nothing to do but drag the monstrous vacuum cleaner—it weighs about thirty pounds—off our cart and try to wrestle it around the floor. Sometimes Carla hands me the squirt bottle of "BAM" (an acronym for something that begins, ominously, with "butyric"; the rest has been worn off the label) and lets me do the bathrooms. No service ethic challenges me here to new heights of performance. I just concentrate on removing the pubic hairs from the bathtubs, or at least the dark ones that I can see.

I had looked forward to the breaking-and-entering aspect of cleaning the stay-overs, the chance to examine the secret, physical existence of strangers. But the contents of the rooms are always banal and surprisingly neat—zipped up shaving kits, shoes lined up against the wall (there are no closets), flyers for snorkeling trips, maybe an empty wine bottle or two. It is the TV that keeps us going, from *Jerry* to *Sally* to *Hawaii Five-O* and then on to the soaps. If there's something especially arresting, like "Won't Take No for an Answer" on *Jerry*, we sit down on the edge of a bed and giggle for a moment as if this were a pajama party instead of a terminally dead-end job. The soaps are the best, and Carla turns the volume up full blast so that she won't miss anything from the bathroom or while the vacuum is on. In room 503, Marcia confronts Jeff about Lauren. In 505, Lauren taunts poor cuckolded Marcia. In 511, Helen offers Amanda $10,000 to stop seeing Eric, prompting Carla to emerge from the bathroom to study Amanda's troubled face. "You take it, girl," she advises. "I would for sure."

The tourists' rooms that we clean and, beyond them, the far more expensively appointed interiors in the soaps, begin after a while to merge. We have entered a better world—a world of comfort where every day is a day off, waiting to be filled up with sexual intrigue. We, however, are only gatecrashers in this fantasy, forced to pay for our presence with backaches and perpetual thirst. The mirrors, and there are far too many of them in hotel rooms, contain the kind of person you would normally find pushing a shopping cart down a city street—bedraggled, dressed in a damp hotel polo shirt two sizes too large, and with sweat dribbling down her chin like drool. I am enormously relieved when Carla announces a half-hour meal break, but my appetite fades when I see that the bag of hot-dog rolls she has been carrying around on our cart is not trash salvaged from a checkout but what she has brought for her lunch.

When I request permission to leave at about 3:30, another housekeeper warns me that no one has so far succeeded in combining housekeeping at the hotel with serving at Jerry's: "Some kid did it once for five days, and you're no kid." With that helpful information in mind, I rush back to number 46, down four Advils (the name brand this time), shower, stooping to fit into the stall, and attempt to compose myself for the oncoming shift. So much for what Marx termed the "reproduction of labor power," meaning the things a worker has to do just so she'll be ready to work again. The only unforeseen obstacle to the smooth transition from job to job is that my tan Jerry's slacks, which had looked reasonably clean by 40-watt bulb last night when I handwashed my Hawaiian shirt, prove by daylight to be mottled with ketchup and ranch-dressing stains. I spend most of my hour-long break between jobs attempting to remove the edible portions with a sponge and then drying the slacks over the hood of my car in the sun.

I can do this two-job thing, is my theory, if I can drink enough caffeine and avoid getting distracted by George's ever more obvious suffering.[7] The first few days after being caught he seemed not to understand the trouble he was in, and our chirpy little conversations had continued. But the last couple of shifts he's been listless and unshaven, and tonight he looks like the ghost we all know him to be, with dark half-moons hanging from his eyes. At one point, when I am briefly immobilized by the task of filling little paper cups with sour cream for baked potatoes, he comes over and looks as if he'd like to explore the limits of our shared vocabulary, but I am called to the floor for a table. I resolve to give him all my tips that night and to hell with the experiment in low-wage money management. At eight, Ellen and I grab a snack together standing at the mephitic end of the kitchen counter, but I can only manage two or three mozzarella sticks and lunch had been a mere handful of McNuggets. I am not tired at all, I assure myself, though it may be that there is simply no more "I" left to do the tiredness monitoring. What I would see, if I were more alert to the situation, is that the forces of destruction are already massing against me. There is only one cook on duty, a young man named Jesus ("Hay-Sue," that is) and he is new to the job. And there is Joy, who shows up to take over in the middle of the shift, wearing high heels and a long, clingy white dress and fuming as if she'd just been stood up in some cocktail bar.

Then it comes, the perfect storm. Four of my tables fill up at once. Four tables is nothing for me now, but only so long as they are obligingly staggered. As I bev table 27, tables 25, 28, and 24 are watching enviously. As I bev 25, 24 glowers because, their bevs haven't even been ordered. Twenty-eight is four yuppyish types, meaning everything on the side and agonizing instructions as to the chicken Caesars. Twenty-five is a middle-aged black couple, who complain, with some justice, that the iced tea isn't fresh and the tabletop is sticky. But table 24 is the meteorological event of the century: ten British tourists who seem to have made the decision to absorb the American experience entirely by mouth. Here everyone has at least two drinks—iced tea and milk, shake, Michelob and water (with lemon slice, please)—and a huge promiscuous orgy of breakfast specials, mozz sticks, chicken strips, quesadillas, burgers with cheese and without, sides of hash browns with cheddar, with onions, with gravy, seasoned fries, plain fries, banana splits. Poor Jesus! Poor me! Because when I arrive with their first tray of food—after three prior trips just to refill bevs—Princess Di refuses to eat her chicken strips with her pancake-and-sausage special, since, as she now reveals, the strips were meant to be an appetizer. Maybe the others would have accepted their meals, but Di, who is deep into her third Michelob, insists that everything else go back while they work on their "starters." Meanwhile, the yuppies are waving me down for more decaf and the black couple looks ready to summon the NAACP.

Much of what happened next is lost in the fog of war. Jesus starts going under. The little printer on the counter in front of him is spewing out orders faster than he can rip them off, much less produce the meals. Even the invincible Ellen is ashen from stress. I bring table 24 their reheated main courses, which they immediately reject as either too cold or fossilized by the microwave. When I return to the kitchen with their trays (three trays in three trips), Joy confronts me with arms akimbo: "What is this?" She means the food—the plates of rejected pancakes, hash browns in assorted flavors, toasts, burgers, sausages, eggs. "Uh, scrambled with cheddar," I try, "and that's..." "NO," she screams in my face. "Is it a traditional, a super-scramble, an eye-opener?" I pretend to study my check for a clue, but entropy has been up to its tricks, not only on the plates but in my head, and I have to admit that the original order is beyond reconstruction. "You don't know an eye-opener from a traditional?" she demands in outrage. All I know, in fact, is that my legs have lost interest in the current venture and have announced their intention to fold. I am saved by a yuppie (mercifully not one of mine) who chooses this moment to charge into the kitchen to bellow that his food is twenty-five minutes late. Joy screams at him to get the hell out of her kitchen, please, and then turns on Jesus in a fury, hurling an empty tray across the room for emphasis.

I leave. I don't walk out, I just leave. I don't finish my side work or pick up my credit-card tips, if any, at the cash register or, of course, ask Joy's permission to go. And the surprising thing is that you *can* walk out without permission, that the door opens, that the thick tropical night air parts to let me pass, that my car is still parked where I left it. There is no vindication in this exit, no fuck-you surge of relief, just an overwhelming, dank sense of failure pressing down on me and the entire parking lot. I had gone into this venture in the spirit of science, to test a mathematical proposition, but somewhere along the line, in the tunnel vision imposed by long shifts and relentless concentration, it became a test of myself, and clearly I have failed. Not only had I flamed out as a housekeeper/server, I had even forgotten to give George my tips, and, for reasons perhaps best known to hardworking, generous people like Gail and Ellen, this hurts. I don't cry, but I am in a position to realize, for the first time in many years, that the tear ducts are still there, and still capable of doing their job.

When I moved out of the trailer park, I gave the key to number 46 to Gail and arranged for my deposit to be transferred to her. She told me that Joan is still living in her van and that Stu had been fired from the Hearthside. I never found out what happened to George.

In one month, I had earned approximately $1,040 and spent $517 on food, gas, toiletries, laundry, phone, and utilities. If I had remained in my $500 efficiency, I would have been able to pay the rent and have $22 left over (which is $78 less than the cash I had in my pocket at the start of the month). During this time I bought no clothing except for the required slacks and no prescription drugs or medical care (I did finally buy some vitamin B to compensate for the lack of vegetables in my diet). Perhaps I could have saved a little on food if I had gotten to a supermarket more often, instead of convenience stores, but it should be noted that I lost almost four pounds in four weeks, on a diet weighted heavily toward burgers and fries.

How former welfare recipients and single mothers will (and do) survive in the low-wage workforce, I cannot imagine. Maybe they will figure out how to condense their lives—including child-raising, laundry, romance, and meals—into the couple of hours between fulltime jobs. Maybe they will take up residence in their vehicles, if they have one. All I know is that I couldn't hold two jobs and I couldn't make enough money to live on with one. And I had advantages unthinkable to many of the long-term poor—health, stamina, a working car, and no children to care for and support. Certainly nothing in my experience contradicts the conclusion of Kathryn Edin and Laura Lein, in their recent book *Making Ends Meet: How Single Mothers Survive Welfare and Low-Wage Work*, that low-wage work actually involves more hardship and deprivation than life at the mercy of the welfare state. In the coming months and years, economic conditions for the working poor are bound to worsen, even without the almost inevitable recession. As mentioned earlier, the influx of former welfare recipients into the low-skilled workforce will have a depressing effect on both wages and the number of jobs available. A general economic downturn will only enhance these effects, and the working poor will of course be facing it without the slight, but nonetheless often saving, protection of welfare as a backup.

The thinking behind welfare reform was that even the humblest jobs are morally uplifting and psychologically buoying. In reality they are likely to be fraught with insult and stress. But I did discover one redeeming feature of the most abject low-wage work—the camaraderie of people who are, in almost all cases, far too smart and funny and caring for the work they do and the wages they're paid. The hope, of course, is that someday these people will come to know what they're worth, and take appropriate action.

---

[1] According to the Department of Housing and Urban Development, the "fair-market rent" for an efficiency is $551 here in Monroe County, Florida. A comparable rent in the five boroughs of New York City is $704; in San Francisco, $713; and in the heart of Silicon Valley, $808. The fair-market rent for an area is defined as the amount that would be needed to pay rent plus utilities for "privately owned, decent, safe, and sanitary rental housing of a modest (non-luxury) nature with suitable amenities."

[2] According to the Monthly Labor Review (November 1996), 28 percent of work sites surveyed in the service industry conduct drug tests (corporate workplaces have much higher rates), and the incidence of testing has risen markedly since the Eighties. The rate of testing is highest in the South (56 percent of work sites polled), with the Midwest in second place (50 percent). The drug most likely to be detected—marijuana, which can be detected in urine for weeks—is also the most innocuous, while heroin and cocaine are generally undetectable three days after use. Prospective employees sometimes try to cheat the tests by consuming excessive amounts of liquids and taking diuretics and even masking substance available through the Internet.

[3] According to the Fair Labor Standards Act, employers are not required to pay "tipped employees," such as restaurant servers, more than $2.13 an hour in direct wages. However, if the sum of tips plus $2.13 an hour falls below the minimum wage, or $5.15 an hour, the employer is required to make up the difference. This fact was not mentioned by managers or otherwise publicized at either of the restaurants where I worked.

[4] I could find no statistics on the number of employed people living in cars or vans, but according to the National Coalition for the Homeless's 1997 report "Myths and Facts About Homelessness," nearly one in five homeless people (in twenty-nine cities across the nation) is employed in a full- or part-time job.

[5] In Workers in a Lean World: Unions in the International Economy (Verso, 1997), Kim Moody cites studies finding an increase in stress-related workplace injuries and illness between the mid-1980s and the early 1990s. He argues that rising stress levels reflect a new system of "management by stress," in which workers in a variety of industries are being squeezed to extract maximum productivity, to the detriment of their health.

[6] Until April 1998, there was no federally mandated right to bathroom breaks. According to Marc Linder and Ingrid Nygaard, authors of Void Where Prohibited: Rest Breaks and the Right to Urinate on Company Time (Cornell University Press, 1997), "The right to rest and void at work is not high on the list of social or political causes supported by professional or executive employees, who enjoy personal workplace liberties that millions of factory

workers can only daydream about.... While we were dismayed to discover that workers lacked an acknowledged legal right to void at work, [the workers] were amazed by outsiders' naive belief that their employers would permit them to perform this basic bodily function when necessary.... A factory worker, not allowed a break for six-hour stretches, voided into pads worn inside her uniform; and a kindergarten teacher in a school without aides had to take all twenty children with her to the bathroom and line them up outside the stall door when she voided."

[7] In 1996, the number of persons holding two or more jobs averaged 7.8 million, or 6.2 percent of the workforce. It was about the same rate for men and for women (6.1 versus 6.2), though the kinds of jobs differ by gender. About two thirds of multiple jobholders work one job full-time and the other part-time. Only a heroic minority—4 percent of men and 2 percent of women—work two full-time jobs simultaneously. (From John F. Stinson Jr., "New Data on Multiple Jobholding Available from the CPS," in the Monthly Labor Review, March 1997.)

QUESTIONS

- ? Ehrenreich finds that low wage laborers must pay many "hidden costs." What are these hidden costs?
- ? Ehrenreich finds that pay is only one of the dimensions that make low wage jobs less than desirable. What others problems do low-wage workers encounter?
- ? Societal map question: Ehrenreich conducts her research shortly after the 1996 TANF (Temporary Assistance to Needy Families) welfare to work reform—an act that placed time limits on welfare (60 months) and required welfare recipients to look for work. Most TANF recipients are single women with children, and most who found work found it in the service sector. Based on the article, what problems do you think these women will face? What solutions do you see?

Maytag in Mexico

By DAVID MOBERG

■ Perhaps someone close to you, or even you, yourself, recently lost a job. If so, you may have been caught up in the large-scale pattern of deindustrialization—the process by which the industrial base of a country declines and industrial jobs disappear. Since the turn of the twenty-first century, economic deindustrialization in the United States has resulted in the overseas relocation of thousands of manufacturing jobs. Many displaced workers must now find jobs in a growing service-based economy where they receive low pay and limited, if any, benefits. When the Maytag Corporation, located for years in Galesburg, Illinois, joined hundreds of other fleeing corporations, author David Moberg followed the story. In the article that follows, Moberg, who has documented a number of stories about the state of American labor, follows the struggles of local citizens and the local economy, linking them to national and global changes.

Galesburg Illinois—MANY Americans dream of getting rich. Aaron Kemp had more modest ambitions. "I wanted to **work** at a decent job and earn a decent wage, with decent benefits, so I can raise my kids, give them a decent education and maybe take them out to Pizza Hut on a Friday night. I don't need a Mercedes, just a ho-hum existence, and now," he says, with sadness and anger in his voice, "it seems hard to even do that."

Eight years ago, Kemp began working at the factory of Maytag Corporation, the largest employer in Galesburg, a western Illinois town of 34,000 and the birthplace of poet Carl Sandburg. In September, Maytag finally closed the plant, after sending a large part of the **work** that 1,600 people had recently been performing to a new Maytag factory in Reynosa, Mexico; another large part to Daewoo, a Korean multinational subcontractor that is expected to build a plant in Mexico; and a few dozen jobs to a plant in Iowa. Now Kemp, a 31-year-old union safety and

From *In These Times* by David Moberg. Copyright © 2004 by In These Times, www.inthesetimes.com. Reprinted by permission.

education official with a muscular build and a small goatee, has a temporary job as a counselor to laid-off workers at two-thirds his old pay.

The local Machinists union fought the shutdown, taking their case to the streets, to the press, to politicians and to Maytag shareholders, even winning national attention when Senator-elect Barack Obama mentioned their cause in his Democratic convention keynote speech. But the union could not stop the Maytag jobs from being added to the tally of 2.7 million manufacturing jobs lost since 2000. Those several million jobs were eliminated for many reasons—including declining demand, rising efficiency and increased imports—but a significant portion are the result of U.S. multinational corporations, like Maytag, moving production out of the country.

Although the U.S. Bureau of Labor Statistics concluded that during the first three months of this year only 4,633 workers lost jobs because of investment shifts overseas, a study for the U.S.-China Economic and Security Review Commission by Kate Bronfenbrenner of Cornell University and Stephanie Luce of the University of Massachusetts found that at least more than five times that number of jobs were lost in the same period. They also estimate that in 2004 more than 400,000 jobs will be shifted from the United States to other countries. That's nearly twice the rate in 2001, and it represents about one-fourth of all mass layoffs in 2004.

Despite the trend toward outsourcing white-collar jobs, Bronfenbrenner and Luce found that more than four-fifths of job shifts were still in manufacturing industries and more than one-third of the estimated 400,000 jobs shifted went to Mexico. But China is in second place, and rapidly rising in popularity. They also found that companies disproportionately target unionized jobs, which represent 39 percent of all jobs shifted out of the United States but only 8.2 percent of the private workforce. The Midwest has been hardest hit, most of all Illinois, which in the first three months of 2004 lost at least 7,555 jobs—almost all to Mexico.

LOCAL LOSSES CUT DEEP

The loss of 1,600 jobs with the Maytag closing is hard on Galesburg, where 5 percent of the town's workforce lost jobs, as well as the small surrounding towns. But the ripple effects—from lost jobs at nearby suppliers (including a workshop for the disabled that employed 100 people working on Maytag subassemblies) to indirect effects of declining consumption and reduced tax revenues—will raise the total job loss in the region to roughly 4,166, according to a Western Illinois University study.

That's only a part of the region's woes. In January, the new Australian owners of Butler Manufacturing, which makes steel buildings, will close their Galesburg plant—dumping both 270 manufacturing employees and the only unionized Butler facility. In the past few years, other area factories have closed or greatly cut back on their workforce, including a rubber hose manufacturer, a ceramics manufacturer, and several small industrial parts and equipment makers.

Some, but not all, of these other job losses involve shifts out of the country. They become part of the national problem posed by the growing trade deficit that may approach a record $ 600 billion this year. As more governments and financial market players have perceived this deficit—and the federal budget deficit—as unsustainable, the value of the dollar has fallen. The deficit increase partly reflects rising oil prices and a growing trade imbalance with China, whose currency, the yuan, is pegged to the dollar and, according to critics, undervalued. But the deficit is also a result of the shift in jobs manufacturing tradable goods.

A declining dollar should reduce this trade deficit. But changes in the American economy may blunt its effect. With the decline in its manufacturing base, the United States has fewer producers of tradable goods for export and relies more on imports for essential goods, even if their price in dollars rises sharply. The United States even runs deficits in agricultural commodities and advanced technology, while the small trade surplus in services has been shrinking. The surge in offshoring of white-collar work undercuts the traditional expectation that the United States would simply shift to theoretically higher skilled jobs as it lost manufacturing.

The attention focused on offshoring call-center or software jobs has reinforced the assumption, at least in elite political circles, that manufacturing is a lost cause, especially if the product can be made in China.

MAYTAG WORKERS ARGUE FOR QUALITY, MORALITY

But Maytag workers had a strategy for saving their jobs. David Bevard, the articulate and thoughtful local union president, wanted Maytag to continue to position itself as a high-quality, premium-priced, Made-in-America classic; he argued that the company was damaging itself by undermining workers at the Galesburg plant who wanted to maintain high standards of quality and by accepting "junk" from offshore suppliers. Union members also wanted their protests to make other employers think twice about shifting jobs overseas. And they saw themselves in a global battle for justice.

Workers losing their $15 an hour jobs in Galesburg have a surprising empathy for the Mexican maquiladora workers who would be doing the same work for roughly one-sixth the wage. "The only people being done more a disservice than the people in Galesburg are the people who are going to have our jobs," Kemp says, sitting around the union hall before the shutdown occurred. "They're the only ones more exploited. It shouldn't be American workers against Chinese or Mexican workers, but working people against greed."

"We represent 1,600 in the Galesburg plant, but as a union representative, I feel I'm representing all workers everywhere and try to speak for all those workers," union vice-president Doug Dennison says. "This is so much bigger than a union issue. It's almost accepted what's happening in Galesburg is OK, that it's OK to do that."

"It's exploitation of the many for the benefit of the few," says Kemp. "Sometimes there's a fine line between what's legal and what's right."

"Morality," Dennison adds. They clearly think that is missing, as well as their power to do much about their situation. While most workers blamed "corporate greed" for the plant closing, they also blamed the government for enabling or encouraging that greed. And among an otherwise strongly Democratic crowd, people remember that it was Bill Clinton who pushed through NAFTA. "People in both parties are allowing this to happen," Toby Ladendorf laments on closing day. "Who's going to defend us?"

CONCESSIONS CAN'T COMPETE WITH BOTTOM LINE

Over the decades, Galesburg workers had grown accustomed both to the security of the Maytag jobs and to intimations of insecurity, especially as the industry consolidated into a handful of domestic appliance makers. When Maytag bought the plant in 1986, workers were encouraged by its reputation for quality. But by 1992, as a precondition to making an investment of $180 million, Maytag was demanding concessions from the union and public assistance to keep the plant open, including $7.5 million in state grants and loans, a $3 million city grant paid through increased sales taxes, and local tax abatements through 2004 worth about $4 million. (After the closing, the state passed new legislation to make expected public benefits of such aid clear and to recover money if the goals are not met. And the Knox County state's attorney is trying to recover excess tax abatements.)

The union tried to cooperate to increase productivity, says Bevard, but management was only interested in cutting jobs. Union business agent Mike Patrick suggested that management adopt the "high performance work organization" model that worked well at companies like Harley-Davidson, giving workers responsibility and authority to use their knowledge at work. "Maytag had no intention of giving employees any control," Patrick says. "They wanted to stay with the command and control model." Indeed, Maytag tried to tighten control further and force more concessions, provoking workers to the brink of a strike in 2002.

Then on October 12, 2002, Maytag announced that the plant would close beginning in 2003. Managers told the union that the plant was "not competitively viable."

Maytag was profitable, but revenue and profits have been stagnant or declining and the company's stock price has dropped. Big box retailers like Home Depot were taking a larger share of the market and demanding lower prices from manufacturers. Also, other refrigerator makers had begun producing in Mexico, and Maytag already had subassembly operations in Reynosa. About three hours of direct labor are needed to build the cheaper refrigerators, and with cheaper Mexican labor that can make a difference of $50 on a $350 refrigerator, not counting the savings accrued from lower social and environmental regulations. Maytag will save money eventually, but there was speculation in Galesburg that Maytag was simply following the crowd offshore or trying to please Wall Street to boost its stock price.

GALESBURG STRUGGLES TO RETOOL

In October, the unemployment rate in Galesburg was 9.1 percent. Knox County is on the state's youth poverty warning list. Galesburg recovered from major workplace closings in the 1980s partly through expansion of factories like Maytag, as well as accepting a state prison that residents previously opposed.

Now, to survive, laid-off workers must retrain as welders, nurses, office managers and computer technicians. But even in these growing occupations, there are far more trainees than available local jobs. Many look to long commutes or relocations in order to find jobs, or they prepare to compete with their kids for $7 to $8 Wal-Mart jobs. Meanwhile, economic development officials try to attract investment but rarely mention manufacturing, except to convert the region's abundant corn and soybeans into marketable products. The town has a new logistics park, entrepreneurial centers, and business incubators, and there's some talk about Galesburg becoming an education laboratory, a tourist center or an "agurb" retirement center for upscale refugees from cities like Chicago, a three-and-a-half-hour drive away.

The town is playing up its historic—and rebounding—strength as a railroad center and its interstate highway connections in the search for warehouses and distribution facilities. Last summer a delegation went to China, looking for investors and Chinese companies seeking distribution centers for the kinds of goods once manufactured in towns like Galesburg. It was a sign, local citizens thought, of how globalized the town was becoming.

"Globalization is such a fraud," says Bevard. "It's just a rush to the bottom for cheap labor. Instead of reducing the United States to the Third World, we should be elevating the standards of those countries." Then, perhaps, the Aaron Kemps of this country could hope once again for a ho-hum but decent life for themselves and their kids.

QUESTIONS

- ? What jobs have disappeared in the early twenty-first century? Why have they disappeared? Where have they gone?
- ? What impact does job flight have on the local citizens and on the local economy?
- ? Societal map question: You own a manufacturing plant in the Midwest, the hardest hit of all areas around the issue of manufacturing flight. Assume that your product is still in high demand and that your plant is still making profits, but all your competitors have moved their plants overseas. Is it possible to keep your Midwest plant open? Is it desirable to do so? Find evidence in the article that it is possible and desirable. Find evidence to indicate that it is neither possible nor desirable. What will you conclude?

Chapter 9

Marriage: Then and Now

By STEPHANIE COONTZ

■ Perhaps no other American social institution is more mythologized than the family. And within families, marriage, itself, holds a highly romanticized place. But social norms and values around marital unions continue to change. What do marriages look like today? Will they become extinct in the future? Sociologist Stephanie Coontz explores these and other questions as she provides a brief overview of historical marital unions and contemporary dilemmas.

HISTORICAL FUNCTIONS OF MARRIAGE

Because marriage served so many political, social, and economic functions, the individual needs and desires of the conjugal couple were a secondary consideration, and sometimes completely irrelevant, in most marital decisions. Government agencies, extended families, and established churches often fought over who had the ultimate control over contracting and enforcing marriage, but for centuries all agreed that marriage decisions were too important to be left in the hands of the couple alone.

In Europe during the first half of the previous millennium, marriage also served as a sorting institution for families and communities. In spite of (or perhaps because of) its vital functions, it was far from a universal state. Younger sons and daughters of the upper class, for example, were frequently denied the right to marry, so as to safeguard the inheritance of the oldest son or to protect the parents from crippling dowry payments. Poor people had more freedom to contract unions, but these unions were often not recognized by the authorities. When marriage was recognized, it was to serve the needs of the state or the couple's family. Unmarried people from the upper classes were supported and controlled by their families of origin; unmarried people of the lower classes often lived as dependents in the households of richer neighbors.

Reprinted from *National Forum: The Phi Kappa Phi Journal*, Vol. 80, No. 3 (Summer 2000). Copyright by Stephanie Coontz. By permission of the publishers.

Beginning in the seventeenth century, marriage became much more widespread in Europe and America, to the point that the only option outside marriage, except for Catholic nuns or priests and the occasional rich widow, was to live at the farthest margins of society. In late-eighteenth-century America, bachelorhood was considered the lowest form of manliness. By the mid-nineteenth century, a middle-class man had very little chance of securing credit unless he was married. Women, for their part, could seldom earn enough on their own to forgo or leave marriage. The word "spinster," originally an honorable word derived from medieval women's dominance of textile production, had by the eighteenth century become an epithet so disgraceful that many women settled for almost any husband rather than accept the label.

Under these conditions, marriage was much more universal and stable than it is today. While the social support for lifelong marriage provided by church, state, and public opinion was helpful to many individual wives and husbands, we should not romanticize this marriage-based redistribution and caregiving system. Within many families of the eighteenth and nineteenth centuries, an often-humiliating subordination to the male head of household, sometimes enforced by violence, was the norm. Women and children usually had a lower standard of living than husbands and fathers, and until the early twentieth century, most children who worked turned the bulk of their wages over to their parents. Elders fared particularly poorly under the Euro-American marriage welfare system. Not until the advent of Social Security did elders cease to be the most impoverished and poorly housed segment of the population. But there were few other ways to organize and coordinate socioeconomic life, so most people made the best of marriage, or they suffered in comparative silence, which was broken only by bouts of violence and rates of spousal homicide much higher than today.

SOCIAL CHANGES AND MARRIAGE

Over the course of the nineteenth century and the first half of the twentieth, other institutions began to take over some of the older functions of the family. The spread of banks, schools, foundations, hospitals, unemployment insurance, Social Security, and pension plans slowly but surely eroded many of the roles that marriage had traditionally played in organizing wealth transfers and social welfare measures. The eclipse of kinship as a major political and economic force lessened the incentive of parents to dictate their children's marriage choices, while the rise of new work opportunities freed many young men from parental controls.

Although considerations of status and practical necessity still compelled most people to marry, courtship and marriage increasingly became an individual decision made independently of family and community pressures. Love and companionship became not just the wistful hope of a husband or wife but the legitimate goal of marriage in the eyes of society. Many couples found new satisfactions and pleasures in both courtship and marriage itself, including new sexual compatibility.

By the early twentieth century, however, the emerging definition of marriage as the vehicle for achieving personal happiness had generated some unanticipated consequences. Great expectations, as historian Elaine Tyler May has pointed out, often led to great disappointments, and people were less likely to assume that such disappointments simply had to be endured. The divorce rate shot up in the 1920s and again in the 1940s. It dipped in the 1950s, but alongside the idealization of married life in that decade, the erosion of the economic necessity for marriage continued. The expansion of a consumer society created new temptations and opportunities for women to earn their own wages. More effective birth control created the possibility of a recreational sexuality separated from marriage. New household appliances and TV dinners made it possible for men to purchase meals and cleaning services that had required a forty-hour work week from wives in the early 1900s.

The long-term erosion of the socioeconomic functions of marriage was obscured in the middle forty years of the twentieth century by certain demographic and cultural trends. From the 1920s to the 1960s, the age of marriage fell, while life spans lengthened. The result was that people spent a longer and longer portion of their lives within marriage. Advice books, popular magazines, and the new profession of marriage counselors urged couples to direct more energy into their domestic life, to work through conflicts, and to improve their sexual compatibility. As a result, marriage began to play a heightened role in people's emotional lives even as its social and economic functions continued to erode.

CHANGES IN THE PAST THREE DECADES

During the past thirty years, however, the long-term trend making marriage less central to social and personal life reasserted itself. The ever-escalating ideal of intimate marriage deepened many relationships but also rendered an unsatisfying marriage less acceptable, lessening the stigma against divorce. Meanwhile, the spread of ever-more effective birth control and of a youth "singles culture" contributed to the steady proliferation of culturally acceptable alternatives to marriage, including nonmarital sexual activity and unwed parenthood. While divorce remained a painful experience that often left long-term scars, the cultural acceptability of alternatives to marriage can be seen in the fact that young people, often the sons and daughters of divorced parents, reported themselves happier at the end of the 1990s than they did in the 1970s, and the biggest increase in happiness came among *unmarried* young people.

Alternatives to marriage have continued to multiply at the turn of the millennium, not just for companionship and sexual relationships, but even as a vehicle for raising children. Since the 1970s, the rising age at first marriage, the growing proportion of divorced individuals in the population, and the increasing tendency not to remarry after divorce have created a situation where marriage no longer organizes most major life transitions. Whereas most young adults once stayed in their parents' home until marriage, sometimes first experiencing a form of communal living in college dorms or the military, they now typically live on their own for extended periods before marriage. At the other end of the life course, more older adults are living on their own after a marriage ends, whether by divorce or death.

And when a person does live with a sexual partner, it is often without benefit of a marriage license. Cohabitation rates have increased tenfold among heterosexual partners during the past twenty-five years, and cohabitating couples, whether heterosexual or gay or lesbian, are increasingly having children out of wedlock, as are many single women who live alone. Combined with new reproductive techniques such as sperm-donor and surrogate-motherhood arrangements, these trends have frayed the tight link that formerly existed between marriage and child-raising.

IS MARRIAGE BECOMING EXTINCT?

Does this mean, then, that marriage is on the verge of extinction? Certainly not. Most cohabitating couples eventually do get married, either to each other or to someone else, and part of the dramatic drop in marriage rates since 1960 is simply a result of the rising age of marriage. In 1960, the median age at first marriage for women was 20.4 years. By 1998, it was twenty-five. The fact that a smaller proportion of all women fifteen and over are married now than in the past does not necessarily mean that a smaller proportion of all women will eventually get married. Indeed, more and more women are marrying for the first time at age forty or older.

Furthermore, in some ways marriage has become more important and prevalent during the past century. The rise in life spans during the past fifty years means that despite the increase in divorce, more couples live to celebrate their fortieth wedding anniversary together than ever before in history. And new groups are now demanding access to marriage. The gay and lesbian movement, for example, whose predecessors in the 1920s and 1970s tended to reject marriage and its norms, has recently placed a major focus on winning legal recognition for same-sex unions and adoptions.

Marriage also continues to be important for people's life satisfaction. In a recent analysis of seventeen Western industrialized nations, married persons reported a significantly higher level of happiness than unmarried ones. And many studies demonstrate that a good marriage increases the financial and emotional resources available to children.

For these reasons, some individuals and organizations have argued that the multiplication of alternatives to marriage has been bad for children and for adults, and that we should devote more attention to "reinstitutionalizing" marriage, penalizing or at least reducing the attractiveness of alternative living arrangements. Unfortunately, most such proposals ignore the fact that the very sources of satisfaction and success in modern marriages stem from precisely the changes in gender roles and social norms that have made marriages more optional and more fragile. They also ignore the fact that bad marriages seem to be harder on individuals than in the past. While it is true, for example, that individuals in good marriages are happier than single individuals, individuals in bad marriages are much more distressed than single people, and the effects of a bad marriage seem to be particularly severe for women.

THE REVIVAL OF TWO-BREADWINNER FAMILIES

At the heart of both the new risks and the new possibilities of modern marriage has been an unprecedented transformation in the division of labor, power, and autonomy between husband and wife. This transformation emerged out of a revival of shared breadwinning activities by men and women in the totally unprecedented context of shared domestic responsibilities and egalitarian values.

I say revival of shared bread-winning because, in some ways, today's two-earner marriages represent a return to more traditional marital patterns, after a short historical interlude that many people mistakenly identify as traditional. Until the early nineteenth century, most husbands and wives worked together farming the land or operating small household businesses. But in the early 1800s, as large-scale production for the market replaced home-based production for local exchange, and as a wage-labor system supplanted widespread self-employment and farming, more and more work was conducted in centralized workplaces removed from the farm or home. A new division of labor then grew up within many families, especially in the Northern middle class. Men began to specialize in work outside the home, withdrawing from their traditional childraising responsibilities. Household work and child care were delegated to wives, who gave up their traditional roles in production and barter. While black women and newly-arrived immigrant women continued to have high labor-force participation, wives in most other groups were increasingly likely to quit paid work outside the home after marriage.

This new division of work between husbands and wives came out of a *temporary* stage in the history of wage labor and industrialization. It corresponded to a transitional period when households could no longer get by primarily on things that they made, grew, or bartered but could not yet rely on purchased consumer goods for most of their domestic needs. For example, families no longer produced their own homespun cotton, but ready-made clothing was not yet available at prices most families could afford, so women still had to sew most of their family's clothes. Many families still had to grow some of their food and most had to bake their own bread. Food preparation and laundering required hours of work each day. Water often had to be hauled and heated. Somebody had to go out to earn money to buy the things the family needed; somebody else had to stay home and turn the things that were bought into things the family could actually use. Given the pre-existing legal, political, and religious tradition of patriarchal dominance, husbands (and youth of both sexes) continued to work outside the home. Wives assumed exclusive responsibility for domestic matters that they had formerly shared with husbands or delegated to older children, servants, or apprentices.

Many women supplemented their household labor with income-generating work that could be done at or around home—taking in boarders, doing extra sewing or laundering, keeping a few animals, or selling garden products. But this often arduous work was increasingly seen as secondary to wives' primary role of keeping house, raising the children, and getting dinner on the table. Wives came to be seen as homemakers and caretakers, men as breadwinners, and emotional expectations of marriage were organized around this split.

The temporary conditions that established this strict physical and psychological specialization of labor between husbands and wives began to be undermined in the early twentieth century. When child labor was abolished, more wives in working-class families had to take paid work to compensate for the lost wages of their children. During the 1920s, an expansion of office jobs in the new urban economy drew thousands more women into the work force. In the Great Depression of the 1930s and during World War II, married women in all but the wealthiest families of America were pulled into work for economic or political emergencies.

Although they were often fired when pressures to re-employ men mounted, many women had developed a taste for work and the skills that they needed to reenter the labor force.

Ironically, wives began their most rapid return to the labor force during the 1950s, the height of the *Ozzie and Harriet* TV-family ideal. Mothers of young children still tended to withdraw from paid work until their children were well established in school. But the need of families for extra income and of businesses for female labor soon outstripped the supply of married women with no young children at home. After 1970, mothers of young children became the fastest-growing group of female workers. And the 1990s, most working mothers were going back to work before their child's first birthday. Today, joint breadwinner marriages are the norm once more, even for couples with children.

AUTONOMY AND EQUALITY

What is unprecedented about today's co-provider marriages is the degree of autonomy women have achieved. In the male breadwinner model, wives were economically dependent on their husbands. In the earlier co-provider model, although women and men contributed equally to subsistence, wives could not translate their economic parity into personal or social equality. Law, religion, and politics enforced wives' subordination to husbands through everything from seating plans at church to domestic rituals at home. Husbands had the right to physically "chastise" their wives, and government could not interfere unless "permanent injury or excessive violence" was used. Women had few legal rights separate from their husbands or fathers, and not many could earn enough to even contemplate striking out on their own.

For these reasons, women's co-provider roles in earlier days did not increase wives' leverage in the household as they do today. Husbands had outside support for refusing to renegotiate the marriage relationship with an unhappy wife, and women had few possibilities for leaving a brutish husband. Today, however, the erosion of the economic and social centrality of marriage has undercut the props of male dominance within the family, and women have made unprecedented strides in translating their economic options into an expanded voice in decisions about the household division of labor.

While in most marriages women continue to do more housework and child-care than men, the gap has been halved since the 1960s, and cultural ideals have changed even more dramatically. A majority of men as well as women now tell pollsters that domestic chores should be shared equally between husband and wife. In January 2000, the Radcliffe Public Policy Center released a poll in which more than 70 percent of men in their twenties and thirties said that they would be willing to give up some of their pay in exchange for more time with their families.

These changing attitudes do not always translate easily into practice. Old habits and assumptions still make it hard for couples to establish a new division of labor. Conflict over housework remains a major source of marital tension. And when a couple has children, the tension can become even more acute. Couples who value fairness are more likely than couples with traditional values to react to the slow pace of change with disappointment and anger.

Here is the paradox that perplexes so many social commentators. The very values and options that have made marriage more fair have also made it more tense, and more easily dissolved. In consequence, some groups and individuals who wish to preserve the benefits of modern marriage find themselves advising people to abandon "unrealistic" expectations of equality and revive a modified male-breadwinner form of marriage. The Promise Keepers, for example, argue that ultimately, "a ship can only have one captain." Even more egalitarian-minded proponents of revitalizing the institution of marriage often argue that daily married life goes more smoothly when values stressing fairness and equity take a back seat to tolerance of older norms that make the wife primarily responsible for the home and the husband primarily responsible for income-earning.

But we cannot resolve the tensions of modern marriage by trying to cut and paste people's new values and opportunities to fit an older blueprint for marital stability. Most men want to be more active parents and helpful husbands than their own fathers were. And every year, fewer women report that they are willing to let men off the hook in resolving the stress of balancing work and home life.

The answer to the role strain and marital conflicts that occur in modern families is not to attempt to revitalize marital norms that arose in a totally different historical context. As therapist Betty Carter has commented, if any other institution in this country was failing half the people who entered it, we would demand that the institution change to fit people's new needs, not the other way around.

It is never easy to rework expectations and roles that have been handed down for generations. But many studies find that trying to sidestep such issues erodes the quality of marriage. Psychologists Philip and Carolyn Cowan have shown that a major reason for the decline in marital satisfaction after childbirth is that couples so often revert to a male breadwinner/female caretaker mode that both of them resent. The longer the divergence in behaviors and interests is allowed to go on, the more the tensions fester. Indeed, researchers Esther Kluwer, Jose Heesink, and Evert Van De Vliert suggest that when it comes to the organization of housework and childcare, "it seems better to fight a constructive war than to nourish a destructive peace." Besides, it is hard to maintain an unbalanced peace when the disadvantaged party can walk away, a point supported by the fact that the majority of divorces are initiated by women.

Of course, new marital norms and values are not just a matter of individual effort and goodwill. They require adjustments in institutional support systems to make it easier for couples to balance work and family commitments. Employers must organize their work policies on the assumption that *all* their workers have caretaking responsibilities. Similarly, government should make sure that parental and other caretaking leaves are subsidized, and that affordable high-quality child care is available. School schedules must be adjusted to reflect the realities of urban life in the twenty-first century.

Such measures will make it more possible for modern marriages to succeed. But, paradoxically, they will also make it more possible for divorced individuals and unwed parents to pursue alternative forms of family life, thereby further deinstitutionalizing marriage. This is why such obvious and humane policy innovations have been opposed or ignored by so many conservative commentators and politicians, who have instead demanded that we focus our energy on reviving older cultural values about marriage.

It is time to admit that there is no way to reverse the past 200 years of social change. Whether we like it or not, marriage is no longer the only way through which people organize their sex lives, their care-giving obligations, their work roles, and their social networks. We cannot ignore the fact that the very changes which make marriage more satisfying and rewarding for many people make non-marriage a more viable and attractive alternative for others. The only way forward at this point in history is to find better ways to make *both* marriage and its alternatives work.

QUESTIONS

- According to Coontz, what are six historical functions of marriage?
- Give examples of how marriage has stayed the same over time. Give examples of how it has changed. Why has it changed? Why has it stayed the same?
- Societal map question: Coontz discusses some problems that people entering (or hoping to enter) marriages today may encounter. Identify two of these problems. What societal changes will be necessary to address these problems and how will the changes occur?

The Desecularization of the World: A Global Overview

By PETER L. BERGER

■ Have you heard people say that religion is no longer an important force in the modern world? Sociologist of religion, Peter L. Berger, disagrees. In the article that follows he claims instead that most of the world is "furiously religious as it ever was and in some places more so than ever." Briefly addressing the current and future religious landscape in the United States and abroad, Berger gives us insight into why some people wrongly believe that religion is no longer powerful, and what religious groups are thriving in modern times.

A few years ago the first volume coming out of the so-called Fundamentalism Project landed on my desk. The Fundamentalism Project was very generously funded by the MacArthur Foundation and chaired by Martin Marty, the distinguished church historian at the University of Chicago. A number of very reputable scholars took part in it, and the published results are of generally excellent quality. But my contemplation of this first volume gave me what has been called an "*aha*! experience." The book was very big, sitting there on my desk—a "book-weapon," the kind that could do serious injury. So I asked myself, why would the MacArthur Foundation shell out several million dollars to support an international study of religious fundamentalists?

Two answers came to mind. The first was obvious and not very interesting. The MacArthur Foundation is a very progressive outfit; it understands fundamentalists to be anti-progressive; the Project, then, was a matter of knowing one's enemies. But there was also a more interesting answer. "Fundamentalism" is considered a strange, hard-to-understand phenomenon; the purpose of the Project was to delve into this alien world and make it more understandable. But to whom? *Who* finds this world strange? Well, the answer to *that* question was easy: people to whom the officials of the MacArthur Foundation normally talk, such as professors at elite American universities. And with this came the aha! experience. The concern that must have led to this Project

---

From *The National Interest*, No. 46 Winter 1996/97 by Peter Berger. Copyright © 1997 by National Affairs, Inc. Reprinted by permission.

was based on an upside-down perception of the world, according to which "fundamentalism" (which, when all is said and done, usually refers to any sort of passionate religious movement) is a rare, hard-to-explain thing. But a look either at history or at the contemporary world reveals that what is rare is not the phenomenon itself but knowledge of it. The difficult-to-understand phenomenon is not Iranian mullahs but American university professors—it might be worth a multi-million-dollar project to try to explain that!

Mistakes of Secularization Theory

My point is that the assumption that we live in a secularized world is false. The world today, with some exceptions to which I will come presently, is as furiously religious as it ever was, and in some places more so than ever. This means that a whole body of literature by historians and social scientists loosely labeled "secularization theory" is essentially mistaken. In my early work I contributed to this literature. I was in good company—most sociologists of religion had similar views, and we had good reasons for holding them. Some of the writings we produced still stand up. (As I like to tell my students, one advantage of being a social scientist, as against being, say, a philosopher or a theologian, is that you can have as much fun when your theories are falsified as when they are verified!)

Although the term "secularization theory" refers to works from the 1950s and 1960s, the key idea of the theory can indeed be traced to the Enlightenment. That idea is simple: Modernization necessarily leads to a decline of religion, both in society and in the minds of individuals. And it is precisely this key idea that has turned out to be wrong. To be sure, modernization has had some secularizing effects, more in some places than in others. But it has also provoked powerful movements of counter-secularization. Also, secularization on the societal level is not necessarily linked to secularization on the level of individual consciousness. Certain religious institutions have lost power and influence in many societies, but both old and new religious beliefs and practices have nevertheless continued in the lives of individuals, sometimes taking new institutional forms and sometimes leading to great explosions of religious fervor. Conversely, religiously identified institutions can play social or political roles even when very few people believe or practice the religion that the institutions represent. To say the least, the relation between religion and modernity is rather complicated.

The proposition that modernity necessarily leads to a decline of religion is, in principle, "value free." That is, it can be affirmed both by people who think it is good news and by people who think it is very bad news. Most Enlightenment thinkers and most progressive-minded people ever since have tended toward the idea that secularization is a good thing, at least insofar as it does away with religious phenomena that are "backward," "superstitious," or "reactionary" (a religious residue purged of these negative characteristics may still be deemed acceptable). But religious people, including those with very traditional or orthodox beliefs, have also affirmed the modernity/secularity linkage, and have greatly bemoaned it. Some have then defined modernity as the enemy, to be fought whenever possible. Others have, on the contrary, seen modernity as some kind of invincible worldview to which religious beliefs and practices should adapt themselves. In other words, *rejection* and *adaptation* are two strategies open to religious communities in a world understood to be secularized. As is always the case when strategies are based on mistaken perceptions of the terrain, both strategies have had very doubtful results.

It is possible, of course, to reject any number of modern ideas and values theoretically, but making this rejection stick in the lives of people is much harder. To do that requires one of two strategies. The first is *religious revolution*: one tries to take over society as a whole and make one's counter-modern religion obligatory for everyone—a difficult enterprise in most countries in the contemporary world. (Franco tried in Spain and failed; the mullahs are still at it in Iran and a couple of other places.) And this *does* have to do with modernization, which brings about very heterogeneous societies and a quantum leap in intercultural communication, two factors favoring pluralism and *not* favoring the establishment (or reestablishment) of religious monopolies. The other possible way of getting people to reject modern ideas and values in their lives is to create *religious subcultures* designed to keep out the influences of the outside society. That is a somewhat more promising exercise than religious revolution, but it too is fraught with difficulty. Modern culture is a very powerful force, and an immense effort is required to maintain enclaves with an airtight defense system. Ask the Amish in eastern Pennsylvania. Or ask a Hasidic rabbi in the Williamsburg section of Brooklyn.

Interestingly, secularization theory has also been falsified by the results of adaptation strategies by religious institutions. If we really lived in a highly secularized world, then religious institutions could be expected to survive to the degree that they manage to adapt to secularity. That has been the empirical assumption of adaptation strategies. What has in fact occurred is that, by and large, religious communities have survived and even flourished to the degree that they have *not* tried to adapt themselves to the alleged requirements of a secularized world. To put it simply, experiments with secularized religion have generally failed; religious movements with beliefs and practices dripping with reactionary supernaturalism (the kind utterly beyond the pale at self-respecting faculty parties) have widely succeeded.

The Catholic Church vs. Modernity

The struggle with modernity in the Roman Catholic Church nicely illustrates the difficulties of various strategies. In the wake of the Enlightenment and its multiple revolutions, the initial response by the Church was militant and then defiant rejection. Perhaps the most magnificent moment of that defiance came in 1870, when the First Vatican Council solemnly proclaimed the infallibility of the Pope and the immaculate conception of Mary, literally in the face of the Enlightenment about to occupy Rome in the shape of the army of Victor Emmanuel I. (The disdain was mutual. If you have ever visited the Roman monument to the Bersaglieri, the elite army units that occupied the Eternal City in the name of the Italian *Risorgimento*, you may have noticed the placement of the heroic figure in his Bersaglieri uniform—he is positioned so that his behind points exactly toward the Vatican.)

The Second Vatican Council, almost a hundred years later, considerably modified this rejectionist stance, guided as it was by the notion of *aggiornamento*, bringing the Church up to date—that is, up to date with the modern world. (I remember asking a Protestant theologian what he thought would happen at the Council—this was before it had convened; he replied that he didn't know but he was sure they would not read the minutes of the last meeting!) The Second Vatican Council was supposed to open windows, specifically the windows of the Catholic subculture that had been constructed when it became clear that the overall society could not be reconquered. In the United States, this Catholic subculture has been quite impressive right up to the very recent past. The trouble with opening windows is that you can't control what comes in, and a lot has come in—indeed, the whole turbulent world of modern culture—that has been very troubling to the Church. Under the current pontificate the Church has been steering a nuanced course between rejection and adaptation, with mixed results in different countries.

This is as good a point as any to mention that all my observations here are intended to be "value free"; that is, I am trying to look at the current religious scene objectively. For the duration of this exercise I have put aside my own religious beliefs. As a sociologist of religion, I find it probable that Rome had to do some reining in on the level of both doctrine and practice, in the wake of the institutional disturbances that followed Vatican II. To say this, however, in no way implies my theological agreement with what has been happening in the Roman Catholic Church under the present pontificate. Indeed, if I were Roman Catholic, I would have considerable misgivings about these developments. But I am a liberal Protestant (the adjective refers to my religious position and not to my politics), and I have no immediate existential stake in what is happening within the Roman community. I am speaking here as a sociologist, in which capacity I can claim a certain competence; I have no theological credentials.

THE GLOBAL RELIGIOUS SCENE

On the international religious scene, it is conservative or orthodox or traditionalist movements that are on the rise almost everywhere. These movements are precisely the ones that rejected an *aggiornamento* with modernity as defined by progressive intellectuals. Conversely, religious movements and institutions that have made great efforts to conform to a perceived modernity are almost everywhere on the decline. In the United States this has been a much commented upon fact, exemplified by the decline of so-called mainline Protestantism and the concomitant rise of Evangelicalism; but the United States is by no means unusual in this.

Nor is Protestantism. The conservative thrust in the Roman Catholic Church under John Paul II has borne fruit in both number of converts and renewed enthusiasm among native Catholics, especially in non-Western countries. Following the collapse of the Soviet Union there occurred a remarkable revival of the Orthodox Church in Russia. The most rapidly growing Jewish groups, both in Israel and in the Diaspora, are Orthodox. There have been similarly vigorous upsurges of conservative religion in all the other major religious communities—Islam, Hinduism, Buddhism—as well as revival movements in smaller communities (such as Shinto in Japan and Sikhism in India). These developments differ greatly in their social and political implications. What they have in common is their unambiguously *religious* inspiration. Consequently, taken together they provide a massive falsification of the idea that modernization and secularization are cognate phenomena. At the very least they show that *counter*-secularization is at least as important a phenomenon in the contemporary world as secularization.

Both in the media and in scholarly publications, these movements are often subsumed under the category of "fundamentalism." This is not a felicitous term, not only because it carries a pejorative undertone but also because it derives from the history of American Protestantism, where it has a specific reference that is distortive if extended to other religious traditions. All the same, the term has some suggestive use if one wishes to explain the aforementioned developments. It suggests a combination of several features—great religious passion, a defiance of what others have defined as the *Zeitgeist*, and a return to traditional sources of religious authority. These are indeed common features across cultural boundaries. And they do reflect the presence of secularizing forces, since they must be understood as a reaction *against* those forces. (In that sense, at least, something of the old secularization theory may be said to hold up, in a rather back-handed way.) This interplay of secularizing and counter-secularizing forces is, I would contend, one of the most important topics for a sociology of contemporary religion, but far too large to consider here. I can only drop a hint: Modernity, for fully understandable reasons, undermines all the old certainties; uncertainty is a condition that many people find very hard to bear; therefore, any movement (not only a religious one) that promises to provide or to renew certainty has a ready market.

Differences Among Thriving Movements

While the aforementioned common features are important, an analysis of the social and political impact of the various religious upsurges must also take full account of their differences. This becomes clear when one looks at what are arguably the two most dynamic religious upsurges in the world today, the Islamic and the Evangelical; the comparison also underlines the weakness of the category of "fundamentalism" as applied to both.

The Islamic upsurge, because of its more immediately obvious political ramifications, is better known. Yet it would be a serious error to see it only through a political lens. It is an impressive revival of emphatically *religious* commitments. And it is of vast geographical scope, affecting every single Muslim country from North Africa to Southeast Asia. It continues to gain converts, especially in sub-Saharan Africa (where it is often in head-on competition with Christianity). It is becoming very visible in the burgeoning Muslim communities in Europe and, to a much lesser extent, in North America. Everywhere it is bringing about a restoration, not only of Islamic beliefs but of distinctively Islamic life-styles, which in many ways directly contradict modern ideas—such as ideas about the relation of religion and the state, the role of women, moral codes of everyday behavior, and the boundaries of religious and moral tolerance. The Islamic revival is by no means restricted to the less modernized or "backward" sectors of society, as progressive intellectuals still like to think. On the contrary, it is very strong in cities with a high degree of modernization, and in a number of countries it is particularly visible among people with Western-style higher education—in Egypt and Turkey, for example, many daughters of secularized professionals are putting on the veil and other accoutrements of Islamic modesty.

Yet there are also great differences within the movement. Even within the Middle East, the Islamic heartland, there are both religiously and politically important differences between Sunni and Shiite revivals—Islamic conservatism means very different things in, say, Saudi Arabia and Iran. Away from the Middle East, the differences become even greater. Thus in Indonesia, the most populous Muslim country in the world, a very powerful revival movement, the Nudhat'ul-Ulama, is avowedly pro-democracy and pro-pluralism, the very opposite of what is commonly viewed as Muslim "fundamentalism." Where the political circumstances allow this, there is in many places a lively discussion about the relation of Islam to various modern realities, and there are sharp disagreements among individuals who are equally committed to a revitalized Islam. Still, for reasons deeply grounded in the core of the tradition, it is probably fair to say that, on the whole, Islam has had a difficult time coming to terms with key modern institutions, such as pluralism, democracy, and the market economy.

The Evangelical upsurge is just as breathtaking in scope. Geographically that scope is even wider. It has gained huge numbers of converts in East Asia—in all the Chinese communities (including, despite severe persecution, mainland China) and in South Korea, the Philippines, across the South Pacific, throughout sub-Saharan Africa (where it is often synthetized with elements of traditional African religion), apparently in parts of ex-Communist Europe. But the most remarkable success has occurred in Latin America; there are now thought to be between forty and fifty million Evangelical Protestants south of the U.S. border, the great majority of them first-generation Protestants. The most numerous component within the Evangelical upsurge is Pentecostalism, which combines biblical orthodoxy and a rigorous morality with an ecstatic form of worship and an emphasis on spiritual healing. Especially in Latin America, conversion to Protestantism brings about a cultural transformation—new attitudes toward work and consumption, a new educational ethos, and a violent rejection of traditional *machismo* (women play a key role in the Evangelical churches).

The origins of this worldwide Evangelical upsurge are in the United States, from which the missionaries first went out. But it is very important to understand that, virtually everywhere and emphatically in Latin America, this new Evangelicalism is thoroughly indigenous and no longer dependent on support from U.S. fellow believers—indeed, Latin American Evangelicals have been sending missionaries to the Hispanic community in this country, where there has been a comparable flurry of conversions.

Needless to say, the religious contents of the Islamic and Evangelical revivals are totally different. So are the social and political consequences (of which I will say more later). But the two developments also differ in another very important respect: The Islamic movement is occurring primarily in countries that are already Muslim or among Muslim emigrants (as in Europe), while the Evangelical movement is growing dramatically throughout the world in countries where this type of religion was previously unknown or very marginal.

Exceptions to the Desecularization Thesis

Let me, then, repeat what I said a while back: The world today is massively religious, is *anything but* the secularized world that had been predicted (whether joyfully or despondently) by so many analysts of modernity. There are, however, two exceptions to this proposition, one somewhat unclear, the other very clear.

The first apparent exception is Europe—more specifically, Europe west of what used to be called the Iron Curtain (the developments in the formerly Communist countries are as yet very under-researched and unclear). In Western Europe, if nowhere else, the old secularization theory would seem to hold. With increasing modernization there has been an increase in key indicators of secularization, both on the level of expressed beliefs (especially those that could be called orthodox in Protestant or Catholic terms) and, dramatically, on the level of church-related behavior—attendance at services of worship, adherence to church-dictated codes of personal behavior (especially with regard to sexuality, reproduction, and marriage), recruitment to the clergy. These phenomena, long observed in the northern countries of the continent, have since World War II rapidly engulfed the south. Thus Italy and Spain have experienced a rapid decline in church-related religion. So has Greece, thereby undercutting the claim of Catholic conservatives that Vatican II is to be blamed for the decline. There is now a massively secular Euro-culture, and what has happened in the south can be simply described (though not thereby explained) by that culture's invasion of these countries. It is not fanciful to predict that there will be similar developments in Eastern Europe, precisely to the degree that these countries too will be integrated into the new Europe.

While these facts are not in dispute, a number of recent works in the sociology of religion, notably in France, Britain, and Scandinavia, have questioned the term "secularization" as applied to these developments. A body of data indicates strong survivals of religion, most of it generally Christian in nature, despite the widespread alienation from the organized churches. A shift in the institutional location of religion, then, rather than secularization, would be a more accurate description of the European situation. All the same, Europe stands out as quite different from other parts of the world, and certainly from the United States. One of the most interesting puzzles in the sociology of religion is why Americans are so much more religious *as well as* more churchly than Europeans.

The other exception to the desecularization thesis is less ambiguous. There exists an international subculture composed of people with Western-type higher education, especially in the humanities and social sciences, that is indeed secularized. This subculture is the principal "carrier" of progressive, Enlightened beliefs and values. While its members are relatively thin on the ground, they are very influential, as they control the institutions that provide the "official" definitions of reality, notably the educational system, the media of mass communication, and the higher reaches of the legal system. They are remarkably similar all over the world today, as they have been for a long time (though, as we have seen, there are also defectors from this subculture, especially in the Muslim countries). Again, regrettably, I cannot speculate here as to why people with this type of education should be so prone to secularization. I can only point out that what we have here is a globalized *elite* culture.

In country after country, then, religious upsurges have a strongly populist character. Over and beyond the purely religious motives, these are movements of protest and resistance *against* a secular elite. The so-called culture war in the United States emphatically shares this feature. I may observe in passing that the plausibility of secularization theory owes much to this international subculture. When intellectuals travel, they usually touch down in intellectual circles—that is, among people much like themselves. They can easily fall into the misconception that these people reflect the overall visited society, which, of course, is a big mistake. Picture a secular intellectual from Western Europe socializing with colleagues at the faculty club of the University of Texas. He may think he is back home. But then picture him trying to drive through the traffic jam on Sunday morning in downtown Austin—or, heaven help him, turning on his car radio! What happens then is a severe jolt of what anthropologists call culture shock.

RESURGENT RELIGION: ORIGINS AND PROSPECTS

After this somewhat breathless *tour d'horizon* of the global religious scene, let me turn to some the questions posed for discussion in this set of essays. *First, what are the origins of the worldwide resurgence of religion?* Two possible answers have already been mentioned. One: Modernity tends to undermine the taken-for-granted certainties by which people lived through most of history. This is an uncomfortable state of affairs, for many an intolerable one, and religious movements that claim to give certainty have great appeal. Two: A purely secular view of reality has its principal social location in an elite culture that, not surprisingly, is resented by large numbers of people who are not part of it but who feel its influence (most troublingly, as their children are subjected to an education that ignores or even directly attacks their own beliefs and values). Religious movements with a strongly anti-secular bent can therefore appeal to people with resentments that sometimes have quite non-religious sources.

But I would refer once more to the little story with which I began, about American foundation officials worried about "fundamentalism." In one sense, there is nothing to explain here. Strongly felt religion has always been around; what needs explanation is its absence rather than its presence. Modern secularity is a much more puzzling phenomenon than all these religious explosions—if you will, the University of Chicago is a more interesting topic for the sociology of religion than the Islamic schools of Qom. In other words, the phenomena under consideration here on one level simply serve to demonstrate continuity in the place of religion in human experience.

Second, what is the likely future course of this religious resurgence? Given the considerable variety of important religious movements in the contemporary world, it would make little sense to venture a global prognosis. Predictions, if one dares to make them at all, will be more useful if applied to much narrower situations. One prediction, though, can be made with some assurance: There is no reason to think the world of the twenty-first century will be any less religious than the world is today. A minority of sociologists of religion have been trying to salvage the old secularization theory by what I would call the last-ditch thesis: Modernization *does* secularize, and movements like the Islamic and the Evangelical ones represent last-ditch defenses by religion that cannot last; eventually, secularity will triumph—or, to put it less respectfully, eventually Iranian mullahs, Pentecostal preachers, and Tibetan lamas will all think and act like professors of literature at American universities. I find this thesis singularly unpersuasive.

Having made this general prediction—that the world of the next century will not be less religious than the world of today—I will have to speculate very differently regarding different sectors of the religious scene. For example, I think that the most militant Islamic movements will find it hard to maintain their present stance *vis-à-vis* modernity once they succeed in taking over the governments of their countries (this, it seems, is already happening in Iran). I also think that Pentecostalism, as it exists today among mostly poor and uneducated people, is unlikely to retain its present religious and moral characteristics unchanged, as many of these people experience upward social mobility (this has already been observed extensively in the United States). Generally, many of these religious movements are linked to non-religious forces of one sort or another, and the future course of the former will be at least partially determined by the course of the latter. In the United States, for instance, militant Evangelicalism will have a different future course if some of its causes succeed in the political and legal arenas than if it continues to be frustrated in these arenas. Also, in religion as in every other area of human endeavor, individual personalities play a much larger role than most social scientists and historians are willing to concede. There might have been an Islamic revolution in Iran without the Ayatollah Khomeini, but it would probably have looked quite different. No one can predict the appearance of charismatic figures who will launch powerful religious movements in unexpected places. Who knows—perhaps the next religious upsurge in America will occur among disenchanted post-modernist academics!

Third, do the resurgent religions differ in their critique of the secular order? Yes, of course they do, depending on their particular belief systems. Cardinal Ratzinger and the Dalai Lama will be troubled by different aspects of contemporary secular culture. What both will agree upon, however, is the shallowness of a culture that tries to get along without any transcendent points of reference. And they will have good reasons to support this view. The religious impulse, the quest for meaning that transcends the restricted space of empirical existence in this world, has been a perennial feature of humanity. (This is not a theological statement but an anthropological one—an agnostic or even an atheist philosopher may well agree with it.) It would require something close to a mutation of the species to extinguish this impulse for good. The more radical thinkers of the Enlightenment and their more recent intellectual descendants hoped for something like this, of course. So far it has not happened, and as I have argued, it is unlikely to happen in the foreseeable future. The critique of secularity common to all the resurgent movements is that human existence bereft of transcendence is an impoverished and finally untenable condition.

To the extent that secularity today has a specifically modern form (there were earlier forms in, for example, versions of Confucianism and Hellenistic culture), the critique of secularity also entails a critique of at least these aspects of modernity. Beyond that, however, different religious movements differ in their relation to modernity. As I have said, an argument can be made that the Islamic resurgence strongly tends toward a negative view of modernity; in places it is downright anti-modern or counter-modernizing, as in its view of the role of women. By contrast, I think it can be shown that the Evangelical resurgence is positively modernizing in most places where it occurs, clearly so in Latin America. The new Evangelicals throw aside many of the traditions that have been obstacles to modernization—*machismo*, for one, and also the subservience to hierarchy that has been endemic to

Iberian Catholicism. Their churches encourage values and behavior patterns that contribute to modernization. To take just one important case in point: In order to participate fully in the life of their congregations, Evangelicals will want to read the Bible; this desire to read the Bible encourages literacy and, beyond this, a positive attitude toward education and self-improvement. They also will want to be able to join in the discussion of congregational affairs, since those matters are largely in the hands of laypersons (indeed, largely in the hands of women); this lay operation of churches necessitates training in administrative skills, including the conduct of public meetings and the keeping of financial accounts. It is not fanciful to suggest that in this way Evangelical congregations serve—inadvertently, to be sure—as schools for democracy and for social mobility.

QUESTIONS

- ? Define and give one example of secularization theory. Define and give one example of desecularization theory. Which, does Berger believe, more accurately reflect reality? Why?
- ? What religions are "resurgent"? Are resurgent religions all the same? What does the future hold for them?
- ? Societal map question: Think about the community (city, town, area) that you grew up in. Describe it—size, average age of the people, their class, race, and the religions represented there. Does your community better fit the theory of secularization or desecularization? Explain.

Chapter 10

Hitting Them Hardest When They're Small

By JONATHAN KOZOL

■ If you could give your early education experience a grade, what would it be? Think back to the teachers, the classrooms, playgrounds, library, food, and technology. Do you believe your experience to be fairly typical? Would it surprise you to find out that the quality of public education varies considerably? Jonathan Kozol, the author of your next reading, has spent most of his life documenting the unequal educational experiences of American children. In this article, taken from his 2005 book "*The Shame of the Nation: The Restoration of Apartheid Schooling in America*," Kozol examines the unequal educational experiences of children in the Bronx.

"Dear Mr. Kozol," said the eight-year-old, "we do not have the things you have. You have Clean things. We do not have. You have a clean bathroom. We do not have that. You have Parks and we do not have Parks. You have all the thing and we do not have all the thing.... Can you help us?"

The letter, from a child named Alliyah, came in a fat envelope of 27 letters from a class of third grade children in the Bronx. Other letters that the students in Alliyah's classroom sent me registered some of the same complaints. "We don't have no gardens," and "no Music or Art," and "no fun places to play," one child said. "Is there a way to fix this Problem?" Another noted a concern one hears from many children in such overcrowded schools: "We have a gym but it is for lining up. I think it is not fair." Yet another of Alliyah's classmates asked me, with a sweet misspelling, if I knew the way to make her school into a "good" school—"like the other kings have"—and ended with the hope that I would do my best to make it possible for "all the kings" to have good schools.

The letter that affected me the most, however, had been written by a child named Elizabeth. "It is not fair that other kids have a garden and new things. But we don't have that," said Elizabeth. "I wish that this school was the most beautiful school in the whole why world."

From *The Shame of the Nation* by Jonathan Kozol, copyright © 2005 by Jonathan Kozol. Used by permission of Crown Publishers, a division of Random House, Inc.

Elizabeth had very careful, very small, and neatly formed handwriting. She had corrected other errors in her letter, squeezing in a missing letter she'd initially forgotten, erasing and rewriting a few words she had misspelled. The error she had left unaltered in the final sentence therefore captured my attention more than it might otherwise have done.

"The whole why world" stayed in my thoughts for days. When I later met Elizabeth I brought her letter with me, thinking I might see whether, in reading it aloud, she'd change the "why" to "wide" or leave it as it was. My visit to her class, however, proved to be so pleasant, and the children seemed so eager to bombard me with their questions about where I lived, and why I lived there rather than New York, and who I lived with, and how many dogs I had, and other interesting questions of that sort, that I decided not to interrupt the nice reception they had given me with questions about usages and spelling. I left "the whole why world" to float around unedited and unrevised within my mind. The letter itself soon found a resting place up on the wall above my desk.

In the years before I met Elizabeth, I had visited many elementary schools in the South Bronx and in one northern district of the Bronx as well. I had also made a number of visits to a high school where a stream of water flowed down one of the main stairwells on a rainy afternoon and where green fungus molds were growing in the office where the students went for counseling. A large blue barrel was positioned to collect rain-water coming through the ceiling. In one make-shift elementary school housed in a former skating rink next to a funeral parlor in another nearly all-black-and-Hispanic section of the Bronx, class size rose to 34 and more; four kindergarten classes and a sixth grade class were packed into a single room that had no windows. Airlessness was stifling in many rooms; and recess was impossible because there was no outdoor playground and no indoor gym, so the children had no place to play.

In another elementary school, which had been built to hold 1,000 children but was packed to bursting with some 1,500 boys and girls, the principal poured out his feelings to me in a room in which a plastic garbage bag had been attached somehow to cover part of the collapsing ceiling. "This," he told me, pointing to the garbage bag, then gesturing around him at the other indications of decay and disrepair one sees in ghetto schools much like it elsewhere, "would not happen to white children."

A friend of mine who was a first-year teacher in a Harlem high school told me she had 40 students in her class but only 30 chairs, so some of her students had to sit on windowsills or lean against the walls. Other high schools were so crowded they were forced to shorten schooldays and to cut back hours of instruction to accommodate a double shift of pupils. Tens of thousands of black and Hispanic students were in schools like these, in which half the student body started classes very early in the morning and departed just before or after lunch, while the other half did not begin their schoolday until noon.

Libraries, once one of the glories of the New York City system, were either nonexistent or, at best, vestigial in large numbers of the elementary schools. Art and music programs had for the most part disappeared as well. "When I began to teach in 1969," the principal of an elementary school in the South Bronx reported to me, "every school had a full-time licensed art and music teacher and librarian." During the next decade, he recalled, "I saw all of that destroyed."

School physicians were also removed from elementary schools during these years. In 1970, when substantial numbers of white children still attended New York City's schools, 400 doctors had been present to address the health needs of the children. By 1993, the number of doctors had been cut to 23, most of them part-time—a cutback that affected most acutely children in the city's poorest neighborhoods where medical provision was perennially substandard and health problems faced by children most extreme. During the 1990s, for example, the rate of pediatric asthma in the South Bronx, already one of the highest in the nation, was exacerbated when the city chose to build a medical waste incinerator in their neighborhood after a plan to build it on the East Side of Manhattan was abandoned in the face of protests from the parents of that area. Hospitalization rates for these asthmatic children in the Bronx were as much as 20 times more frequent than for children in the city's affluent communities. Teachers spoke of children who came into class with chronic wheezing and, at any moment of the day, might undergo more serious attacks, but in the schools I visited there were no doctors to attend to them.

Political leaders in New York tended to point to shifting economic factors, such as a serious budget crisis in the middle 1970s, rather than to the changing racial demographics of the student population, as the explanation for these steep declines in services. But the fact of economic ups and downs from year to year, or from one decade to the next, could not convincingly explain the permanent shortchanging of the city's students, which took place routinely in good economic times and bad, with bad times seized upon politically to justify these cuts while, in the good times, losses undergone during the crisis years had never been restored.

"If you close your eyes to the changing racial composition of the schools and look only at budget actions and political events," says Noreen Connell, the director of the nonprofit Educational Priorities Panel in New York, "you're missing the assumptions that are underlying these decisions." When minority parents ask for something better for their kids, she says, "the assumption is that these are parents who can be discounted. These are kids that we don't value."

The disrepair and overcrowding of these schools in the South Bronx "wouldn't happen for a moment in a white suburban school district like Scarsdale," says former New York State Commissioner of Education Thomas Sobol, who was once the superintendent of the Scarsdale schools and is now a professor of education at Teachers College in New York. "I'm aware that I could never prove that race is at the heart of this if I were called to testify before a legislative hearing. But I've felt it for so long, and seen it operating for so long, I know it's true...."

During the 1990s, physical conditions in some buildings had become so dangerous that a principal at one Bronx school, which had been condemned in 1989 but nonetheless continued to be used, was forced to order that the building's windows not be cleaned because the frames were rotted and glass panes were falling in the street, while at another school the principal had to have the windows bolted shut for the same reason. These were not years of economic crisis in New York. This was a period in which financial markets soared and a new generation of free-spending millionaires and billionaires was widely celebrated by the press and on TV; but none of the proceeds of this period of economic growth had found their way into the schools that served the truly poor.

I had, as I have noted, visited many schools in other cities by this time; but I did not know children in those schools as closely as I'd come to know, or soon would know, so many of the children in the New York City schools. So it would be these children, and especially the ones in elementary schools in which I spent the most time in the Bronx, whose sensibilities and puzzlements and understandings would impress themselves most deeply on my own impressions in the years to come, and it would be their questions that became my questions and their accusations and their challenges, when it appeared that they were making challenges, that came to be my own.

This, then, is the accusation that Alliyah and her classmates send our way: "You have.... We do not have." Are they right or are they wrong? Is this a case of naïve and simplistic juvenile exaggeration? What does a third grader know about these big-time questions about what is fair and what is not, and what is right and what is wrong? Physical appearances apart, how in any case do you begin to measure something so diffuse and vast and seemingly abstract as having more, or having less, or having not at all?

In a social order where it seems a fairly common matter to believe that what we spend to purchase almost anything we need bears some connection to the worth of what we get, a look at what we think it's in our interest to invest in children like Alliyah or Pineapple may not tell us everything we need to know about the state of educational fair play within our nation, but it surely tells us *something* about what we think these kids are worth to us in human terms and in the contributions they may someday make to our society. At the time I met Alliyah in the school-year 1997–1998, New York's Board of Education spent about $8,000 yearly on the education of a third grade child in a New York City public school. If you could have scooped Alliyah up out of the neighborhood where she was born and plunked her down within a fairly typical white suburb of New York, she would have received a public education worth about $12,000 every year. If you were to lift her up once more and set her down within one of the wealthiest white suburbs of New York, she would have received as much as $18,000 worth of public education every year and would likely have had a third grade teacher paid approximately $30,000 more than was her teacher in the Bronx.

The dollars on both sides of the equation have increased since then, but the discrepancies between them have not greatly changed. The present per-pupil spending level in the New York City schools is $11,700, which may be compared to a per-pupil spending level in excess of $22,000 in the well-to-do suburban district of Manhasset. The present New York City level is, indeed, almost exactly what Manhasset spent per pupil 18 years ago, in 1987, when that sum of money bought a great deal more in services and salaries than it can buy today. In dollars adjusted for inflation, New York City has not yet caught up to where its wealthiest suburbs were a quarter-century ago.

Gross discrepancies in teacher salaries between the city and its affluent white suburbs have remained persistent too. In 1997, the median salary for teachers in Alliyah's neighborhood was $43,000, as compared to $74,000 in suburban Rye, $77,000 in Manhasset, and $81,000 in the town of Scarsdale, which is only about 11 miles from Alliyah's school. Five years later, in 2002, salary scales for New York City's teachers rose to levels that approximated those within the lower-spending districts in the suburbs, but salary scales do not reflect the actual salaries that teachers typically receive, which are dependant upon years of service and advanced degrees. Salaries for first-year teachers in the city now were higher than they'd been four years before, but the differences in median pay between the city and its upper-middle-income suburbs had remained extreme. The overall figure for New York City in 2002–2003 was $53,000, while it had climbed to $87,000 in Manhassett and exceeded $95,000 in Scarsdale.

Even these numbers that compare the city to its suburbs cannot give an adequate impression of the inequalities imposed upon the children living in poor sections of New York. For, even within the New York City schools themselves, there are additional discrepancies in funding between schools that serve the poorest and the wealthiest communities, since teachers with the least seniority and least experience are commonly assigned to schools in the most deeply segregated neighborhoods. The median salary of teachers in Pineapple's neighborhood was less than $46,000 in 2002–2003, the lowest in the city, compared to $59,000 in one of Manhattan's recently gentrified communities, and up to $64,000 in some neighborhoods of Queens.

None of this includes the additional resources given to the public schools in affluent communities where parents have the means to supplement the public funds with private funding of their own, money used to build and stock a good school library for instance, or to arrange for art and music lessons or, in many of these neighborhoods, to hire extra teachers to reduce the size of classes for their children.

This relatively new phenomenon of private money being used selectively to benefit the children only of specific public schools had not been noted widely in New York until about ten years ago when parents of the students at a public school in Greenwich Village in Manhattan raised the funds to pay a fourth grade teacher, outside of the normal budget of the school, when class size in the fourth grade otherwise was likely to increase from 26 to 32, which was the average class size in the district at the time but which, one of the parents said, "would have a devastating impact" on her son. The parents, therefore, collected $46,000—two thirds of it, remarkably, in just one night—in order to retain the extra teacher.

The school in Greenwich Village served a population in which less than 20 percent of students were from families of low income, a very low figure in New York, compared, for instance, to Pineapple's neighborhood, where 95 percent of children lived in poverty. The Greenwich Village school, moreover, was already raising a great deal of private money—more than $100,000 yearly, it was now revealed—to pay for music, art, and science programs and for furniture repairs.

The chancellor of the New York City schools initially rejected the use of private funds to underwrite a teacher's pay, making the argument that this was not fair to the children in those many other schools that had much larger classes; but the district later somehow came up with the public funds to meet the cost of hiring the extra teacher, so the parents won their children the advantage they had sought for them in any case.

As it turned out, the use of private subsidies to supplement the tax-supported budgets of some schools in affluent communities was a more commonly accepted practice than most people in the city's poorest neighborhoods had known. The PTA at one school on the Upper West Side of Manhattan, for example, had been raising nearly $50,000 yearly to hire a writing teacher and two part-time music teachers. At a school in a middle-class section of Park Slope in Brooklyn, parents raised more than $100,000 yearly to employ a science teacher and two art instructors. In yet another neighborhood, parents at an elementary school and junior high had raised more than $1 million, mostly for enrichment programs for their children.

In principle, the parents in poor neighborhoods were free to do fund-raising too, but the proceeds they were likely to bring in differed dramatically. The PTA in one low-income immigrant community, for instance, which sponsored activities like candy sales and tried without success to win foundation grants, was able to raise less than $4,000. In the same year, parents at P.S. 6, a top-rated elementary school serving the Upper East Side of Manhattan, raised $200,000. The solicitation of private funds from parents in communities like this had come to be so common, said the president of the New York City Board of Education, "you almost expect a notice from the schools saying there's going to be tuition." A good deal of private money, moreover, as The Times observed, was "being collected under the table" because parents sometimes feared that they would otherwise be forced to share these funds with other schools. "We can do it," said the leader of the parent group at one of the schools where lavish sums of private money had been raised, "but it is sad that other schools that don't have a richer parent body can't. It really does make it a question of haves and have-nots."

In view of the extensive coverage of this new phenomenon not only by New York City papers but by those in other cities where the same trends are observed, it is apparent that this second layer of disparities between the children of the wealthy and the children of the poor is no secret to the public any longer. Yet, even while they sometimes are officially deplored, these added forms of inequality have been accepted with apparent equanimity by those who are their beneficiaries.

"Inequality is not an intentional thing," said the leader of the PTA in one of the West Side neighborhoods where parents had been raising private funds, some of which had been obtained as charitable grants. "You have schools that are empowered and you have schools that have no power at all.... I don't bear any guilt for knowing how to write a grant," he said, a statement that undoubtedly made sense to some but skirted the entire issue of endemic underbudgeting of public schools attended by the children of poor people who did not enjoy his money-raising skills or possible connections to grant makers.

A narrowing of civic virtue to the borders of distinct and self-contained communities is now evolving in these hybrid institutions which are public schools in that they benefit from the receipt of public funds but private in the many supplementary programs that are purchased independently. Boutique schools within an otherwise impoverished system, they enable parents of the middle class and upper middle class to claim allegiance to the general idea of public schools while making sure their children do not suffer gravely for the stripped-down budgets that have done great damage to poor children like Alliyah and Pineapple.

"There are cheap children and there are expensive children," writes Marina Warner, an essayist and novelist who has written many books for children, "just as there are cheap women and expensive women." When Pineapple entered P.S. 65 in the South Bronx, the government of New York State had already placed a price tag on her forehead. She and her kindergarten classmates were $8,000 babies. If we had wanted to see an $18,000 baby, we would have had to drive into the suburbs. But the governmentally administered diminishment of value in the children of the poor begins even before the age of five or six when they begin their years of formal education in the public schools. It starts during their infant years and toddler years when hundreds of thousands of children in low-income neighborhoods are locked out of the opportunity for preschool education for no reason but the accident of birth and budgetary choices of the government, while children of the privileged are often given veritable feasts of rich developmental early education.

In New York City, for example, affluent parents pay surprisingly large sums of money to enroll their youngsters in extraordinary early-education programs, typically beginning at the age of two or three, that give them social competence and rudimentary pedagogic skills unknown to children of the same age in the city's poorer neighborhoods. The most exclusive of the private preschools in New York, which are known to those who can afford them as the "Baby Ivies," cost as much as $22,000 for a full-day program. Competition for admission to these pre-K schools is so intense that "private counselors" are frequently retained, at fees as high as $300 hourly, according to The Times, to guide the parents through the application process.

At the opposite extreme along the economic spectrum in New York are thousands of children who receive no preschool opportunity at all. Exactly how *many* thousands is almost impossible to know. Numbers that originate in governmental agencies in New York and other states are incomplete and imprecise and do not always differentiate with clarity between authentic pre-K programs that have educative and developmental substance and those less expensive childcare arrangements that do not. But even where states do compile numbers that refer specifically to educative preschool programs, it is difficult to know how many of the children who are served are of low income since admissions to some of the state-supported programs aren't determined by low income or they are determined by a complicated set of factors of which poverty is only one.

There is another way, however, to obtain a fairly vivid sense of what impoverished four-year-olds receive in segregated sections of our cities like the Bronx. This is by asking kids themselves while you are with them in a kindergarten class to tell you how they spent their time the year before—or, if the children get confused or are too shy to give you a clear answer, then by asking the same question to their teacher.

"How many of these children were in pre-K programs last year or the last two years?" I often ask a kindergarten teacher.

In middle- and upper-class suburbs, a familiar answer is "more than three quarters of them," "this year, almost all of them," or "virtually all...." In poor urban neighborhoods, by comparison, what I more often hear is "only a handful," "possibly as many as a fourth," "maybe about a third of them got *something* for one year...." The superintendent of the district that includes Pineapple's former school estimated in the fall of 2002 that only between a quarter and a third of children in the district had received even a single year of preschool and that less than five percent had been provided with the two years of pre-K instruction that are common in most affluent communities.

Government data and the estimates of independent agencies tend to substantiate the estimates of principals and teachers. Of approximately 250,000 four-year-olds in New York State in 2001–2002, only about 25 percent, some 60,000, were believed to be enrolled in the state-funded preschool program—which is known as "Universal Pre-K" nonetheless—and typically in two-and-a-half-hour sessions rather than the more extended programs children of middle-class families usually attend. Then too, because these figures were not broken down by family income levels and because the program did not give priority to children of low income, it was difficult to know how many children in the poorest neighborhoods had been excluded from the program.

Head Start, which is a federal program, is of course much better known than New York's Universal Pre-K and it has a long track-record, having been created 40 years ago by Congress at a time when social programs that expanded opportunities for children of low income were not viewed with the same skepticism that is common among many people who set public policy today. In spite of the generally high level of approval Head Start has received over the years, whether for its academic benefits or for its social benefits, or both, 40 percent of three- and four-year-olds who qualified for Head Start by their parents' income were denied this opportunity in 2001, a percentage of exclusion that has risen steeply in the subsequent four years. In some of the major cities, where the need is greatest, only a tiny fraction of low-income children in this age bracket are served. In New York City, for example, less than 13,000 four-year-olds were served by Head Start in 2001; and, in many cases, Head Start was combined with Universal Pre-K, so the children served by Head Start on its own were relatively few.

There are exceptions to this pattern in some sections of the nation. In Milwaukee, for example, nearly every four-year-old is now enrolled in a preliminary kindergarten program, which amounts to a full year of all-day preschool education, prior to a second kindergarten year for five-year-olds, according to the superintendent of Milwaukee's schools. In New Jersey, full-day pre-K programs have been instituted for all three- and four-year-olds in 31 low-income districts, one of the consequences of a legal action to reduce inequities of education in that state. More commonly in urban neighborhoods, large numbers of children have received no preschool education and they come into their kindergarten year without the minimal social skills that children need in order to participate in class activities and without even such very modest early-learning skills as knowing how to hold a pencil, identify perhaps a couple of shapes or colors, or recognize that printed pages go from left to right.

A first grade teacher in Boston pointed out a child in her class who had received no preschool and, as I recall, had missed much of his kindergarten year as well, and introduced me to the boy so I could sit beside him for a while and derive my own conclusions, then confirmed my first impression when she told me in a whisper, "He's a sweetheart of a baby but knows almost absolutely nothing about anything that has to do with school!"

Two years later, in third grade, these children are introduced to what are known as "high-stakes tests," which in many urban systems now determine whether students can or cannot be promoted. Children who have been in programs like the "Baby Ivies" since the age of two have been given seven years of education by this point, nearly twice as many as the children who have been denied these opportunities; yet all are required to take, and will be measured and in many cases penalized severely by, the same examinations.

Which of these children will receive the highest scores—those who spent the years from two to four in lovely little Montessori schools and other pastel-painted settings in which tender and attentive grown-ups read to them from storybooks and introduced them for the first time to the world of numbers, and the shapes of letters, and the sizes and varieties of solid objects, and perhaps taught them to sort things into groups or to arrange them in a sequence, or to do those many other interesting things that early-childhood specialists refer to as prenumeracy skills, or the ones who spent those years at home in front of a TV or sitting by the window of a slum apartment gazing down into the street? There is something deeply hypocritical in a society that holds an inner-city child only eight years old "accountable" for her performance on a high-stakes standardized exam but does not hold the high officials of our government accountable for robbing her of what they gave their own kids six or seven years before.

There are obviously other forces that affect the early school performance of low-income children: levels of parent education, social instability, and frequently undiagnosed depression and anxiety that make it hard for many parents I have known to take an active role in backing up the efforts of their children's teachers in the public schools. Still, it is all too easy to assign the primary onus of responsibility to parents in these neighborhoods. (Where were these parents educated after all? Usually in the same low-ranking schools their children now attend.) In a nation in which fairness was respected, children of the poorest and least educated mothers would receive the most extensive and most costly preschool preparation, not the least and cheapest, because children in these families need it so much more than those whose educated parents can deliver the same benefits of early learning to them in their homes.

The "Baby Ivies" of Manhattan are not public institutions and receive no subsidies from public funds. In a number of cities, on the other hand, even this last line of squeamishness has now been crossed and public funds are being used to underwrite part of the costs of preschool education for the children of the middle class in public institutions which, however, do not offer the same services to children of the poor. Starting in spring 2001, Chicago's public schools began to operate a special track of preschool for the children of those families who were able to afford to pay an extra fee—nearly $6,000—to provide their children with a full-day program of about 11 hours, starting at the age of two if parents so desired. In a city where 87 percent of students in the public schools were black or Hispanic, the pay-for-preschool program served primarily white children.

Almost all these preschools were "in gentrified or gentrifying neighborhoods," The Chicago Tribune reported. "The fresh paint and new toys" in one of these programs on the North Side of Chicago were not there simply "to make preschool a happier place for the new class of toddlers" but "to keep their parents from moving to the suburbs." These and other "gold-plated academic offerings" which the city was underwriting to attract or to retain the children of the middle class had already begun to slow the "brain drain" from the public schools, The Tribune said. In the same year in which the pay-for-pre-K program was begun, 7,000 children from low-income families, many of whom were deemed to be "at risk," were waiting for pre-school spaces that the city was unable to provide.

Undemocratic practices like these, no matter how strategically compelling they may seem, have introduced a radical distorting prism to an old, if seldom honored, national ideal of universal public education that affords all children equal opportunity within the borders of a democratic entity. Blurring the line between democracy and marketplace, the private subsidy of public schools in privileged communities denounces an ideal of simple justice that is often treated nowadays as an annoying residue of tiresome egalitarian ideas, an ethical detritus that sophisticated parents are encouraged to shut out of mind as they adapt themselves to a new order of Darwinian entitlements.

QUESTIONS

? Doesn't public education mean equal education? Why and how do public educational experiences vary? (Think about atmosphere, programs, teachers, building conditions, No Child Left Behind achievement tests, and student opportunities).

? What children are most likely to experience poor educational opportunities? Why?

? Societal map question: Parental fundraising to produce "boutique" schools is proposed as one strategy to provide services, teachers, or other essentials that public schools might be unable to afford. Argue for and against this proposition.

Let Them Eat Fat
The heavy truths about American obesity

By GREG CRITSER

■ "Becoming obese," reveals author Greg Critser in your next reading, "is a normal response to the American environment." Read this article closely to discover how obesity is created by our society and how it, in turn, poses problems for people and society.

Not long ago, a group of doctors, nurses, and medical technicians wheeled a young man into the intensive care unit of Los Angeles County-USC Medical Center, hooked him to a ganglia of life-support systems—pulse and respiration monitors, a breathing apparatus, and an IV line—then stood back and collectively stared. I was there visiting an ailing relative, and I stared, too.

Here, in the ghastly white light of modern American medicine, writhed a real-life epidemiological specter: a 500-pound twenty-two-year-old. The man, whom I'll call Carl, was propped up at a 45-degree angle, the better to be fed air through a tube, and lay there nude, save for a small patch of blood-spotted gauze stuck to his lower abdomen, where surgeons had just labored to save his life. His eyes darted about in abject fear. "Second time in three months," his mother blurted out to me as she stood watching in horror. "He had two stomach staplings, and they both came apart. Oh my God, my boy..." Her boy was suffocating in his own fat.

I was struck not just by the spectacle but by the truth of the mother's comment. This *was* a boy—one buried in years of bad health, relative poverty, a sedentary lifestyle, and a high-fat diet, to be sure, but a boy nonetheless. Yet how surprised should I have been? That obesity, particularly among the young and the poor, is spinning out of control is hardly a secret. It is, in fact, something that most Americans can agree upon. Along with depression, heart disease, and cancer, obesity is yet another chew in our daily rumination about health and fitness, morbidity and mortality. Still, even in dot-com America, where statistics fly like arrows, the numbers are astonishing. Consider:

Copyright © 2000 by Harper's Magazine. All rights reserved. Reproduced from the March issue by special permission.

- Today, one fifth of all Americans are obese, meaning that they have a body mass index, or BMI, of more than 30. (BMI is a universally recognized cross-measure of weight for height and stature.) The epidemiological figures on chronic corpulence are so unequivocal that even the normally reticent dean of American obesity studies, the University of Colorado's James O. Hill, says that if obesity is left unchecked almost all Americans will be overweight within a few generations. "Becoming obese," he told the *Arizona Republic*, "is a normal response to the American environment."

- Children are most at risk. At least 25 percent of all Americans now under age nineteen are overweight or obese. In 1998, Dr. David Satcher, the new U.S. surgeon general, was moved to declare childhood obesity to be epidemic. "Today," he told a group of federal bureaucrats and policymakers, "we see a nation of young people seriously at risk of starting out obese and dooming themselves to the difficult task of overcoming a tough illness."

- Even among the most careful researchers these days, "epidemic" is the term of choice when it comes to talk of fat, particularly fat children. As William Dietz, the director of nutrition at the Centers for Disease Control, said last year, "This is an epidemic in the U.S. the likes of which we have not had before in chronic disease." The cost to the general public health budget by 2020 will run into the hundreds of billions, making HIV look, economically, like a bad case of the flu.

Yet standing that day in the intensive care unit, among the beepers and buzzers and pumps, epidemic was the last thing on my mind. Instead I felt heartbreak, revulsion, fear, sadness—and then curiosity: Where did this boy come from? Who and what had made him? How is it that we Americans, perhaps the most health-conscious of any people in the history of the world, and certainly the richest, have come to preside over the deadly fattening of our youth?

The beginning of an answer came one day last fall, in the same week that the Spanish language newspaper *La Opinión* ran a story headlined "Diabetes epidemia en latinos," when I attended the opening of the newest Krispy Kreme doughnut store in Los Angeles. It was, as they say in marketing circles, a "resonant" event, replete with around-the-block lines, celebrity news anchors, and stern cops directing traffic. The store, located in the heart of the San Fernando Valley's burgeoning Latino population, pulsed with excitement. In one corner stood the new store's manager, a young Anglo fellow, accompanied by a Krispy Kreme publicity director. Why had Krispy Kreme decided to locate here? I asked.

"See," the manager said, brushing a crumb of choco-glaze from his fingers, "the idea is simple—accessible but not convenient. The idea is to make the store accessible—easy to get into and out of from the street—but just a tad away from the—eh, mainstream so as to make sure that the customers are presold and very intent before they get here," he said, betraying no doubts about the company's marketing formula. "We want them intent to get at least a dozen before they even think of coming in."

But why this slightly non-mainstream place?

"Because it's obvious..." He gestured to the stout Mayan doñas queuing around the building. "We're looking for all the bigger families."

Bigger in size?

"Yeah." His eyes rolled, like little glazed crullers. "*Bigger in size.*"

Of course, fast-food and national restaurant chains like Krispy Kreme that serve it have long been the object of criticism by nutritionists and dietitians. Despite the attention, however, fast-food companies, most of them publicly owned and sprinkled into the stock portfolios of many striving Americans (including mine and perhaps yours), have grown more aggressive in their targeting of poor inner-city communities. One of every four hamburgers sold by the good folks at McDonald's, for example, is now purchased by inner-city consumers who, disproportionately, are young black men.

In fact, it was the poor, and their increasing need for cheap meals consumed outside the home, that fueled the development of what may well be the most important fast-food innovation of the past twenty years, the sales gimmick known as "supersizing." At my local McDonald's, located in a lower-middle-income area of Pasadena,

California, the supersize bacchanal goes into high gear at about five P.M., when the various urban caballeros, drywalleros, and jardineros get off work and head for a quick bite. Mixed in is a sizable element of young black kids traveling between school and home, their economic status apparent by the fact that they've walked instead of driven. Customers are cheerfully encouraged to "supersize your meal!" by signs saying, "If we don't recommend a supersize, the supersize is free!" For an extra seventy-nine cents, a kid ordering a cheeseburger, small fries, and a small Coke will get said cheeseburger plus a supersize Coke (42 fluid ounces versus 16, with free refills) and a supersize order of french fries (more than double the weight of a regular order). Suffice it to say that consumption of said meals is fast and, in almost every instance I observed, very complete.

But what, metabolically speaking, has taken place? The total caloric content of the meal has been jacked up from 680 calories to more than 1,340 calories. According to the very generous U.S. dietary guidelines, 1,340 calories represent more than half of a teenager's recommended daily caloric consumption, and the added calories themselves are protein-poor but fat- and carbohydrate-rich. Completing this jumbo dietetic horror is the fact that the easy availability of such huge meals arrives in the same years in which physical activity among teenage boys and girls drops by about half.

Now consider the endocrine warfare that follows. The constant bombing of the pancreas by such a huge hit of sugars and fats can eventually wear out the organ's insulin-producing "islets," leading to diabetes and its inevitable dirge of woes: kidney, eye, and nerve damage; increased risk of heart disease; even stroke. The resulting sugar-induced hyperglycemia in many of the obese wreaks its own havoc in the form of glucose toxicity, further debilitating nerve endings and arterial walls. For the obese and soon to be obese, it is no overstatement to say that after supersized teen years the pancreas may never be the same. Some 16 million Americans suffer from Type 2 diabetes, a third of them unaware of their condition. Today's giggly teen burp may well be tomorrow's aching neuropathic limb.

Diabetes, by the way, is just the beginning of what's possible. If childhood obesity truly is "an epidemic in the U.S. the likes of which we have not had before in chronic disease," then places like McDonald's and Winchell's Donut stores, with their endless racks of glazed and creamy goodies, are the San Francisco bathhouses of said epidemic, the places where the high-risk population indulges in high-risk behavior. Although open around the clock, the Winchell's near my house doesn't get rolling until seven in the morning, the Spanish-language talk shows frothing in the background while an ambulance light whirls atop the Coke dispenser. Inside, Mami placates Miguelito with a giant apple fritter. Papi tells a joke and pours ounce upon ounce of sugar and cream into his 20-ounce coffee. Viewed through the lens of obesity, as I am inclined to do, the scene is not so *feliz*. The obesity rate for Mexican-American children is shocking. Between the ages of five and eleven, the rate for girls is 27 percent; for boys, 23 percent. By fourth grade the rate for girls peaks at 32 percent, while boys top out at 43 percent. Not surprisingly, obesity-related disorders are everywhere on display at Winchell's, right before my eyes—including fat kids who limp, which can be a symptom of Blount's disease (a deformity of the tibia) or a sign of slipped capital femoral epiphysis (an orthopedic abnormality brought about by weight-induced dislocation of the femur bone). Both conditions are progressive, often requiring surgery.

The chubby boy nodding in the corner, waiting for his Papi to finish his *café*, is likely suffering from some form of sleep apnea; a recent study of forty-one children with severe obesity revealed that a third had the condition and that another third presented with clinically abnormal sleep patterns. Another recent study indicated that "obese children with obstructive sleep apnea demonstrate clinically significant decrements in learning and memory function." And the lovely but very chubby little girl tending to her schoolbooks? Chances are she will begin puberty before the age of ten, launching her into a lifetime of endocrine bizarreness that not only will be costly to treat but will be emotionally devastating as well. Research also suggests that weight gain can lead to the development of pseudotumor cerebri, a brain tumor most common in females. A recent review of 57 patients with the tumor revealed that 90 percent were obese. This little girl's chances of developing other neurological illnesses are profound as well. And she may already have gallstones: obesity accounts for up to 33 percent of all gallstones observed in children. She is ten times more likely than her non-obese peers to develop high blood pressure, and she is increasingly likely to contract Type 2 diabetes, obesity being that disease's number-one risk factor.

Of course, if she is really lucky, that little girl could just be having a choco-sprinkles doughnut on her way to school.

What about poor rural whites? Studying children in an elementary school in a low-income town in eastern Kentucky, the anthropologist Deborah Crooks was astonished to find stunting and obesity not just present but prevalent. Among her subjects, 13 percent of girls exhibited notable stunting; 33 percent of all kids were significantly overweight; and 13 percent of the children were obese—21 percent of boys and 9 percent of girls. A sensitive, elegant writer, Crooks drew from her work three important conclusions: One, that poor kids in the United States often face the same evolutionary nutritional pressures as those in newly industrializing nations, where traditional diets are replaced by high-fat diets and where labor-saving technology reduces physical activity. Second, Crooks found that "height and weight are cumulative measures of growth...reflecting a sum total of environmental experience over time." Last, and perhaps most important, Crooks concluded that while stunting can be partially explained by individual household conditions—income, illness, education, and marital status—obesity "may be more of a community-related phenomenon." Here the economic infrastructure—safe playgrounds, access to high-quality, low-cost food, and transportation to play areas—was the key determinant of physical-activity levels.

Awareness of these national patterns of destruction, of course, is a key reason why Eli Lilly & Co., the $75 billion pharmaceutical company, is now building the largest factory dedicated to the production of a single drug in industry history. That drug is insulin. Lilly's sales of insulin products totaled $357 million in the third quarter of 1999, a 24 percent increase over the previous third quarter. Almost every leading pharmaceutical conglomerate has like-minded ventures under way, with special emphasis on pill-form treatments for non-insulin-dependent forms of the disease. Pharmaceutical companies that are not seeking to capture some portion of the burgeoning market are bordering on fiduciary mismanagement. Said James Kappel of Eli Lilly, "You've got to be in diabetes."

Wandering home from my outing, the wondrous smells of frying foods wafting in the air, I wondered why, given affluent America's outright fetishism about diet and health, those whose business it is to care—the media, the academy, public-health workers, and the government—do almost nothing. The answer, I suggest, is that in almost every public-health arena, the need to address obesity as a class issue—one that transcends the inevitable divisiveness of race and gender—has been blunted by bad logic, vested interests, academic cant, and ideological chauvinism.

Consider a story last year in the *New York Times* detailing the rise in delivery-room mortality among young African-American mothers. The increases were attributed to a number of factors—diabetes, hypertension, drug and alcohol abuse—but the primary factor of obesity, which can foster both diabetes and hypertension, was mentioned only in passing. Moreover, efforts to understand and publicize the socioeconomic factors of the deaths have been thwarted. When Dr. Janet Mitchell, a New York obstetrician charged with reviewing several recent maternal mortality studies, insisted that socioeconomics were the issue in understanding the "racial gap" in maternal mortality, she was unable to get government funding for the work. "We need to back away from the medical causes," she told the *Times*, clearly exasperated, "and begin to take a much more ethnographic, anthropological approach to this tragic outcome."

In another example, a 1995 University of Arizona study reported that young black girls, who are more inclined toward obesity than white girls, were also far less likely to hold "bad body images" about themselves. The slew of news articles and TV reports that followed were nothing short of jubilant, proclaiming the "good news." As one commentator I watched late one evening announced, "Here is one group of girls who couldn't care less about looking like Kate Moss!" Yet no one mentioned the long-term effects of unchecked weight gain. Apparently, when it comes to poor black girls the media would rather that they risk diabetes than try to look like models.

"That's the big conundrum, as they always say," Richard MacKenzie, a physician who treats overweight and obese girls in downtown L.A., told me recently. "No one wants to overemphasize the problems of being fat to these girls, for fear of creating body-image problems that might lead to anorexia and bulimia." Speaking anecdotally, he said that "the problem is that for every one affluent white anorexic you create by 'overemphasizing' obesity, you foster ten obese poor girls by downplaying the severity of the issue." Judith Stern, a professor of nutrition and internal medicine at UC Davis, is more blunt. "The number of kids with eating disorders is positively dwarfed by the number with obesity. It sidesteps the whole class issue. We've got to stop that and get on with the real problem."

Moreover, such sidestepping denies poor minority girls a principal, if sometimes unpleasant, psychological incentive to lose weight: that of social stigma. Only recently has the academy come to grapple with this. Writing in a recent issue of the *International Journal of Obesity*, the scholar Susan Averett looked at the hard numbers: 44 percent of African-American women weigh more than 120 percent of their recommended body weight yet are less likely than whites to perceive themselves as overweight.[1] Anglo women, poor and otherwise, registered higher anxiety about fatness and experienced far fewer cases of chronic obesity. "Social stigma may serve to control obesity among white women," Averett reluctantly concluded. "If so, physical and emotional effects of greater pressure to be thin must be weighed against reduced health risks associated with overweight and obesity." In other words, maybe a few more black Kate Mosses might not be such a bad thing.

While the so-called fat acceptance movement, a very vocal minority of super-obese female activists, has certainly played a role in the tendency to deny the need to promote healthy thinness, the real culprits have been those with true cultural power, those in the academy and the publishing industry who have the ability to shape public opinion. Behind much of their reluctance to face facts is the lingering influence of the 1978 bestseller, *Fat Is a Feminist Issue*, in which Susie Orbach presented a nuanced, passionate look at female compulsive eating and its roots in patriarchal culture. But although Orbach's observations were keen, her conclusions were often wishful, narcissistic, and sometimes just wrong. "Fat is a social disease, and fat is a feminist issue," Orbach wrote. "Fat is not about self-control or lack of will power.... It is a response to the inequality of the sexes."[2]

Perhaps so, if one is a feminist, and if one is struggling with an eating disorder, and if one is, for the most part, affluent, well-educated, and politically aware. But obesity itself is preeminently an issue of class, not of ethnicity, and certainly not of gender. True, the disease may be refracted though its concentrations in various demographic subgroupings—in Native Americans, in Latinos, in African Americans, and even in some Pacific Island Americans—but in study after study, the key adjective is *poor:* poor African Americans, poor Latinos, poor whites, poor women, poor children, poor Latino children, etc. From the definitive *Handbook of Obesity*: "In heterogeneous and affluent societies like the United States, there is a strong inverse correlation of social class and obesity, particularly for females." From *Annals of Epidemiology*: "In white girls...both TV viewing and obesity were strongly inversely associated with household income as well as with parental education."

Yet class seems to be the last thing on the minds of some of our better social thinkers. Instead, the tendency of many in the academy is to fetishize or "postmodernize" the problem. Cornell University professor Richard Klein, for example, proposed in his 1996 book, *Eat Fat*, "Try this for six weeks: Eat fat." (Klein's mother did and almost died from sleep apnea, causing Klein to reverse himself in his epilogue, advising readers: "Eat rice.") The identity politics of fat, incidentally, can cut the other way. To the French, the childhood diet has long been understood as a serious medical issue directly affecting the future of the nation. The concern grew directly from late-nineteenth-century health issues in French cities and the countryside, where tuberculosis had winnowed the nation's birth rate below that of the other European powers. To deal with the problem, a new science known as puériculture emerged to educate young mothers about basic health and nutrition practices. Long before Americans and the British roused themselves from the torpor of Victorian chub, the French undertook research into proper dietary and weight controls for the entire birth-to-adolescence growth period. By the early 1900s, with birth rates (and birth weights) picking up, the puériculture movement turned its attention to childhood obesity. Feeding times were to be strictly maintained; random snacks were unhealthy for the child, regardless of how "natural" it felt for a mother to indulge her young. Kids were weighed once a week. All meals were to be supervised by an adult. As a result, portion control—perhaps the one thing that modern obesity experts can agree upon as a reasonable way to prevent the condition—very early became institutionalized in modern France. The message that too much food is bad still resounds in French child rearing, and as a result France has a largely lean populace.

What about the so-called Obesity Establishment, that web of researchers, clinicians, academics, and government health officials charged with finding ways to prevent the disease? Although there are many committed individuals in this group, one wonders just how independently minded they are. Among the sponsors for the 1997 annual conference of the North American Association for the Study of Obesity, the premier medical think tank on the subject, were the following: the Coca-Cola Company, Hershey Foods, Kraft Foods, and, never to be left out, Slim Fast Foods. Another sponsor was Knoll Pharmaceuticals, maker of the new diet drug Meridia. Of course, in a society where until recently tobacco companies sponsored fitness pageants and Olympic games, sponsorship hardly denotes corruption in the most traditional sense. One would be hard-pressed to prove any kind of censorship, but such underwriting effectively defines the parameters of public discussion. Everybody winks or blinks at the proper moment, then goes on his or her way.

Once upon a time, however, the United States possessed visionary leadership in the realm of childhood fitness. Founded in 1956, the President's Council on Youth Fitness successfully laid down broad-based fitness goals for all youth and established a series of awards for those who excelled in the effort. The council spoke about obesity with a forthrightness that would be political suicide today, with such pointed slogans as "There's no such thing as stylishly stout" and "Hey kid, if you see yourself in this picture, you need help."

By the late 1980s and early 1990s, however, new trends converged to undercut the council's powers of moral and cultural suasion. The ascendancy of cultural relativism led to a growing reluctance to be blunt about fatness, and, aided and abetted by the fashion industry's focus on baggy, hip-hop-style clothes, it became possible to be "stylishly stout." Fatness, as celebrated on rap videos, was now equated with wealth and power, with identity and agency, not with clogging the heart or being unable to reach one's toes. But fat inner-city black kids and the suburban kids copying them are even more disabled by their obesity. The only people who benefit from kids being "fat" are the ones running and owning the clothing, media, food, and drug companies. In upscale corporate America, meanwhile, being fat is taboo, a surefire career-killer. If you can't control your own contours, goes the logic, how can you control a budget or a staff? Look at the glossy business and money magazines with their cooing profiles of the latest genius entrepreneurs: to the man, and the occasional woman, no one, I mean *no one*, is fat.

Related to the coolification of homeboyish fat—perhaps forcing its new status—is the simple fact that it's hard for poor children to find opportunities to exercise. Despite our obsession with professional sports, many of today's disadvantaged youth have fewer opportunities than ever to simply shoot baskets or kick a soccer ball. Various measures to limit state spending and taxing, among them California's debilitating Proposition 13, have gutted school-based physical-education classes. Currently, only one state, Illinois, requires daily physical education for all grades K-12, and only 19 percent of high school students nationwide are active for twenty minutes a day, five days a week, in physical education. Add to this the fact that, among the poor, television, the workingman's baby sitter, is now viewed at least thirty-two hours a week. Participation in sports has always required an investment, but with the children of the affluent tucked away either in private schools or green suburbias, buying basketballs for the poor is not on the public agenda.

Human nature and its lazy inclinations aside, what do America's affluent *get* out of keeping the poor so fat? The reasons, I'd suggest, are many. An unreconstructed Marxist might invoke simple class warfare, exploitation fought through stock ownership in giant fast-food firms. The affluent know that the stuff will kill them but need someone (else) to eat it so as to keep growing that retirement portfolio. A practitioner of vulgar social psychology might argue for "our" need for the "identifiable outsider." An economist would say that in a society as overly competitive as our own, the affluent have found a way to slow down the striving poor from inevitable nipping at their heels. A French semiotician might even say that with the poor the affluent have erected their own walking and talking "empire of signs." This last notion is perhaps not so far-fetched. For what do the fat, darker, exploited poor, with their unbridled primal appetites, have to offer us but a chance for we diet- and shape-conscious folk to live vicariously? Call it boundary envy. Or, rather, boundary-free envy. And yet, by living outside their boundaries, the poor live within ours; fat people do not threaten our way of life; their angers entombed in flesh, they are slowed, they are softened, they are *fed*.

Meanwhile, in the City of Fat Angels, we lounge through a slow-motion epidemic. Mami buys another apple fritter. Papi slams his second sugar and cream. Another young Carl supersizes and double supersizes, then supersizes again. Waistlines surge. Any minute now, the belt will run out of holes.

---

[1] Certainly culture plays a role in the behavior of any subpopulation. Among black women, for example, obesity rates persist despite increases in income. A recent study by the National Heart, Lung, and Blood Institute concludes that obesity in black girls may be "a reflection of a differential social development in our society, wherein a certain lag period may need to elapse between an era when food availability is a concern to an era of affluence with no such concern." Other observers might assert that black women find affirmation for being heavy from black men, or believe themselves to be "naturally" heavier. Such assertions do not change mortality statistics.

[2] At the edges of the culture, the inheritors of Susie Orbach's politics have created Web sites called FaT GIRL and Largesse: the Network for Size Esteem, which claim that "dieting kills" and instruct how to induce vomiting in diet centers as protest.

QUESTIONS

- ? What does Critser mean when he says that obesity is a class issue? Why do people fail to see it as such? Do anorexia and/or bulimia might also have class origins?
- ? What health complications are likely for obese children and adults? How do these complications impact society as a whole?
- ? Societal map question: Informed by Critser's information, think carefully about obesity as a socially-created problem. If you were to design a policy (a plan or course of action to influence or change a certain part of society) to decrease obesity, where would you start? To answer this question identify what you think are two primary social causes of obesity. Then, explain how you would target one of those causes to decrease obesity.

Chapter 11

Gangstas, Thugs, and Hustlas: Identity and the Code of the Street in Rap Music

By CHARIS A. KUBRIN

■ Music and lyrics can provide special insight into social worlds that are often not examined by scholars. In the article that follows, Charis E. Kubrin examines gangsta rap lyrics to understand the presentation of "street code" that centers on respect, violence, material wealth, and violent retaliation. Analyzing 103 platinum rap albums and 403 songs, Kubrin illustrates that street code provides justification and accounting for violence that "establishes identity, reputation, and exerts social control."

Rap music has undergone major transformations in the last two decades. One of the most significant occurred in the early 1990s with the emergence of "gangsta rap." *The St. James Encyclopedia of Popular Culture* identifies gangsta rap as the most controversial type of rap music, having received global attention for "its vivid sexist, misogynistic, and homophobic lyrics, as well as its violent depiction of urban ghetto life in America" (Abrams 2000:198). Its roots can be traced to early depictions of the hustler lifestyle and blaxploitation movies of the 1970s, which glorified blacks as criminals, pimps, pushers, prostitutes, and gangsters. Mainly associated with West Coast artists (Keyes 2002:4), gangsta rap is considered a product of the gang culture and street wars of South Central Los Angeles, Compton, and Long Beach, and the resurgence of the retromack culture (pimp attitude and style) of East Oakland (Perkins 1996:18). Since its early pioneers were gang members, gangsta rap relates to the life experiences of the rappers themselves, and its lyrics portray gang and ghetto life from a criminal's perspective (Krims 2000:70).

Gangsta rap departed from earlier rap forms, which were often characterized as socially conscious and more politically Afro-centric (Keyes 2002:88, 158–59; Martinez 1997; Perkins 1996:19). Even today, gangsta rap differs from other types of rap mainly in that it is the musical expression of ghettocentricity, an expression that engages the "black youth cultural imagination that cultivated varying ways of interpreting, representing, and understanding the shifting contours of ghetto dislocation" (Watkins 2001:389). Scholars agree that other rap forms reflect a generic concern for chronicling the "black" experience, while gangsta rap is specifically interested in the black underclass in the ghetto (Keyes 2002:122; Rose 1994:12, 114; Smith 1997:346). Today gangsta rap purportedly provides an insiders' look into black urban street life via crime and violence (Keyes 2004:4; Kitwana 1994:19).

Sociological scholarship on identity, culture, and violence in inner-city communities has largely overlooked rap music. Much of the existing literature assumes that the street code is a product of neighborhood processes and neglects additional sources such as popular culture which may reflect, reinforce, or even advocate street-code norms. This study builds on the existing literature through a content analysis of rap music that explores how the code is present not only in "the street," but also in rap music. This research, however, does not suggest that rap directly causes violence; rather, it examines the more subtle discursive processes through which rap helps to organize and construct violent social identity and account for violent behavior.

Theoretically, the study considers how structural conditions in inner-city communities have given rise to cultural adaptations—embodied in a street code—that constitute an interpretive environment where violence is accountable, if not normative. It focuses on the complex and reflexive relationship between the street code, rap music, and social identity. Empirically, the study examines how rappers' lyrics actively construct violent identities for themselves and for others. It explores the ways in which violence is justified and accounted for in terms that clearly resonate with the code of the street. I address these issues through a content analysis of 403 songs on rap albums from 1992 to 2000. As I will argue, the lyrics offer portrayals of violence that serve many functions including establishing identity and reputation and exerting social control.

SOCIAL-STRUCTURAL CONDITIONS IN INNER-CITY COMMUNITIES: THE CONTEXT

Whereas studies of violent crime typically have been situated within an exclusively structural or subcultural theoretical framework, recent research argues that the causes of violence are both socio-structural and situational (Bruce, Roscigno, and McCall 1998; Fagan and Wilkinson 1998; Kubrin and Wadsworth 2003; Kubrin and Weitzer 2003; Sampson and Wilson 1995). Growing recognition of the utility of an integrative approach has led researchers to consider the relationship between structural disadvantage, cultural and situational responses to such disadvantage, and the perpetuation of violence within African American communities.

Structurally, the combined effects of poverty, unemployment, family disruption and isolation from mainstream America define the neighborhood context for residents in many inner-city neighborhoods. These "concentration effects" contribute to social disorganization (Sampson and Wilson 1995) and violence (Krivo and Peterson 1996; Kubrin and Weitzer 2003). The social, political, and economic forces that have shaped these conditions include, among other things, globalization and deindustrialization (Rose 1994:21–61; Wadsworth 2004; Wilson 1996), residential segregation (Keyes 2002:44–45; Massey and Denton 1993), punitive criminal justice policy (Tonry 1995), and a legacy of slavery and discrimination (Hawkins 1985). The concentrated disadvantage found in many urban African American communities is not paralleled in predominantly white neighborhoods.

An important element of such disadvantaged communities is the opportunity structure available for residents. The inner city affords limited avenues for adolescents to obtain the types of social status and social roles available to youth in other environments (Rose 1994:27). Street-oriented peer groups dominate social roles, and few opportunities exist for broader participation in community life, such as after-school groups, volunteer organizations, or supervised athletics. Alternatives to conventional status attainment are thus limited to manifestations of physical power or domination, verbal agility, or displays of material wealth (Wilkinson 2001:235).

At the same time, illegitimate avenues for success abound. For many poor, young, black males, the opportunity for dealing drugs is literally just around the corner (Anderson 1999:114; Keyes 2002:184) and represents one of the most viable "job" options in the face of limited employment opportunities (Kitwana 2002:39). This is not to say that impoverished blacks bypass hard work as a prerequisite for success in life; young blacks, like most Americans who are given the opportunity to work, have demonstrated their willingness to do so (Newman 1999). But the continual demand for economic and social success, coupled with limited legitimate avenues and numerous illegitimate avenues by which to attain it, creates a unique situation unparalleled in white and middle-class black communities (George 1998:43).

The prevalence of drugs—and of crack cocaine in particular—generates more than increased illegitimate opportunities. Crack and the drug trade create neighborhood battles for the control over markets where violence is used as social control (George 1998:42; Keyes 2002:183). Elijah Anderson (1990) explains this phenomenon in his ethnography of Northton, a poor, urban, black community: "Dealers have certain corners and spaces 'sewed up,' marked off as their own territory, and may prevent other dealers from selling either at a particular corner or even in the general area. At times these corners are bought and sold, leading to turf disputes and violence to decide who owns them. A 'king of the hill' competition may ensue, awarding the corner to whoever can claim it" (p. 85). Contributing to the violence, the ready availability of guns in these communities increases the stakes, often turning what would have been an assault into a homicide (Fagan and Wilkinson 1998; Wilkinson 2001:232).

Tenuous police-community relations contribute to these problems (see especially Anderson 1990:190–206). Residents of disadvantaged black communities, arguably those most in need of police protection, tend to be wary of the police, in part because of concerns about racial profiling and the possibility of being wrongfully accused. These practices cause residents who might otherwise assist the police to avoid them, to not cooperate with investigations, to assume dishonesty on the part of officers, and to teach others that such reactions are prudent lessons of survival on the streets (Anderson 1990; Kennedy 1997:153; Kubrin and Weitzer 2003). Anderson (1990) notes, "Because the young black man is aware of many cases when an 'innocent' black person was wrongly accused and detained, he develops an 'attitude' toward the police. He becomes concerned when he notices 'the man' in the community… The youth knows…that he exists in a legally precarious state. Hence he is motivated to avoid the police and his public life becomes severely circumscribed" (p. 196). For many poor and working-class blacks, police and brutality are synonymous (Rose 1994:106).

Scholars have documented the disparities between black and white communities. In many cities, racial differences in poverty, joblessness, and family disruption are so great that the worst urban contexts in which whites reside are considerably better than the average context of black communities (Sampson 1987:354). These inequalities are even greater considering that incarcerated blacks, typically the most economically and socially disadvantaged social bloc, are not included in census counts (Western 2002).

In addition to racial inequality, patterns of economic bifurcation within the African American community have become more pronounced: "At one end of this bifurcated class structure are poor and working class blacks in ghetto communities that experience social, economic, spatial, and demographic isolation. On the other end is a black middle and lower-middle class buoyed by increased access to higher education and professional employment" (Watkins 2001:381). Although black middle-class residents may fare better than their lower-class counterparts, Mary Pattillo-McCoy (1999) finds that almost half of the black middle-class is concentrated in the lower-middle-class region, distinguished by its close proximity to the black working poor. Moreover, she finds that middle-class blacks do not perform as well as similarly situated whites on standardized tests, are more likely to be incarcerated for drug offenses, are less likely to marry and more likely to be single parents, and are less likely to be working. Thus, we should be cautious in celebrating the achievements of the "fragile black middle-class" (Kitwana 2002:42).

In sum, the extreme, concentrated disadvantage and isolation of black inner-city communities coupled with the quantity and potency of drugs and availability of guns have created a situation unparalleled in American history; such conditions represent "previously unseen challenges in African American life" (Kitwana 1994:45; 2002:xx). These are the social-structural community characteristics from which a "code of the street" has emerged.

THE CODE OF THE STREET AND NEIGHBORHOOD SUBCULTURE

In his ethnography of the moral life of the inner city, Anderson (1999) argues that a street code provides the principles governing much interpersonal public behavior. Given the bleak conditions, black youth in disadvantaged communities have created a local social order complete with its own code and rituals of authenticity (Anderson 1999; Henderson 1996; Keyes 2002:6; Kitwana 2002; Perkins 1996:20). This street code articulates powerful norms and characterizes public social relations among residents, particularly with respect to violence. Neighborhood structural conditions generate the subculture, so cultural differences reflect adaptations to structural inequality.

Social identity and respect are the most important features of the code. Respect—defined as being treated right or granted the deference one deserves (Anderson 1999:33)—often forms the core of a person's self-esteem. One way to acquire respect is by developing a reputation for being violent, by creating a self-image based on "juice" (Anderson 1999:72). On the streets, the image one projects is paramount, and at the top of the hierarchy is the "crazy," "wild," or "killer" social identity (Wilkinson 2001:246). A person's public bearing must send the message that he or she is capable of violence when necessary. In his study of inner-city Philadelphia communities, Anderson (1999:72) found that youth often created altercations with the sole purpose of building respect. Similarly, Deanna Wilkinson (2001) found that young men committed robberies in order to impress their peers and upgrade their social status. A third study found that youth from inner-city New York communities used violence for recognition (Fagan and Wilkinson 1998). In short, violence is thought to be the single most critical resource for achieving status among those who participate in street culture (Wilkinson 2001:243).

In this context, the gun becomes a symbol of power and a remedy for disputes. Since the 1970s, guns have been a central part of the changing character of youth violence (Fagan and Wilkinson 1998:106). For those who subscribe to the code, guns are the tactical choice for settling scores and asserting dominance in matters of honor, territory, and business (George 1998:42). The easy accessibility of guns in the inner city has raised the stakes of the street code even higher. Jeffrey Fagan and Deanna Wilkinson (1998) found that guns dominated social interactions; youth reported having one close by in case it would be needed during a conflict. Regarding one youth Fagan and Wilkinson state, "It was understood that using a gun to harm his opponent was the best way to handle the situation both in terms of what was expected on the street and what an individual had to do to maintain a respected identity" (p. 139). For many youth, guns have become symbols of respect, identity, and power in addition to having strategic survival value.

Building a violent reputation not only commands respect but also serves to deter future assaults. For those invested in street culture, or for those who simply wish to survive (Keyes 2002:6, 166), a key objective of their demeanor is to discourage others from "testing" or "challenging" them. In some cases, manifest nerve—stealing another's possessions, mouthing off, pulling a trigger—builds a reputation that will prevent future challenges. However, when challenges arise or transgressions occur, violence is viewed as acceptable, appropriate, and even obligatory: "In the most socially isolated pockets of the inner city, this situation has given rise to a kind of people's law based on a form of social exchange whose by-product is respect and whose caveat is vengeance or payback" (Anderson 1999:66). If a person is assaulted, for instance, it is essential in the eyes of his peers and others for him to seek revenge, otherwise he risks being victimized. Walking away from conflict is risky to one's health:

> *To run away would likely leave one's self-esteem in tatters, while inviting further disrespect. Therefore, people often feel constrained to pay back—to seek revenge—after a successful assault. Their very identity, their self-respect, and their honor are tied up with the way they perform on the streets during and after such encounters. And it is this identification, including a credible reputation for payback, that is strongly believed to deter future assaults. (Anderson 1999:76)*

In instances of payback, violence is considered an appropriate reaction to crime, not a crime itself, and the offender operates on the assumption that the victim provoked his own injury (or death) through an act of wrongdoing. As Donald Black (1983) explained decades ago, much crime is moralistic and involves the pursuit of justice; it is a mode of conflict management, a form of punishment—in some cases, it may even be capital punishment (see also Polk 1994:113). Much inner-city violence involves residents who characterize their conduct as a perfectly legitimate exercise of social control, as vengeful "self-help" (Kubrin and Weitzer 2003). These residents are determined to show that justice is done, even if this means they will be defined as criminals; they do what they think is right and willingly suffer the consequences.

Violent social control is directly related to the availability (and effectiveness) of authoritative agents of dispute resolution such as the police—vengeful self-help emerges in the absence or weakness of third-party control (Black 1984:41; Horwitz 1990:128). In other words, crimes of self-help are more likely where the law is less accessible, such as, for example, in poor minority communities where residents have relatively less legal protection. When called, the police may not respond, which is one reason many residents feel they must be prepared to defend themselves and their loved ones (Anderson 1999:34). Indeed, a study of extremely disadvantaged communities in St. Louis found that problems confronting the residents were often resolved informally—without calling the police—and that neighborhood cultural codes supported this type of problem solving, even when the "solution" was a retaliatory killing (Kubrin and Weitzer 2003). That residents frequently bypass the police to resolve disputes on their own confirms the street code as a "people's law based on street justice;" the code begins where the influence of the police ends and the personal responsibility for one's safety picks up (Anderson 1999:27).

Finally, the code of the street encompasses other related dimensions of street life in inner-city communities. For example, the code highlights the appreciation for material wealth as another way to establish self-image and gain respect. Nice cars, expensive jewelry, and the latest clothing fashions not only reflect one's style, but also demonstrate a willingness to possess things that may require defending. Likewise, respect and recognition are gained through sexual promiscuity and conquest. For young men, sex is considered an important symbol of social status, which results in the objectification of women. The more women with whom a young man has sex, the more esteem he accrues. And given the harsh conditions in extremely disadvantaged communities, the street code recognizes a growing sense of nihilism in black youth culture, an outgrowth of living in an environment filled with violence and limited opportunities. Clearly these dimensions of the street code reinforce, and are reinforced by, respect and violence.

In sum, worsening conditions in inner-city communities over the last several decades have given rise, in large part, to the street code. These same conditions also define the context in which rap music has emerged. In studying rap, scholars maintain that "popular forms of music contain significant cultural traditions that cannot be severed from the socio-historical moment in which they take place" (Rose 1994:xiv; see also Keyes 2002:228; Watkins 2001). The production of rap, and gangsta rap in particular, corresponded with crucial shifts in the material worlds inhabited by young minority males. S. Craig Watkins (2001) notes, "the hyper-segregated conditions of the postindustrial ghetto became a fertile reservoir of cultural production" (p. 389). Rap music "anticipated the racial mood shifts and growing discontent of a generation of young black Americans who were either disillusioned by the racial hostilities brought on by participation in the societal mainstream or dislocated from the center of social and economic life altogether" (Watkins 2001:381). A question arises: what is the connection between inner-city life, the code of the street, rap music, and social identity? This is the focus of the next section.

THE STREET CODE, RAP MUSIC, AND SOCIAL IDENTITY

A naturalistic approach to understanding the culture-music-identity nexus would treat the street code as an explanation of behavior that operates much like a set of subcultural directives (see Gubrium and Holstein 1997:19–37; Holstein and Jones 1992). The subculture shapes and constrains residents' behaviors, particularly with respect to violence. From this point of view, the code would be viewed as a source of motivations and sanctions that lead to violence (see Anderson 1999) and, as such, behavior would stem from rule compliance, or noncompliance, with the tenets of the code (see Part I of Wieder 1988). From this perspective, the street code projects a compelling normative order, and rap lyrics would be viewed as reproductions of the code offered up to describe black urban street life. Put most simply, the street code could be viewed naturalistically as a source or inspiration for rap lyrics; the code-inspired lyrics would then be understood to reflect—whether accurately or inaccurately—black urban youth culture. An analysis using this approach would treat rap lyrics as more or less verifiable reports of street life and violence in poor urban communities (see, for example, Allen 1996).

Alternatively, one could frame the street code as an interpretive resource used to constitute what is and what is not deviant (Gubrium and Holstein 1997:48; Part II of Wieder 1988). This "constitutive" perspective treats the code as a source of indigenous explanation whereby reality is organized and made sensible through language use: "It is a form of *social action* through which social actors assemble the intelligible characteristics of their own circumstances. Descriptions, accounts, or reports, then, are not merely *about* some social world as much as they are *constitutive of* that world" (Holstein and Jones 1992:305). Such an approach has been applied to studies of inmate accounts of "doing time" (Holstein and Jones 1992) and the informal code that permeates talk and conduct in a halfway house for convicted substance abusers (Wieder 1988).

In the latter work, Lawrence D. Wieder (1988) treats the convict code as a set of locally developed instructions for understanding resident conduct. In describing this approach, Jaber F. Gubrium and James A. Holstein (1997) explain, "It became clear to Wieder that residents were doing much more than merely reporting on the features of their lives when they 'told the code.' They were trying to accomplish things in the telling, 'doing things with words' to create the very social structures they were otherwise apparently just describing. They were, in practice, actively marking the border between deviance and nondeviance through talk and interaction" (p. 49). Wieder recognized that the code represents more than a normative structure available to members of a setting as well as to the researcher of their behavior: it is a set of interpretive guidelines that was variably conjured up by the residents themselves who used it to account for matters that required explanation. In other words, "the code was a living embodiment of social control, serving as a shared accountability structure for residents' actions" (Gubrium and Holstein 1997:49–50).

Applying this perspective to the current study, I argue that both the street code and rap lyrics are constitutive elements of contemporary black urban culture. Here culture is akin to an interpretive tool kit (Swidler 1990) that is useful for understanding residents' experiences. As I will demonstrate, rap lyrics are discursive actions or artifacts that help construct an interpretive environment where violence is appropriate and acceptable. The lyrics—like the street code in Anderson's study—create the sense of a normative climate of violence. They provide sometimes graphically detailed instructions for how to interpret violent, degrading conduct and in so doing create possibilities for social identity in relation to violence. From this point of view, a lyrical analysis is less concerned with how well rappers' accounts comport with objective reality and instead focuses on how such accounts are used by rappers to reflexively accomplish a sense of reality—for themselves and for others. In the process, rappers articulate "vocabularies of motive" (Mills 1940) and "grammars of motive" (Burke 1945) to explain and account for street reality. In line with these classic approaches to rhetorical analysis, the constitutive approach is concerned with how words and grammar are used to constitute rather than report historical reality and its causes. Thus, for the purpose of analysis, I suspend belief (or doubt) in the motivations and explanations rappers offer for events and actions, and focus instead on account making as a persuasive project that constitutes situated realities.

This is not to suggest that the street code is insubstantial or without explanatory value. But neither the code nor culture more generally is deterministic. The code and rap music do not cause violence; violent conduct is far more complex than that. Because listeners interpret music in multiple ways, rap and its lyrics are appropriated and embedded into specific individual, familial, and community fields of reference. That rap music is a "localized form of cultural expression" is clearly evident in the work of Andy Bennett (1999a, 1999b:77) and of Tricia Rose (1994), who explains "Los Angeles county, Oakland, Detroit, Chicago, Houston, Atlanta, Miami, Newark and Trenton, Roxbury, and Philadelphia developed local hip hop scenes that link various regional postindustrial urban experiences of alienation, unemployment, police harassment, social, and economic isolation to their local and specific experience via hip hop's language, style, and attitude" (p. 60).

Lyrics have situational and situated meaning. Moreover, their reception may be oppositional. For example, Keith Negus and Patricia Roman Velazquez (2002:141) point out that listeners may disagree with or reject lyrics resulting in disaffiliation, ambivalence, and disengagement with (rap) music. Anticipated disaffiliation may even be part of the lyrics' design (as in instances of irony, sarcasm, or hyperbole). That media content has multiple meanings and that audiences actively construct this meaning implies no direct relationship between music and identity (or behavior). The street code and rap music lyrics do not compel one to act, but they do provide an accountability structure or interpretive resource that people can draw upon to understand violent identity and conduct.

That listeners of rap music are "actively involved in the construction of meaning" (Bennett 1999b:86) implies a complex and reflexive culture-music-identity relationship, as Simon Frith (1996), Negus and Velazquez (2002), and William F. Danaher and Vincent J. Roscigno (2004) all suggest. Instead of music lyrics reflecting pre-existing identities, in this view, they help to organize and construct identity. Frith (1996) states, "The issue is not how a particular piece of music reflects the people, but how it produces them, how it creates and constructs an experience" (p. 109). Likewise, the development of cultural forms will be structured by the reciprocal and mutually influential dynamics of production and reception (Danaher and Roscigno 2004:52).

In short, rap lyrics instruct listeners in how to make sense of urban street violence and how to understand the identities of those who participate in (or avoid) it. They do so in ways that resemble what Anderson's (1999) informants told him about street violence. Both sets of instructions—the everyday telling of the code by residents and the rappers' telling of the code in music lyrics—provide potent and complementary sources of local culture. Through the telling of the code, both in the streets and in the music, residents and rappers actively construct identities and justify the use of violence. As I will show, the rap lyrics provide vivid "vocabularies of motive" (Mills 1940), which structure violent identities and justify violent conduct, providing a way for listeners to understand and appreciate violent conduct.

DATA, METHODS, AND ANALYSIS

To examine the street code in rap lyrics, I identified rap albums from 1992 to 2000 that had gone platinum (that is, had sold over 1,000,000 copies) during that period ($N = 130$). I examined rap albums generally, rather than only gangsta rap albums, because rap albums typically mix genres (Krims 2000:87), and many songs with street code elements would have been excluded from the analysis if only gangsta rap albums had been included. The criterion that an album had sold over 1,000,000 copies ensured that the music had reached a wide segment of the population.

The 1992 to 2000 period was chosen because gangsta rap emerged in the late 1980s/ early 1990s (Kelley 1996:147; Keyes 2002:104; Kitwana 2002:xiv; Krims 2000:83; Smith 1997:346; Watkins 2001:389), and while still popular today, beginning around 1999, it became highly commercialized (Kitwana 1994:23; Krims 2000:71; Smith 1997:346; Watkins 2001:382). Therefore, the year 2000 represents a turning point in the rap music industry whereby production values more clearly addressed commercial competition, pushing cultural production and reproduction aside. I chose to examine this time frame to capture a period when the fiscal priorities of the music industry were not so clearly dominating cultural commentary.

The 130 albums had 1,922 songs. For the analysis I drew a simple random sample of 632 songs (roughly 1/3 of the sample) and coded each song in two stages. First, I listened to a song in its entirety while reading the printed lyrics in order to get an overview of the song. Second, I listened to the song again and coded each line to determine whether six street code elements were present (0 = no, 1 = yes): (1) respect, (2) willingness to fight or use violence, (3) material wealth, (4) violent retaliation, (5) objectification of women, and (6) nihilism. These elements were identified based upon a close examination of Anderson's (1999) work. They encompass the major points raised throughout his general discussion of the "code of the street." Although this article's focus is violence, I report the percentage of songs that discussed related themes for comparison. I coded the data conservatively, identifying themes only where it was clear that the lyrics reflected the street code. In cases of uncertainty about the meaning of a word or phrase, I consulted *The Rap Dictionary*, a comprehensive online dictionary of rap and hip-hop terms. As most themes are intricately linked, in those instances where lyrics referred to more than one theme at a time, each scored a "1" to create overlapping categories. Finally, in the relatively few cases where lyrics criticized or made light of the street code, I scored those as "0" so as to include only statements that endorsed the code.

The findings are based on a sample size of 403 songs (64 percent of the total sample). During the course of coding, after song 350, I no longer encountered lyrics that described new aspects of the street code themes. I coded another 53 songs to ensure that I had reached saturation (Glaser and Strauss 1967:111). In all, 1,588 minutes of music were coded for the analyses.

To assess intercoder reliability, an independent researcher identified a random subset of the sample (n = 64, 16 percent of the final sample) and listened to the songs, read the lyrics and coded the cases. Agreement percentages were computed, which reflect how often the researcher and I agreed that the street code theme was present (or absent) in the lyrics. Although the percentages vary slightly by theme, overall they suggest fairly strong agreement: 70.3 percent for respect, 79.7 percent for willingness to fight or use violence, 75 percent for material wealth, 82.8 percent for retaliation, 73.4 percent for objectification of women, and 87.5 percent for nihilism.

The first analyses I present are quantitative and describe the occurrence of violence (and the other themes) in the sample. The second analyses are qualitative and determine how rappers portray violent identities—both their own and those of others—and account for the use of violence in everyday street lives. Using content analysis, I looked for instances of violence (and related issues) in the lyrics and illustrate the results using representative quotations. During coding, I looked for evidence of violence, respect for being violent, the role of guns and other weapons, violent personae, violent retaliation, justification for the use of violence, and community support for violence. Since subthemes did arise in the process of coding the lyrics (e.g., violent retaliation for snitching, projecting a mentally unstable violent persona), I carefully searched for additional meanings in the data and incorporated them into the findings. In this way, the findings not only address how violence is characterized in rap music, but they also contribute to the theoretical framework for understanding the street code.

THE "STREET CODE" IN RAP LYRICS

The street code is clearly a staple of rap music lyrics. I found each street code theme prominently represented in the lyrics, albeit to varying degrees. Respect was the most commonly referenced theme (68 percent of the songs), followed closely by violence (65 percent). Material wealth and violent retaliation were mentioned in 58 percent and 35 percent of the songs, respectively. Finally, nihilism was present in 25 percent, and only 22 percent had references to the objectification of women, despite the common assumption that misogyny pervades rap music.

The qualitative review of the data underscores the centrality of violence in rap music and suggests that violence has several components. The discussion below considers the two most prominent functions served by violent imagery in rap lyrics: (1) establishing social identity and reputation, and (2) exerting social control. The discussion below includes 45 direct quotations by 21 different rappers. These quotations do not exhaust the universe of violence examples, but are representative.

Constructing Violent Social Identity and Reputation

In extremely disadvantaged neighborhoods, residents learn the value of having a "name," a reputation for being violent, as a means of survival. To build such a reputation is to gain respect among peers (Anderson 1999:67). Accordingly, rappers often project images of toughness in their music, referring to themselves and others as assassins, hustlers, gangstas, madmen, mercenary soldiers, killas, thugs, and outlaws. Some rappers are even more colorful in their depictions: "untamed guerillas" (Hot Boys; "Clear Da Set"), "3rd world nigga" (Master P; "Making Moves"), "thuggish, ruggish niggas" (BTNH; "2 Glocks"), "hellraiser" (2Pac; "Hellrazor"), "trigger niggas"

(Master P; "Till We Dead and Gone"), "the nigga with the big fat trigger" (Ice Cube; "Now I Gotta Wet'Cha"), "no limit soldier" (Silkk the Shocker; "I'm a Soldier"), "young head busta" (Hot Boys; " 'Bout Whatever"), "wig splitas" (Juvenile; "Welcome 2 the Nolia"), "cap peelers" (Mystikal; "Mystikal Fever"), "grave filler" (Juvenile; "Back that Ass Up"), "gat buster" or "trigger man" (Jay-Z; "It's Hot"), "raw nigga" (Layzie Bone; "2 Glocks"), and "Sergeant Slaughter" (Killer Mike; "Snappin' and Trappin' ").

To bolster this image of toughness, rappers describe how dangerous they and others are—or can be, if necessary. The Notorious B.I.G. raps, "Armed and dangerous, ain't too many can bang with us," while 2Pac boasts, "A little rough with a hardcore theme / Couldn't rough something rougher in your dreams / Mad rugged so you know we're gonna rip / With that roughneck nigga named 2Pacalypse (2Pac, 'Strugglin' "). Cypress Hill references 187, the California Penal Code for murder, as a way to drive home their violent image: "1 for the trouble, 8 for the road / 7 to get ready when I'm lettin' off my load / I'm a natural-born cappeela', strapped [armed] illa / I'm the West Coast settin' it on, no one's reala' " (Cypress Hill, "Stoned Raiders"). Master P describes the viciousness of his posse:

We couldn't run from niggas cause we 'bout it 'bout it
I'm from the set where my niggas get rowdy rowdy
We gon' hang niggas
We gon' bang niggas
We gon' slang niggas
Cause we trigger niggas. (Master P, "Till We Dead and Gone")

In projecting a tough image, rappers allude to violent reputations whether for "kickin' ass" or for "keepin' an extra clip" in their gun: "I'm an assassin known for kickin' ass / Show me who them niggas are, and watch me start blastin' / It's Mr. Magic, known for causin' havoc / As long as I'm on your side, see there's no need for panic" (C-Murder, "Watch Yo Enemies"); "I was born and raised for this gangsta shit / C-Murder be known for keepin' an extra clip / My pops say look 'em in the eye before I kill 'em / P crank the 'llac [Cadillac] up and let's go get 'em" (C-Murder, "How Many").

Young inner-city males take reputation or "rep" seriously and exert effort into building it in order to gain respect (Fagan and Wilkinson 1998:148). Often rappers will instruct listeners on how to develop "rep" on the street: "Rep in New York is the cat burglar, the fat murderer / Slippin' the clip in the Mac [Mac 10 submachine pistol] inserterer / Hurtin' your pockets, droppin' your stock to zero profit / Holding heroes hostage and mansions for ransom like DeNiro mob flicks" (Big Punisher, "Fast Money"); "Sterling [B.G.'s friend] lived a soldier, died a soldier / Had respect for knockin' heads clean off the shoulder" (B.G., "So Much Death"); "Kickin' niggas down the steps just for rep" (Notorious B.I.G., "Ready to Die"). In these examples, rappers authorize the use of violence to establish identity. In other words, the lyrics "accomplish [identity] in the telling" (Gubrium and Holstein 1997:49).

At the top of the hierarchy is the "crazy" or "wild" social identity (Fagan and Wilkinson 1998:151). As a way to display a certain predisposition to violence, rappers often characterize themselves and others as "mentally unstable" and therefore extremely dangerous. Consider Snoop Dogg and DMX, both of whom had murder charges brought against them in the 1990s: "Here's a little something about a nigga like me / I never should have been let out the penitentiary / Snoop Dogg would like to say / That I'm a crazy motherfucker when I'm playing with my AK [AK-47 assault rifle]" (Snoop Dogg, "DP Gangsta");

Since I run with the devil, I'm one with the devil
I stay doin' dirt so I'm gonna come with the shovel
Hit you on a level of a madman, who's mind's twisted
Made niggas dreams caught the last train, mines missed it,
Listed as a manic, depressin' with extreme paranoia,
and dog I got somethin' for ya!

Have enough of shit, startin' off hard then only gettin' rougher!
Tougher, but then came the grease, so if you wanna say peace,
Tame the beast! (DMX, "Fuckin' Wit' D")

An important element of the "crazy" persona is having a reputation for being quick tempered (Katz 1988:99). In the chorus of "Party Up," DMX warns others that even when he's at the club partying, the slightest thing may set him off: "Y'all gon' make me lose my mind (up in here, up in here) / Y'all gon' make me go all out (up in here, up in here) / Y'all gon' make me act a fool (up in here, up in here) / Y'all gon' make me lose my cool (up in here, up in here)" (Chorus, DMX, "Party Up"). These lyrics show how the code is brought into play to account for matters that require explanation, in this case, for explaining a mood shift that may result in violence. DMX and others account for their violent behavior, which they render acceptable and appropriate given the circumstances. The lyrics supply a vocabulary of motive which, C. Wright Mills (1963) argues, offers "accepted justifications for present, future or past programs or acts" (p. 443).

Verbal assertions of one's violent tendencies are important in establishing identity, but physical assertions are necessary as well (Anderson 1999:68). So, while projecting the right image is everything, backing up the projection with violent behavior is expected. For this reason, some rappers project images of toughness by describing acts of violence that they have perpetrated on others. The Notorious B.I.G. explains how he point blank kills someone: "As I grab the glock, put it to your headpiece / One in the chamber, the safety is off release / Straight at your dome [head] homes, I wanna see cabbage / Biggie Smalls the savage, doin' your brain cells much damage" (Notorious B.I.G., "Ready to Die"). It is common for rappers to provide detail when describing violent situations. Some songs contain literally dozens of lines describing in rich detail incidents that precipitate violence, the persons involved, violent acts, weapons, ammunition, and the bloody aftermath. The descriptions often make explicit reference to elements of the street code: "Must handle beef, code of the street / Load up the heat, if these niggas think they could fuck around / Real niggas do real things / By all means, niggas knowin' how we get down" (Nas, "Shoot 'Em Up"). Here the rapper, Nas, accounts for his violent actions in ways analogous to what Wieder (1988) reported in his study of a halfway house. Wieder explains, "It [the code] was a device for accounting for why one should feel or act in the way that one did as an expectable, understandable, reasonable, and above all else acceptable way of acting or feeling" (p. 175). Nas's notion that one "must handle beef" not only accounts for his violent conduct; it also instructs listeners how to understand violent circumstances and violent responses, given the situation.

Firearms are often used to claim the identity of being among the toughest. In fact, guns—referred to by rappers as street sweepers, heaters, ovens, and pumps—have become *the* tactical choice for demonstrating toughness and for settling scores, as suggested by the Notorious B.I.G., "Fuck tae kwon do, I tote the fo'-fo' [.44 magnum]" ("One More Chance") and Dr. Dre, "Blunt in my left hand, drink in my right, strap [gun] by my waistline, cause niggas don't fight" ("Ackrite"). Both rappers acknowledge the important role of the gun in the ghetto and justify its use.

Further, rappers acknowledge an increase in gun use by showing how times have changed in the inner city (George 1998:42). Fagan and Wilkinson (1998:138) found that inner-city young males often characterized their neighborhood as a "war zone" and described the streets as dangerous and unpredictable, a sentiment echoed in many of the songs. For example, in "Things Done Changed" the Notorious B.I.G. reminisces about the past as he explains how conditions in the ghetto have become much more violent:

Remember back in the days, when niggas had waves,
Gazelle shades, and corn braids
Pitchin' pennies, honies had the high top jellies
Shootin' skelly, motherfuckers was all friendly
Loungin' at the barbeques, drinkin' brews
With the neighborhood crews, hangin' on the avenues
Turn your pagers to nineteen ninety three

Niggas is gettin' smoked [killed] G, believe me
(Notorious B.I.G., "Things Done Changed").

The Notorious B.I.G. goes on to describe in detail how violence began to escalate as drugs, fighting, gambling, and general disorganization set in. Violent circumstances and experiences are frequently offered as emerging norms as rappers depict the "reality" of street life—for them and for others. When rappers portray life in the streets as dangerous and unpredictable, they implicitly authorize the use of violence to establish identity and supply a vocabulary of motives for describing and understanding violent conduct.

As a result of worsening conditions, guns have become an everyday accessory in the ghetto. One study found that most young males carry guns and describe them as central to their socialization (Fagan and Wilkinson 1998:140). For many, carrying a gun is as common as carrying a wallet or keys. Rapper 2Pac makes this point clear in the chorus of "High Speed." He is asked, "Whatcha gonna do when you get outta jail?" and answers matter-of-factly: "I'm gonna buy me a gun." The lesson to learn is summed up in the chorus of C-Murder's "Watch Yo Enemies": "Watch your motherfuckin' enemies / And you might live a long time / Watch your motherfuckin' enemies / Stay strapped [carry a gun] cause the ghetto is so wicked now." C-Murder both rationalizes his decision to carry a gun and instructs the listener that in everyday life one must "stay strapped" to stay secure. The lyrics are implicit, interpretive instructions for understanding "life in the streets"—not just for rappers, but for others as well.

Collectively, rap lyrics show how toughness and a willingness to use violence are articulated as central features of masculine identity and reputation. The rappers implicitly and explicitly use the code of the street to construct identities and in so doing they resemble Anderson's (1999) respondents from inner-city communities in many important respects. As the above passages illustrate, rappers typically characterize life on the streets as violent and unpredictable and implicate this violence and their participation in it in their own identity work. The lyrics provide an implicit recipe for how to create a violent, but viable, street identity. The lyrics suggest that one learns the value of having a reputation for being tough in order to survive. The lyrics also enlist guns as signs of toughness; their possession is a significant identity marker. The lyrics tout "rep" as a means of gaining and sustaining respect among peers and preventing future challenges. In sum, the lyrics provide both a formula and a justification for violent street identities.

Portraying Violence as Social Control

As the problems of the inner city become more acute and police-community relations grow increasingly tentative, residents claim they must assume primary responsibility in matters of conflict (Kubrin and Weitzer 2003). This often results in violence intended as punishment or other expression of disapproval. Most frequently violent social control is precipitated through disrespect. Rappers are virtually fixated on "respect"; they tell listeners that no one should tolerate disrespect and are clear about the consequences of such behavior, which can include death for the "perpetrator." Whether referenced only in passing or explained in more detail, the message is clear. There may be severe penalties for disrespect:

Y'all punk muthafuckas ain't got no nuts
I only be dealin' with real niggas
Them other niggas, they get they ass put in check
When they try to flex and disrespect me
And that's when I gotta get even with niggas, retaliation
(Krayzie Bone, "Thugz All Ova Da World");

Gotta push the issue
On the fools that dis you

Whether pump or pistol
When it's up in yo' gristle [face]
Hand yo' mama a tissue
If I decide to kiss [kill] you (Ice Cube, "Ask About Me").

In the latter passage, Ice Cube not only warns others about the repercussions of disrespecting him, but also makes explicit the rules of the game concerning disrespect: payback is a must. Cube's lyrics instruct listeners that on the streets when one is disrespected one responds with violence. In this way, he constructs an interpretive environment where violence is accountable and acceptable, as both a means of constructing identity and of enforcing social control on the street.

Disrespect can come in a variety of flavors including disrespect by testing or challenging someone, disrespect through victimizing—usually robbing—someone, and disrespect by snitching. Each was serious enough to warrant violent self-help again and again in rap songs.

Responding to Challenges. Rappers are often vague in what constitutes being "tested" or "challenged"—two words commonly encountered in the lyrics. What they make very clear, however, is the *reaction* to being "tested" or "challenged," summed up succinctly by the Notorious B.I.G., "Fifty-shot clip if a nigga wanna test," and Bone Thugs-N-Harmony, "A nigga wanna test, catch slugs, put 'em in the mud"; "187 is a lesson for them niggas that want to test, bring more than one cause me shotgun will be buckin' your chest."

One form of testing or challenging involves "fucking with" someone or with his or her family, friends, or "posse." To do so, according to the code, is to invite a virtual death sentence. In "It's On," Eazy-E bluntly states, "You try to fuck with E nigga run run run, cause it it's on motherfucker, then it's on G." DMX describes the implications of "fuckin' wit' D": "Fuckin' wit' me, y'all know somebody has / Told you about fuckin' wit' D, stuck in / A tree is what you will be, like a cat / And I'm the dog at the bottom, lookin' up" (DMX, "Fuckin' Wit' D"). In a song appropriately titled "Murder III," Mystikal is furious as he recounts the story of his sister's death at the hands of her boyfriend. Mystikal tells the boyfriend, "I'm living for revenge": "I know what you did, I'm comin' to get'cha, you cannot live / Look, you sleep forever is the fuckin' price / Shit, a throat for a throat, a life for a life" (Mystikal, "Murderer III"). And consider the lyrics from a Juvenile song: "I ain't gonna let a nigga disrespect my clique / And I ain't gon' let a nigga come and take my shit / That'll make me look like a stone cold bitch / So ain't no way I ain't gon' grab my AK and let my shit spit" (Juvenile, "Guerilla"). Note Juvenile's reference to looking like a "stone cold bitch" if he does not to respond to "niggas disrespecting his clique." Here he strongly justifies the use of violent social control in order to not lose respect—a fundamental aspect of the code. As such, the lyrics serve as a vehicle by which Juvenile and other rappers explain and justify their actions. The message that one is not a pushover must be loud and clear. In this context, projecting the right image is everything, an image that must be substantiated with violent behavior (Fagan and Wilkinson 1998:136).

The code in the lyrics justifies a reciprocal exchange of punishments in cases where one's friends and family are victimized. This position is not difficult to justify. According to the street code, even verbal disrespect cannot go unpunished (Kubrin and Weitzer 2003). This seemingly mild form of disrespect is enough to provoke violent retaliation in numerous songs: "Talk slick, you get your neck slit quick / Cause real street niggas ain't havin' that shit" (Notorious B.I.G., "Machine Gun Funk"). In another song, Ice Cube warns that you should "check yo self"—watch what you say and do—because otherwise the consequences will be "bad for your health": "So come on and check yo self before you wreck yo self / Check yo self before you wreck yo self / Yeah, come on and check yo self before you wreck yo self / Cause shotgun bullets are bad for your health" (Chorus, Ice Cube, "Check Yo Self").

Resisting Victimization. Inner-city communities pose high levels of risk for victimization. Yet an important part of the street code is not to allow others to "get over on you," to let them know that you are not to be messed with. So those who want to present themselves as streetwise signal to potential criminals (and anyone else) that they are not the ones to be targeted for victimization (Anderson 1999). Rap lyrics invoke such signals letting listeners know that being disrespected through robbery victimization is a costly transgression: "You play with my life when you play with my money / Play around but this'll be the last time you think somethin's funny" (DMX,

"One More Road to Cross"). Method Man insists that violent retaliation is an automatic response to robbery: "Niggas try to stick [rob] me, retaliation, no hesitation" ("Sub Crazy"). And the Wu-Tang Clan warns others that they can get "wild with the trigger" if need be: "Shame on a nigga who try to run game on a nigga / Wu buck wild with the trigger! / Shame on a nigga who try to run game on a nigga / We buck- I fuck yo' ass up! What?" (Wu-Tang Clan, "Shame on a Nigga"). Rappers' lyrics actively define the border between what is acceptable and unacceptable behavior—in other words, what will or will not provoke violent retaliation, as well as what is an appropriate and warranted response. By invoking rules and elaborating their application to specific cases, these rappers describe and constitute their activities as rational, coherent, precedented, and orderly (Gubrium and Holstein 1997:45). The concluding message to the would-be offender: "If you ever jack [rob] this real nigga, you'd besta kill me or pay the price" (C-Murder, "Ghetto Ties").

Don't Snitch. Violence as social control is perhaps best personified in cases of snitching, where rappers are not at all reluctant to administer capital punishment: "My next door neighbor's having a convo with undercovers / Put a surprise in the mailbox, hope she get it / Happy birthday bitch, you know you shouldn't a did it" (2Pac, "Only Fear of Death"). In many rappers' eyes, the worst case scenario is to "end up Fed": "And I don't know who the fuck you think you talkin' to / No more talkin'—put him in the dirt instead / You keep walkin'—lest you end up red / Cause if I end up Fed, y'all end up dead" (DMX, "Party Up"). DMX concludes with, "Sun in to sun out, I'ma keep the gun out, Nigga runnin his mouth? I'ma blow his lung out." Entire songs may be devoted to warning others about the repercussions of snitching and testifying, as is Nas' song "Suspect" with the chorus: "To the suspect witness don't come outside / You might get your shit pushed back tonight" (Nas, "Suspect"). These excerpts provide a glimpse of why, after a violent incident, residents of extremely disadvantaged communities are often unwilling to cooperate with the police out of fear of retribution (Kubrin and Weitzer 2003). The lyrics virtually instruct observers to keep quiet and perpetrators to enforce silence. The code in the lyrics is strikingly similar to the one Anderson (1999) observed, whereby people "see but don't see" (p. 133). The neighborhood mantra is "Niggas do unto these snitches before it's done unto you" (2Pac, "Hell 4 a 'Hustler' "), which clearly coveys that snitching is unacceptable and offers guidelines for how one should respond when encountering a snitch. Again, the theme of justified violence is clear.

Retaliation. In cases of snitching or disrespect, violent retaliation is portrayed as punishment and is characterized as an acceptable and appropriate response as part of the street code. In many instances violent retaliation is claimed to be not only appropriate but also obligatory: "You fucked with me, now it's a must that I fuck with you" (Dr. Dre, "Fuck with Dre Day"); "Otis from the thirteenth bit the dust / It's a must we strap up and retaliate in a rush" (B.G., "So Much Death"). In "Retaliation," B.G. describes acts of retaliation and expresses the sentiment that retaliation is expected, a given, known to all, and therefore, clearly justified. It's simple: "You done took mine, I'ma take yearn": "Ain't that cold? I heard a nigga downed my nigga / My partner just paged me and say they found my nigga / It's a bust back thang can't be no hoes / I got a hundred rounds plus for my Calico." And later in the song: "You sleep six feet I tear down the whole street / Bust ya head up leave ya deader yo blood redder / Nigga what, keep ya mouth shut retaliation is a must." Ms. Tee warns all in the chorus: "Niggas....they comin' to get'cha / You betta watch ya back before they muthafuckin' split cha" (B.G., "Retaliation"). Retaliation, of course, builds "juice." According to the lyrics, it is also a way to deter future assaults, as Rappin 4-Tay explains to 2Pac: "Pac I feel ya, keep servin' it on the reala / For instance say a playa hatin' mark is out to kill ya / Would you be wrong, for buckin' a nigga to the pavement? / He gon' get me first, if I don't get him—fool start prayin' " (2Pac, "Only God Can Judge Me"). Again, we see how rappers justify the use of violence, this time as a deterrent.

Anderson (1999:33) suggests that everyone knows there are penalties for violating the street code. In their music, rappers use the implicit rules of the code as explanations for street behavior. By reference to aspects of the code, the lyrics mark what is acceptable and unacceptable behavior (e.g., don't challenge, victimize, snitch). The lyrics make sense of violence as an arguably accountable response to a wide variety of "offenses," while simultaneously identifying just what those "offenses" might be. The above passages show how the code is variably conjured up by rappers to instruct listeners on how to understand and account for their own and others' everyday actions. In this way, the code becomes a living embodiment of social control as it both serves to define offensive behaviors and accounts for the violence that might be forthcoming in response (Gubrium and Holstein 1997:49–50).

RAP MUSIC AND CULTURAL CODES

That violence constitutes a large part of rap music, particularly gangsta rap, is axiomatic. This study found that nearly 65 percent of the songs sampled make reference to some aspect of violence and many songs were graphic in their violent depictions. It is precisely for this reason that gangsta rap is controversial and unpopular with some segments of the population. Still, rappers tell important stories through their music. Some use their street knowledge to construct first-person narratives that interpret how social and economic realities affect young black men in the context of deteriorating inner-city conditions. Other narratives may be more mythical than factual. Regardless of their source or authenticity, rap lyrics serve specific social functions in relation to understandings of street life and violence.

In rap music, social identity and respect are the most important features of the street code. Lyrics instruct listeners that toughness and the willingness to use violence are central to establishing viable masculine identity, gaining respect, and building a reputation. As Anderson (1999) might suggest, the lyrics show how violent confrontations settle the question of "who is the toughest and who will take, or tolerate, what from whom under what circumstances" (p. 69). As was evident in many passages, references to guns are used to bolster these violent identities.

In cases of disrespect, the code—as evident in the lyrics—makes clear that payback is imminent. Rappers' lyrics delineate the rules and actively mark the border between acceptable and unacceptable behavior. Moreover, the lyrics teach listeners how to appropriately respond in the event that rules are violated; they authorize the use of violent retaliation in certain situations and thereby prescribe violent self-help as a method of social control. As the lyrics showed, the code requires constant application and articulation with concrete events and actions in order to make the events and actions meaningful and accountable.

In examining how rappers use violence to establish social identity and reputation and exert violent social control, the study has carefully considered the relationship between the street code, rap music, and identity and behavior. As argued earlier, one approach is to treat the code as an explanation of behavior that operates much like subcultural counter-directives. From this view, the street code is a compelling normative order and rap lyrics are reproductions of the code that describe black urban street life. Any examination, therefore, would treat the lyrics as more or less accurate reports of street life and violence in poor urban communities.

The current analysis provides a different framing. Rather than encouraging residents to be deviant, here the code is seen as an interpretive resource—as a source of indigenous explanation whereby reality is organized and made sensible through language use—in this case, lyrics. As explained earlier, the code supplies an interpretive schema for seeing and describing violent identity and behavior, and the lyrics are treated as reality-producing activities. In terms of analysis, this has led us beyond the artists' own explanations (the simple telling of the street code) in order to determine what is accomplished by the use of the code as an explanation of behavior. In other words, the focus has shifted from what is said by rappers to how they say it and what is socially realized in the process. I have bracketed rappers' claims about the causes of behavior in order to examine what is accomplished by making the claims. This has meant suspending belief in whether or not rappers' claims are true (Burke 1945; Gubrium and Holstein 1997:51). My analysis is indifferent to whether the reality rappers portray in their lyrics is an "actual" or "literal" one. What is important is that rap artists *create* cultural understandings of urban street life that render violence, danger, and unpredictability normative.

Of course, this cultural understanding legitimizes certain aspects of the street code while ignoring other important and arguably more positive aspects of urban life. Anderson (1999) devotes a significant portion of his book to discussing "decent" families and daddies and reminds us "to be sure, hustlers, prostitutes, and drug dealers are in evidence, but they coexist with—and are indeed outnumbered by—working people in legitimate jobs who are trying to avoid trouble" (p. 24). But what we mostly hear in rap lyrics are rappers touting the virtues of violence with little of the more mundane, yet positive, elements that emanate from the black community. This is not to say that the lyrics are inaccurate. But as a cultural force, gangsta rap music offers a particular characterization of urban life. While this version of local culture may be at odds with other versions, it is the one that gets the most "air play," so to speak. In that sense, it widely promotes an accountability structure in which violence is legitimized and condoned.

This raises another important issue: the characterization of rap music and its messages in the context of mainstream culture. Although Theresa A. Martinez (1997) and others (e.g., Negus 1999) recognize rap as a resistant, oppositional, countercultural form of expressive culture, they also argue that this culture "may be embedded within and even contribute to a dominant hegemonic framework" (Martinez 1997:272). I agree wholeheartedly. Rap music does not exist in a cultural vacuum. Rather, it expresses the cultural crossing, mixing, and engagement of black youth culture with the values, attitudes, and concerns of the white majority. Many of the violent (and patriarchical, materialistic, sexist, etc.) ways of acting that are glorified in gangsta rap are a reflection of the prevailing values created, sustained, and rendered accountable in the larger society. Toughness and a violent persona have been central to masculine identity in myriad American social contexts. And young men come to identify the connections between masculinity-power-aggression-violence as part of their own developing masculine identities (Messerschmidt 1986:59). In short, gangsta rap is just one manifestation of the culture of violence that saturates American society as a whole—in movies, video games, sports, pro-wrestling, and other venues. Therefore, it is important to recognize that the values that underpin some rap music are very much by-products of broader American culture.

Indeed, in some cases rap music does not warrant the excessive criticism it receives. Recall that one finding from the analysis is that "objectification of women" or "misogyny" is not as pervasive in rap lyrics as originally thought. Likewise, it does not appear to be a significant part of the rappers' code—nowhere near as central as respect and violence. Of all the street code themes, "objectification of women" was least prominent in the lyrics. A greater percentage of the songs mentioned issues related to nihilism, a topic frequently overlooked in the literature and by critics. This is not to suggest that rappers be "let off the hook" for their violent and misogynistic lyrics but that critics recognize that rap music and misogyny are not synonymous and acknowledge the variability in topics covered by rappers.

Findings from this study suggest that violence researchers might look beyond traditional data sources (e.g., census reports and crime statistics) for the empirical traces of "culture in action" (Swidler 1990) that render violence acceptable. As I have argued, rap music does not cause violence but extends the purview of the street code of violence and respect. Rappers' telling the street code in their music in conjunction with the everyday telling of the code by inner-city residents in community research (Anderson 1999; Fagan and Wilkinson 1998; Kubrin and Weitzer 2003) provide two potent sources of local culture—a culture of the streets in which violence is cast as a way of life.

QUESTIONS

? How does gangsta rap normalize violence?

? Give examples of how street code establishes identity, reputation, and how it exerts social control. Why are each of these elements important? (Make sure you think about the social conditions that this music arises from.)

? Societal map question: Media plays an increasingly important role in our lives. Researchers have shown that much media promotes a "culture of violence." Give examples of violence in two of the following areas: advertising, movies, sports, video games, regular television programming. If you were to create a study to identify a culture of violence in one of the examples listed above, how would you go about it? What themes do you think you would find?

Stuff:
The Secret Lives of Everyday Things

By JOHN C. RYAN & ALAN THEIN DURNING

■ Take a minute to list all the "stuff" that you used and or threw away today—what you ate and drank (and the packaging), applied (e.g. deodorant), wore, etc. Can you identify where this stuff originated and where it goes after you consume it? The typical American is not likely to know. They are likely, however, to throw out an average of four pounds of such "stuff" daily, according to the authors of the following excerpt, John C. Ryan and Alan Thein Durning. In the following article these authors draw your attention to the origins, destinations, environmental and societal impact of our daily consumption.

MY NAME IS DANA, AND I AM A CONSUMER

"Today, as soon as I got out of bed, I started consuming. I had a cup of coffee. I ate breakfast. I read a newspaper. I put on my clothes. I commuted to work. All day long I went about my ordinary business, consuming stuff and unwittingly affecting places and people around the world.

I don't usually think of myself as a consumer. Though I don't spend much time worrying about the environment, I don't have a wasteful lifestyle either. I recycle. I have a compost bin in my garden. I've even biked to work before.

But cleaning out my basement recently got me thinking. Though it felt good to throw out all that junk, my back was sore for a week afterward. Wading through all the objects of my life was a chore. Making them in the first place must have been one, too.

There I was, piling old paint cans into a cardboard box, when something caught my eye. It was a sticker that had fallen off the back of who-knows-what stowed in the basement. It said, "Made in Taiwan." I'd seen thousands of such stickers in my life without ever giving them a second thought. Taiwan. Taiwan. Not just a word on a sticker. It's an island. A country. A real place with real people across an ocean from me.

From *The Futurist*, March 1998 by John C. Ryan and Alan Thein Durning. Copyright © 1998 by World Future Society. Reprinted by permission.

Suddenly, the overloaded shelves around me looked different. I was stripped of the illusion that stuff comes from stores and is carted "away" by garbage trucks: Everything on those shelves came from a real place on the earth and will go to some other place when I'm done with it. Everything had a history—a trail of causes and effects—and a future. Everything had a life, of sorts. If you tried very hard, you could put a "Made in _____" sticker on each car wax bottle, speaker component, or old magazine on those shelves.

I started wondering where the things in my life come from. As coffee beans, newspapers, and soda cans make their ways toward me, what wakes do they leave behind, rippling outward across the world? And what had to happen for millions of people like me to go about our ordinary business, using lots of stuff?

The first step toward solving any problem is recognizing it. I've started by looking at the things in my life in a new way and learning what I can about their secret lives."

What We Don't Know about Stuff Can Hurt Us

The above "confession" comes from a fictional North American consumer, a middle-class resident of Seattle awakening to the wake caused by an ordinary day's activities.

North Americans have grown more concerned and knowledgeable about the environment in recent years. And many environmental problems—urban smog, water pollution, lead in our air—are less pronounced than they were just a couple of decades ago.

But Americans throw out about four pounds of garbage each in their daily trash. Though they see only a fraction of it, Americans consume 120 pounds—nearly their average body weight—every day in natural resources extracted from farms, forests, rangelands, and mines.

Consumption on the North American scale—our own body weight each day—is possible only because of chains of production that reach all over the planet. Most of the production, and most of its impacts, are hidden from view—in rural hinterlands, fenced-off industrial sites, and far-off nations.

What happens around the world to support a day in the life of a North American is surprising, dramatic, even disturbing. Multiplied by the billion members of the world's consumer societies, it adds up to stresses greater than the world can withstand.

It does not have to be this way. A quiet revolution in our way of life—different technologies, more balanced lifestyles, greener infrastructure, and better laws—could give us a future where ordinary life in prosperous societies has only innocuous impacts. Ushering in these changes can seem impossible. It is not. Just like a jigsaw puzzle, all the needed pieces are already there. But it takes some effort to get them into place.

A BRIEF HISTORY OF DANA'S COFFEE

"In the morning, my brain manages to hold one coherent thought: caffeine. I stagger into the kitchen to brew a cup of coffee.

It took 100 beans—about one-sixtieth of the beans that will grow on the coffee tree this year. The tree is on a small mountain farm in the Antioquia region of Colombia, which had been cleared of most of its native cloud forests at the turn of the century.

For most of this century, coffee grew on this farm in the shade of taller fruit and hardwood trees, whose canopies harbored numerous birds, from keel-billed toucans to Canada warblers. In the 1980s, farm owners sawed down most of the shade trees and planted high-yielding varieties of coffee. This change increased their harvests. It also increased soil erosion and decimated birds, including wintering songbirds that breed near my home. Biologists report finding just 5% as many bird species in these new, sunny coffee fields as in the traditional shaded coffee plantations they replaced.

Workers earning less than a dollar a day picked my coffee berries by hand and fed them into a diesel-powered crusher, which removed the beans from the pulpy berries that encased them. The pulp was dumped into the

Cauca River. For each pound of beans, about two pounds of pulp was dumped into the river. As the pulp decomposed, it consumed oxygen needed by the fish.

The beans traveled to New Orleans on a freighter that was made in Japan and fueled by Venezuelan oil. The shipyard built the freighter out of Korean steel. The Korean steel mill used iron mined on aboriginal lands in the Hamersley Range of Western Australia.

At New Orleans, the beans were roasted for 13 minutes at 400° F. The roaster burned natural gas pumped from the ground in Texas. The beans were packaged in four-layer bags constructed of polyethylene, nylon, aluminum foil, and polyester. They were trucked to a Seattle warehouse in an 18-wheeler, which got six miles per gallon of diesel. A smaller truck then took the roasted beans to my neighborhood grocery store.

In my kitchen, I pour eight ounces of tap water into the plastic–and–steel drip coffeemaker. The water comes by pipe from a processing plant; originally it came from the Chester Morse Reservoir on the Cedar River on the west slope of the Cascades.

An element heats the water to more than 200° F. The hot water seeps through the ground coffee and dissolves some of its oils and solids. The brew trickles into a glass carafe; I pour it into a mug with a "Made in Taiwan" sticker hidden underneath. Later, I will wash the mug, using much more water than I will have drunk from it.

I measure out two teaspoons of sugar, which came from cane fields—former sawgrass marshes—south of Lake Okeechobee in Florida. Water that used to flow across these marshes and into the Everglades is now drained into canals and sent directly to the ocean, or else it is used to irrigate the fields, where it picks up nutrients and pesticides.

I stir in an ounce of cream. The cream came from a grain-fed dairy cow in the Skagit Valley north of Seattle. The cow likes to wade into a stream to drink and to graze on streamside grasses and willows. As a result, the water has gotten warmer and muddier, making life difficult for the coho salmon and steelhead trout living in the stream.

Two hours after I finish my morning cup, my body has metabolized the coffee. Most of the water and some nutrients now pass into the Seattle sewer system. They are carried by Cedar River water and mixed with other organic and inorganic wastes. They travel under the streets of the city to Seattle's West Point sewage treatment plant on the shores of Puget Sound, next to Discovery Park.

There, the solids are filtered, concentrated, digested, and sterilized by screens, settling tanks, bacteria, and chlorine. An engineer deems the sewage sludge clean enough for agriculture, and a trucker hauls it to pulpwood tree farms for use as fertilizer and soil conditioner. An underwater pipe carries the treated liquids a mile into Puget Sound. The flushing of the tides will eventually carry the liquids into the Pacific Ocean."

An Alternative Scenario for Dana's Coffee

What can be done to change this history and future of a cup of coffee?

First, find some shade. Coffee grown under the shade of mixed trees requires few or no chemical inputs: The leaf litter replenishes soil nutrients, and the variety of tree species benefits birds and discourages pest outbreaks. Many brands of shade coffee—often labeled as organic or cooperatively produced—are available.

Second, go local. Organic mint tea is grown in Oregon's Willamette Valley with no chemical inputs and requires much less energy to be processed and transported (200 miles to Seattle) than coffee.

Besides, caffeine makes you jumpy, coffee stains your teeth, and who likes coffee breath, anyway? Drinking a little less of the stuff might do you some good.

Watch Your Wake

Confronting resource consumption is North Americans' principal environmental challenge, although few realize this fact because the impacts of consumption are mostly invisible to the consumer. The United States, with less than 5% of world population, consumes 34% of the world's energy and a similar share of other commodities.

A team of researchers at the University of British Columbia recently estimated that the typical North American consumes resources each year equivalent to the renewable yield from 12 acres of farmland and forestland. For all the world's people to consume at that rate is a mathematical impossibility. It would require four Earths' worth of productive land. In other words, we're three planets short. And we're at least nine planets—or atmospheres—short of safely absorbing the greenhouse gases that would result if all the world's people pumped pollution aloft at the North American rate.

Unfortunately, this high-consumption way of life is now the international vision of progress. The world longs to live the American dream, with steaks on the grill and two cars in the garage. Yet, consumption on the North American scale—our own body weight per day—cannot last, and expanding it to all the world's people is only a fantasy. Until there is a shift toward lower resource consumption and higher quality of life in North America itself, there is little prospect of arresting ecological decline worldwide.

Broadly speaking, three factors determine how much a society consumes: population, per capita consumption, and the array of technologies it uses. Environmentalists have long debated which factor deserves the most attention, just as they have debated whether individual, corporate, or government behavior is most responsible for our global predicament.

These debates, to some degree, are moot: The gap between how our economy operates and how a sustainable economy operates is so wide that we need progress on all fronts to achieve sustainability. Slowing population growth is essential. So is speeding the spread of resource-efficient technologies, from laptops to clotheslines. And so is reducing individual consumption—through less materialistic lifestyles as well as improvements in efficiency.

In our personal lives, we can seek to align our behavior with our values. We can live more simply, at once reducing environmental impacts, saving money, and leading by example. In our public lives—in our workplaces and in our democracy—we can advocate for dramatic reforms in the systems that shape our consumption patterns.

We can, for example, advocate the elimination of perverse taxpayer subsidies such as those that make aluminum too cheap and un-dammed rivers too rare. And we can promote an overhaul of the tax system. If governments taxed pollution and resource depletion rather than paychecks and savings, prices would help unveil the secret lives of everyday things. Environmentally harmful goods would cost more and benign goods would cost less. The power of the marketplace would help propel the "un-stuffing" of North American life.

"Un-Stuffing" Our Lives

There is much that consumers can do now to reduce the impacts of their consumption. Here are a few suggestions for what to do about our stuff:

- *Newspapers:* Share a subscription with a friend. Read the newspaper at the library. Buy papers only when you're actually going to read them. Lobby your paper to maximize its recycled content and use no pulp from old-growth forests.

- *Clothes:* Wash only full loads of laundry, and avoid using hot water; dry your clothes on a clothesline. Wear T-shirts in summer instead of turning on the air conditioning. Buy and sell at "vintage" (used) clothing stores. Look for organic cotton products and undyed cotton.

- *Shoes:* Buy durable shoes; when they wear out, have them repaired instead of buying new ones. Choose locally made goods over those made far away. Buy secondhand shoes or those made from recycled materials.

- *Cars:* If you need a car, get a fuel-efficient one and drive it as little as possible. Combine trips, carpool, take the bus, ride a bike. Patronize nearby stores rather than far-off ones. Move to a transit- and pedestrian-friendly neighborhood.

- *Computers:* Turn off your computer—or at least the screen—whenever you're not using it. If you need to upgrade your computer, have new memory or circuit boards added rather than replacing the whole thing. If you need a new computer, refurbish a used one or buy a laptop rather than a new desktop. Laptop computers weigh about one-tenth as much as desktop computers and require about one-third the energy.
- *Hamburgers:* Eat less beef. Almost any kind of farm-raised meat is an inefficient use of resources, but red meat is the most wasteful of all. Try a veggie burrito next time.

One of the best ways to reduce material consumption is to focus on the nonmaterial things often lacking in our lives. We sometimes consume for lack of something better to do. Feeling lonely or dissatisfied, we shop. Lacking community, we travel. Concentrating on friendship and community may make us happier while, almost without our noticing, it trims our consumption. Is it only a coincidence that "conversation" and "conservation" are spelled with the same letters?

QUESTIONS

? The authors include a number of resource consumption facts. Explain how much Americans consume and how their consumption compares with international rates?

? What are the three factors that determine how much a society consumes? Give examples of each.

? Societal map question: Argue that it is possible to change American patterns of consumption. Identify and explain one way in which individuals could change their consumption patterns. Identify and explain one way that the entire society could change its consumption patterns. Now, argue that it is not possible to change our consumption patterns. Explain why. Do you believe that consumption patterns can be changed?